George James Spurrell

Notes on the Hebrew Text of the Book of Genesis

With two appendices

George James Spurrell

Notes on the Hebrew Text of the Book of Genesis
With two appendices

ISBN/EAN: 9783337317485

Printed in Europe, USA, Canada, Australia, Japan

Cover: Foto ©Lupo / pixelio.de

More available books at **www.hansebooks.com**

NOTES

ON

THE HEBREW TEXT

OF THE

BOOK OF GENESIS

WITH TWO APPENDICES

BY

G. J. SPURRELL, M. A.

LATE SCHOLAR OF BALLIOL COLLEGE, OXFORD

Oxford

AT THE CLARENDON PRESS

M DCCC LXXXVII

PREFACE.

THE present volume of notes was undertaken at the suggestion of Prof. Driver, and is mainly intended for students beginning the Hebrew language. The notes are taken chiefly from the best German commentaries, and do not aim at originality. The Versions have also been used, and references are given to various grammars, the writer's object being to adapt the book to the wants of students using different grammars. The Commentaries used are those by Tuch[1], Delitzsch[2], and Dillmann[3], to whom the writer is chiefly indebted; reference is also made to Mr. Wright's[4] Notes on Genesis, and (occasionally) to the commentary by the late Dr. Kalisch[5]. The Versions are quoted partly from the London Polyglot, and partly from separate editions.

---

[1] The 2nd edition, by Arnold and Merx, Halle, 1871.

[2] The 4th edition, Leipzig, 1872.

[3] The references to Dillmann are to the 4th edition of his *Genesis*, in the *Kurzgefasstes Exeg. Handbuch zum alten Test.*, Leipzig, 1882. A 5th edition appeared in 1886, but as some of the sheets had already been printed off, the references to the 4th edition have been kept, and any changes in the 5th edition noted on the margin.

[4] *The Book of Genesis in Hebrew*, by C. H. H. Wright, London, 1859.

[5] *Historical and Critical Commentary on the Old Test.*, *Genesis*, London, 1858.

For the LXX, Lagarde's text has been used[1], reference being occasionally made to the text contained in the London Polyglot, and to Tischendorf's edition. The Targum of Onqelos, or Babylonian Targum, has been taken from the edition by Dr. Berliner[2], the text in the London Polyglot being compared, while the Targum of Pseudo-Jonathan and the Jerusalem Targum are quoted from the London Polyglot[3]. For the Peshiṭṭā (Syriac) version the Polyglot and the edition by Lee[4], which is based on the text in the London Polyglot, have been used, while the Vulgate has been taken from a Paris edition[5] and the Polyglot. The other Greek versions (Aquila, Symmachus, and Theodotion) are usually cited second-hand, reference being also made to Field's edition of Origen's Hexapla[6]. The Arabic version of Saadiah has been quoted from the Polyglot: the Hebrew-Samaritan text and the Samaritan version are also cited from the same source[7]. The Grammars to which reference has been made are those of Gesenius, Davidson, Stade,

---

[1] *Genesis Graece*, edidit P. A. de Lagarde, Leipzig, 1868.

[2] In two parts, Berlin, 1884. The first part containing the text after the 'editio Sabioncta' of 1557, and the second part, the notes, introduction, and indices.

[3] The Targum of Pseudo-Jonathan and the Jerusalem Targum (which only exists in a fragmentary form) are really two recensions of one and the same Targum, the Jerusalem Targum; see Bleek's *Einleitung*, ed. Wellhausen, p. 606 f.; Eng. trans., ed. Venables, vol. ii. p. 439 f.

[4] London, 1823.

[5] Published by Garnier Brothers, without date.

[6] Oxford, 1875.

[7] The reader should consult the various 'Introductions' to the Old Testament on these versions (especially that of Wellhausen-Bleek, 1878 or 1886), or read the articles in Smith's *Dictionary of the Bible*.

Ewald, Olshausen, Böttcher (occasionally), Müller (for the Syntax only), and the treatise on the Tenses by Prof. Driver[1].

The text of Genesis that has been followed in compiling the notes is that of Baer (with a preface by Delitzsch), and the same text has been used in quoting passages from other books, the edition of Theile[2] being only cited in those portions of the Old Testament that have not yet been edited by Baer[3].

Two appendices have been added to the book: one on the structure of Genesis, as it was deemed necessary that the student should have some information about the modern views as to the criticism of the Pentateuch; and the other on the names of God, which could not be adequately discussed within the limits of a note.

The writer has to acknowledge the great obligations he is under to Prof. Driver for the valuable help he has rendered

---

[1] Gesenius' *Grammar*, translated by Davies, and edited by Mitchell, London, 1880 (since reprinted). Davidson's *Grammar*, Edinburgh, 8th edition, 1887. Stade, *Lehrbuch der hebräischen Grammatik*, Leipzig, 1879. Ewald, *Lehrbuch der hebräischen Sprache*, 8te Ausgabe, Göttingen, 1870: the Syntax (the third part of the Lehrbuch) has been translated by Kennedy, Edinburgh, 1879. Olshausen, *Lehrbuch der hebräisch. Sprache*, Braunschweig, 1861. Böttcher, *Lehrbuch der hebräisch. Sprache*, Leipzig, 1868. Aug. Müller, *Outlines of Hebrew Syntax*, translated by Robertson (being a translation of the third part of Müller's *Hebräische Schulgrammatik*, Halle, 1878), 1st edition, 1882; 2nd edition, 1887. Driver, *Hebrew Tenses*, 2nd edition, Oxford, 1881.

[2] 3rd edition, Leipzig, 1867.

[3] The following portions of the Bible have been published by Baer: *Genesis*, Leipzig, 1869; *Isaiah*, ib., 1872; *Job*, ib., 1875; *Minor Prophets*, ib., 1878; *The Psalms*, ib., 1880; *Proverbs*, ib., 1880; *Daniel, Ezra, Nehemiah*, ib., 1882; *Ezekiel*, ib., 1884; and *Canticles, Ruth, Lamentations, Ecclesiastes, Esther*, ib., 1886.

him in preparing these notes, and for kindly revising the proof-sheets. His thanks are also due to the Delegates of the Clarendon Press for their assistance in publishing the book, and to Mr. Pembrey, their Oriental reader, for the care which he has taken in passing the sheets through the press.

G. J. SPURRELL.

Oxford, July, 1887.

CONTENTS.

ABBREVIATIONS USED[1].

A. V. = The Authorized Version of 1611.

A. V. R. = The Authorized Version Revised, 1885.

Aq. = Aquila's Greek Version.

Aram. = Aramaic.

B. and D. = Baer and Delitzsch.

B. Jubil. = *The Book of Jubilees* (Ethiopic), ed. Dillmann, Kiel, 1859.

Baumg. = Baumgarten.

Ber. Rabb. = Bereshith Rabba.

Berl. Ak. M. B. = *Monatsberichte der König. Preuss. Akad. der Wissenschaften zu Berlin.*

Bernst. = Bernstein.

Bib. Sam. = *Bibliotheca Samaritana*, ed. Heidenheim, Heft i, Leipzig, 1884.

Boch. = Bochart.

Boh. = von Bohlen.

Bött. = Böttcher.

Böttcher, *Neue Aehr.* = *Neue Hebräische Aehrenlese* (in 3 vols.), by Böttcher, Leipzig, 1849–65.

Burck. = Burckhardt.

Chald. = Chaldee[2].

Dav. = Davidson.

Del. = Delitzsch.

Del., *Par.* = *Wo lag das Paradies?* by Friedrich Delitzsch, Leipzig, 1881.

Di. = Dillmann.

Ecclus. = Ecclesiasticus.

Eich. = Eichhorn.

Einl. = *Einleitung.*

Ewald, *J. B.* = *Jahrbücher der biblischen Wissenschaft*, Göttingen, 1848 and following years.

Ewald, *Komp. der Gen.* = *Die Komposition der Genesis*, by G. H. A. Ewald, Brunswick, 1823.

Frankel, *Vorstudien* = *Vorstudien zu der Septuaginta*, Leipzig, 1841.

Frankel, *Einfluss* or *Einfl.* = *Über den Einfluss der palästin. Exegese auf die Alexand. Hermeneutik*, by Z. Frankel, Leipzig, 1851.

Ges. = Gesenius' *Hebrew Grammar* (vide Preface).

Ges., *Th.* or *Thes.* = Gesenius' *Thesaurus*, Leipzig, 1829–58.

Gesch. = *Geschichte.*

Gr. Ven. = *Versio Veneta* (see Bleek's *Introduction* (Eng. trans.), vol. ii. p. 430).

H. W. B. = Gesenius' *Handwörterbuch über das alte Test.*, ed. Mühlau and Volck, 9th ed., Leipzig, 1883; 10th ed., ib., 1886[3].

Hier. or Hieron. = Hieronymus (Jerome).

Hieron., *Quaest.* = Hieronymus'

---

[1] Most of the commoner abbreviations, with which the student will be familiar, are not given here.

[2] It should be pointed out that the languages usually called Chaldee, Syriac, and Samaritan are really three dialects of the Aramaic, and should be embraced under the term Aramaic.

[3] The 10th edition of the *H. W. B.* is in the main a reprint of the 9th, but is augmented by the addition of much illustrative matter derived from Inscriptions, and contributed by Prof. D. H. Müller.

Quaestiones Hebraicae in libro Geneseos, at the end of Lagarde's *Genesis Graece*, Leipzig, 1868.

Jos. = Josephus.

Kal. = Kalisch.

Ke. = Keil.

Kn. = Knobel.

Lag. = Lagarde.

Lenor. = Lenormant.

Levy, *Chald. W. B.* = Levy, *Chaldäisches Wörterbuch* (2 vols. in one, Leipzig, 1881).

Luth. = Luther.

Luzz. = Luzzatto.

M. R. = *Outlines of Hebrew Syntax*, by Aug. Müller, translated by Robertson (vide Preface).

M. and V. = Mühlau and Volck.

Mid. Bem. = Midrash Bemidbar, i. e. Midrash on the book of Numbers.

Nöld. = Nöldeke.

Nöld., *Unters.* or *Untersuch.* = *Untersuchungen zur Kritik des alten Test.*, by Th. Nöldeke, Kiel, 1869.

Oehl. = Oehler.

Ols. = Olshausen.

Onom. or Onomas. = Onomasticon.

Onq. = Onqelos.

Pesh. = Peshiṭṭā Version, also quoted as Syriac.

Proleg. or *Prol. Crit.* = *Prolegomena Critica in Vet. Test. Hebr.*, by H. L. Strack, Leipzig, 1873.

Rawl. = Rawlinson.

Riehm, *H. W. B.* = Riehm's *Handwörterbuch des Biblischen Alterthums*, Bielefeld and Leipzig, 1875 and following years.

Rob., *Pal.* = Robinson's *Palestine* (1st ed.), London, 1841.

Roed. = Roediger.

s. p. = small print.

Saad. = Saadiah's Arabic Version.

Sam. = The Samaritan Version, and the Hebrew Text in Samaritan characters when both agree; the former is also cited as Sam. Ver., and the latter as Heb.-Sam.

Sch. or Schr. = Schrader.

Schrader, *K. G. F.* = *Keilinschriften und Geschichtsforschung.*

Schrader, *K. A. T.*[2] = *Die Keilinschriften und das alte Testament*, 2nd ed., Giessen, 1883. (The first volume of an English translation, with the pages of the original on the margin, has been published by the Rev. O. Whitehouse, London, 1885: Williams and Norgate. The references in the notes are to the German edition.)

Symm. = Symmachus' Greek Version.

Targ. = Targum.

Targ. Jer. = Jerusalem Targum.

Targ. Ps.-Jon. or Jon. = The Targum of Pseudo-Jonathan.

Targg. = Targums.

Th. or Theod. = Theodotion's Greek Version.

Tisch. = Tischendorf.

Vss. = Versions.

Vulg. = Vulgate.

Wel. or Well. = Wellhausen.

Winer, *R. W. B.* = *Biblisch. Real-Wörterbuch*, Leipzig, 1847–48, 3rd ed.

Z. D. M. G. = *Zeitschrift der Deutschen Morgenländischen Gesellschaft.*

וְגוֹמֵר "=וגו׳ i. e. *et caetera.*

NOTES ON GENESIS.

1.

1. בראשית. '*In the beginning*,' as ἐν ἀρχῇ, in John 1, 1; not ἐν τῇ ἀρχῇ. בראשית is without the article, like בְּאָחוֹר, Prov. 29, 11; בְּיָד, Is. 28, 2; קָרִי, Lev. 26, 27.

The Vss. and most commentators render, '*In the beginning God created*,' etc.: the same rendering is perhaps indicated by the accents, בראשית being marked off by *Ṭifcha* from what follows[1]. If this rendering be adopted, בראשית must not be taken relatively, i. e. '*first of all*,' in opposition to a second or third, which might follow; for this is against the, sense, as heaven and earth include all; and we should rather expect בָּרִאשֹׁנָה; but it must be taken absolutely, '*at first*' ('*uranfänglich*'): hence the choice of the expression בְּרֵאשִׁית, which does not occur elsewhere.

רֵאשִׁית = the beginning of a series, always relative to a genitive either expressed or (as here, Is. 46, 10. Deut. 33, 21) understood. As רֵאשִׁית everywhere else (except in these two passages) is followed by a genitive, Ewald, Bunsen, and others follow Rashi and Ibn Ezra, and render, '*At first, when God created*, etc. . . . (ver. 3) *then God said, Let there be light*.' A similar construction to Ex. 6, 28 בְּיוֹם דִּבֶּר יהוה, where

---

[1] In 3, 1[b] and 5[b]. Deut. 28, 47[b] (מֵרֹב כֹּל׃). 61[a] (בְּסֵפֶר הַתּוֹרָה). Ex. 9, 24[b] (מֵאָז הָיְתָה לְגוֹי׃), we find *Ṭifcha*, the word so accented being closely connected in sense with the next following word. From these and similar passages it seems that the argument from the accents ought not to be pressed in this verse.

יוֹם in the construct state is followed by a sentence as its genitive; so in Gen. 39, 20[b]. Num. 3, 1. Deut. 4, 15. Hos. 1, 2. Ps. 90, 15[b], etc.; see Ewald, § 332 d. וַיֹּאמֶר, in ver. 3, would then be the imperfect with waw conv. in answer to בְּרֵאשִׁית; cf. 19, 15 (כְּמוֹ precedes). 27, 34 וַיִּצְעַק ... בִּשְׁמֹעַ עֵשָׂו; Is. 6, 1 וָאֶרְאֶה ... בִּשְׁנַת מוֹת הַמֶּלֶךְ; and see Ewald, § 344 a; Driver, § 127 β. (Boettcher (*Neue Aehr.* I. 2–9) and others prefer to read בְּרֹא as in 5, 1, which would be the more common construction; but this is not necessary.) According to this interpretation verse 2 becomes a parenthesis, which is unnatural, as a long and heavy sentence at the beginning of the book would hardly be expected; cf. also Ryssel, *De Elohistae Pentateuchi sermone* (Lipsiae, 1878), p. 76. On the reading of the LXX, cf. Geiger, *Urschrift*, etc., pp. 344, 439, 444, who, following the tradition that this was one of the thirteen places that were altered for Ptolemy, considers that Rashi's construction was the traditional one, that of the LXX being an innovation.

בָּרָא '*created*,' the common word in P (see Appendix I) in this connection, is restricted to the divine workmanship, and always implies the production of something new (in matter or form, as ver. 21), being used literally and metaphorically (e.g. Ps. 51, 12). It is never followed by an accusative of the material used, and thus implies the unconditioned operation (absolute causality) of the agent. Its original meaning is generally given as '*to cut*' (cf. the Pi‘el in Josh. 17, 15. 18, and Ges. in *Thes.* sub voce), then '*to shape*,' '*form*,' and so '*create*,' but it does not in itself express the idea of creation out of nothing; cf. the Arabic خلق, prop. '*to smooth*,' '*polish*,' then '*to create*,' the word used by Saadiah here. In the Pi‘el it is used of man, '*to cut with effort*:' contrast the intensive stem with Qal, the simple stem, used of

the free-creating of God without any effort; cf. Ew., § 126 a.
The Samaritan renders ברא by אָ̃שׁ2∇, which Del. explains
as equivalent to ἐθεμελίωσε; see Heidenheim, *Bib. Sam.*, Heft
i. p. 70, who mentions other explanations that have been
suggested.

אֱלֹהִים, plural of אֱלוֹהַּ. The derivation of אלוה is disputed; see Appendix II. אלהים *pluralis excellentiae*, with a
singular verb; see Ges., § 108. 2 b; M. R., § 64. So we find
בְּעָלִים and אֲדֹנִים, used in a similar way, of human superiors;
and Is. (19, 4) says אדנים קשה, singular and plural as here.
אלהים is only joined with a plural verb in special cases; cf.
the note on 20, 13, and Ewald, § 318 a.

אֵת הַשָּׁמַיִם. אֵת or אֶת־, the sign of the acc. when
defined (Ges., § 117. 2; M. R., § 32).   It corresponds to the
Phoenician אֵיַת, which was probably the original form of את
(a noun substantive from אוה; cf. Schröder, *Phoen. Gram.*,
§ 123); cf. the Arabic اِيّا, Chaldee יָת, Syriac ܝܬ (found
twelve times in the Syriac O. T.).   It is usually explained as
meaning '*essence*,' or '*existence*,' but according to usage has
so little emphasis, that it is merely inserted to mark the
definite object; cf. further, Ges., *Thes.*, p. 169 a, where its
etymology is discussed.

שָׁמַיִם, found only in the plural (unless we regard the
form as a dual) in Hebrew.

2. תֹהוּ וָבֹהוּ. תֹהוּ = '*wasteness*,' or '*bareness*.' Sometimes the word is used metaphorically, e. g. of idols, as vain,
unrewarding, 1 Sam. 12, 21. Is. 44, 9.   In Hebrew the root
תהה is not found.

בֹהוּ = '*emptiness*,' '*desolation*.' This word is always found
in immediate or parallel connection with תֹהוּ; it only occurs
twice again, viz. Jer. 4, 23. Is. 34, 11 (possibly borrowed from

this passage). A root בהה is not found in Hebrew. In Arabic we find بَهِيَ='*vacua et inanis fuit*' domus.

תֹּהוּ=תֹּהֶו and בֹּהוּ=בָּהֶו, like קֹדֶשׁ from קָדֵשׁ, are both segholates, from verbs ל"ה, properly ל"ו. On the segholates (so called from the helping vowel seghol, which replaces the shewa under the second consonant), see Ges., § 93; on תהו and בהו in particular, § 85, V; Stade, § 198 a; also Dav., §§ 29 and 45.

The ו before בהו has a pretonic qameç, joining together the two nouns, which are closely connected, so 2, 9. 8, 22 יוֹם וָלַיְלָה; see Ges., § 104. 2, N. B. e; Dav., § 15 d; cf. especially Rem. with Ges., § 104. 2, N. B. e.

רוח אלהים. '*The Spirit of God*,' the life-giving and life-preserving power (Ps. 104, 29), not a '*wind sent by God*,' as apparently Onqelos, וְרוּחָא מִן קֳדָם יְ‏, and others (e. g. Ephrem and Saadiah), for מרחפת does not suit this rendering, and the dividing of the waters in ver. 7, which separated the earth from the water, forbids us to think of a wind sent by God to dry up the earth.

מרחפת. The usual fem. form with the participle, cf. Ges., § 94. 2. Observe that this fem. form is accented, like the segholates, on the penult. The word occurs again in Deut. 32, 11, of an eagle brooding over its young. The original meaning of the root is '*to be loose*' or '*slack*,' and so '*to hover with loose wing*,' the figure here being that of a bird hovering over its young. The root is more widely used in Syriac, the Pa'el ܐܦܪܚ being equivalent to the Heb. root in Deut. l. c., which the Pesh. renders as here with ܡܪܚܦ; cf. Bernstein, *Syr. Chrest.*, p. 173. 4, and *Lex.*, p. 480, the Syriac word having also the notion of fructifying and fertilizing. The Talmud, *Tract. Chag.*, c. 2, fol. 15, refers thus to this passage, ‏כיונה מרחפת על בניה ואינה נוגעת‏ ‘ *as a dove hovering over its young without touching them ;*’ cf. also Matt. 3, 16, and the paraphrase of Milton, *Par. Lost*, Bk. 7, 235 :—

> ‘ *His brooding wings the Spirit of God outspread,*
> *And vital virtue infused, and vital warmth*
> *Throughout the fluid mass.*’

3. ‏יְהִי‏, imperf. apoc. from ‏יְהְיֶה‏, for ‏יְהְי‏ weakened from ‏יַהְיִי‏ (like ‏פְּרִי‏ from ‏פִּרְיְ‏, weakened from ‏פַּרְיְ‏, Ges., § 24, 1 b; so ‏דְּמְכֶם‏ thinned from ‏דַּמְכֶם‏, see Ges., § 27. 3. Rem. 3), cf. Ges., § 75. Rem. 3 e and § 93. Rem. 6; Dav., § 45.   On the thinning of ‏ַ‏ into ‏ִ‏, see Wright, *Arab. Gram.*, i. § 90. Rem. ad fin.

‏וַיְהִי‏.   The grave Metheg before the half-open syllable (see Dav., foot-note, p. 16) only with ‏ויהי‏ and ‏ויחי‏ ‘*when they stand before Metheg [? Maqqeph] or with the accent Pashta,*’ Ges., § 16. 2; Stade, § 54 c.

4. ‏וַיַּרְא‏.   Imperf. with waw conv.   On the apocopated form ‏יַרְא‏ out of ‏יִרְאֶה‏, see Ges., § 75. Rem. 3 c; Dav., § 45. The so-called waw conversive or consecutive is confined to the language of the ancient Hebrews and their neighbours the Moabites, whose language, as we now know, was so closely allied to their own.   Besides the O. T. it occurs on the Siloam inscription, first deciphered by Prof. Sayce, and is frequent on the inscription of Mesha, commonly called the Moabite stone : it is also found in later Hebrew writings composed in imitation of Biblical Hebrew.   If we remember that the tenses in Hebrew do not indicate the *date*, but the *state* of an action, i. e. whether it be *complete* or *incomplete*, the explanation of this peculiar Hebrew construction will not be far to seek.   The imperf. denotes an action as entering on completion.   When we have a series of events, each single event need not necessarily be regarded as completed

and independent, but each may be regarded as related to the preceding one, one event stepping into its place after the other, the date at which each successive event comes in being determined by the ו, which connects the new event with a point previously marked in the narrative. Thus here ברא, ver. 1, is the starting-point in the narrative, to which ויאמר first and then ויהי are related: and the narrative developes itself, each fresh event stepping into the place prepared for it by its predecessor. This construction begins to fall into disuse in later Hebrew. It should be remembered that an imperf. with waw conv. never refers to the future unless its preceding perfect to which it is related is the so-called prophetic perfect, which describes future events which are certain to take place as already accomplished, and so regarded as past, e. g. Is. 9, 5. See further, Prof. Driver, *Heb. Tenses*, c. vi, 2nd ed.; also Ges., §§ 49, 129; M. R., § 16 f.; Dav., § 23. Ewald aptly terms this construction the *relatively-progressive imperfect.*

וירא ... כי טוב. Hebrew says, '*And He saw the light, that it was good:*' English more tersely, '*He saw that the light was good;*' so 6, 2. 12, 14. 49, 15. See Ewald, § 336 a, 2.

בֵּין ... בֵּין, in ver. 6 בין ... ל: the former scheme (בין ... בין) is by far the most common, the latter (בין ... ל) only occurs twice again in the Pentateuch, viz. Lev. 27, 33. 20, 25, being rare, and generally confined to late writers; cf. however 2 Sam. 19, 36 בין טוב לרע.

5. קָרָא לַיְלָה, the tone is here thrown back to avoid the concurrence of two tone syllables; so 3, 19 תֹּאכַל לֶחֶם, 4, 17 בָּנָה עִיר, and often; see Ges., § 29. 3 b, and the note on 4, 17.

יום אחד. 'One day,' so A. V. R., not as the A. V., '*the first day.*' אחד has not, strictly speaking, a corresponding ordinal, though it is possible to use ראשון as such. Here אחד may stand, as at the head of a series the ordinal is not needed; see Ewald, § 269 a. So 2, 11. 4, 19. 2 Sam. 4, 2.

6. וַיְהִי for וַיְּהִי, by Ges., § 24. 1 a: on the pointing of waw, cf. § 104. 2 a; Dav., § 15 d. Rem.

ויהי מבדיל. When any special stress is laid upon the continuance of the action, the participle with היה is used by the best writers, but is more frequently affected by later writers (e. g. 2 Kings 17 it occurs nine times), and is exceedingly common in the Mishna. So in 4, 17 ויהי בנה, 37, 2 היה רעה; cf. Ges., § 134. 2 c; M. R., § 14. 2 a; Driver, § 135. 5. Ryssel, *De Elohistae Pentateuchi sermone,* p. 58. For the Mishna usage, see *Lehrb. der Neuhebräisch. Sprache,* § 96 b, by Strack and Siegfried.

בין מים למים. ל with pretonic qameç; so לָשֶׁבֶת, לָבוֹא, לָתֶת, etc.; cf. Ges., § 102. 2 c; Dav., § 14. 1 d.

רקיע from רקע, Qal='*to strike,*' '*stamp,*' '*make firm;*' Pi'el, '*to spread out by striking:*' according to LXX, Aq., Symm., Theod. στερέωμα, Vulg. '*firmamentum.*'

7. וַיַּעַשׂ. The form is (1) יַעֲשֶׂה, then (2) by apocopation יַעֲשׂ like a segholate, e. g. נַעַר, then (3) with a helping vowel (here pathach on account of the guttural ע) יַעַשׂ (like נַעַר), the ע preserving the original pathach with the prefix יְ, as in the Arabic; cf. يَقْتُل (the regular form=the Heb. יִקְטֹל), see Wright, *Arab. Gram.,* i. p. 62; cf. further, Ges., § 75. Rem. 3 d; Dav., § 45; Driver, § 46, foot-note 2.

7[b]. At the end of ver. 6 the LXX read καὶ ἐγένετο οὕτως instead of at the end of ver. 7, which suits ver. 6[b] better than ver. 7[b]; as elsewhere, e. g. vers. 9. 11. 15. 24. 30,

וַיְהִי כֵן immediately follows what God says. Possibly it has been misplaced in the Mass. text, and the LXX preserve it in the original position.

8ᵃ. שָׁמָיִם. After this word the LXX have in their text καὶ εἶδεν ὁ Θεὸς ὅτι καλόν, which is wanting in the Mass. text, but would be expected here (as in vers. 3. 10) at the end of the second day's work. In the account of the third day's work it occurs twice, in LXX and Mass. text, ver. 10 and ver. 12. Possibly the addition in the LXX text is, as Frankel, *Einfluss*, p. 60, points out, due to a reviser who wished to make 8ᵃ parallel with 3. 10. 12. The Mass. text may have again omitted the formula of divine approval here, as the complete division of the waters was not made until the third day.

9. וְתֵרָאֶה, jussive, although the shortened form is not used; cf. 41, 34. Ruth 1, 8 Ktb. Job 3, 9. In the regular verb, with the exception of the Hif'il stem, the ordinary imperfect must serve as jussive, there being only one form for both tenses; see Ges., § 48, especially 2 and 4; Dav., § 23. On the syntax of the jussive, see Driver, c. iv, and M. R., § 8.

11. דֶּשֶׁא='*grass*' or '*grasslike plants*,' the first verdure that covered the earth young and fresh, appearing after rain, 2 Sam. 23, 4. Job 38, 27, or after the old grass had gone, Prov. 27, 25.

עֵשֶׂב. A wider term including herbs useful for men, Ps. 104, 14. Gen. 3, 18.

תַּדְשֵׁא, a Hif'il denominative from דֶּשֶׁא='*to make or produce*' דֶּשֶׁא; so מָטָר '*rain*,' הִמְטִיר '*to make rain*,' שֹׁרֶשׁ '*a root*,' הִשְׁרִישׁ '*to send out roots*.' Hif'il the causative stem, expressing with denominatives the idea of producing or putting forth that of which the original noun is the name, Ges., § 53. 2. Rem. 2. So מזריע זרע.

The construction of a verb with a cognate accusative is common in Hebrew, so in 27, 34 ויצעק צעקה, Zech. 1, 14 קנאתי...קנאה, and often; see Ges., § 138. Rem. 1; M. R., § 36; the same construction occurs again in ver. 20.

Render, '*Let the earth bring forth young grass, herbs yielding seed*,' with the accents, עשׂב being in apposition to דשׁא; see Ges., § 113; M. R., § 71. 2; not as the LXX, βοτάνην χόρτου (also Aq. and Th.), Vulg. '*herbam virentem*,' connecting דשׁא in the cstr. state with עשׂב. But דשׁא is never used thus in the O. T., it may be preceded by יֶרֶק '*greenness*,' '*viror*,' 2 Kings 19, 26. Ps. 37, 2. Is. 37, 27, but cannot be followed by עשׂב as genitive.

עֵץ פרי '*fruit trees*,' עץ being used collectively, lit. '*trees of fruit*.' The use of words in the singular to denote collective ideas is especially frequent in Hebrew; cf. אדם, coll. '*mankind*' (without a plural), אויב = '*enemies*,' נפשׁ '*living beings*.' Often the fem. ending is employed to express a collective idea, so עננה '*clouds*,' ארחה '*caravan*,' גולה '*captives*.' The same principle is implied in the use of כל before a following genitive singular, e. g. כָּל־עֵץ, in Eng. '*every tree*,' lit. '*the whole of trees;*' see Ges., § 108. 1 c; M. R., § 61.

עֵץ פרי. On the cstr. state with a following gen., where in English we find an adj., cf. Ges., § 106. 1; M. R., § 79. 3.

לְמִינוֹ '*after its kind*.' Emphasis is laid on the fact that each was adapted for continuance; the עשׂב flowered and so produced its seed; the עץ bore fruit containing seed or stones necessary for reproduction. מין is a common word in P (see Appendix I).

אשׁר זרעו בו '*in which is its seed*,' i. e. for propagation (Di.).

12. וַתּוֹצֵא. Hif'il, imperf. apoc. with waw conv. from יָצָא, a verb פ״י, properly פ״ו. The form is יַוְצִיא=יוֹצִיא, cf. יַקְטִיל.

לְמִינֵהוּ for לְמִינוֹ. The suffix ־ֵהוּ for וֹ—except in words that are derived from verbs ל״ה, such as מַעֲשֵׂה, שָׂדֵה, מִקְנֵה, etc.—outside this word (where it is found fourteen times), only occurs in אוֹרֵהוּ for אוֹרוֹ, Job 25, 3; פִּילַגְשֵׁהוּ for פִּילַגְשׁוֹ, Judg. 19, 24; מוֹטֵהוּ for מוֹטוֹ, Nah. 1, 13; see Ges., § 91. 1, note b; Ewald, § 247 d; Stade, § 345 c, who remarks that the è of these forms is to be explained as an extension of a short e,—which has arisen out of short a (cf. § 84. 4),—which is still preserved before the suffix of the second pers. masc. sing. in pause, e. g. נַפְשֶׁךָ, שְׁמֶךָ.

14. יְהִי מְאֹרֹת. On the construction here, see Ges., § 147 a, d; M. R., § 133.

מָאוֹר. Nouns formed by prefixing מ denote often instruments or places, e. g. מַפְתֵּחַ 'a key,' מַזְלֵג 'a fork,' מִרְעֶה 'a pasture,' מַאֲרָב 'a lurking-place;' see further, Ges., § 84. 14; Ewald, § 160 b; and Stade, § 268 ff. Render, 'luminaries.'

וְהָיוּ. The perf. with waw conv. in continuation of the jussive יְהִי, so in 28, 3 וְהָיִיתָ ... יְבָרֵךְ אֹתְךָ, 31, 44 נִכְרְתָה וְהָיָה ... בְּרִית, Ex. 5, 7; cf. Ges., § 126. 6; M. R., § 24. 1 a; Driver, § 113. 2 a.

לְאֹתֹת וגו״ may be rendered in three different ways: I. As a ἓν διὰ δυοῖν, '*for signs of seasons, and for days and for years;*' see Ges., § 155. 1 a, and cf. 3, 16. II. '*For signs and for set times, and for days and for years.*' III. '*For signs, as well for times, as also for days and years.*' Against III. Del. remarks that the correlatives 'as well,' 'as also' are not sufficiently clearly expressed by וְ ... וְ, as, for example, in Ps. 76, 7; nor is this rendering suitable to the simplicity of the narrative. On I. it may be remarked that though the hendiadys may be possible in 3, 16, it is by no means necessary there, and Job 10, 17. 2 Chron. 16, 14 (cited by Ges. l. c.) are not parallel. II. is the simplest and best rendering, and is adopted by the Vss., Del., Di., Kn., and others.

אותות. 'The luminaries were to be אותות, i.e. signs, partly in an ordinary way as marks of the different regions of heaven, of the weather, and partly in an extraordinary way, e.g. through eclipses of the sun and moon, the appearances of comets, etc., which were regarded by the ancients as foreshadowing extraordinary events (Joel 3, 3 f. Jer. 10, 2. Matt. 24, 29).' Knobel in Di.

מועדים. מועד from יער (וער), '*to fix*,' denotes any '*stated place*,' as in the phrase אהל מועד '*tent of meeting*,' or as here, '*any fixed, stated time*;' cf. 17, 21. The מועדים here mean set times or seasons, in particular, stated annual feasts, also periods in animal (cf. Jer. 8, 7, of the stork) and vegetable life, and the seasons suitable to the various occupations and employments of man.

ולימים ושנים. On the pointing וְ, cf. Ges., § 104. 2 c; Dav., § 15. 1 c. '*For days and for years*,' i. e. for distinguishing and counting the days, some being short, others long, according to the season of the year: the years also being long and short, according as they are reckoned by the sun or moon. The מאורות had a threefold aim: (1) to divide the day and night; (2) to fix the calendar; (3) to give light on the earth.

16. The lights more exactly defined שני. On the various ways in which the numerals may be connected with substantives, see Ges., § 120. 1; M. R., § 96. 1 b. On the article with גדולים, see Ges., § 111. 2; M. R., § 85.

את המאור הגדול. On this method of expressing the comparative, cf. Ges., § 119. 1; M. R., § 86.

ואת המאור . . . הכוכבים. '*And the lesser light with the stars to govern the night.*' ואת הכוכבים is closely attached to את המאור הקטן; see 2, 9. 12, 17. 34, 29.

18. ולַהבדיל, the ל is pointed with ־ַ by Ges., § 10. 2. Rem.; see also Stade, § 105.

20. נפֶשׁ חיה '*living beings,*' an explanatory apposition to שֶׁרֶץ; so the Syriac: not as the LXX, Vulg., etc., as a genitive after שֶׁרֶץ; see on ver. 11 דשא עשב. שָׁרַץ and שֶׁרֶץ are frequently found in P.

יעופף. Pilel from עוּף, a denom. from עוֹף; on this form of the intensive stem, cf. Ges., §§ 72. 7 and 55. 2; Dav., § 40. 6. Pilel, because a great number of birds is meant; at the same time expressing the idea of '*up and down,*' '*to and fro;*' cf. Di. in loc.

על פני רקיע '*in front of,*' on the side turned towards the earth, i. e. in the air, for which Hebrew has no special expression (Del., Di.).

21. תנינים. LXX, κήτη; Syr. ܬܢܝܢܐ; Vulg. '*cete.*' From תנן '*to stretch out,*' and used Ex. 7, 9. Deut. 32, 33, for a serpent, but more frequently for the crocodile, see Is. 27, 1. 51, 9; and also for other marine animals, Job 7, 12. Ps. 148, 7. Render, '*sea monsters.*'

כל נפֶשׁ החיה. חיה is an adj., not a substantive (its use as a substantive is only poetical, being then equivalent to the prose חיים). נפֶשׁ is practically limited and determined by כל, hence the adj. has the article, though it is absent with the noun: so again in 9, 10. This usage is rare, but is met with occasionally at all periods of the language; see Ges., § 111. 2 a; M. R., § 85. Rem. c; Ewald, § 293 a; and

Journal of Phil., xi. 229 (where nearly all the examples are collected).

אֲשֶׁר שָׁרְצוּ הַמַּיִם אֲשֶׁר ' *wherewith the waters swarm.*' אֲשֶׁר is the acc. after שׁרץ. Verbs of *abounding in*, and *wanting*, govern the acc.; see Ges., § 138. 3; M. R., § 35; and 9, 2.

לְמִינֵהֶם *scriptio defectiva*, for לְמִינֵיהֶם; cf. 4, 4 חֶלְבְּהֶן.

עוֹף כָּנָף ' *birds* (coll.) *of wing.*' On the construction of a subs., where in English an adj. is used, see Ges., § 106. 1; M. R., § 79.

לְמִינֵהוּ. See on ver. 12.

22. וַיְבָרֶךְ. On the position of the tone, cf. the note on ver. 7.

24. וְחַיְתוֹ. חַיְתוֹ with the old, so-called case ending וֹ. Probably the ending וֹ was that of the nominative; compare the Arabic nominative ending *u*, but in Hebrew its distinctive use as a mark of the nom. was lost. These terminations וֹ or וֹ, also the ending ִי., have no meaning in Hebrew, and are retained as mere binding vowels in particular phrases (ִי. especially in participles before a preposition) as archaisms, or in imitation of archaisms; see Ges., § 90. 3 b; Dav., § 17; Stade, § 344; and cf. בְּנוֹ בְעֹר in Num. 24, 3. 15, and מַעְיְנוֹ מָיִם in Ps. 114, 8.

חַיַּת הָאָרֶץ is one of the characteristic expressions of P.

26. נַעֲשֶׂה ' *let us make.*' The voluntative is hardly ever found with ה cohortative in verbs ל״ה and ל״א; cf. Ges., §§ 75. 6 and 128; M. R., § 8; and Driver, c. iv, esp. § 47.

We have the plural again in 11, 7 and Is. 6, 8, and it has been explained in various ways.

I. The Fathers here see a reference to the Trinity, and many moderns have followed them; but as Del. (*Comm.*, 4th ed., p. 101) and Oehl. (*Theol. of O. T.*, § 36) remark, the *mysterium Trinitatis* is not sufficiently manifest in the O. T. to warrant this interpretation. II. Tuch and others account for the plural on the ground that in a case of reflection or self-consultation, the subject stands as the object, in antithesis to itself, the speaker conceiving himself as addressing himself; cf. Del. on Is. 6, 8; Tuch, *Comm.*, 2nd ed., p. 23. But as Del. and Di. point out, there is no proof of the existence of such a plural. III. Kn. and others explain the plural from the custom which monarchs have of using the first person plural in decrees, etc.; but though this occurs continually in the Qoran, and is found in the Bible, Ezr. 4, 18. 1 Macc. 10, 19. 11, 31. 15, 9 (of Persian and Greek rulers), it was never used in this way by the Hebrews. IV. Di., *Comm.*, p. 29, proposes a new explanation; his words are, ‘We should rather remember that the Hebrew who speaks of God as אלהים in the plural, regarded Him as the living, personal conception of a fullness of power and might; God could thus, differently from men, speak of Himself in the plural.’ A plausible explanation, but perhaps hardly so natural as the one Del. adopts. V. Del. and others seem to be right when they refer the plural, as in Is. 6, 8, to the angels. God announces to them His resolve to create man, without however allowing them to participate in His creation: cf. Del. here, and for the idea 1 Kings 22, 19–22. Dan. 4, 14. 7, 10. Job 1. Luke 2, 9. This is an old interpretation, and is the one adopted by Philo (διαλέγεται ὁ τῶν ὅλων πατὴρ ταῖς ἑαυτοῦ δυνάμεσιν, quoted by Del., p. 101), Targ. Jon., which has וַאֲמַר יְיָ לְמַלְאָכַיָּא דִמְשַׁמְּשִׁין קוֹמוֹי וגו'' (‘*Y. spake to His angels who minister before Him*,’ etc.), Rashi, Ibn Ezra. Is. 40, 13. 14 and 44, 24 are cited against this view, but are not conclusive: for as Del. on this passage remarks, ‘A co-ordinate sharing in the act of *creation* He does not grant them, any more than in Is. 6, 8 in the act of *sending:* but He invites their participation or interest in what He is doing, as the creating of a being, who although of the earth, yet stands in a close relation to them and to Him, is the point now in question.'

אדם *'mankind,'* collective, as the pl. ירדו shows.

אדם, so called, according to one view, as belonging to the earth (אֲדָמָה), *'the earth-born,'* γηγενής, γήϊνος. Another derivation is from אָדַם *'to be red;'* cf. Joseph., *Ant.,* i. 1. 2 (Ἄδαμος σημαίνει πυρρὸς ἐπειδήπερ ἀπὸ τῆς πυρρᾶς γῆς φυραθείσης ἐγεγόνει); so many moderns, e.g. Ges., Tuch. Another derivation is from the meaning of the root preserved in Arabic, *'to attach oneself to,'* so אדם=*'animal sociabile.'* All these are uncertain. 'It is obvious that the derivation from אדמה cannot be philologically defended, but any certain etymology for אדם has not as yet been found, any more than one for the Latin *homo;'* cf. Di., p. 52; Del., p. 117.

בצלמנו וגו״. צלם = *'figure,'* *'image,'* εἰκών. דמות is more abstract=*'likeness,'* ὁμοίωσις. 'The Greek and Latin Fathers make a distinction between צלם and דמות, referring צלם to the physical or inborn, דמות to the ethical or receptive side of the Divine image (Ebenbild),' Di. But the absence of ו between the two words (only the LXX have καί), and a comparison of ver. 27, where only the one, with 5, 1, where only the other occurs, do not favour this view. The two words are almost synonymous, the second being added to emphasize the first (Di.).

דגת, collective, *'fishes'*=דגי הים, 9, 2. Ps. 8, 9.

27. ברא אתו *'made He him,'* i.e. mankind. אדם conceived as collective, mankind in general being spoken of.

זכר ונקבה ברא אתם *'male and female made He them,'* the two sexes are mentioned, hence the plural אֹתָם.

28. ‏פרו ורבו‏. ‏פרה‏ joined with ‏רבה‏ is characteristic of P.

‏הרמשת‏. The art. supplies the place of the relative in English; see Ges., § 109. R.; M. R., § 92. Rem. a; Ewald, § 335 a.

29. ‏נָתַתִּי‏ for ‏נְתַנְתִּי‏; see Ges., § 66. 2. Rem. 3. '*I give*,' the prophetic perf., 'the event being regarded as so certain, it is already conceived of as actually come to pass;' cf. Ges., § 126. 4; M. R. 3. 1 a; more fully, Driver, §§ 13, 14. See 9, 13. 15, 18. 17, 20. 23, 11. 13. 41, 41.

‏אשר בו‏, lit. '*which is in it*,' i. e. '*wherein*,' see Ges., § 123. 1.

30. ‏את כל ירק וגו״‏. The verb ‏נתתי‏ here seems to have dropped out. To make the acc. dependent on the ‏נתתי‏ in ver. 29 is difficult, as ‏לכם יהיה‏ intervenes. The Vulg. paraphrases '*ut habeant ad vescendum*.' The Arab. adds جَعَلْتُهُ '*I have appointed it*' or '*set it*.'

‏כל ירק עשב‏='*all verdure of herbs*;' cf. Ex. 10, 15 ‏ולא נותר כל ירק בעץ‏.

‏עשב‏='*herb*,' in its widest sense, the green of it being emphasized as that which animals commonly live on.

31. ‏יום הששי‏. Common words like ‏יום‏ are sometimes treated as definite in themselves, and may then dispense with the article; cf. 2, 3 ‏יום השביעי‏ (also Ex. 20, 10). 1 Kings 7, 12 ‏חצר הגדולה‏, also ver. 8 ‏חצר האחרת‏, Ez. 40, 28. 31. 2 Chron. 23, 20 ‏שער העליון‏, Neh. 3, 6 ‏שער הישנה‏, also *Journ. Phil.*, xi. 229 f. On the relation in which the Cosmogony of Genesis stands to modern science, comp. Prof. Driver in the *Expositor*, Jan. 1886, pp. 23–45.

2.

1. ‏צבאם‏, applied zeugmatically to ‏השמים והארץ‏. The phrase '*host of heaven*' is common in the O. T., e. g. 1 Kings

22, 19 (='*the angel hosts*'). Josh. 5, 14 f. (='*army* or *host of God*'). Ps. 103, 21 (of the elements). The phrase '*host of the earth*,' here due to the צבא השמים, is not common elsewhere, we find instead מלא הארץ, Is. 34, 1.

2. ויכל. '*And God ended*,' not as a pluperfect as some render. It is very doubtful whether an imperf. with waw conv. can stand for a pluperfect, if no perfect in a pluperfect sense precedes, and is scarcely consistent with the meaning . of the idiom; cf. on 1, 4. When a writer wishes to mark that a pluperfect sense is necessary, he usually separates the ו from the verb, which then naturally passes over into the perfect (ואלהים כלה). For a full discussion of the question and an examination of the instances in which waw conv. with the imperfect has been supposed to be equivalent to a pluperfect, see Driver, § 76. Obs.

כלה = here '*to bring to an end*,' '*to leave off*;' cf. Ex. 34, 33. 1 Sam. 10, 13. Ez. 43, 23 (where כלה occurs with מן). This '*leaving off* or *resting*' fills up the seventh day, just as the work of creation the six preceding days. 'God did not create anything on the seventh day,' Kn. The Sam., LXX, Syr., Ber. Rab. read ששי for שביעי; an intentional alteration to avoid the idea that God created anything on the seventh day.

מְלַאכְתּוֹ from מְלָאכָה, which has arisen out of מַלְאָכָה, the weak letter א surrendering its vowel to the preceding vowelless consonant, and the pathach under the prefix מ disappearing and its place being taken by shewa vocal; cf. Stade, § 110 c and § 112 b; Ges., § 23. 2 and § 95. iii. In the form with the suffix וֹ, the pathach under the ל is due to the syllable being short and unaccented.

3. ויברך. If the penult. is an open syllable waw conv. frequently draws back the tone on to it, leaving the last

syllable a short unaccented syllable; see Dav., § 23. 3 b; Driver, § 69; Ges., § 49. 2 b. Cf. 1, 11. 22, and often.

את יום השביעי. Cf. on 1, 31.

אשר ברא אלהים לעשות. Two renderings are possible, (I) '*which God created in respect of making*,' *quae creaverat Deus faciendo*. The inf. cstr. being used to define a preceding verb, as in Judg. 9, 56 אשר עשה .... להרג; 2 Kings 19, 11 עשו .... להחרימם; Ps. 103, 20 עשי דבריו לשמע; cf. Ges., § 45. 2; Ewald, § 280 d; M. R., § 113 ad fin. But as ברא in this construction would be followed by אשר (=מלאכה), which is against the usage of the language, and for which עשה מלאכה would stand, Di. (II) prefers rendering with Ewald, § 285 a, '*in making which he created*,' i. e. '*which he made creating*,' אשר being acc. after לעשות, and the latter word being defined by ברא; cf. הפליא להעזר, הגדיל לעשות, הרבה להתפלל. The LXX have ὦν ἤρξατο ὁ Θεὸς ποιῆσαι, a paraphrase. The Syriac ܐ̇ܘܕܝ' ܕ(ܝܠܗܐ) ܕܥܒܕ, as the Hebrew, so Onq. דִּבְרָא יְיָ לְמֶעְבָּד. Vulg. '*quod creavit Deus ut faceret*.'

4: אלה תולדות. '*These are the generations of the heavens and the earth when they were created*.' תולדות,—which only occurs in the pl. cstr. state,—when it stands before a proper name signifies '*generations*,' not as a *nom. act.*, but in the sense '*those who are brought forth*,' so =*family*, '*the details about those who spring from any one*;' hence in the title of a book or chapter, '*the history of the families springing from any one*.' LXX, γένεσις; in this passage βίβλος γενέσεως. Here תולדות = the '*creatures*,' i. e. '*the things brought into existence when heaven and earth were created*.' Elsewhere תולדות always refers to what follows, e. g. 5, 1. 6, 9. 10, 1, but in this chap. no history of the heavens and the earth follows, so Schrader and others suppose that this half verse properly ought to precede 1, 1, its present position being perhaps due to the compiler of the book, who inserted it here in order to form a transition to 2, 4 b, ff. The אלה (as it stands now) points backwards, and may be rendered, '*Such then are the generations:*' so Job 18, 21. Ps. 73, 12. Gen. 10, 21. 31, 32. Cf. further, Del., *Comm.*, p. 111; Di., p. 37; Tuch, p. 49. The heading אלה תולדות is peculiar to P: so 5, 1. 6, 9. 10, 1, etc.

יהוה אלהים, the combined name '*Yahweh Elohim,*' is only found once again in the Pent. (viz. Ex. 9, 30) outside Genesis, but occurs in Joshua. On the Tetragrammaton, יהוה, cf. Appendix II. P uses אלהים till Ex. 6, 3.

ארץ ושמים. Only once again, in Ps. 148, 13.

בהבראם. Inf. Nif'. with בּ prefixed, and the suff. of the third pers. pl. masc., from ברא. The ה is written smaller than the other letters, and is marked by the Massoretes ה" זְעֵירָא, i. e. *He small.* Tuch remarks on this: 'The ה minusc. in בהבראם (cf. 5, 2) has a critical significance, and points to a variant reading, Qal (viz. בְּבָרְאָם), not Hof'., as Rosenmüller thinks. Similarly Lev. 1, 1.' Cf. Di., p. 38, who apparently endorses this view. Other instances of letters written smaller or larger than the other letters will be found in Strack, *Pro-legomena critica*, p. 92, e.g. *litterae majusculae* in Lev. 11, 42, נָחֹון, with waw larger than the other three letters; in Num. 14, 17, י in יִגְדַּל; in Deut. 34, 12, ל in יִשְׂרָאֵל; and *litterae minusculae* in Deut. 32, 18, י in תֶּשִׁי; Esth. 9, 9, שׁ in פַּרְמַשְׁתָּא: see also Bleek (*Introduction*, § 357 f.) [Eng. transl.], or Keil (*Introduction*, § 205) [Eng. transl.]. A list of the '*litterae majusculae et minusculae*' will be found in *Ochla we Ochla* (ed. Frensdorff), Nos. 82–84; Buxtorf, *Tiberias* (1665 ed.). They are not expressly mentioned in the Talmud, and probably in

the course of time became more numerous.   Buxtorf, l. c.,
enumerates thirty-one instances of the *lit. majusc.*, and thirty-
two of the *lit. minusc.*   The Jews give fanciful explanations.
The two following—viz. on this passage, and 23, 2—are cited
from the *Tiberias*, p. 147 ff.   '*ה״* in voce בהבראם "*quando creata
fuerant illa*," nempe, coelum et terra, Gen. 2, 4.   Ad indicandum, fore ut omnia creata minuantur et intereant : et ut littera
ה constat ex lineis dissolutis et ab invicem separatis, sic creata
cuncta dissolventur, sicut scriptum est : "*Coeli velut fumus
evanescent, et terra ut pannus veterascet, et habitatores ejus
similiter morientur*," Is. 51, 6.   Hebraei litterarum mysteria
sectantes, notant innui transpositionem hujus litterae, ut ex
בהבראם fiat באברהם "*propter Abraham*," i. e. propter fideles
creatum esse mundum : illi enim soli Deum propter admi-
randa creationis opera laudant.'   And on the small ב in
23, 2 (p. 152) : 'ad indicandum, planctum et luctum propter
mortuos, viris minuendum esse, ne modum excedat, quod
et Abrahamum fecisse, externo litterae signo indicatum fuit.'
See another Jewish explanation of Gen. 2, 4, from the Talmud, *Tract. Menachoth*, fol. 29, col. 2, in Hershon, *The
Pentateuch according to the Talmud*, p. 92 (Eng. transl.).

Render,'*When they were created*,' lit. '*in their being created;*'
a common use of the inf. cstr., like the Greek construction
ἐν τῷ, with the inf.; see Ges., § 132. 1, 2, 3; M. R., § 111 b.

4ᵇ. The narrative begins here.   '*In the day of God's
making*,' i. e. '*when God made*,' etc.   On the construction, see
Ges., § 133. 2, 3 ; M. R., § 111 a, § 118.

ביום,=lit.'*in the day of*,' is freely used for '*at the time of;*'
so 3, 5 ביום אכלכם; Is. 11, 16 ביום עלותו; Jer. 11, 7 ביום
העלתי.   עֲשׂוֹת=בְּרֹא in P.

The apodosis to 4ᵇ, ביום עשות, may be either ver. 7 or ver. 5.

If we take ver. 7 as the apodosis, then vers. 5, 6 will be a parenthesis descriptive of the earth's condition before God created mankind, and we should have to render it as follows:—
'*When Yahweh Elohim made earth and heaven (now no shrub of the field was yet on the earth, and no herb of the field had yet sprung up; for Yahweh Elohim had not sent rain upon the earth, and there was no man to till the ground; and a mist used to go up and water all the surface of the ground), then Yahweh Elohim formed,*' etc.   So Di.

If we make ver. 5 the apodosis, then the rendering would be, '*When Yahweh Elohim made earth and heaven, then there was no shrub of the field,*' etc.   So Tuch.

Against the first rendering it may be urged that the construction is too involved, and seems to identify a *period* (ver. 6), with a *point* (ver. 7) of time.   To make וכל שׂיח the apodosis to 4ᵇ is against the division of the verses and the syntax (Del.); cf., however, on the latter point, Driver, §§ 123 and 124, who cites Ex. 25, 9. Josh. 3, 3, and other instances of the imperf. separated from ו, after a time determination, and treats this passage similarly.   The argument, too, from the division of the verses is hardly conclusive. Del. takes apparently 4ᵇ and 4ᵃ, after the analogy of 5, 1, as belonging together, and regards vers. 5 and 6 as independent sentences introductory to ver. 7, which beginning with ויצר ('*so he formed*') expresses the main point, viz. the creation of man.

5. On the imperf. after טֶרֶם, cf. Ges., § 127. 4 a; M. R., § 6. 1; Ewald, § 337 c; Driver, § 27 b.   Ewald, l. c., remarks that טרם for the most part stands in circumstantial clauses, preceded by the subject.

כל indefinite, and with the negative = '*none*,' Germ. *kein*: cf. Ges., § 152. 1; M. R., § 142; Ewald, § 323 b. On אין, see Ges., § 152. 1; Ewald, § 321 a; M. R., § 140.

On the position of אֵין in the sentence, cf. Num. 20, 5 וּמַיִם אֵין, M. R., § 79. 6 b. Rem. a.

6. יַעֲלֶה. The imperf. used in a frequentative sense, and followed by a perfect with waw conv. וְהִשְׁקָה. The companion construction to the imperf. with waw conv. is that of the perfect with waw conv. According to Ewald, § 234 a, b. this construction was originally due to the opposite construction of the perfect, followed by an imperfect with waw conv.; just as the two tenses are in many aspects opposite one to the other, so the peculiar idiomatic use of the one, generated a corresponding idiomatic use of the other as its counterpart. Ols., cited by Professor Driver, *Tenses*, p. 141, remarks that this use of the perfect rests originally on a 'play of the imagination,' in virtue of which an action when brought into relation with a preceding occurrence as its *consequence*, from the character of inevitability it then assumes, is contemplated as actually completed. In this construction 'the nascent action (i. e. the action of the imperf.) is conceived of as advancing to completion (the action of the perfect with waw conv.), as no longer remaining in suspension, but as being (so to say) precipitated.' Driver, *Tenses*, p. 141. Compare c. viii, where a full discussion of this idiom will be found, and the rules concerning the shifting of the tone one place forward with the waw conv. are noted. When the waw and the verb are separated, the imperf. reappears. Cf. also Ewald, § 136 b and § 342 b, 1; M. R., §§ 23 and 25; Ges., § 126. 6 d. Other instances of the imperf. as a frequentative, followed by a perf. with waw conv., are 6, 4. 29, 2. 3 יִשְׁקוּ . . . וְנֶאֶסְפוּ . . . וְגֹלְלוּ . . . וְהִשְׁקוּ; 2 Kings 3, 25 יַשְׁאוּם . . . וְהֵשִׁיבוּם 1 Kings 14. 28 וְהֵשִׁיבוּ; יַשְׁלִיכוּ . . . וּמִלֵּאוּהָ, etc.

אֵד only occurs in this passage and Job 36, 27. The LXX render here by πηγή, and in Job, l. c., by νεφέλη, which is also Onqelos' rendering here (עֲנָנָא). Syr. and Vulg. have respectively ܡܰܒܽܘܥܳܐ and '*fons.*' Saadiah agrees with the ordinary rendering '*mist*,' '*vapour*,' ﻧﺪﻯ. The word אֵד appears to be confined to Hebrew. Ges. in the *Thesaurus*, p. 35 (as Professor Driver has pointed out to me), is in error when he says that the word אֵד is used in the Targ., Job 3, 5. Prov. 23, 33. He has accidentally written ' Targum ' for '*the Commentary of Rabbi Levi ben Gerson*' (of Provence, died 1370), cited by Buxtorf, *Lexicon. Chald. Talm. et Rabb.*, p. 69. The mistake is repeated in the 9th ed. of the *H. W. B.* of Gesenius, p. 10 b.

7. וַיִּיצֶר. On the form of this פ״י verb, see Ges., § 70. 1; Dav., § 39. 2.

הָאָדָם. On the derivation of אדם, compare the note on 1, 26. The author connects אדם with אדמה, as though he would imply that man bore in his name a mark of his earthly origin. On the article with אדם, cf. Ges., § 109. 2; Ewald, 277 c; M. R., § 66. Rem. a.

עָפָר is a second accusative, specifying or defining the material used in the operation; see Ewald, § 284 a. 1; M.R., § 45. 5; Driver, § 195. 1 (Tertiary predicate). Cf. Ex. 20, 25.

חַיִּים. The masc. plural used to form an abstract noun. ' The plural may serve to collect together the scattered items into a higher idea, so as to form the signification of an abstract,' Ewald, § 179, who gives as other instances נדדים '*flittings*,' Job 7, 4; עועים '*perverseness*;' סנורים '*blindness*;' cf. also Stade, § 324 b, who remarks ' that חיים is the only word of this sort in general use, the other instances that occur being archaisms, and belonging to the conventional

language of the Law, or of Poets or Prophets.' See also
Ges., § 108. 2 a.

לְנֶפֶשׁ . . . וַיְהִי. In the sense of '*become*,' הָיָה לְ, cf. 17, 4.
18, 18, etc., is more frequent than הָיָה, followed by the simple
subst., as in 4, 20. 21. 19, 26.

נֶפֶשׁ in Heb. = the breath of life that is in every individual being. Man derives this breath of life from God
immediately (Job 27, 3. Is. 42, 5), animals from the earth
(1, 20. 24), and so only mediately from God, yet participating in God's spirit (Job 34, 14 f. Ps. 104, 30). In this
direct inspiration lies man's pre-eminence over the animal
world, stress being laid on the manner in which man 'became a living soul.' He comes into existence as a personal
being in a personal relation with God. Cf. Oehl., § 70. Onq.
renders נפשׁ חיה by רוּחַ מְמַלְּלָא '*a talking spirit*.'

8. גַּן בְּעֵדֶן. '*A garden in Eden*.' עֵדֶן as an appellative
means '*loveliness*,' '*delight*,' but is here clearly the name of the
place where the garden was situated. The LXX render here
παράδεισον ἐν Ἐδέμ; ver. 15 (incorrectly) παραδείσῳ τῆς τρυφῆς, so
3, 24, and Vulg. '*Paradisum voluptatis*.' Syr. has ܟܕܢ ܡܫܐܙ̈ܦ,
Saadiah جِنَاناً فِي عَدْنٍ. Schr., *K. A. T.*, 2nd ed., p. 26 f., says
'Eden,' Heb. עֵדֶן, has originally nothing to do with עֶדֶן, pl.
עֲדָנִים '*loveliness*,' but is a word that came over to the Hebrews
from the Babylonians, meaning properly '*field*,' '*plain*;' in
Assyrian *i-di-nu*. עֵדֶן, pointed with ־ֵ־, to distinguish it
perhaps from עֶדֶן with ־ֶ־ , is a pr. n., the name of a district
in Mesopotamia, or Assyria, which, according to 2 Kings 19,
12. Is. 37, 12, came under the rule of Assyria. עֵדֶן has not
yet been identified; cf. further, Di., p. 51; Del., p. 120.

מִקֶּדֶם is local, not temporal (for וַיִּטַּע is against this), =
'*eastwards*,' '*on the east of*' (a further definition of the position

of Eden; cf. 3, 24. 11, 2. 13, 11), i.e. from the standpoint of the narrator in Palestine.

9. ויצמח. The shortened form of the Hif'. imperf.; see Ges., § 65. 1 c. Rem.; Dav., § 37. 1, 2.

ועץ הדעת טוב ורע = 'and *the tree of knowledge of* (lit. *of the knowing*) *good and evil;*' i.e. the tree, the partaking of the fruit of which would cause persons to know good and evil.

טוב ורע cannot be genitive after דעת, as a word defined by being in the construct state does not take the article, but must be regarded as the accusative; cf. Jer. 22, 16 הלא היא הדעת אתי '*was not that the knowing me?*' see Ewald, § 236 a; M. R., § 110. Rem.; Ges., § 133. 1. The article prefixed to an inf. cstr. is very rare.

טוֹב וָרָע. On the pointing of ו with ‾, see on 1, 2.

10. '*And a river was going out of Eden, to water the garden; and from thence it separated itself, and became four branches.*'

יוצא. The part. denoting continuous, unintermittent action; see Driver, § 21; M. R., § 14. 2 a.

יפרד. On the imperf. as a freq. in past time, see Driver, § 30 a; M. R., § 6. 2 a.

והיה; cf. on והשקה, ver. 6.

11. פִּישׁוֹן =, according to Gesenius, '*streaming,*' or '*stream,*' from a root פוש '*to burst forth.*' It is not found again in the Canonical books of the Old Testament, but is mentioned in Ecclesiasticus 24, 25, together with the Tigris. The Arabic of Saadiah has اَلنِّيل '*the Nile.*' The other versions follow the Heb. text. Its position is more closely defined by the mention of the land (חוילה) round which it flows. Joseph. (*Ant.*, i. 1. 3), the Fathers (Euseb., Aug., Hier.),

and others identify it with the Ganges; Reland and others
consider it is the Phasis; Del. and the moderns, the Indus.
החוילה occurs only here with the art.; in 10, 7. 29, it is mentioned partly among the Cushites, and partly among the sons
of Joqtan, together with Ophir.   It also occurs in the phrase
(25, 18) מחוילה עד שׁור; cf. 1 Sam. 15, 7.

Ḥavila in 25, 18 and 1 Sam. 15, 7 seems to have been the
eastern frontier of the Ishmaelites and Amalekites on the
Persian gulf.   The moderns identify the Ḥavila of this verse
with India; according to their view פּישׁון is the Indus.   That
one of the rivers here mentioned was an Indian one, was the
view prevalent among the ancients; and the identification of
חוילה with India, and פּישׁון with the Indus, is strengthened by
the fact that the products of the land of חוילה, viz. זהב, בדלח,
שׁהם, are mentioned by ancient writers as being found in
India; the gold of the Indus district being celebrated among
classical writers, as that of Ophir was among biblical: cf.
Her., iii. 106; Diod. Sic., ii. 36; Curt., viii. 9. 18.   Cf. 1 Kings 10,
11. Ps. 45, 10. Job 22, 24: see further, Del., p. 123; Di., p. 59[1].
חוילה has the article by Ewald, § 277 c; cf. ver. 7.   It seems
to indicate, as Di. remarks, that the Hebrews had not then
forgotten the original meaning of the word, '*the sand land*'
par excellence.   The חוילה mentioned in 10, 7 (cf. 1 Chron. 1, 9)
among the sons of Cush seems to denote a place distinct
from those intended here, and in 25, 18. 1 Sam. 15, 7, which is
perhaps to be identified with the modern Zeila on the Abyssinian
coast, south of Bab-el-Mandeb.   Cf. the note on 10, 7.

הוּא הסבב = '*that is the one encompassing the whole land
of Ḥavila.*'   The article with the predicate by Ges., § 110. 4,

---

[1] The name may possibly = '*Sandland*,' or '*Land of golden sand*,' connected with חול '*sand*.'

note; Driver, § 135. 7. סֹבֵב without the article would =
'*is encompassing.*' The word סבב does not of necessity
imply a complete surrounding; cf. Num. 21, 4. Judg. 11, 18.
Ps. 26, 6.

On the relative construction אֲשֶׁר שָׁם, cf. Ges., § 123. 1;
M. R., § 156 d.

12. וְהַדָּב. The ו is pointed וּ by Ges., § 104. 2 c. On the
‑ָ under the ו, to emphasize the sibilant, see Ges., § 10. 2.
Rem. b; Stade, § 105. Cf. 3, 17 (תֹאבְּלֶנָּה). 25, 22. 27, 26.
29, 3. 8 (גְלָלִי). ו is marked with metheg, as in Judg. 5, 12,
וּשְׁבֵה: see Ges., § 16. 2, 1 a; Stade, § 52 d.

הוּא in the Pent., with the exception of eleven places, is
of common gender. The punctuators, however, by pointing
it הִוא, indicate that they meant it to be read as הִיא, the usual
form of the fem.: cf. Ewald, § 184 c; Ges., § 32. iii. 6; Stade,
§ 171 c. 2. This has usually been explained as an archaism,
but Nöld., *Z. D. M. G.*, xx. (1866), p. 458, has pointed out
that this cannot be philologically sustained, if we compare the
other Semitic languages, all of which exhibit a fem. הִיא. He,
shewing that the double form must have existed *before* the
different branches of the Semitic race had parted from their
common home, rejects the supposition that the fem. הִיא was
at an early date lost, and again introduced into the language
at a later period from the Aramaic, but admits that he has no
plausible solution of the anomaly to offer. Only he is con-
vinced 'that it cannot be explained as an archaism (dass es
mit dem Archaismus nichts ist); at the most it might be an
artificial archaism.' Stade, § 171 c. 2, regards it as 'a mistake of tradition,' and adds, 'probably the use of הוא for both
genders arose from a MS., which both for הוא and היא wrote
defectively הא, as it is found on the Moabite stone and

Phoenician inscriptions. This הא was thoughtlessly always miswritten הוא.' Del., in the '*Zeitschrift für Kirchliche Wissenschaft und Kirchliches Leben*,' i. p. 393 ff., has accepted Nöldeke's statement that it cannot be an archaism, and accounts for the fem. as follows: 'Though through all Hebrew, even in the post-biblical literature (cf. p. 395 of his article), the distinction of gender was not sharply defined; yet at the time of the revision of the text, the use of הוא for the fem. was regarded as a mistake (for outside the Pentateuch it is unheard of, and not found in the Hebrew-Samaritan Pentateuch). In the recension of the text however it was presupposed that in the language at the time of Moses, although it possessed for the fem. the form היא, the use of הוא as of double gender prevailed, and the distinction of gender was at the lowest stage of its development.'

Stade's view, which is adopted by Kautzsch (cf. Ges., *Gram.*, l. c., foot-note), that היא and הוא were both originally written הא, and that the last redactors of the text have almost everywhere written this הוא without regard to gender, is borne out by the הא on the Moabite stone, line 6, ויאמר גם הא=בֵּית בָּמֹות כִּי, and line 27, וַיֹּאמֶר נַם־הוּא=בת במת כי הרס הא הָרֻם הוּא (cf. Mic. 5, 1, בית לחם, masculine); and the Phoenician inscription of Eṣmunazar, king of Sidon, line 22, הממלכת הַפַּמָלָכָה הַהִיא=הא in Heb.; cf. Schröd., *Phœn. Gram.*, pp. 144, 225. This is probably the best explanation of the anomaly[1]. The art. is pointed according to Ges., § 35. 2 A; Dav., § 11 b. הוא is here defined by the art. by Ges., § 111. 2; M. R., § 85.

<hr>

[1] It is not certain that היא=הוא is confined to the Pentateuch. It seems to be found in the *Codex Petropolitanus* (916 A.D.), edited by Dr. Strack, 1876. Delitzsch denies this (see p. 394 of his article), but admits that the distinction between ו and י is very slight.

הַבְּדֹלַח . ‘*Bdellium*,’ a transparent kind of gum, with a pleasant smell, and of wax-like appearance; found, according to Pliny, in India, Arabia, Media, and Babylonia: so Jos., Aq., Symm., Theod., and Vulg. In Greek the by-forms βδέλλα, μάδελκον occur. The LXX have ἄνθραξ here, but in Num. 11, 7 (the only other passage where the word occurs) κρύσταλλος, regarding בדלח as a stone, but this would have required אֶבֶן before it. The Syriac has ܒܶܪܽܘܠܳܐ (reading ר for ד), which apparently can be used of pearls or crystals. Saad. and others render *pearls* (so also Ges. in *Th.*), which meaning would be suitable here—between זהב and שהם—but hardly in Num. 11, 7 (Del.), and according to Tuch was first derived from this passage in order that some object of equal value with זהב and שהם might be mentioned; but cf. 1 Kings 10, 2. 10. The etymology is doubtful.

הַשֹּׁהַם . The art. as in הַזָּהָב, according to Ges., § 109. 3. Rem. 1 b; M. R., § 68. The LXX here give ὁ λίθος ὁ πράσινος, perhaps meaning the beryl, Vulg. ‘*lapis onychinus*,’ Syr. ܒܶܪܽܘܠܳܐ, Onq. בּוּרְלָא. Elsewhere variously rendered, onyx, sardonyx, sardius, which all belong to the same species (chalcedony), or beryl (more correctly chrysopras): cf. *H. W. B.*, 9th ed., Di. in loco. The etymology is doubtful.

13. גִּיחוֹן. A similar formation to פִּישׁוֹן. From גִּיחַ ‘*to burst forth*.’ This river flowed round the land of כּוּשׁ, and is quite distinct from the גיחון mentioned in 2 Chron. 32, 30. 1 Kings 1, 33. 38. 45. 2 Chron. 33, 14. The LXX have here Γεών, Vulg. ‘*Gehon*,’ so the other Vss. The LXX in Jer. 2, 18 translate the Heb. שִׁיחוֹר, Nile, by Γεών; cf. Ecclesiasticus 24, 27. Josephus and the Fathers also consider the Nile the river here meant, so many moderns. כּוּשׁ is Ethiopia. Thus if גיחון is the Nile, we have a river, taking its source in Asia, flowing round the African כּוּשׁ! Others consider כּוּשׁ as representing

only the Asiatic Cushites, and identify גיחון with either the
Ganges or Oxus. Reland identifies it with the Araxes. Del.
and Di. decide for the Nile, explaining the anomaly above
noted, as having arisen through the ignorance of the ancients
of geography; see their commentaries in loco.

14. חדקל,='*the Tigris,*' occurs again Dan. 10, 4. The
Heb. name agrees with the Sumerian *Idigna*, and the Bab.-
Assyr. *Idiglat* (Schr., *K. A. T.*, 2nd ed., 32 f.; Del., *Par.*, 170).
In Aramaic the name is דִּיגְלַת (so Onq. here); the Pesh.
has ܕܹܩܠܰܬ, Arab. دِجْلَة. 'The Aryan name (Old Persian
Tigra, Pahlawi דגרת, Greek Τίγρης, Τίγρις), according to the
express tradition of the ancients (Strabo, xi. 14, 8; Pliny,
vi. 31; Curt., iv. 9), designates the river as "*the arrow-
swift,*" Old Baktrian *tighra*="*pointed,*" *tighri*="*arrow.*"'
Dillmann.

קדמת. Render, '*in front of Assyria,*' i. e. from the
standpoint of the narrator; so LXX κατέναντι, Pesh. ܩܕܡܬ.
Others (the Targg., Aq., Tuch) render '*east of,*' thus including Mesopotamia in the term אשור; but then the narrator
could not have spoken of the Tigris as being east of Assyria,
for he must have known that Assyria extended far east of the
Tigris. Mesopotamia, too, is called ארם נהרים in 24, 10; for
this meaning of קדמת, cf. 4, 16.

פרת. '*The Euphrates,*' not further defined, as being
familiar to every Hebrew reader. It is often mentioned in
O. T. as '*the great river,*' or '*the river*' κατ' ἐξοχήν. Together
with the Heb.-Aramaic name, we have now the Old Persian
'*Ufratu,*' and the Babylonian-Assyrian '*Burattuv,*' '*Purâtu.*'
A Semitic etymology is still unknown; see Di. in loc., and
M. and V. in *H. W. B.*, 9th ed., p. 692 b.

15. וינחהו. The Hif'. imperf. with waw conv. from

נוח: see Ges., § 72. Rem. 9; Dav., § 40, esp. Rem. c. N. B. הֵנִיחַ='*to cause to rest*,' הִנִּיחַ '*to place*,' '*set*,' '*lay down*.'

לִעבדה ולשׁמרה. The inf. cstr. with suffixes follows the analogy of the segholate nouns: see Ges., § 61. 1; Dav., § 31. 4.

16. וַיְצַו עַל '*laid a command on him*.' More usually צוה,= '*to command*,' is followed by an acc., or the prep. לְ, or אל (cf. 28, 6), the words of the command being introduced by לאמר.

אכל תֹּאכל. '*Thou mayest indeed eat*.' The inf. abs. being prefixed to the verb. 'The inf. abs. expresses the idea of the verb simply, without conditions of person, mood, etc.; hence, when it precedes the finite verb, there is first the idea bare, and then the idea modified; and the effect of the whole is to express with some variety of emphasis the *fact* (not the *quality*) of the action as now predicated in the finite verb.' Dav., § 27, rule at end. See also Ewald, § 312 a; Ges., § 131. 3 a.

On the potential use of the imperf., see Driver, § 38 a; Ges., § 127. 3 d; M. R., § 7. 2 b.

אכל is one of the five verbs that form their imperf. with holem in the first syllable: see Ges., § 68. 1; Dav., § 35.

17. '*But from the tree of knowledge of good and evil, thou shall not eat of it*.' On the preposition with the suffix, repeating the substantive (a use allied to that of the *casus pendens*), see Driver, § 197. 6. Obs. 1; Ewald, § 309 a, ad fin.

אכלך is an instance of an inf. cstr. with the suffix departing from the analogy of segholate nouns: cf. ver. 15, and see Ges., § 61. 1. Rem. 2.

18. לא טוב היות‎. The inf. cstr. as the subject to a
sentence: cf. Ges., § 132. 1 a; M. R., §§ 112 b and 115.

אעשׂה לו‎. The ל of לו‎ has a *dag. forte conjunctivum*
or *euphonicum:* see Ges., § 20. 2; Dav., § 7. 4, foot-note; cf.
ver. 28. The LXX and Vulg. here have read the plural, to
bring the text into conformity with 1, 26.

עזר כנגדו‎, lit. '*a help as before him,*' i. e. '*a help corresponding to him,*' '*meet for him,*' A.V. LXX have here κατ'
αὐτόν, in ver. 20 ὅμοιος αὐτῷ; so the Syr. and Vulg. In Rab-
binic, כנגד‎ ='*corresponding to:*' see Ges., *Thes.*, p. 847. עזר‎
is used concretely, as in Ps. 70, 6: cf. Nah. 3, 9.

19. רייצר‎ is written defectively for וייצר‎, which occurs in
ver. 7. The verb must not be rendered as a pluperfect. It
appears that the narrator conceived the formation of animals
as posterior to that of man. For the question of the use
of the imperf. with waw conv. as a pluperfect, cf. the note
on ver. 2.

כל חית השׂדה‎, P כל חית הארץ‎ (1, 25. 30; cf. 2, 10).

מה‎. On the punctuation of מה‎, see Ges., § 37. 1; Dav.,
§ 13. 'The punctuation is quite like that of the article.'

מה יקרא‎ '*what he would call them;*' cf. Driver, § 39 b.

וכל אשׁר יקרא‎. The imperf. according to Driver, § 38 a,
'*all whatever he called them.*'

נפשׁ חיה‎ appears to be added very abnormally, in explanation of לו‎. Possibly these words are a gloss, as they
read very harshly. Such a redundancy as we find in the text
here is common in Aramaic, which would say לְהּ לְנַפְשָׁא חַיְתָא‎;
and there are genuine examples of it in the O. T., e.g. Ex. 2,
6. 1 Sam. 21, 14 (see Ges., § 121. 6. Rem. 3; M. R., § 72.
Rem. a), but none so harsh as this (note especially the masc.
לו‎). In late Hebrew this redundancy might be an Aramaism,

but that can hardly be the case in this passage. ‏נפשׁ חיה‎ = 'living creatures,' ‏נפשׁ‎ being collective. ‏חיה‎ is a fem. adj. (‏חיה‎ = 'life' is only poetical; see on 1, 21). As the text stands we have ‏לו‎ masc. followed by ‏נפשׁ חיה‎ fem., which is difficult. Del. supposes that ‏נפשׁ חיה‎ (cf. ‏נפשׁ‎ in 46, 27. Num. 31, 28) was construed *ad sensum* as a masc.; but these passages are scarcely parallel.

20. ‏וְלָאָדָם‎, so pointed by Ols. The word is not used as a proper name until 4, 25. In these three chapters (1–3) it is, with the exception of this verse and 3, 17. 21, always pointed with the article. Cf., however, M. R., § 66. Rem. a.

‏לא מצא‎. I. Impersonally, ' *One did not find for mankind.*' II. '*For himself* (‏לנפשׁו‎=‏לאדם‎) *he (man) did not find.*' III. '*For mankind (God) did not find.*' III. is not probable, as we have ‏האדם‎ already as subj. at the beginning of the verse. If I. be adopted, ‏מצא‎ would be impers. by Ges., § 137. 2; M. R., § 123. 2, and ‏לאדם‎ could stand without the art., as in 1, 26. Tuch adopts II. Del. and Di. propose a rendering that differs slightly from any of these: '*He (man) did not find for man,*' i. e. '*for a human being, like himself,*' etc.; almost the same as II, though they do not take ‏לאדם‎ as directly equivalent to ‏לנפשׁו‎.

21. ‏תחתבה‎ '*in its place;*' the suffix is a verbal one, cf. Ges., § 103. 1. Rem. 3; Stade, § 347 c. 3: with the nominal suffix it would be ‏תַּחְתֶּיהָ‎.

23. '*This now is . . . this shall be called woman.*' The connection of ‏אשׁה‎ with ‏אִישׁ‎ is preserved by the Vulg., which renders them by ' *virago* ' and ' *vir,*' respectively, probably following Symm., who has ἀνδρίς and ἀνήρ; so Luther, *Männin.*

‏לְקֳחָה‎. The form is made more distinct by the fuller shewa; see Ges., § 10. 2, and § 52. 1, s. p. The dag. in the ‏ק‎

has fallen away in accordance with the rule, that any doubled letter pointed with shewa, if it be not one of the aspirates (בגדכפת), may drop its doubling; see Dav., § 7. 4, foot-note a; Ges., § 20. 3 b, where the letters that commonly admit of this loss of the dag. are mentioned. Hence the Raphe.

24. '*Therefore doth a man leave his father and his mother and cleave unto his wife, and they become one flesh.*' The imperf. as freq. followed by the perf. with waw conv., in present time, as before (ver. 6) in past time; so Ps. 17, 14. 49, 11. 73, 10–11; Driver, § 113. 4 a. These words are the narrator's comment, as in 26, 33. 32, 33, as they would be unnatural if assigned to the man, who had no knowledge of a father or mother.

The LXX, Pesh., Vulg., and Sam. insert שְׁנֵיהָם '*and they two become;*' and the text is quoted thus in the N. T., Matt. 19, 5. Mark 10, 7; cf. 1 Cor. 6, 16. Eph. 5, 31. It may have fallen out of the Heb. text through the שניהם of ver. 25.

25. עֲרוּמִים marked by the Massoretes, מ' בדגש '*mem with dagesh.*' On the apparent anomaly of a long vowel in a toneless syllable, see Dav., p. 8; Stade, § 327 a. This word occurs again, with the same points, in Job 22, 6.

יתבשׁשׁוּ. Hithpolel of בוֹשׁ; see Ges., § 72. 7; Dav., § 26. 3 c. Render, '*were not ashamed,*' i. e. '*not in the habit of being ashamed.*' The imperf. according to Driver, § 30 a; Ewald, § 136 c.

3.

1. וְהַנָּחָשׁ הָיָה עָרוּם מִכֹּל חַיַּת. '*Now the serpent was more cunning than all the beasts of the field,*' etc. On the use of מִן in expressing the comparative, see Ges., § 119. 1; M. R., § 49. 2.

אַף כִּי, lit. = 'and that . . . !' is placed first in the sentence to denote astonishment, which may be expressed by a note of interrogation. Render, ' And (is it really the case) that ?' cf. Ewald, § 354 c; M. R., § 143 b. There is no necessity to suppose that the ה interrog. has fallen out.

לֹא . . . . כֹּל = ' not any ;' see Ges., § 152. 1 ad fin.; M. R., 142; cf. 2, 5.

3. תְּמֻתוּן. This form of the plural of the imperfect in וּן, which always in Hebrew has the tone, is the common ending in the pl. imperf. 3rd pers. masc. and 2nd masc. in classical Arabic (the abbreviated form being reserved for the subj. and jussive moods), and in Aramaic, but is not found in Ethiopic in the written language. It is tolerably common in Hebrew, and is probably not to be regarded as a mark of antiquity, but as a weightier form, being especially frequent in the elevated prose style and in poetry. ' I. It is found in various cases of pause, as here, and Ex. 1, 22 תחיון. II. As an emphatic form, e. g. in Deut. 1, 29 לא תערצון ולא תיראון; Josh. 4, 6 כי ישאלון: especially after particles or nouns, which expect a verb after them, e. g. כה, אשר כל, פן, למען, לא, למה, הדבר אשר. III. As a rhythmical form to ensure a fuller sound for the word, Hab. 3, 7 ירגזון; Ps. 4, 3 תאהבון. IV. As an audible connecting link, similar to the -εν, -σιν before ἀ, ἁ in Greek: so 32, 20 תדברון before אל עשו. Judg. 6, 31 תושיעון before אתו: most commonly before א, but also before ע, ה, ו, and מ. Many common verbs, as אמר, שוב, ידע, דבר, etc., have preserved the וּן; while others, as ירד, ישב, נתן, etc., do not receive it any longer. It is found in all classes of verbs, with the single exception of verbs ע"ע, and is very frequent in verbs ל"ה and ע"ו. Qal, as a light form, has it more frequently than the heavier reflexive forms. It occurs more commonly in the 3rd pers. than the 2nd pers. pl.

as this form is far more frequent, but is by no means uncommon in the 2nd pers. pl. in certain verbs, e. g. אמר, עשׂה, שׁמע, דבר, שׁמר. It is found in the oldest prose, e. g. in Gen. (twelve times), Ex. (twenty-eight times), Num. (seven times), Josh. (nine times), Judg. (eight times), 1 Sam. (eight times); being especially frequent in Exodus, which contains many old pieces; also in old poetry, e. g. Ex. 15. 2 Sam. 22 (once), and some Psalms and old prophets, e. g. Is., Mic., Joel, Hos., Amos. In Job, Deut., Is. 24–27, 40 ff., Ps. 58, 89, 104, etc., it is more artificial (a revived archaism). In the gnomic poetry (Prov.) it is rare, and does not occur in the erotic and purely elegiac (Song of Songs, Lam.). Leviticus has it very rarely, Ezekiel never. More modern prose writings (Ruth, Kings) have it only in colloquial passages. The books of Chronicles have preserved it in some passages from more ancient sources, while it rejects it in others. In Ezra, Neh., Esther, Dan. (Heb.), Eccles. there are no examples of ן.' See further, Böttcher, *Lehrbuch*, ii. § 930 (from whom the above paragraph slightly abbreviated is borrowed), where a full list of the passages, where the ending ן occurs, is given; and cf. Wright, *Arab. Gram.*, i. p. 63; Ges., § 72. 7. Rem. 4 and § 47. 3. Rem. 4; Dav., § 21. Rem. a. It may be observed that some of Böttcher's distinctions seem doubtful and arbitrary.

4. לֹא מוֹת תמוּתוּן. The negative should stand between the inf. and the verb; see Ges., § 131. 3. Rem. 1; Ewald, § 312 b. 1; who cite Amos 9, 8. Ps. 49, 8 as parallel to this passage. Its unusual position here is probably due to a desire to keep the formula מוֹת תמוּת from 2, 17 unchanged. Render, ' *Ye shall by no means die.*'

5. ידע. The participle as a true present, so 19, 13 כי המכסה אני 18, 17; משׁחיתים אנחנו (the subject does not

precede, as a slight emphasis is laid on the verb; cf.
Driver, § 135. 4), Driver, § 135. 2 and Obs.; cf. Ges.,
§ 134. 2 a.

ונפקחו ... ביום אכלכם. '*In the day ye eat ... your
eyes shall be opened.*' The perf. with waw conv. after a time
determination; see Driver, § 123 β; M. R., § 132 b; cf. § 26.
Waw in this usage is to be noticed. It assumes a stronger
demonstrative force than it has in the ordinary cases of the
perf. with waw conv. (cf. Driver, § 119), when used to introduce the predicate or the apodosis; so in Ex. 16, 6 ערב
וידעתם '*at evening, (then) ye shall know.*' 1 Kings 13, 31
במותי וקברתם אתי '*when I die, (then) ye shall bury me.*'
Ez. 24, 24 b בבאה וידעתם '*when it comes, (then) ye shall
know.*'

כאלהים '*as gods.*' Targ. Onq. כְּרַבְרְבִין '*as princes,*'
perhaps intentionally to avoid an anthropomorphic idea. Targ.
Jon. כְּמַלְאָכִין רַבְרְבִין דְּחַכְּמִין '*as mighty princes who know,*'
connecting יודעי with אלהים, which is grammatically possible.
The Samaritan has ᛦᛦᛦᛦᛦ '*like angels.*'

6. לְהַשְׂכִּיל. The LXX, Syr., Vulg., and some moderns
render, '*to look at,*' or '*regard,*' a meaning which השכיל
never has. Render, '*to become wise,*' lit. '*to gain insight,*' Del.
'*um einsichtig zu werden.*' Rashi's note here is כמו שאמר
לה יודעי טוב ורע '*compare his saying to her, "knowing good
and evil."*'

וַיֹּאכַל. Pausal form of יֹאכַל; cf. Ges., § 29. 4 c, note,
with § 68. 1. The LXX and Sam. read ויאכלו (plural), the
waw might have arisen out of the following waw in ותפקחנה.
The plural is not necessary.

7. כי עירומם הם. The pronoun stands here by Ges.,
§ 121. 1; M. R., § 125; cf. ver. 11.

עלה תאנה, lit. '*leaf of a fig*,' i.e. '*fig-leaf*,' here collective, '*fig-leaves*.'

ויעשׂו להם '*and they made themselves*.' The personal pronoun is used for the reflexive, as often with this verb; cf. Ges., § 124. 1 b; M. R., § 89 a.

8. קול, not '*the voice*,' but '*the sound*,' as in 2 Sam. 5, 24. 1 Kings 19, 12.

לרוח היום· '*About the cool of the day*,' so 8, 11 לעת ערב '*about eventide;*' 17, 21 למועד הזה '*about this date;*' also Is. 7, 15 לדעתו '*about* (*the time of*) *his knowing;*' cf. Ges., § 154. 3ᵉ; M. R., § 51. 2. In the East, towards evening a cool breeze springs up (cf. Song of Songs 2, 17. 4, 6) and the Oriental goes out; so 24, 63 לפנות הערב. The LXX render well τὸ δειλινόν. In 18, 1 the noontide is called חם היום '*the heat of the day*' (LXX, excellently, μεσημβρίας); Abraham being described as sitting in the door of his tent.

9. אַיֶּכָּה. The suffix (as it is pointed) is a verbal one; cf. Ges., § 100. 5; M. R., § 39; אַיֶּכָּה standing for אַיֶּנְכָּה; cf. Prov. 2, 11 תִּנְצְרֶכָּה, and with the nun, Jer. 22, 24 אֶתְּקֶנְךָ; see Ges., § 58. 4; Dav., § 31. 5. Stade, § 355 b. 3, remarks that 'It is due to false analogy if the Pausal suffix ךָ— is transferred from the verb to a noun,' and cites with this passage, Prov. 25, 16 דַּיֶּךָ, and other instances. It is possible, however, that the vowel points in these cases are not to be trusted as they stand in our texts.

The ה at the end of איכה is merely a *scriptio plena* (found both in obj. and subj. suffixes),—as Prov. 2, 11 תנצרכה; cf. ver. 12 נתתה. Ex. 15, 11 כמכה (twice). 1 Sam. 1, 26 עמכה,— and in no way affects the sense.

10. אנכי. The Mass. note here is מלעל, i.e. the word is, contrary to rule, accented on the penult.; cf. Ges., § 29. 4 c;

Dav., § 10. 5 b. As a rule the vowel in pause is lengthened, this cannot take place here as the vowel is already long. The accents :—, —, and (sometimes) —'— usually effect this lengthening, when it is possible, in pause. Here the minor distinctive accent —, (*Tifcha*) exercises a pausal influence, there being a sufficient break in the sense for the voice naturally to rest; cf. Driver, § 103, and 15, 14 יַעֲבָדִ֣י (the tone drawn back and the vowel lengthened), which the Massoretes have not noticed. אתה and עתה, like אנכי, transfer the accent to the penult. in pause.

11. כי עירם אתה is really the object to מי הגיד, see M. R., § 161 b, where it is designated 'an object sentence;' cf. 1, 4.

לבלתי וגו״. בלתי is used regularly to negative the inf. cstr. after ל; cf. Ges., § 152. 1; M. R., § 140. Rem. a.

המן. On the pointing of ה interrog., see Ges., § 100. 4, s. p.; Dav., § 49. 2. Here ה introduces a simple interrogative sentence (cf. Ges., § 153. 2; M. R., § 143), the answer being uncertain (affirmative or negative). הלא=Latin *nonne*, the answer expected being in the affirmative.

12. האשה . . . עמדי, a *casus pendens*. '*The woman which etc. . . . she gave me*.' הוא is resumptive and is inserted for emphasis; see Driver, § 123. Obs.; cf. 15, 4 כי אם אשר יצא יהוה . . . הזאת הוא ישלח 7, 24; ממעיך הוא יירשך. The *casus pendens* is often used to relieve a long and unwieldy sentence.

ואכל. The pausal form of the 1st person. In ver. 6 we have ותאכל and ויאכל as the pausal forms of the 3rd pers. fem. sing. and 3rd pers. masc. sing. respectively; see Ges., § 68. 1.

13. מה זאת עשית : cf. 12, 18. M. R., § 93. Rem. c, renders, '*What, this, hast thou done?=what hast thou done*

there?' taking זֹאת in opposition to מַה. The A. V. and Syr. render it as a relative sentence, '*what is this thou hast done?*' Del. adopts the former rendering, remarking that the corresponding question in Arabic, whether the demonstrative belongs to the interrogative, or whether it should be rendered as our Eng. Ver. does, was a subject of dispute among the Arabic grammarians. He points out that the Massoretic punctuation favours the first rendering. LXX render slightly differently, τί τοῦτο ἐποίησας; so Vulg. *quare hoc fecisti?* On the dag. in the ז of זֹאת, see on 2, 18.

14. אָרוּר אַתָּה מִכָּל וגו׳ LXX, ἐπικατάρατος σὺ ἀπὸ πάν-των κ.τ.λ. Vulg. *maledictus es inter omnia*, etc. Render as the Vulg. '*Cursed art thou among all beasts,*' i. e. '*marked out by a curse from,*' etc. The other renderings, '*cursed by all beasts,*' i. e. '*these shall hate and abhor the serpent,*' or '*more cursed than,*' as apparently A. V., are untenable: for, as Knobel points out, the curse comes from God, not from the beasts, who had no reason to curse, and is aimed at the serpent only; not at the other beasts, as there is no ground assigned for cursing these. For this use of מִן, cf. Ex. 19, 5. Deut. 14, 2. Judg. 5, 24.

כֹּל יְמֵי חַיֶּיךָ, acc. of time; cf. Ges., § 118. 2; M. R., § 42.

15. הוּא יְשׁוּפְךָ רֹאשׁ וגו׳ רֹאשׁ and עָקֵב are accusatives of limitation; cf. Ges., § 139. 2, s. p.; M. R., § 44 and Rem. a; Ewald, § 281 c; so 37, 21 לֹא נַכֶּנּוּ נֶפֶשׁ; Deut. 33, 11 מָחַץ מָתְנַיִם; Jer. 2, 16 יִרְעוּךְ קָדְקֹד. Hebrew in this respect is analogous to Greek; cf. τυφλὸς τά τ᾽ ὦτα τόν τε νοῦν τά τ᾽ ὄμματ᾽ εἶ, '*blind both in ears and mind and eyes art thou;*' βλέπω κολοιὸν τὤμματ᾽ ἐκκεκομμένον, '*I see a jackdaw pecked out as to his eyes.*' שׁוּף occurs again Job 9, 17. Ps. 139, 11. The only meaning which can be philologically defended is '*crush.*'

This meaning suits Job 9, 17, but not Ps. 139, 11. The alternative rendering is, '*lie in wait for*,' a kindred form with שאף '*to pant after*;' it suits Ps. 139, 11 (cf. Del. in loc.) better than '*crush*,' but a word='*cover*' is required: hence some read there יְשׁוּכֵּנִי, so Ew., Ges. in *Th.* שׁוּף='*to crush*' is justified by the Aramaic usage of שׁוּף and ܫܳܦ or ܫܽܦ, e.g. in Onq., Deut. 9, 21 וְשָׁפִית יָתֵיהּ '*and I crushed it*,' i.e. the calf; Targ. on Job 14, 19 אַבְנַיָּא שָׁיְפָא מַיָּא '*the water crushes the stones*.' And in Syriac, Ex. 32, 20 (Pesh.) ܘܫܳܦ ܚܰܡ̈ܶܗ ܒܫܺܝܢܳܐ (=Heb. ויטחן) '*and crushed* (better *scraped*) *it with a file*.' [It should be remarked that in Syriac the roots ܫܰܦ and ܫܽܦ are confounded one with the other, as Bernstein points out l. c.] Cf. Levy, *Chald. Wörterb.*; Bernst., *Lex. Syr.* sub voc. Di. admits that the meaning '*crush*' suits the first part of the clause, i.e. the man's crushing the serpent's head, but denies its application to the serpent, and adopts the rendering '*lie in wait for*,' which he attempts to justify by appealing to שאף; but this meaning is not so certain as the meaning '*crush*,' and the double acc. after the rendering '*lie in wait for*' is difficult. שׁוּף is applied to the serpent in the second half of the verse by a kind of zeugma, the same verb being used to express the mutual nature of the enmity (Kal.); compare Del., and Tuch, 2nd ed., who compares '*feriri a serpente*,' Pliny, xxix. 4. 22. The Vss. render variously. In the LXX the reading varies, both τηρήσει ... τηρήσεις and τειρήσει ... τειρήσεις occurring. The Vulg. has '*ipsa conteret caput tuum, et tu insidiaberis calcaneo ejus*;' but שׁוּף cannot have a different meaning in each half of the sentence. Syriac has ܗܽܘ ܢܕܽܘܫ ܢܶܦܚܳܟ ܘܐܰܢ̱ܬ ܬܶܡܚܽܘܢܳܝܗܝ ܒܥܶܩܒܶܗ, using different words in the two parts of the clause, but giving שׁוּף a similar sense in each half. Onq. paraphrases יְהֵא הוּא דְכִיר [לָךְ] מָה דְעָבַדְתְּ לֵיהּ מִלְּקַדְמִין וְאַתְּ תְּהֵי נָטַר לֵיהּ לְסוֹפָא:

' *he will remember against thee what thou hast done to him from
the beginning, and thou wilt guard against him to the end.*'
Targg. Jon. and Jer. paraphrase widely, but seem to have
rendered שׁוּף ' *crush.*'

16. הרבה ארבה ' *with a multiplying, I will multiply,*'
i. e. '*I will greatly multiply;*' cf. the rule on 2, 16.   רבה has
two forms for the inf. abs. Hif'il : (1) הַרְבֵּה (which would be
the regular form) used as an adverb; (2) הַרְבָּה, see Ges.,
§ 75. iv. Rem. 15 : only here and 16, 10. 22, 17.

עצבונך והרונך.   Not a hendiadys, '*the pain of thy conception,*' Ges., § 155. 1 a, but '*thy pain and (especially) thy
conception :*' waw attaching the *particular* הרונך to the *general*
עצבנך; cf. Ps. 18, 1. Is. 2, 1.   הרון is an abnormal formation,
which occurs nowhere else in the O. T.   The abs. state
is הֵרָיוֹן (Hos. 9, 11. Ruth 4, 13), cstr. הֵרְיוֹן; with suffix הֵרְיוֹנֵךְ
and shortened הֵרוֹנֵךְ; see Stade, § 297.

תשׁוקתך.   The LXX here, and 4, 17, render with ἀπο-
στροφή, possibly reading תשׁובתך; cf. their rendering in 1 Sam.
7, 17. Frankel, *Einfluss*, p. 10, suggests that the LXX rendering is a free euphemistic translation of the Heb. word.   The
word תשׁוקה is only found once again outside the book of
Genesis, viz. in the Song of Songs 7, 11 אני לדודי ועלי תשׁוקתו;
LXX, ἐγὼ τῷ ἀδελφιδῷ μου, καὶ ἐπ' ἐμὲ ἡ ἐπιστροφὴ αὐτοῦ.

17. ולאדם.   On the pointing וְלָאָדָם, adopted by some,
see the note on 2, 20.   The punctuators, excepting here,
ver. 21 and 2, 20, always point אדם with the article up to
4, 25, where it is first used as a proper name.

בעבורך.   The LXX (ἐν τοῖς ἔργοις) and Vulg. ('*in opere
tuo*') seem to have read עבודך, which they apparently took as
עֲבוֹדָתְךָ.   Tuch considers the variant as perhaps due to the
parallel passage 4, 12.

18. ‫קוץ ודרדר‬. Cf. Hos. 10, 8. Only in Isaiah do we find the phrase ‫שמיר ושית‬, e. g. Is. 5, 6. ‫דרדר‬ occurs but once again in Hos. l. c.

‫ואכלת‬. Notice the place of the tone, which has been thrown forward one place by waw conv. with the perfect; see for details, Driver, § 110 : cf. also Ges., § 49. 3; Dav., § 23. 3.

19. ‫תאכל לחם‬. The tone is drawn back on to the penult., to avoid the concurrence of two tone syllables; see Ges., § 29. 3 b.

‫עד שובך אל האדמה‬. On the construction, see Ges., §§ 132. 1, 133; M. R., § 111 b; and above 2, 4. Render, '*until thou return;*' ‫שובך‬ (as Arabic shews; see Wright, *Arab. Gram.*, i. p. 311) is to be regarded as the genitive after ‫עד‬, taken as a subst.

‫כי ממנה‬. Some render, '*from which thou wast taken,*' lit. '*which from it thou wast taken;*' ‫כִּי‬ being regarded as equivalent to the relative ‫אשר‬; so in 4, 25; cf. Ges., § 123. 1; M. R., § 156: so all the Vss. here and in 4, 25, except the Sam., which has ‫א·2·ה‬ here and ‫ה·צ‬ in 4, 25. But as the passages cited in defence of this are not conclusive, it is better to render '*for*' here and in 4, 25. '*Until thou returnest unto the ground; for thou wast taken from it*' (pause, this half of the verse being marked off from the second half by *Ath-nach* [‫־ֽ‬], the second strongest prose accent): '*for dust thou art,*' etc.

20. ‫חוה‬ = '*Life*' or '*Living,*' not '*Life-giver.*' It is equivalent to ‫חַיָּה‬, the form used here being antiquated in Heb., but preserved in Phoenician (Di.). LXX here Ζωή, in the other passage where it occurs (4, 1) Εὔα. Ζωή is probably intentionally used by the LXX, being occasioned by the explanatory addition ‫כי הוא היתה וגו׳‬.

22. '*And Yahweh Elohim said, Behold the man hath become*

as one of us, so as to know . . . and now that he may not stretch forth his hand and take,' etc.

כאחד ממנו. On the construct state before the preposition, see Ges., § 116. 1; M. R., § 73. Rem. a. It is especially frequent with אחד and מן, Lev. 13, 2. Num. 16, 15. 1 Sam. 9, 3. 1 Kings 19, 2, etc.

לדעת וגו״=*'so as to know:'* cf. 1 Sam. 12, 17 לשאל לכם מלך; Prov. 26, 2 כצפור לנוד כדרור לעוף. On this usage of the inf. with ל, see Driver, § 205; Ewald, § 280 d.

פן is used here independently, as in Ex. 13, 17; cf. Ewald, § 337 b; M. R., § 164 b; 'without indicating that the sentence which it introduces is dependent on another.' The formula, *'For he said . . . lest,'* occurs frequently, and always implies that some precaution is taken by the speaker to prevent what he fears happening; e. g. Ps. 38, 17 (compare Del., *Die Psalmen*, p. 323, 4th ed.). Gen. 38, 11. 42, 4. Ex. 13, 17, etc.

ולקח. The perfect with waw conv. after the imperfect with פן; so 19, 19 ומתי . . . פן תדבקני; Ex. 1, 10 פן ירבה והיה. Three times (Ps. 2, 12. Jer. 51, 46. Prov. 31, 5) we find the imperfect repeated after פן, instead of a perf. with waw conv.; see Driver, § 115 end, and § 116.

וְחַי. Perf. with waw conv. pointed with pretonic qameç; so 19, 19 וָמַתִּי (notice the tone; cf. the note there); 44, 22 וָמֵת: see on 1, 2.

חי is perf. from חָיַ: see Ges., § 67; Dav., § 42.

24. את הכרובים *'the cherubim.'* These appear in the Old Testament always in connection with God's manifesting himself to the world. In the tabernacle they hovered over the ark (Ex. 25, 18 ff.). In Solomon's temple they are represented as stationed on the floor of the Holy of Holies, spreading out their wings from one side to the other (1 Kings 6, 23.

1 Chron. 28, 18). In Ez. 1 and 10 they form God's living chariot, in which he appears to the prophet; and in Ps. 18, 11. 2 Sam. 22, 11 God is represented as riding on a cherub to judgment: cf. Ps. 80, 2. 1 Sam. 4, 4. 2 Sam. 6, 2, where God is described as "יושב הכ‎. From 1 Kings, l. c., we find that the cherub had an upright form, partly human, with one face (Ex. 25, 20), two wings (1 Kings 6, 24), and possibly hands. In Ez. 1 and 10 a somewhat fuller and different description of the cherubim is given: 'with the similitude of a man, four wings' (Ez. 1, 11. 23), two of which served to cover their bodies, and with two of which they flew; and under their wings human hands (Ez. 1, 8. 10, 7. 8, 21), with four faces (Ez. 1, 10. 10, 14), one human, one that of a lion, one that of an ox, and one that of an eagle, and the soles of their feet like those of a calf (Ez. 1, 7). Lastly (Ez. 1, 18. 10, 12; cf. Rev. 4, 6), their whole body was studded with eyes. It is uncertain whence the Hebrews derived their idea of the cherubim; possibly the winged forms on the Assyrio-Babylonian and Egyptian monuments exercised some influence on their conception of the cherub, but it is doubtful whether they borrowed the idea from either the Egyptians or Assyrians (cf. the authorities cited below).

The etymology of the word is uncertain. (i) Some connect it with the Aramaic ڡڼ‎, כְּרַב‎ *aravit;* so כְּרוּב‎ = *arator, bos:* cf. Ez. 10, 14 with 1, 10. (ii) Another view is that כְּרוּב‎ is transposed for רְכוּב‎ = 'chariot,' i. e. 'the divine chariot:' cf. 1 Chron. 28, 18, where the כרובים‎ are explained by תבנית המרכבה‎; so Rödig. in Ges., *Thes.;* M. and V., *H. W. B.,* 9th ed. (iii) Hyde (quoted by Ges., *Thes.,* p. 710) considers that כרוב‎ = קרוב‎, i.e. 'he who is near God,' 'his servant.' (iv) Maurer on Is. 6, 2 explains כרוב‎ as from כרב‎ = כרם‎, Arab. كَرُمَ‎ 'nobilis *fuit.'* (v) Another view is that כרוב is to be connected with the Arab. كرب *'adstringere,'* so כרוב *'a strong being'* (Rosenmüller); cf. viii. (vi) Ges. in the *Thes.* proposes a derivation from כרב=חרם, Arab. حرم *'prohibuit a communi usu.'* כרוב= *'custos,' 'satelles,'* i.e. Dei, 'qui profanos arcet.' All these are most precarious and improbable. (vii) Vatke, see Ges., *Thes.*, 711, assigned a Persian origin to the word, regarding it as the same as the Greek γρύψ, γρυπός, 'quod a Pers. گرفتن (greifen) *prehendere, tenere,* derivabat Chr. Th. Tychsen (Heeren's *Ideen,* i. p. 386), vel idem esse volunt atque γρυπός *naso adunco nostrove praeditus.'* (viii) Del., *Par.*, 154, connects it with an Assyrian root '*karâbu*' (from which an adj. '*karûbu*' is derived)='*to be great, powerful;*' cf. Schr., *K. A. T.*², p. 39. The word reads like a foreign one, but it seems that nothing can be affirmed as to its meaning with certainty. See further, Di. in *Schenkel's Bibel Lex.*, 1. 509 ff.; Keil., *Bib. Arch.*, 2nd ed., i. 92 ff.; Winer, *R. W. B.*; Riehm, *H. W. B.*, art. *Cherubim;* Del. *Comm.* and Di. *Comm.* on this passage; also Cheyne, art. *Cherub,* in *Ency. Brit.*

ואת להט החרב '*and the blade of the waving sword.*'

החרב. The article is pointed according to Ges., § 35. 2 A; Dav., § 11 b; and is placed before the genitive, and *not* before the cstr. state, by Ges., §§ 110. 2, 111. 1; M.R., § 76. II. a.

המתהפכת, lit.=*'the one turning itself about:'* cf. on 2, 11; also M. R., § 92. Rem. a. The form is a participle fem. sing. Hithpa'el of הפך, being formed as a segholate noun, and so accented on the penult.: see Ges., § 95. Rem. 2. 3. 4; Dav., p. 196, esp. 2.

את דרך עץ החיים *'the way to the tree of life:'* so 16, 7 דרך שור *'the way to Shur;'* 38, 14 דרך תמנתה *'the way to Timnah;'* 48, 7 בדרך אפרת *'on the way to Ephrath.'* Hebrew uses the cstr. state (implying belonging) to denote ideas which are made clearer in English by the use of a preposition.

4.

1. ידע '*to get to know,*' '*make the acquaintance of,*' so euphemistically = '*concubuit cum ea;*' used again in this sense vers. 17. 25. 24, 16, and often. This meaning has passed over into Hellenistic Greek; cf. γιγνώσκειν, often used by the LXX for the Hebrew ידע, e. g. here. Cf. also in the New Testament, Luke 1, 34 ἐπεὶ ἄνδρα οὐ γιγνώσκω. The Pesh. has ܣܚܡ, which is again used in the same sense in their version of Matt. 1, 25 οὐκ ἐγίνωσκεν αὐτήν = ܘܠܐ ܚܟܡܗ.

קין '*Kain,*' elsewhere a nom. app. = '*spear,*' 2 Sam. 21, 16, or a nom. prop. of a people, Num. 24, 22. Judg. 4, 11. The text here seems to connect קין with the root קנה '*to gain,*' '*acquire;*' but this explanation must not be regarded as an etymology. The name was given, not because it was derived from קנה, but as recalling to mind this word : compare such proper names as נוח, שמואל, משה (not *derived from,* but *recalling to mind* משה). Gesenius derives קין here from קין = '*to forge,*' Arab. قَانَ, قَيْنٌ, '*a smith,*' Syr. ܩܝܢܐ; and supposes that קַיִן in this passage means '*spear,*' as in 2 Sam. 21, 16.

את יהוה. LXX, διὰ τοῦ Θεοῦ. Syr. ܠܡܪܝܐ '*for the Lord.*' Onq. מִן קֳדָם יְיָ '*from before Yahweh.*' Vulg. '*per Deum.*' The Targ. of Ps.-Jon. has קָנִיתִי לְגַבְרָא יַת־מַלְאָכָא דַיְיָ '*I have gotten as man the angel of the Lord,*' possibly meaning the Messiah. The את has been variously explained. I. Di. and others render '*with Yahweh,*' i. e. through his assistance, with his help; so LXX, though it is uncertain whether διά is a free rendering, or whether they had מֵאֵת for את in their text, and similarly the Vulg. and Onqelos. Elsewhere, to be sure,

we find עם used in this sense, and not את; cf., for example.
1 Sam. 14, 45 כי עם אלהים עשׂה; still את may be regarded as synonymous with עם, as may be inferred from
its alternative usage with עם in the phrase '*to be with one,*'
i. e. help him; cf. 26, 3 עמך with 21, 10 את הנער. 28, 15. 31,
3 עָ, but 26, 24. 39, 2 את. II. *a.* Others (Luther, etc.)
render, '*I have gained a man, the Lord;*' את יהוה being a
second acc. of nearer definition, so 6, 10 שׁלשׁה בנים את שם;
26, 34; Judg. 3, 15; Eve supposing she had given birth to
the Messiah; see Ps.-Jon., above. *b.* Or as Umbreit, '*I possess as a man, Yahweh,*' אישׁ acc. of the predicate. But
against *a* it may be urged that there is nothing in the text to
justify the idea that Eve thought she had given birth to the
Messiah (cf. also 3, 15); and against *b* that it gives no
explanation of the name of the child.

2. ותסף ללדת '*and she bare again;*' cf. ver. 12. The
finite verb in Hebrew corresponds to the adverb in our idiom.
We find other verbs used in Hebrew to express adverbs, e. g.
מהר '*to hasten;*' cf. Ges., § 142. 1. 2; M. R., § 114 a.

ויהי הבל רעה צאן וקין. וקין is placed before the verb
to which it belongs in order to slightly emphasize the contrast between the occupations of Kain and Abel. M. R., § 131.
1 b. Rem. c, compares μὲν ... δέ in Greek. הבל has been
explained as meaning '*a breath,*' '*nothing,*' possibly with
reference to his short life; but it is doubtful if the name can
be brought into connection with this meaning. In Assyrian
'*Habal*' is a common word for son.

רֹעֵה is a participle in the cstr. state, '*a shepherd of;*'
רֹעֶה would be the abs. state, and צאן would then be in the
acc. case. Both constructions are possible, cf. 22, 12 יְרֵא אֱלֹהִים
with Ex. 9, 20 הַיָּרֵא אֶת־דְּבַר יְהוָֹה; see other examples in Ges.,
§ 135. 1; M. R., § 121.

3. מִפְּרִי. The prep. מִן must be taken here in a partitive sense, 'some of,' cf. 8, 20 ויתן לך אלהים 27, 28; ויקח מכל־הבהמה; מטל; Ex. 12, 7. Ges., § 154. 3 c; M. R., § 94 a.

מנחה. 1. 'a gift,' 2. 'an offering (to God),' but not to be taken in this passage in its more restricted sense 'the meal offering,' as opposed to זבח, 'the meat offering.' The LXX render it here by θυσίαν.

4. 'And Abel too brought.' גם with the pronoun repeated is emphatic; cf. ver. 26 ולשת גם הוא.

וּמֵחֶלְבֵּהֶן, scriptio defectiva, for וּמֵחֶלְבֵיהֶן. The sing. would be חֶלְבֵּהֶן. Other instances of scriptio defectiva are, 1, 21 לְמִינֵהֶם. Job 42, 10 רֵעֵהוּ for רֵעֵיהוּ. Ex. 33, 13 דְּרָכֶךָ for דְּרָכֶיךָ; see Ges., § 91. 2. Rem. 1. 'The singular would be permissible here (Lev. 8, 16. 25), but would not express the plurality of animals so distinctly' (Di.). The plural here, as in Lev. 6, 5,='fat pieces.' In the Levitical service the offering of the first-born of the flock and their fat portions is enjoined; cf. Num. 18, 17.

וַיִּשַׁע. Impf. Qal from שָׁעָה, apocopated from יִשְׁעֶה, יִשַׁע=יִשְׁעְ; cf. Ges., § 75. Rem. 1. 3 a, b, c; so יִחַר from יֶחֱרֶה. in ver. 5. The verb שעה is rare in prose.

5. וַיִּחַר לְקַיִן. So 18, 30. 32. 31, 36, and often. I. Either אף may be understood, 'it (anger) was hot for Kain,' or II. חרה may be taken impersonally, 'it was hot to Kain.' On this impersonal use of the 3rd perf. sing., cf. Ges., § 137. 2; M. R., § 124.

7. Render, 'Is there not, if thou doest well, lifting up? and if thou doest not well, at the door sin croucheth; and towards thee is its desire, but thou oughtest to rule over it.' שְׂאֵת (for שְׂאֵת inf. cstr. of נשא, cf. Ges., § 76. 2 a) must be explained from the phrase נשא פנים='to lift up (one's own) face,' the

opposite of נפלו פנים in verse 6; so Tuch, Ke., Del., and Di.: compare also the usage of language in Job 10, 15. 11, 15. 22, 26. Lifting up of the face = '*cheerfulness, joy;*' falling of the face, '*sadness* or *moroseness.*' The Vss. render variously. LXX has οὐκ ἐὰν ὀρθῶς προσενέγκῃς, ὀρθῶς δὲ μὴ διέλῃς, ἥμαρτες ἡσύχασον, possibly connecting שְׂאֵת with מַשְׂאֵת 43, 34, and taking פתח in the sense of dividing, and perhaps reading חָטָאתָ רְבִץ; cf. their rendering of רבץ in Job 11, 19. Frankel, *Einf.*, p. 67, considers that this translation refers to some proverb current at the time the translation was made. Pesh. has, هَا'ۗ لٰعفۡ مٰدۡكٰا ٥ۢۗ إۡ لٰعفۡ كٰلٰ لٰوۡكٰا مٰۢۚۗا ۥٰدۡتٰۢ '*Behold if thou doest well thou receivest; and if thou doest not well, at the door sin croucheth,*' taking שאת in the sense of receiving; so Vulg. '*Nonne si bene egeris recipies, sin autem male, statim in foribus peccatum aderit,*' but this is not in keeping with the context. Onq. has, הֲלָא אִם־תּוֹטֵיב עוֹבָדָךְ יִשְׁתְּבֵיק לָךְ וְאִם לָא תוֹטֵיב עוֹבָדָךְ לְיוֹם דִּינָא חִטְאָה נְטִיר עָתִיד לְאִיתְפָּרְעָא מִנָּךְ אִם־לָא־תְתוּב וְאִם־תְּתוּב יִשְׁתְּבֵק לָךְ '*If thou doest thy work well thou will be pardoned; but if thou doest not thy work well, for the day of judgment thy sin is laid up, ready to take vengence upon thee, if thou dost not repent; but if thou repentest thou shalt be forgiven,*' paraphrasing, but taking שאת in the sense '*forgive:*' this rendering of Onqelos' is also out of harmony with the context.

חטאת רבץ. '*Sin is at the door* (cf. Prov. 9, 14) *a lurker.*' Sin is compared to a ravenous beast lying in wait for its prey; perhaps a lion is here intended (cf. the Arabic name for the lion الرابض '*the lier in wait*'); cf. 1 Pet. 5, 8. Sin being personified is viewed as masc., so we have רבץ, and the masc. suffixes in תשוקתו and בו; cf. Ges., § 147. Rem. 2; M. R., § 135. 4 a; Ewald, § 318 a. See also Kalisch, *Heb. Gram.*, I. § 77. 13.

8. ויאמר קין וגו׳. LXX, Itala, Pesh., Vulg., Sam., Targ. Jer. have given in their translations נלכה השדה, which does not stand in the Mass. text. Frankel, *Einfl.*, p. 55, objects to נלכה on the ground that a Hebrew would say נֵצֵא, not נֵלְכָה, and regards the addition in the LXX as a gloss; but though this is the more usual phrase, yet we have 27, 5 וילך עשׂו השדה; Ruth 2, 2 אלכה נא השדה. Some MSS. note a lacuna here [פסקא]; two expressly note no lacuna (בלא פסקא, Wright); and according to Del. it is doubtful whether the פסקא is found in the best authorities. Some (Bött., Kn.), unwilling to accept a lacuna, read וישׁמר, cf. 2 Sam. 11, 16 ' *he laid in wait for.*' Tuch, comparing Ex. 19, 25, where he takes ויאמר אליהם (as אמר is always followed by what is said) in the sense ' *Moses spake to the people what God had said to him,*' ver. 27 (cf. Ewald, § 303 b, 2), renders, ' *And Kain said it,*' viz. what God had said to him. This is, according to Di., ' something psychologically quite improbable.'

בהיותם וגו׳, lit. ' *In their being in the field,*' i. e. ' *when they were in the field.*' LXX, ἐν τῷ εἶναι αὐτοὺς κ.τ.λ., cf. 2, 4 בהבראם and the note there.

10. מה עשׂית. מה pointed with ־ַ before the guttural with ־ָ, according to Ges., § 37. 1; Dav., § 13, ' מה assumes a pointing quite like the article.'

קול דמי. I. ' *Hark, thy brother's blood crying!*' קול is used as an interjection, as in Jer. 10, 22. Is. 13, 4; cf. Ges., § 148. 1 : צעקים being in apposition to דמים, Ewald, § 317 c. II. M. R., § 135. 3 c, takes it apparently as an instance of the predicate agreeing with the genitive instead of the cstr. state, as is always the case, for example, with כל; M. R. renders, ' *The voice of thy brother's blood-drops cry.*' The Sam. reads צעק. דמים=blood violently shed.

11. ‏ארור אתה מן האדמה‏. Cf. 3, 14. I. ‘*Cursed art thou away from the ground*,’ or II. ‘*Cursed art thou from*,’ etc., i. e. the curse shall strike thee from the ground, cf. ver. 12. I. is adopted by Tuch and Del., II. by Ibn Ezra, Keil, Kn. The rendering ‘*Cursed art thou by*’ is untenable, as curses are represented in the Old Testament as coming from God or man, never from the ground. The rendering ‘*More cursed art thou than*’—though 3, 17. 8, 21 may be cited in its favour— does not suit the context here; cf. ver. 14, which favours I, more stress being laid in the narrative on Kain’s banishment than on the unfruitfulness of the soil, or on the difference in the curses laid on Kain and the ground.

‏אשׁר פצתה את פיה‏. Cf. Is. 5, 14 ‏לכן הרחיבה שׁאל נפשׁה ופערה פיה לבלי חק‏.

12. ‏לא תסף תת‏. The jussive with ‏לא‏ is rare, cf. 24, 8. Joel 2, 2. Ez. 48, 14. Ewald, § 320 a. 1; Driver, § 50. Obs.

‏כחה‏. Cf. Job 31, 39 ‏אם כחה אכלתי‏.

‏נע ונד‏. The LXX paraphrased to reproduce the paronomasia, στένων καὶ τρέμων; Hier., ‘*vagus et profugus*.’

13. ‏גדול עוני מנשׂא‏, lit. ‘*Greater is my punishment than bearing*,’ i. e. ‘*my punishment is too great to bear*.’ ‏מן‏ before the inf. cstr., as in Ps. 40, 6 ‏עצמו מספר‏. 1 Kings 8, 64 ‏קטון מהכיל‏.

‏עון‏ = ‘*sin*,’ including its consequence, punishment, which is represented as a burden heavy to bear; cf. Is. 24, 20. Ps. 38, 5.

‏נשׂוא‏, inf. cstr. with the ‏נ‏ retained, Ges., § 76. 2 a; cf. Num. 20, 21 ‏נתן‏ and Gen. 38, 9 ‏נתן‏, by the side of the more usual form ‏תת‏. The Vss. mostly render, ‘*My transgression is greater than forgiving*,’ i. e. ‘*too great to be forgiven*,’ which is grammatically possible, but not so suitable here, as in ver. 14, Kain speaks of his punishment, not with a view to its removal through the forgiveness of his offence, but with a desire that it should be mitigated.

14. כל מצאי =‘ *every one that findeth me*,’ lit. ‘ *my finder*.’ The participle may either govern its case like the verb, or may stand as a substantive in the cstr. state followed (as here) by a suffix or a genitive; cf. Ges., § 135. 1; M. R., § 121; cf. also § 80. 2 a and Gen. 32, 12 יָרֵא אֹתוֹ ‘ *timens eum*,’ 23, 10. 18 באי שער עירו ; Ex. 1, 4 יצאי ירך יעקב. Comp. note on 4, 2.

15. כל הרג קין, *casus absolutus*, ‘ *Every one that slayeth Kain, he (Kain) shall be avenged*’ (cf. ver. 24); or ‘ *vengeance shall be taken*,’ so Kn.; and this is perhaps preferable, the change of subject involved in the first way being a little harsh, though perhaps supported by ver. 24. כל הרג קין =‘ *every one, or any one, that killeth*,’ is virtually a hypothetical sentence, ‘ *if any one kills Kain;*’ cf. Ges., § 145. 2. Rem.; Ewald, § 357 c (Prov. 23, 24. 1 Sam. 2, 13, cited by Gesenius, are some- what different, the apodosis being introduced by ו. Job 41, 18 is a better parallel).

שבעתים =‘ *sevenfold*,’ so ארבעתים, 2 Sam. 12, 6, ‘ *fourfold;*’ see Ges., § 97. Rem. 1. It may be interpreted, with Tuch, as meaning, Kain’s murder shall be avenged with a vengeance seven times greater than the vengeance taken on Abel’s; sevenfold meaning, as in Prov. 24, 16, ‘ *manifold*,’ ‘ *many times.*’

יקם does not mean ‘ *shall be punished, shall suffer punish- ment*,’ so perhaps LXX, ἑπτὰ ἐκδικούμενα παραλύσει, but ‘ *shall be avenged;*’ cf. Ex. 21, 21.

וישם יהוה לקין אות. The אות was given to Kain for his protection, and not as a token of the truth of what God had said, for Kain did not express any doubt as to the truth of what he had been told, and stress is rather laid in the narrative on Kain's immunity from death in the event of any one attacking him.

וישם לקין. '*And gave him a sign.*' לקין='*for Kain's protection*,' rather than '*on Kain*,' which would require על or ב, cf. Ex. 10, 2. Is. 66, 19. · What this אות was, cannot be determined; some have conjectured that Kain had a mark set on his forehead, perhaps a horn; others (Haitsma quoted by Di., p. 95) an inscription set somewhere on his person, commencing with כל, and ending with יקם; but there is nothing in the narrative to throw any light on the nature of the אות given to Kain. The LXX have ἔθετο Κύριος ὁ Θεὸς σημεῖον τῷ Κάϊν; Pesh. ; Onq. וְשַׁוִּי יְיָ לְקַיִן אָתָא וגו".

לבלתי הכות אתו, not לבלתי הכותו, because that might mean '*that he might not smite;*' cf. Ges., § 121. 4. Rem. The usual order is here departed from, and the object coming after the infinitive precedes the subject; cf. Ges., § 133. 3; Ewald, § 307 b: see also Is. 20, 1 בשלח אתו סרגון. Prov. 25, 8 בהכלים אתך רעך. כל ... לבלתי='*that no one,*' just as לא כל='*no one;*' cf. 3, 1 לא תאכל מכל עץ '*thou shalt eat of no tree.*'

16. נוד must be the name of a place, as we may infer from וישב, and its position after ארץ and before קדמת; not as the Vulg. '*profugus in terra,*' connecting נוד with נד '*to wander:*' so also Onq., who renders גְּלִי וּמְטַלְטַל. The position of נוד is as uncertain as that of the garden of Eden. The narrative gives us no real ground for assuming that it was eastwards of Eden, for this can neither be inferred from קדמת (LXX, κατέναντι; cf. 2, 14) nor from 3, 24 (Di.). נוד='*banishment.*'

17. חנוך='*dedication,*' from חנך '*to dedicate,*' prob. a denom. from the root of חך '*a gum*' (for חֵנֵךְ), prop. '*to rub*

the gums;' so in Arabic; it being customary to rub the gums of new-born children with date syrup, which was regarded as an act of dedication or initiation into life; cf. Del., p. 171. Prov. 22, 6.

ויהי בנה עיר *'and he was building a city,'* i.e. at the time when חנוך was born, the city was not completed, otherwise the narrator had written בָּנָה (perf.) or וַיִּבֶן (impf. with waw consec.). Other instances where the subst. verb היה is added to the participle to mark more prominently the duration of the action (i. e. that it is incomplete) are to be found in 37, 2 היה רעה *'was shepherding;'* 39, 22 הוא היה עשה; Driver, § 135. 5; M. R., § 14. 2 a; Ges., § 134. 2 c. Ryssel, however, *De Elohistae Pentateuchi sermone*, p. 59, takes this passage differently, his words are 'Prorsus aliter res se habet Gen. 4, 17, ubi participium loco nominis ponitur [" *Städtebauer* "].' This, however, seems harsh and unnatural. For conjectures as to the city חנוך, see Di., p. 96, who says, 'We are not in a position to identify it geographically.'

בֹּנֶה עִיר. The retrogression of the tone in בנה is due to the following tone-syllable in עיר. Two tone-syllables usually do not come together, either the first word is accented on the penult., or deprived of all accent by being connected with the second by Maqqef; cf. Ges., § 29. 3 b; Driver, § 100 : so 1, 5 לִצְחק בֵּנוּ 39, 14. בְּהֹולֶד לו 21, 5. תֹּאבַל לֶחֶם 3, 19. קֹרָא לֵילה.

18. וַיוֹלַד ... עִירָד. The passive verb is followed by the acc. case, as in 17, 5. 21, 5. 27, 42. 40, 20, and often; cf. Ges., § 143. 1 a; Ewald, § 295 b; M. R., § 47.

The meanings of some of the *nomina propria* which follow are very obscure.

עִירָד may mean *' he who flees,'* or *' the one who flees,'* from ערד, Arab. عرد *' to flee.'* LXX give it by Γαιδάδ, which is inter-

esting as throwing light on their pronunciation of the Heb. ע ;
cf. עמורה, Γόμορρα; עזה, Γάζα; עתליה, Γοθολία; רעואל, ʽΡαγουήλ ;
עתניאל, Γοθονιήλ ; רעמה, ʽΡεγμά; see Frankel, *Vorstudien*, p. 112.

מחויאל, of which מחייאל is another form, perhaps means
'*blotted out by God*,' or '*stricken of God*,'=מְחוּי אֵל. LXX,
Μαλελεήλ. מתושאל may mean '*man that is of God*,' being
composed of מְתוּ, i.e. מת with the old case ending וּ, which
is found again in מתושלח and פנואל ; cf. Ges., § 90. 3 b; Stade,
§ 344 a : of שֻׁ, possibly the abbreviated form of the relative
pronoun אשר : and of אל ' *God*.' מת is preserved in Ethiopic,
where it often has the meaning '*husband*,' as Is. 54, 1. Luke 2,
36. Gen. 2, 23, in the Ethiopic version ; see Di., *Ethiop. Lex.*,
p. 183. The abbreviated form שֻׁ is not found in the Pentateuch, unless we adopt the view of some interpreters who
consider בשגם in 6, 3 to consist of ב, שֻׁ, and גם ; and שלה in
49, 10 to be equivalent to שֶׁלֹּה, i. e. אֲשֶׁר לֹו. It is found in
Judg. 5, 7. 6, 17, where it may be due to a north Palestinian
dialect, and in the Song of Songs ; also in later writings, e. g.
Eccles., Lam., late Pss.; while in Phoenician (see Schröder, *Phön.
Gram.*, pp. 162–166, and the inscriptions cited by him, note 2,
p. 162) שֻׁ is the common form, אשר, the full form, being never
used. This explanation of the name מתושאל is corroborated
by the Assyrian ; compare Hommel, *Z. D. M. G.*, xxxii. 714,
and Lenormant, *Les Origines de l'Histoire* (1880), i. p. 263.
A less probable explanation is '*Man of Entreaty*'('*Bittmann*'),
from שָׁאֵל and מֶת. The LXX have Μαθουσάλα.

ועירד ילד. ילד is generally used of the mother, and the
Hif. הוליד of the father; cf. 10, 8 ff. 22, 23.

לֶמֶךְ cannot be explained from the Hebrew. In Arabic
يَلْمَك='*a strong young man*;' possibly למך is to be connected
with this.

19. Lamech was the first to introduce polygamy, in opposition to the divine injunction in 2, 24.

The names of the wives are given here because it is necessary for the understanding of the song.

עָדָה =‘ *adornment;*’ צִלָּה ‘ *shade:*’ but these two meanings are not quite certain.

שְׁתֵּי constr. of שְׁתַּיִם. According to Ges., § 97. 1. Rem. 1, the dag. lene after a vocal shewa is due to the fact that the full form of word was אֶשְׁתַּיִם. According to Stade, p. 216, ‘ שְׁתַּיִם is formed after the analogy of שְׁנַיִם from שִׁתַּיִם.’

20. The names in this verse are very obscure; cf. Di. for explanations that have been attempted.

יושב אהל ומקנה . Jabal was the father of those who dwelt (the sing. taken collectively) in tents, and had cattle, i. e. the first to introduce nomad life. ישׁב is connected by zeugma with מקנה; cf. Hos. 2, 20. Is. 42, 5. Josh. 4, 10. ישׁב with the acc. or gen. of the place that is dwelt in, so Ps. 22, 4 יושב תהלות ישראל; cf. Is. 33, 14, where יגור is construed with an acc. of the place dwelt in.

מקנה ‘*possession,*’ then ‘*possession of cattle,*’ a wider idea than צאן; it comprehends also (e. g. 26, 14. 47, 17) larger cattle, sometimes camels and asses; cf. Ex. 9, 3. Job 1, 3.

21. אבי כל תפש כנור וגו׳ . ‘ *The father of all those who handle harp and pipe.*’ LXX somewhat freely, ὁ καταδείξας ψαλτήριον καὶ κιθάραν. כִּנּוֹר, according to Ewald (*Lehrbuch*, § 79 d, § 118 a), who seeks to connect it with κιθάρα, is abbreviated from כַּנְתָּר or כִּנְתֹּר. According to *H. W. B.*, 9th ed., it is from כִּנֵּר; cf. כִּנֶּרֶת, Arab. كِنَارَة, Aramaic כִּנָּרָא, כִּנּוֹרָא, ܟܶܢܳܪܳܐ; from כנר 'an assumed onomatopoetic root. Josephus, *Arch.*, vii. 12. 3, describes it as being ten-stringed, and says that it was touched with the plectrum, but cf. 1 Sam.

16, 23. 18, 10. 19, 9. where David is said to touch it with his hand.

עוגב occurs only four times in the Old Testament; here, Job 21, 12. 30, 31 (see Baer in loco, p. 50). Ps. 150, 4; and is taken by the LXX (κιθάραν) and Pesh. (כֿנֿ֟אֿ) as a string-instrument; it is better to take it with Targ. Jer., LXX in Ps. 150, and Rabb. as = '*pipe*,' perhaps '*a shepherd's pipe*.' In the Hebrew translation of the Aramaic parts of Daniel it is used in 3, 5. 10, 15 for סומפוניה.

22. לטש כל חרש. '*A sharpener of every kind of instrument of brass and iron*.' The A. V. takes לטש in a metaphorical sense '*a sharpener*,' i. e. '*instructor of every worker in brass*,' etc.; A. V. R. '*forger*;' Marg. '*an instructor*.' חרש= '*an instrument*' does not occur again in the O. T.; the passage (1 Kings 7, 14) cited in *H. W. B.*, 9th ed., being an instance of its ordinary meaning, '*workman*.'

The rendering above given is that of Tuch, Del., and most moderns. Dillmann, however, in his note on the passage remarks: 'This explanation, which since Tuch is the one usually adopted, is hardly the meaning of the Massoretes, who—judging from the accent on לטש and the pronunciation חֹרֵשׁ (where one would rather expect חָרָשׁ)—perhaps supplied (cf. Targ.?) אֲבִי from ver. 21, '*a hammerer, (father) of every brass and iron smith*.' The falling out of אבי must have been very old, as the Vss. do not give it. The LXX have σφυροκόπος χαλκεὺς χαλκοῦ καὶ σιδήρου, taking חרש as a masculine, so Vulg. '*malleator et faber in cuncta opera aeris et ferri*,' supporting to some extent Dillmann's view. Onq. paraphrases רַבְּהוֹן דְּכָל־יָדְעֵי עִיבִידַת נְחָשָׁא וּבַרְזְלָא, but apparently did not view חרש as = '*an instrument*.' Ps.-Jon. has much the same as Onq., רַב לְכָל־אוּמָן דְּיָדַע בְּעִבִידַת '*the master of every workman*

who understands the working in' etc.; also taking חרש as a
participle. If חרש be taken as a subst. it is a participle neuter;
cf. יוֹתֵר *'that which remains over,' 'that which is gained,'* so
'an advantage, benefit, gain,' נבל; in Isa. 28, 4 נבל ציצת. נעמה
=*'die Liebliche, the amiable, lovely one.'*

23, 24. Lamech's Song. It consists of three verses, each
containing two lines. It may be rendered thus:

23 (a). *'Ada and Zillah hear my voice;'*

    (β). *'Ye wives of Lamech, give ear unto my speech:'*

    (a). *'Surely a man have I slain for wounding me,'*

    (β). *'And a young man for bruising me:'*

24 (a). *'If Kain shall be avenged sevenfold,'*

    (β). *'Then Lamech seven and seventyfold.'*

With ver. 23, cf. Isa. 28, 23. 32, 9.

23. שְׁמַעַן for שְׁמַעְנָה; cf. קְרָאן, Ex. 2, 20, and Ges., § 46.
Rem. 3; Stade, p. 334, § 612 a.

כִּי not *'for,'* nor=the ὅτι *recitativum*, of the N. T., introducing the words of the speaker (as e. g. 21, 30); but=
'certainly, surely;' cf. Ex. 4, 25.

לפצעי . . . לחברתי. The suffixes are *objective;* cf. Ges.,
§ 114. 2; M. R., § 78. Cf. LXX, εἰς τραῦμα ἐμοὶ . . . εἰς μώλωπα
ἐμοί. So Vulg.

ל = *'on account of;'* cf. M. R., § 51. 4; Ges., § 154. 3 e;
see Num. 16, 34 לקולם.

The perfects may best be taken, with the Vss., as real perfects, and not as perfects of certainty. Lamech has killed
men and will not, should necessity occasion it, hesitate to
kill others. Jewish fancy narrates that Lamech killed Kain
(אִישׁ) and Tubal Kain (יֶלֶד). But only one act is intended,
the repetition being due to the parallelism common in Hebrew
poetry.

The song is probably a triumphal song on the invention of war weapons. Lamech boasts that if Kain would be avenged sevenfold, surely he, with his instruments, would be able to take a far greater vengeance (seventy-sevenfold). For a mere wound inflicted on him, he has punished the inflicter with death; and in the possession of his weapons he feels himself superior to his ancestors, and able to dispense with divine protection. The poetical words האזין and אמרה and the parallelism which is observed throughout the three verses are noticeable.

25. שֵׁת = *Satz, Setzling*, and then *Ersatz*, ' *substitute.*'

כִּי שָׁת־לִי. Qameç remains, notwithstanding the Maqqef, and is on this account marked with Metheg; see Ges., § 16. 2 b; cf. § 9, p. 44. 1 d. כי הרגו קין; cf. on 3, 19.

26. ולשת גם הוא. The pronoun is repeated separately, to emphasize the noun; cf. Ges., § 121. 3; Ewald, § 311 a; M. R., § 72. 1. Rem. a; so 10, 21 ולשם ילד גם הוא.

אנוש = ' *man,*' from אנש ' *to be weak ;*' or from אנש = the Arabic أَنِسَ ' *to attach oneself to,*' so *animal sociabile.*

אז הוחל. The indeterminate 3rd pers. sing.; see Ges., § 137. 3 d; M. R., § 124: cf. Lam. 5, 5 לא הונח לנו. The LXX have οὗτος ἤλπισεν, perhaps reading הֵחֵל and זֶה; cf. Frankel, *Einfluss*, p. 41, on their reading. Onq. has בְּכֵין בְּיוֹמוֹהִי חָלוּ בְּנֵי אֲנָשָׁא מִלְצַלָּאָה בִּשְׁמָא דַיְיָ ' *thus in his days the children of men ceased praying in the name of the Lord ;*' so Ps.-Jon., taking הוחל as = ' *profanari,*' and paraphrasing to avoid the idea of profaning Y.'s name, so that the commencement of idolatry is here mentioned. This, however, is not probable. Aq. has correctly τότε ἤρχθη, also Symmachus ἀρχὴ ἐγένετο. Di. remarks on this verse : ' It is a question whether the reading הֵחֵל (= זֶה) ?, i.e. " *This one began,*" which is expressed by the Vulg. ("*iste coepit*"), and B. Jubil., and probably by the LXX, was not the original one, and אז הוחל (so, read as a passive, already in Aquila and Symmachus, but with the meaning ἀρχή) stood in connection with the view taken by the Targum.'

לקרא בשם. Not merely '*to call with Yahweh's name,*' '*to mention Him;*' but '*to worship Him.*'

5.

A short notice of the generations from Adam to Noah, connecting the history of the creation, the first chief event, with that of the flood, the second important event in the narrative. The number of generations from Adam to Noah is ten. In the accounts of the first nine generations, the name of the first-born is always given, the age of the father at the time of his birth, the number of years which the father lived after the birth of his first-born, and the total length of his life. In the case of each, mention is made that he begat sons and daughters (ויולד בנים ובנות). In the notice of Noah however, no mention is made of the number of years he lived after the birth of his three sons, nor of the total number of his years when he died, this being narrated, chaps. 7, 11. 9, 28. On the deviations in the chronology followed by the Hebrew text, the LXX, and the Samaritan, cf. Di., p. 105, and the authorities cited by him, p. 107; Del., *Comm.*, p. 182, and more especially for the LXX chronology; Frankel, *Einfluss*, p. 70. The following table, taken from Di., p. 105, gives the variations in the chronology of the Hebrew, LXX, and Samaritan texts.

In each of the three tables marked Heb. Text, Sam. Ver., Septuagint, the first column gives the years each patriarch lived until he begat children; the second, the number of years in each life after the birth of the first child; and the third, the total number of years each individual lived.

	HEB. TEXT.			SAM. VER.			SEPTUAGINT.		
Adam	130	800	930	130	800	930	230	700	930
Seth	105	807	912	105	807	912	205	707	912
Enos...	90	815	905	90	815	905	190	715	905
Kenan	70	840	910	70	840	910	170	740	910
Mahalalel... ...	65	830	895	65	830	895	165	730	895
Jared	162	800	962	62	785	847	162	800	962
Henoch	65	300	365	65	300	365	165	200	365
Methusalah ...	187	782	969	67	653	720	167	802	969
Lamech	182	595	777	53	600	653	188	565	753
Noah	500	...	...	500	...	...	500	...	...
Up to the flood .	100	...	(950)	100	...	(950)	100	...	(950)

1. כפר תולדות only here: elsewhere in P תולדות alone; cf. 2, 4. 6, 9. Num. 3, 1.

3. ויחי אדם שלשים. מאה שנה is equally common with מאת שנה; cf. Ges., § 120. 1, note; M. R., § 98. The acc. is acc. of time, in answer to the question '*how long?*' cf. M. R., § 42 a; Ges., § 118. 2 b.

ויולד, viz. a son or child. Olshausen proposes to insert בן here, but unnecessarily, the object being contained in the verb, as in 6, 4 וילדו להם; 16, 1 לא ילדה לו.

5. כל ימי אדם וגו". The predicate always, in the case of כל, agrees with the genitive, and not with the noun in the construct state: cf. Ges., § 148. 1, note; M. R., § 135. 3 a.

תשע מאת שנה ושלשים שנה. The noun שנה repeated with the ten; cf. Ges., § 120. 3; M. R., § 97. Rem. c. חַי is perf. from חיי, as in 3, 22.

6. חמש שנים ומאת שנה. The noun repeated with

the lesser number (from 3–9 inclusive) in the pl., and with
the greater in the singular; Ges., § 120. 3; M. R., § 97.
Rem. c.

22. ויתהלך חנוך את; so Noah, 6, 9, walked with God;
cf. a similar use of the Qal in Mic. 6, 8. Mal. 2, 6. התהלך את
is used of confidential intercourse with God, a closer relationship to God than is implied in '*walking before God*' (17, 1),
or, '*walking after God*' (Deut. 13. 5); cf. 1 Sam. 25, 15 of the
intercourse between David's followers and Nabal's servants.
The LXX have here Εὐηρέστησε δὲ 'Ενὼχ τῷ Θεῷ, perhaps to
avoid an anthropomorphic idea; cf. Ecclus. 44, 16. 49, 14, and
Heb. 11, 5 πίστει 'Ενώχ. Onq. paraphrases וְהַלֵּיךְ חֲנוֹךְ בְּדַחַלְתָּא
דַיְיָ '*Enoch walked in the fear of Yahweh.*' The Pesh. renders
as the LXX, ܐ̇ܠܗܐ '*Enoch pleased God.*'

24. ואיננו כי לקח אתו. '*And he was not, for Elohim
took him;*' cf. the usage of אֵין in Is. 17, 14. Ps. 103, 16.
1 Kings 20, 40, of sudden disappearance. On its use in the
narrative style, cf. Ewald, § 321 a; M. R., § 128, 2 a. כי לקח
א"תו, that is, without dying, otherwise we should expect
וימת: cf. 2 Kings 2 (Elijah's removal from earth to heaven,
without tasting death). The reason for כי לקח אתו is to be
found in the first half of the verse, viz. his piety; cf. Heb. 11,
5, and Onq.; not, as some suppose, the danger of his relapsing
into sin: so Ber. Rabb. c. 24. Frankel, *Einfluss*, p. 43, cites
this passage as one of the places where the LXX translators
had the Haggada in view. LXX have καὶ οὐχ εὑρίσκετο, ὅτι
μετέθηκεν αὐτὸν ὁ Θεός. So Vulg. Onq. וְלֵיתוֹהִי אֲרֵי (לָא) אֲמִית
יְיָ יָתֵיה (cf. Frankel, p. 44, note d, who omits לא, so Berliner
in his edition of Onqelos [ed. 1884, Berlin], p. 5; cf. part 2,
p. 3)='*And he was not, for Yahweh did (not) slay him.*' The
Pesh. follows the Heb. text. In Ecclus. 44, 16 Enoch is called

παράδειγμα μεταvoλαs ταῖs γενεαῖs, and in the book of Enoch (translated by Dillmann) and the N. T. book of Jude, 14 et seq., he is described as a seer and prophet, who announced the coming of God, to punish the world for its sin.

29. **ויקרא את שמו נח** .נוח=*'rest;'* the explanation given in the text, זה ינחמנו, is not strictly an etymology at all, as נוח cannot be connected with נחם, which is an entirely different stem; but the similarity in sound led the narrator to connect in thought נוח with נחם, just as מֹשה is a reminiscence of מֹשה *'to draw out,'* yet cannot be etymologically connected with that word. The LXX render ינחמנו as though they read it יְנִיחֵנו (not יַנִּיחֵנו, which would rather mean *'to set, place'*). Rashi perceiving the etymological difficulty, fancifully explains ינחמנו as though it were=יניח ממנו ' *make to rest from us.'* His words are ינח ממנו את עצבון ידינו עד שלא בא נוח לא היה להם כלי מחרישה והוא הכין להם והיתה הארץ מוציאה קוצים ודרדרים כשזורעים חטים מקללתו של אדם הראשון ובימי נוח נחה וזהו ינחמנו ' *He will make the toil of our hands cease from us: before Noah came they had no instruments to plough with, but he made them some, and the earth used to bring forth thorns and thistles when they sowed wheat, on account of the curse of the first man, but in the days of Noah (the earth) had rest, and this is the meaning of* ינחמנו.'

ממעשנו ומעצבון וגו" . *'From our work and labour (arising) from the ground;'* better than מן־האדמה ' *because of the ground,'* as A.V.; for the curse comes to man from the ground, which brought forth קוץ ודרדר when it was tilled (3, 18).

6.

1. לרב is inf. cstr. of רבב ' *to be many,' 'gross sein;'* רבה= *'to become many,' 'gross werden.'* The apodosis of the sentence begins with 2^b, at ויקחו.

2. טבות is used in a physical sense here =‘*comely;*’ cf.
Ex. 2, 2.

מכל אשר בחרו. מִן is used to particularise the idea
as in 7, 22. 9, 10; cf. Ewald, § 278 c.

בני האלהים. This phrase, elsewhere in the O. T.,
always means ‘*the angels,*’ with reference to their nature as
beings of a higher, diviner type (being called מלאכים, with
regard to their office as messengers executing the divine
commands); so Job 1, 6. 2, 1. 38, 7. Dan. 3, 25 (‘*a son of
the gods*’), but never בני יהוה. The same meaning is usually
assigned to it here by ancient interpreters, e. g. Philo,
Book of Enoch, etc.; cf. Jude 6. 2 Peter 2, 4; the moderns
also mostly explain it in the same way; so Del., Di.,
Tuch, Knobel, Schrader, etc. As, however, the idea of a
carnal connection between the angels and daughters of men
was very repugnant to a refined mode of thought, and
especially objectionable to the Christian mind (cf. Matt. 22,
30), many attempts were made to explain these words in
a way that would not cause offence. Thus, Targg., Onq.
and Ps.-Jon. both render בְּנֵי רַבְרְבַיָּא ‘*sons of nobles,*’ from the
use of אלהים in Ex. 21, 6; 22, 7 (which, however, are
very different passages from this). Rashi has בני השׂרים
והשׁפטים ‘*the sons of princes and judges;*’ others explain
בני האלהים similarly as the sons of those of higher rank,
opposed to בנות האדם the daughters of those of lower rank. In
favour of this interpretation, Pss. 82, 6. 49, 3 are quoted. But
in the first of these passages the expression is not the same,
and the application evidently different; in the second,
the opposite to אדם is אישׁ, not אלהים; further האדם, in
vers. 1 and 4 (=‘*the human race*’), is against this view.
Another explanation is that adopted by the Fathers, e. g.
Ephrem Syrus, Theodoret (cf. Del., p. 191), who interpret the

sons of God in a spiritual sense as the pious ones, those who lead the lives of angels; viewing these as the descendants of Seth, and regarding the בנות האדם as the daughters of the wicked, the offspring of the line of Kain. But there is nothing in either chap. 4 or 5 to bear out this view, and the expression 'sons of God' as a name for pious men is not usual in the O. T.; and it is scarcely conceivable that האדם in ver. 2[b] is to be taken in a different sense from the האדם in ver. 1[a], which would be required if this view were adopted. The Vss. render variously. The reading of the LXX is uncertain, υἱοὶ τοῦ Θεοῦ is found, and also ἄγγελοι τοῦ Θεοῦ; cf. Lagarde, *Genesis Graece*, p. 20. The Pesh. has here ܒܢܝ ܐܠܗܐ merely transliterating the Heb. words; so in Job 1, 6. 2, 1; Aquila, υἱοὶ τῶν Θεῶν, on which Hieron., *Quaest.* ed. Lagarde, p. 11, says, '*Deos intelligens sanctos sive angelos;*' Symm., οἱ υἱοὶ τῶν δυναστευόντων (agreeing with the old Jewish view); Itala (from LXX), '*angeli Dei;*' Vulgate, '*filii Dei.*'

3. לא ידון רוחי. רוחי is rather the breath of life which Yahweh Elohim (2, 7) breathed into man's nostrils when he created him ('the principle of physical and spiritual life,' Di.), than the Holy Spirit (as the Targg. of Ps.-Jon., Jer.; Symm., etc.) working in man, and judging him; for the determination on Yahweh's part to deprive man of His spirit, as the latter half of the verse shows, really means depriving him of life.

יָדוֹן is not jussive, but (as in יָבוֹא from בוא not בּיא) has the intransitive punctuation of the imperf.; cf. Ew., § 138 b; Stade, § 490 c. The Vss. (LXX, Pesh., Onq., Vulg.) either read ידור, or according to others ילון, or guessed at the meaning of the word, rendering it '*abide*' or '*remain.*' It is now generally rendered either '*be abased,*' so Dillmann, from the Arabic; or '*rule,*' Del.; דון being = דין, whose primary meaning is '*rule*' and then '*judge;*' cf. Nif'. נָדוֹן (cf. אדן, from which is derived אדון '*ruler,*' '*lord*'). The latter meaning is perhaps better supported than the former, as the meaning '*be abased*' ascribes to the word a signification which it has ceased to have in Hebrew. The Targg. (Ps.-Jon., Jer.) and others take it as synonymous with דין, and render '*judge,*' but this does not suit the context so well as '*be abased,*' or '*rule.*' The A. V. renders '*my spirit shall not strive,*' so Joseph Kimchi and Rashi, regarding דון as equivalent to דין, and giving it the meaning of the Nif'al נדון (cf. נשפט), a meaning which in Nif'al depends on the reciprocal signification of the conjugation, and so cannot be assigned to Qal.

בְּשַׁגַּם הוּא בָשָׂר. The best attested reading is that adopted by Baer and Del. in their edit. of *Genesis,* Leipz., 1869, בְּשַׁגַּם with pathach. The reading in the ordinary editions is בְּשַׁגָּם with qameç. The meaning of these words is disputed. There are two general explanations. That adopted by Delitzsch, '*For that he too is flesh,*' or '*For that he indeed is flesh,*' בְּשַׁגַּם being treated as compounded of בְּ the prep., שַׁ[1] a fragment of אֲשֶׁר (cf. on 4, 18), and the particle גַּם *also;* cf. בַּאֲשֶׁר, 39, 9. But against this it may be urged that (*a*) the abbreviation of the relative אֲשֶׁר never

---

[1] It should be mentioned that Fritz Hommel and others consider that the fragment שׁ has nothing to do with the rel. אֲשֶׁר, but that שֶׁ, שַׁ, originally ﺵ, is only another form of the Aramaic relative conjunction זְ, דְ. See *Z.D.M.G.* xxxii. 711 ff., and a note in the American Journal, *Hebraica,* April, 1885, p. 249, where a third view of the relation between שׁ and אשר is mentioned, which makes שׁ the original relative, and derives אשר from it by prefixing an independent pronominal stem *a*, and affixing lă (which appears also in the Arabic relative alladi الَّذِى), ל being then hardened to ר; cf. Sperling, *Die nota relationis im Hebräischen,* Jena, 1876.

occurs in the Pentateuch, though defended by some by an
appeal to the pr. n. מְתוּשָׁאֵל, 4, 18; מִישָׁאֵל, Ex. 6, 22. Lev.
10, 4; which are not, however, of any weight for prose usage,
and both of which may be explained otherwise: and that (*b*) גַם
is here superfluous.   The second explanation is that adopted
by Di., who reads בְּשַׁגָּם, and takes it as inf. cstr. from
שָׁגָה=שָׁגַג, with the affix of the third pers. m. pl. (cf. Ges., § 67,
note 3; Ewald, § 238 b), and renders, '*On account of their
error* or *transgression he* (*mankind*) *is flesh.*' Against this it
may be urged (*a*) that הוּא is masc. sing., while שַׁגָּם has the
third pl. m. affix; cf., however, Ewald, § 319 a, where other
instances of a similar *Enallage numeri* are to be found: (*b*)
that שָׁגַג is scarcely the word that would be expected in this
connection, and it is here hardly general enough: (*c*) that
the reading with qameç is not so well attested as that with
pathach; cf. Del., p. 195. The text is probably corrupt:
but the emendations that have been proposed are not satisfactory: e.g. גַם בַּאֲשֶׁר, or גַם בְּנַפְשָׁם, לָבָשׁ. The Vss. give—
LXX, διὰ τὸ εἶναι αὐτοὺς σάρκας; Pesh. ܡܛܠ ܕܒܣܪ ܗܘ;
Onq. בְּדִיל דְּאִינוּן בִּשְׂרָא; Vulg. '*quia caro est,*' all expressing
the sense '*For that.*'

וְהָיוּ יָמָיו מֵאָה וגו׳. '*So his days shall be,*' or '*so let
his days be,*' etc., i.e. he shall have a respite of a hundred and
twenty years. This seems better than the other explanation,
that human life should be limited to a hundred and twenty
years; for many post-diluvian Patriarchs reached a far higher
age, e.g. Abraham, 25, 7; and it cannot be regarded as
a general statement to which there might be exceptions, as
the exceptions are too numerous (all the post-diluvian Fathers,
from Shem to Terach, reach a higher age than the limit here
assigned; cf. 11, 10 et seq.).

4. הַנְּפִילִים. According to the ancients (LXX, Pesh.,

Onq., Sam., Saad.), a name for giants; cf. Num. 13, 33 וישם
ראינו הנפלים בני ענק. No clear etymology can be found in
Hebrew; perhaps the word was derived from a Canaanitish
dialect. It has been connected with the root נפל ' *to fall:*'
thus many of the Fathers consider these נפילים to have been
fallen angels; but there is nothing in the narrative to justify
this, and the narrator appears to distinguish the נפילים from
the בני האלהים. Others render ' *Robbers, Tyrants,*' lit. those
who fall upon others; so Aq. οἱ ἐπιπίπτοντες; Symm. οἱ βίαιοι;
but נפל only means ' *to fall upon,*' ' *attack* ' in certain connec-
tions; cf. Josh. 11, 7. Job 1, 15. Gen. 43, 18. Others (Tuch,
Knobel) connect the word with a root נפל, supposed to
possess the sense of פלא, and consider it to allude to their
extraordinary size, but this is precarious. Other conjectures
will be found in Lenormant, *Les Origines de l'histoire*, etc.
(1880), I. chap. vii.

הָהֵם is always pointed with ◌ֵ, although ◌ֶ would be
expected here; cf. ver. 19 הָחִי; and Ges., § 35. 2 A. The
article stands with הם, because the noun which it qualifies is
defined; cf. Ges., § 122. 1; Dav., § 13. Rule 1.

אשר יבאו . . . וילדו. Render, ' *When the sons of God
went in . . . and they bare.*' אשר, connecting the new sentence
with a preceding particle of time (אחרי כן), may be rendered
' *when ;*' cf. 45, 6. 1 Sam. 20, 31. 2 Sam. 19, 25 after יום;
Deut. 4, 10. Ps. 95, 9[a] and [b]. The imperf. as a frequentative past, followed by the perf. with waw consec.; cf. Driver,
§ 113. 4 a: cf. 2, 6. 29, 2. Ex. 33, 7–11. The subject to וילדו
is the בנות האדם : cf. for the change of subject, 9, 27. 15, 13.

המה refers to the נפילים in the first half of the verse, not
to an object to וילדו, which has been left out, as this would be
very forced.

אַנְשֵׁי הַשֵּׁם is co-ordinate with אֲשֶׁר מֵעוֹלָם. ' *The men of repute;*' cf. Num. 16, 2 אנשי שם. A word in the construct state cannot take the article, so it is defined by the article being attached to the following genitive, Ges., § 111. 1; M. R., § 76. N. B. Whether such a combination as אנשי השם means I. '*The men of repute,*' or II. '*Men of the repute,*' or III. '*The men of the repute,*' can only be decided by the context. Hebrew has only one way of defining the first, or the second, or both parts of a construct state, and following genitive combination.

5. רַבָּה is accented *milra'*, and so is an adj., and not the perfect fem., from רבב, which would be *mil'el*.

כל יצר מחשבות לבו. ' *Every form of the thoughts of his heart,*' יצר, I. '*form, shape,*' physically; II. tropically applied to what is fashioned in the mind, imagination; cf. 8, 21. Is. 26, 3. The LXX paraphrase πᾶς τις διανοεῖται ἐν τῇ καρδίᾳ, on which cf. Frankel, *Einfluss*, p. 10.

רק רע ' *only evil,*' i. e. ' *utterly, hopelessly, nothing but evil :*' cf. a similar use of רק in Deut. 28, 33 רק עשוק ורצוץ; Is. 28, 19 והיה רק זועה.

6. ויתעצב אל לבו. ' *And was pained in his heart.*' LXX, καὶ διενοήθη. Onq. וַאֲמַר [בְּמֵימְרֵהּ] לְמִיתְּבַר תּוּקְפְהוֹן כִּרְעוּתֵיהּ ' *And spake by his Word, to break their strength according to his will.*' Ps.-Jon. וְאִידְּיָן עֲלֵיהוֹן בְּמֵימְרֵהּ ' *And disputed with his Word concerning them ;*' so Sam. and Targ. Jer. All intentional, in order to avoid an anthropomorphic idea.

7. בהמה = usually ' *tame,*' ' *domestic animals ;*' here used of ' *tame* and *wild animals,*' as in ver. 20; 7, 23. 8, 17.

9. אלה תולדות. Cf. on 2, 4.

נח איש צדיק תמים. Render, ' *Noah was an upright*

man, perfect among his contemporaries;' according to the accents and the order of the words.

10. שלשה בנים. Masc. nouns take the numeral in the fem. form, and vice versa; see Ges., § 97; Dav., § 48. The number 2 *agrees* in gender with the word which it enumerates, and is an exception to this rule. The numerals from 2–10 are substantive, אחד, fem. אחת, *one* is an adj.

11. ותמלא הארץ חמס. Verbs of *abounding* and *wanting* take in Hebrew the accusative, Ges., § 138. 3 b; M. R., § 35; cf. ver. 13 מלאה הארץ חמס.

√ 13. קץ כל בשר בא לפני. ' *The end* (i. e. *the destruction) of all flesh (man and beast) has come before me.'* Not ' *The end of all flesh has come to my knowledge,'* which would rather be בא אלי (cf. 18, 21. Ex. 3, 9), but ' *has come before my mind, is determined on by me'* (cf. Job 10, 13. 23, 14).

כָּל־בָּשָׂר is characteristic of P.

מפניהם '*from before them,'* i. e. ' *because of them, through their influence;'* cf. Ex. 8, 20 תשחת הארץ מפני הערב. The pl. suffix is used because בשר must be taken collectively.

את הארץ '*with the earth.'* So LXX, Onq., Vulg. Pesh. has ܒܐܪܥܐ ' *on the earth;'* Sam. ᐃᐯᐯᐊ בצב '*from the earth,'* perhaps reading (wrongly) מאת by repeating the final ם of משחיתם.

14. תבת עצי גפר. תבה only occurs in Gen., chaps. 6–9, and Ex. 2, 3. 5; it is most probably an Egyptian word; see Gesenius, *Th.* sub voce, and M. V., *H. W. B.,* p. 875. The Semitic etymologies given by Del., *Comm.,* p. 206 (from תוב, a secondary formation of אוב ' *to be hollow'*), and Dietrich, *Abhandl. zur Semit. Wortforschung,* p. 33 (who regards the word as Semitic, and as standing ' in lebendigem zusammen-

hange' (in actual connection) with אָבֶה 'a reed;' comparing the derivation of תבה from אָבֶה with those of חֵבֶל, ܚܒܠ, from אבל; תֹּם, from תאם; in all of which the א is suppressed), are untenable. The LXX here have κιβωτόν; in Exodus θίβιν; the Vulg. has 'arcam' here, and in Exodus 'fiscellam;' Targg. תֵּיבוֹתָא, Syr. ܩܐܒܘܬܐ, which is the Greek κιβωτός.

עֲצֵי גֹפֶר only occurs here. עֵצִים='wood' when cut down, 'logs,' as opposed to עֵץ, 'trees' growing; so חִטָּה, and חִטִּים, sing.'wheat' growing, and pl.'wheat' when cut down, 'grain;' כסף 'silver' in general, כְּסָפִים 'pieces of silver,' Ges., § 108. 4. Rem. 1; Stade, § 311 c.

גֹפֶר, connected with גָפְרִית sulphur and כפר pitch, is a resinous coniferous tree (Nadelbaum), perhaps the old name for the cypress, which was used by the Phoenicians for ship-building, and is elsewhere called בְּרוֹשׁ. גֹפֶר only occurs here. The LXX, Itala, and Vulg. did not understand the meaning of the word, and resorted to conjecture. The LXX have ξύλων τετραγώνων; the Itala, 'ligna quadrata;' the Vulg. 'ligna laevigata.' Onq. and Ps.-Jon. render 'cedar trees;' the Syriac has ܩܝܣܐ ܕܟܐܦܐ, which Walton renders 'de ligno viminis;' but this is doubtful. Possibly it should be rendered 'juniper wood;' see Löw, Aram. Pflanzennamen, s. v.

קִנִּים. 'In cells shalt thou make the ark;' קנים being acc. of manner, after a verb of making; cf. Ex. 38, 3 כל כליו עשה נחשת 'all its vessels he made brass,' i. e. so that they consisted of brass; Deut. 27, 6 אבנים שלמות תבנה את מזבח יהוה; cf. Ewald, § 284. 1 b; Ges., § 139. 2 end; M. R., § 45. 5 b.

עָשָׂה . . . וְכָפַרְתָּ. The perf. with waw conv. in continuation of an imperative; cf. Driver, § 112 (1); M. R., § 24. 1 a; cf. 8, 17. Lev. 24, 14 וסמכו . . . הוצא את המקלל. 2 Sam.

11, 15 וְשַׁבְתֶּם ... הָבוּ אֶת אוּרִיָּה. וְכִפַּרְתָּ has the tone thrown forward on to the last syllable, after the waw conv.; cf. Driver, §§ 106 and 110; Dav., § 23. 3 b; M. R., § 23. כָּפַר is a denominative from כֹּפֶר. See Ges., § 52. 2; Dav., § 26. 3. Rem. a.

בַכֹּפֶר. The article is used here with a material which was well known; cf. Ges., § 109. Rem. 1 b; M. R., § 68.

15. וְזֶה אֲשֶׁר תַּעֲשֶׂה, lit. 'this is what thou shalt make it;' i.e. 'this is how thou shalt make it.'

16. צֹהַר, prop. = 'light,' and then 'an inlet for light,' so 'window.' So all Vss. except the LXX, and most moderns. צֹהַר is regarded as a feminine, so חַלּוֹן, Ez. 41, 16. 26; cf. Ges., § 107. 4 a or c; Ewald, § 174 d (γ), who classes צֹהַר, as fem., among the nouns denoting places in which man is wont to move, or things which man uses, comparing חָצֵר 'a court,' Ez. 10, 4. 5; מַחֲנֶה 'camp,' in Gen. 32, 9; רְחוֹב 'a street,' Dan. 9, 25. It is not necessary to render צֹהַר collectively 'windows;' cf. 8, 6; צֹהַר as opposed to חַלּוֹן is merely an opening for light, חַלּוֹן being a lattice-work window, which could be opened or shut at will.

וְאֶל אַמָּה תְּכַלֶּנָּה מִלְמַעְלָה, either I. 'Up to a cubit (not further) shalt thou complete it from above:' so Kn., Del.; or II. 'Up to a cubit above (upwards) shalt thou complete it,' Di.; both being grammatically possible, as מִלְמַעְלָה may either mean 'above,' or 'from above.' According to I. the window in the side of the ark would have the space of a cubit between it and the roof. Dillmann considers the opening to have been a cubit high, and to have run round the four sides of the ark, being interrupted merely by the beams supporting the roof; so that there was really a continuous row of צֹהַר; and claims כלה as suiting this meaning. Delitzsch's view is open to the objection that it leaves the size of the צהר undefined, and one window in one side would scarcely suffice for the lighting of the whole ark. Dillmann's view is possibly less objectionable, but it is questionable whether the Hebrew text can bear the meaning he puts upon it. The text seems merely to say that a window or opening was to be made in the ark, its place being left undefined, and this opening was to be continued until it reached a distance of a cubit from the roof (מלמעלה *from above*), or to the height of a cubit (מלמעלה *above, upwards*). The opening may have been in the roof, for the absence of a notice about the covering of such a light-hole may be explained on the ground that the narrative says very little about the construction of the window. Tuch's explanation that the window was intended for Noah's cell, while the animals were in darkness, cannot be derived from the text as it stands, nor his view that the window was a cubit square.

17. ואני הנני מביא. The participle as future (*futurum instans*), which it represents as already 'beginning;' frequently with הנה preceding it; cf. Ges., § 134. 2 b. cf. Rem. 1; M. R., § 14. Rem. a; Driver, § 135. 3.

את המבול מים. Not '*the flood of waters*,' but in app. '*the flood [even] waters*.' So Ps. 60, 5 יין תרעלה, lit. '*wine, reeling*.'

מים. On the subst. in apposition, cf. Ges., § 118. 3; M. R., § 76. Rem. b; Ewald, § 287 h; Driver, § 188. The emendation מָיִם is unnecessary and unsuitable.

גוע in the Pent. and Josh. is peculiar to P.

18. והקימתי. הקים ברית and נתן ברית, 9, 12 are marks of P.

19. והחי; cf. on ver. 4.

זכר ונקבה, characteristic of P.

20. לְמִינֵהוּ. See on 1, 20. רֶמֶשׂ and רָמַשׂ belong to the language of P.

21. קִֹת.לֶךָ . . . וְאָסַפְתָּ ; cf. on ver. 14. אכלה is another characteristic of P.

22. כֵן עשׂה is rare outside P.

7.

1. וּכָל בֵּיתְךָ. Cf. the fuller description of Noah's family in P, 6, 18. 7, 7. 13. 8, 16. 18.

2. שׁבעה שׁבעה. 'Seven by seven,' i.e. 'by sevens;' see Ges., §§ 108. 4, 120. 5; M. R., § 72. 2; Ewald, § 313 a; cf. Zech. 4, 2. Num. 3, 47. 17, 17 מטה מטה 'rod, rod,' 'a rod each;' 2 Kings 17, 29 גוי גוי 'nation, nation,' i.e. 'every single nation:' cf. also Mark 6, 39 συμπόσια συμπόσια; 40 πρασιαὶ πρασιαί. The repetition of a noun indicates that the action expressed in the sentence is performed on different individuals of the class denoted by the noun; thus the repetition serves to express the *distributive* relation. Some think that seven individuals of each kind were to be selected, the seventh possibly being intended for sacrifice (Del.). But the addition of אִישׁ וְאִשְׁתּוֹ seems to indicate that 'seven pairs' were intended. In the case of the unclean animals we have שׁנים once, i.e. 'one pair,' and we may reasonably presume that had the narrator intended seven individual animals here, we should have had שׁבעה once. This also suits ver. 9 better (the animals went in שׁנים שׁנים by twos). שׁבעה שׁבעה in the next verse is to be taken in the same way.

4. כי לימים עוד שׁבעה. 'For after yet seven days.'

For this use of the preposition לְ, cf. 2 Sam. 13, 23 וַיְהִי
לִשְׁנָתַיִם יָמִים; Ex. 8, 19 לְמָחָר יִהְיֶה הָאוֹת הַזֶּה; M. R., § 51. 2.

אַרְבָּעִים יוֹם. Certain nouns are used after the numerals
in the singular; cf. Ges., § 120. 2. Rem.; M. R., § 97.

וּמָחִיתִי. P uses שָׁחֵת or הִשְׁחִית; cf. 6, 13. 17.

כָּל הַיְקוּם. הַיְקוּם, which always has the ' without a
dagesh, is a subst. formed from the analogy of the imperfect;
cf. ܡܶܬܽܘ, in Syriac, by transposition, from ܩܽܘܡܶܐ. Render,
'*Every existing thing.*'

6. בֶּן שֵׁשׁ מֵאוֹת שָׁנָה. The adj. is expressed by joining
to a subst., denoting a reference or relationship, a genitive
expressing the attribute or thing; cf. Ges., § 106. 2 a; M. R.,
§ 79. 6 d.

וְהַמַּבּוּל הָיָה מַיִם. '*When the flood was, waters,*' etc.
מַיִם is an explanatory apposition to הַמַּבּוּל; cf. Ewald, § 287 h;
Driver, § 188; M. R., § 76. Rem. b. הָיָה = '*accidit,*' '*came;*'
LXX, ἐγένετο. The second half of the verse is a circ. clause;
see Ewald, § 341 d; Driver, § 169: cf. 19, 4. 24, 45. The
A. V. R. keeps the old rendering, '*the flood of waters,*' which
is a paraphrase adopted for the sake of English idiom.

7. וַיָּבֹא נֹחַ וּבָנָיו. '*And Noah came in and his sons,*' etc.
When the predicate *precedes* a compound subj., it frequently
stands in the sing.; Ges., § 148. 2; M. R., § 138.

11. בִּשְׁנַת שֵׁשׁ מֵאוֹת ... לְחַיֵּי, lit. '*in the year of six
hundred years to the life of N.,*' i. e. '*in the six hundredth year
of N.'s life.*' The cardinals, for numbers beyond ten, are
used for the ordinals; cf. Ges., § 120. 4; M. R., § 100 a;
Ewald, § 287 k.

לְחַיֵּי נֹחַ. The genitive is often expressed thus by לְ,
when a writer wishes to avoid a string of construct states, or—

as here—when any word intervenes between the construct state and the genitive. Cf. Ges., § 115. 2 ; M. R., § 83.

וארבות = lit. '*the latticed windows*,' from ארב '*to intertwine*.' The LXX have αἱ καταῤῥάκται, Vulg. '*cataractae*,' Aq. and Symm. αἱ θυρίδες : cf. ארבת ממרום, Is. 24, 18 ; also Job 38, 16. Prov. 8, 28 on the whole verse.

13. בעצם היום הזה. '*On this very day;*' see Ges., § 124. 2. Rem. 3 ; M. R., § 90 ; Ewald, § 286 f ; and cf. 17, 23 ; Ex. 24, 10 כעצם השמים '*as the very heavens;*' Josh. 10, 27 עד עצם היום הזה '*until this very day.*'

בא. It is not necessary to take this in a pluperfect sense, the rendering '*came*' is quite suitable.

שלשת. Here the numeral very exceptionally *agrees* in gender with its substantive ; cf. Ges., § 97. 1, note, p. 250 ; Ewald, § 267 c : other instances are Ez. 7, 2 Ktb. ; Zech. 3, 9. 4, 2. Job 1, 4.

14. כל צפור כל כנף. The same phrase occurs in Ez. 17, 23 ; cf. also 39, 4. Ps. 148, 10. Lit. '*every bird of every wing*,' i.e. '*all sorts of birds*,' '*every species of birds.*' צפור is properly '*a small bird*,' so called from its twittering or chirping.

16. הבאים = '*those that came*,' lit. '*the ones coming :*' see Ges., § 109, note ; M. R., § 92. Rem. a. The article is equivalent to the rel. pronoun : cf. Neh. 4, 12 הבונים '*those that built;*' Ex. 1, 1 הבאים מצרימה '*those who came to Egypt.*'

19. מאד מאד (cf. 17, 2. 6. 20) is repeated to imply intensity ; cf. Ges., § 151. 2 ; M. R., § 72. 1. מאד מאד is peculiar to P ; so 17 l. c., Num. 14, 7.

20. חמש עשרה אמה. אמה is acc. of measure, answering to the question '*how far ?*' Ges., § 118. 1 ; M. R., § 41 c.

21. בעוף ובבהמה. ב is used to specify the whole according to its contents; cf. M. R., § 52. 1; cf. 8, 17. 9, 2. 23, 18.   This construction of ב is a mark of P.

22. חָרְבָה, with firm ָ under ח, the noun being of the form יַבָּשָׁה.

23. וימח.   The better-attested reading has no dag. in the מ; so the form would be apoc. impf. Qal from מחה, and would mean 'He (God), or it (the flood) blotted out,' the first rendering being the best.   The reading with dag. in the מ would be imperf. apoc. Nif'., for which we should rather expect וַיִּמָּ֯ with ָ , but cf. Ewald, § 224 c and Ps. 109, 13. 14: the acc. could stand after a passive, as in 4, 18; but a passive would hardly be expected with וַיִּמָּחוּ following in the same verse.   The accent on the penult. points to the imperf. Qal: in the imperf. Nif'. it could not be drawn back, as the penult. would be a closed syllable.

ואשר אתו. אשר = 'ii qui,' containing in itself the demonstrative pronoun, Ges., § 123. 2; cf. M. R., § 158. 2.

8.

3. וישובו המים ... הלוך ושוב.   The inf. abs. הלוך is added to שוב to emphasize the continuance of the abating of the waters, just as in vers. 5. 7; 12, 9: cf. Ges., § 131. 3, note 3; Ewald, § 280 b; M. R., § 37 b.

4. ותנח is impf. Qal with waw conv. from נוח, like וַיָּסַר from סור, וַיָּזַר from זור, וַיָּנַע from נוע: cf. Ges., § 72. Rem. 4; Stade, § 484 d.

על הרי אררט. אררט is in the O. T., 2 Kings 19, 37 = Is. 37, 38 and Jer. 51, 27 (together with מני and אשכנז), the

name of a land. In the passage in Isaiah, the LXX translate
אררט by 'Αρμενία, and acc. to Schrader, *K. A. T.*², p. 52 ff.,
Armenia is called in Assyrian *U-ra-ar-ti*. Hieron., on Is. 37,
38, describes Ararat more closely as the fruitful plain lying
at the foot of mount Taurus, through which the Araxes flows;
and Moses of Chorene calls this part of Armenia *Ajrarat*.
Kiepert (*Berl. Ak. M. B.*, 1869, 228 A; *Geogr.* 75) connects
the 'Αλαρόδιοι of Herodotus, iii. 94, vii. 79, with this name
(Di.). The hills of Ararat mentioned in this verse are
usually identified with the highest of the mountains in the
land of Ararat, which rises on the right bank of the Araxes
to a considerable height, and is always covered with snow.
This mountain is named Masis, and is situated twelve hours
south-west of the town of Eriwan: see further, Di., p. 138 and
the works cited there.

5. היו הלוך וחסור. The more usual cstr. with היה to
emphasize the continuance of the action would be the
participle: cf. on 1, 6; see Ewald, § 280 b.

באחד לחדש. יום is omitted by Ges., § 120. 4. Rem. 2;
M. R., § 100 a. Rem. a.

7. הערב. The article is generic. The individual as
representative of its species is distinguished from the animals
belonging to other species; cf. Ges., § 109. 3. Rem. 1 c; Ewald.
§ 277 a; M. R., § 68; 1 Sam. 17, 34 ובא הארי; 1 Kings 20, 36
והכך האריה. Others explain the article on the ground that
Noah had only one raven with him in the ark, which is
somewhat difficult to prove, or had merely a male raven;
but ערב is used of both the male and female bird, and does
not admit of a distinction of gender: cf. יונה used of both
sexes; so דבורה ' *bee ;*' cf. Ewald. § 175 b; Ges., § 107. 1 c, d.

יבשת is inf. cstr. with the fem. ending, like יכלת, Num.

14, 16. This ending is usual only with verbs פ״י and פ״ן;
cf. Ges., § 83. 1; Stade, §§ 199 c. 2, 208 c, 619 g; Ewald,
§ 239. 2 (who classes these instances as abstract formations
with an inf. force).

8. הֲקָלֽוּ. On the pointing of ה interrog., see Ges., § 100.
4; Dav., p. 122. The indirect question is here identical in
form with the direct; cf. Ges., § 153. 2 s. p.; M. R., § 146;
Ewald, § 324 c (a).

9. מָנֽוֹחַ 'a resting-place.' Cf. the note on 1, 14.

10. וַיָּֽחֶל is, according to form, Qal or Hif'. imperf. (of
חוּל or חִיל); according to usage, Hif'. Only one other instance
is cited in Ges., H. W. B., 9th ed., viz. Judg. 3, 25. Di. wishes
to emend after Ols. to וַיְיַחֵל; cf. ver. 12, as the meaning
'wait' elsewhere is expressed by the Pi'el or Hif'il of יחל, or
(ver. 12) by the Nif'.; but he apparently overlooks Judg. 3, 25.

וַיּֽוֹסֶף שַׁלַּח. In the combination of a verb and inf. construct, two constructions are possible: (a) The verb governs
the inf. cstr. as an acc., as here and ver. 12; (β) ל the prep.
is prefixed to the inf. cstr., as in 11, 8 וַיַּחְדְּלוּ לִבְנוֹת; cf. M. R.,
§§ 112 a, 113; Ges., § 142. 1, 2.

11. עֲלֵה זַיִת טָרָף 'a fresh olive leaf.' טָרָף, prop.=
'a plucked (leaf),' from טרף 'carpere;' cf. طَرُفَ 'to be fresh,
new,' prop. 'to be freshly plucked.'

'That the olive tree is found in Armenia, Strabo shows,
xi. 14. 4: and that it also thrives under water is attested by
Theophr., Hist. pl. iv. 8; Plin., N. H., xiii. 50.' Tuch in Di.

12. וַיִּיָּחֶל is impf. Nif'. from יחל. In Ez. 19, 5 (the only
other example of a Nif'al form of this verb) we have נוֹחֲלָה.
Ges., § 69. Rem. 5, explains it as an instance of the Nif'al of
a verb פ״י, written with י instead of ו; cf. יִיָּרֶה, Ex. 19, 13.

1 Sam. 13, 8 וַיֹּחֶל Ktb.; so Ewald, § 140 b. Stade possibly is right in emending to וַיְיַחֶל; see §§ 115 note, and 504 a.

13. בְּרִאשֹׁן. See on ver. 5 (בְּאֶחָד); cf. Ges., § 120. 4 and the note on 7, 11.

16. Render, '*Go thou forth from the ark with thy wife*,' etc. Notice the difference between the English and Hebrew idiom. English says, '*Go forth with*,' Heb. '*Go forth, thou and thy wife.*'

17. בָּעוֹף. Cf. the note on 7, 21.

הוֹצֵא ... וְשָׁרְצוּ. Cf. the note on 6, 14. The Ktb. הוֹצֵא is the regular imper. Hif'. from יצא, הוֹצֵא arising out of הַוְצֵא; see Ges., § 24. 2 b; Dav., § 9. Rem. b. One fails to see why the Massoretes should prefer the irregular Kri הַיְצֵא to the regular Ktb. Other instances of the Hif'il of verbs פ"י retaining their י as a consonant when we should expect י‑ or וֹ, are Hos. 7, 12 אַיְסִירֵם; Prov. 4, 25 יַיְשִׁרוּ; 1 Chr. 12, 2 מַיְמִינִים; cf. Ges., § 70, 2. Stade, § 120, considers all the instances cited (except 1 Chr. 12, 2) suspicious. Cf. Ps. 5, 9 where, as here, for the Ktb. הוֹשַׁר the Kri הַיְשַׁר is substituted.

21. וַיָּרַח יי׳ אֶת רֵיחַ הַנִּיחֹחַ. וירח is impf. Hif'. from רוּחַ, shortened from יָרִיחַ, after the waw conv.; cf. Ges., § 72. Rem. 7; Stade, § 499 f.

רֵיחַ הַנִּיחֹחַ. '*The odour of satisfaction.*' נִיחֹחַ is a similar formation to נִיצוֹץ, the only other instance of this formation of nouns; Stade, § 233. Ewald, § 156 b, forms ניחח from the verbal stem נוֹחַ, and cites as a third instance of the same formation כִּידוֹר, Job 15, 24, which Stade has apparently overlooked (see § 216, however). The רֵיח ניחח is the pleasant odour which rose up from the sacrifice. In the technical language of the sacrifice (Opfersprache) it is the common expression used for the favourable acceptance of an offering, or rather of the sentiments and wishes to which the sacrifice gives expression (Di.).

אל לבו = '*to himself*,' thus a paraphrase for the reflexive pronoun: for other methods of supplying the reflexive pr. in Heb., see Ges., § 124. 1; M. R., § 89 b.   The LXX paraphrase here with διανοηθείς, Symm. has εἶπε Κύριος πρὸς ἑαυτόν, Onq. has וַיֵּאֲמַר יְיָ בְּמֵימְרֵיהּ, '*Y. spake by his Word*,' so Ps.-Jon. The Pesh. follows the Heb. text with ܒܠܒܗ.   The same idiom recurs 24, 45. 27, 41.

22. The composite subject when *followed* by its predicate, takes the latter in the plural; when the predicate precedes, it may stand in the sing.; cf. the note on 7, 7.

זרע וקציר are '*the seed time and harvest*,' dividing the year into two halves, which are described as '*seed time and harvest*,' also '*cold and heat*,' which roughly correspond to the זרע and קציר respectively. '*The summer and winter*' again correspond to the חם and קר.   The season or half-year, which is called זרע, חרף, and קר, began possibly with the fifteenth of Tisri, and ended on the fifteenth of Nisan; while the other half of the year, called קציר, קיץ, and חם, extended from the fifteenth of Nisan to the fifteenth of Tisri.   The Jewish expositors, following Rashi, consider the seasons mentioned here as six, each of two months' duration. The punctuation is noticeable: יום וָלַיְלָה, קיץ וָחֹרֶף, קר וָחֹם, in pairs, the second member of each pair being connected by ו with pretonic qameç.

9.

2. וּמוֹרַאֲכֶם וְחִתְּכֶם.   Render, '*And the fear of you, and the dread of you.*' The suffixes are objective.   The genitive in Heb. may be either subjective or objective, the latter embracing

many different shades of meaning, often being represented
in English by a preposition, e. g. 3, 24 דרך עץ החיים, see
the note there, and cf. Ges., § 121. 5; M. R., § 78; Ewald,
§ 286 b; 16, 5. 27, 13. 50, 4. Previous to the flood, the beasts
lived at peace with man, and without fear, now they must
fear and dread him (Di.). בכל אשר וגו׳=‘*with all wherewith the ground swarms, and with all the fishes of the sea,
into your hand they are given.*’　The ב of ‘concomitance,’
as in Ex. 10, 9. 15, 19. 1 Kings 10, 2. Jer. 11, 19, and often.

אשר (acc., see on 6, 11), as in Lev. 20, 25 ובכל אשר תרמש
האדמה.

בידכם.　ידכם out of יָדְכֶם (cf. אָחִיו for אָחָיו, from אַחִים),
Stade, § 81 b; Ges., § 27. Rem. 2 a.　‘*Into your power they
are given*,’ a power even over their lives; cf. Lev. 26, 25.
Deut. 1, 27, etc. [misquoted 1, 57, Kn. in Di.].

　3. אשר הוא חי, lit. ‘*which, it is alive*.’　הוא does not
take the place of the copula ‘*is*,’ but resumes the relative אשר.
Compare ver. 18 חם הוא אבי; 2, 14. 19.　Cf. Driver, § 199
end, with Ges., § 121. 2; M. R., § 156 a, where אשר is described
as the link connecting the two sentences, ‘*every creeping thing*’
and ‘*it is alive;*’ so Num. 9, 13. 14, 8. 27. 35, 31. 1 Sam.
10, 19.

　לְאָכְלָה.　אכלה always occurs in this particular phrase,
and always with another dative (except Jer. 12, 9).　אכלה (as
distinguished from אכל, מאכל, and אכילה)=לאכל generalized;
a thing that is given on a particular occasion לֶאֱכֹל, is given
for a continuance לְאָכְלָה; see Prof. Driver, *Journ. of Phil.*,
No. 22, p. 217.

　4. בנפשו דמו.　ב=‘*with*,’ as in 32, 11 בְּמַקְלִי ‘*with my
staff;*’ Ps. 42, 11 ברצח בעצמותי ‘*with crushing in my bones.*’
דמו is an explanatory app. to נפשו, defining it more closely,

84 GENESIS,

M. R., § 71. 2 a. The LXX with their πλὴν κρέας ἐν αἵματι
ψυχῆς seem to have transposed the words, and read בְּדַם נֶפֶשׁ.
Frankel, *Einfluss*, p. 53 note, explains it by the Halacha,
which refers the command forbidding the '*Blutgenuss*' chiefly
to the blood that flows out and causes death (*Kerithoth*, 20 b
דם שהנפש יוצאה בו '*the blood wherein the life goes out*'). The
blood is not actually the life itself, but through the blood the
life becomes apparent to the senses, and is conceived as
existing; cf. Lev. 17, 11. 14. Deut. 12, 23.

5. אֶת דמכם לנפשׁתיכם . '*But the blood of your lives*
(i. e. *belonging to*) *will I require; from the hand of every living
creature will I require it : and from the hand of man, from the
hand of each one's brother will I require the life of man.*'
Tuch and others render, '*your blood for your lives*,' i. e. '*for
their protection;*' לנפשׁתיכם being *dat. commodi;* so Deut. 4, 15
ונשמרתם מאד לנפשׁתיכם, and Josh. 23, 11; see Ewald, § 217 d, a ;
but this is not suitable to the context: in 4 the דם and נפשׁ
are practically identical. Better לנפשׁתיכם='*belonging to your
souls;*' so the LXX, τὸ ὑμέτερον αἷμα τῶν ψυχῶν ὑμῶν, Vulg.
'*sanguinem enim animarum vestrarum*,' Pesh. ܕܟܘܿܢ ܕܡܟܘܢ
ܘܢܦܫܬܟܘܢ; cf. Ges., § 115. 2. Other renderings, which are
not so good, are Del.'s, '*according to your souls*,' as ver. 10,
defining distributively the whole to which the part belongs;
or '*whoever's soul it is, to whom it belongs;*' or '*your blood as
your souls*,' i. e. '*so far as your souls are contained in it*,'
according to vers. 4. 5ᵇ, לַ as in Job 39, 16 (*as though not
her own*); Ewald, § 217 d. דִּמְכֶם is thinned from דַּמְכֶם, Ges.,
§ 93. 2. Rem. 3.

מִיד כל חיה . '*From the hand of every beast.*' According
to Ex. 21, 28 f., the ox that gored any one, so that he or she
died, was to be stoned to death (סקול יסקל).

מיד איש אחיו=*'from the hand of each one's brother.'*
Inverted for the more usual איש מיד אחיו, as Zech. 7, 10
ורעת איש אחיו; cf. תְּרֵין in Aramaic, and ἀλλήλων in Greek,
and contrast Zech. 11, 7 where the usual order is observed
(איש ביד רעהו); cf. Ewald, § 301 b; Ges., § 124. 2. Rem. 1.
4; M. R., § 94. Rem. a; 15, 10. 42, 25. 35. Pesh., Vulg.,
Sam. apparently corrected the text with איש ואחיו. מיד איש
אחיו is co-ordinate with מיד אדם.

6. בָאדם. The LXX ἀντὶ τοῦ αἵματος αὐτοῦ, either reading
בְּדָם or confusing in sound באדם and בדם; compare their
rendering of לכן as though it were=לא כן, viz. 4, 15. 30, 15.

באדם. The ב must be regarded as ב of instrument;
cf. Hos. 1, 7. 1 Sam. 28, 6. Ps. 18, 3, but this is not usual;
passives in Heb. are generally construed with מן of the agent,
as in ver. 11 ממי . . . יכרת, or ל, as in 14, 19 ברוך לאל עליון;
cf. Ges., § 143. 2; M. R., § 49. 4 and § 51. 3. Rem. a.

צלם אלהים is an expression characteristic of P.

9. ואני הנני מקים. When the pronoun precedes הנה,
אני is the form used; when it follows, אנכי is preferred; see
Journ. Phil., No. 22, p. 226.

הקים ברית. ברית, when used with הקים, always has a
suffix; the phrase הקים ברית denotes the perpetuation of
a covenant already, at least in idea, existing, rather than the
formation of one altogether new, which is expressed by
כרת ברית; see *Journ. Phil.,* l.c.

אתכם ואת זרעכם *'with you and with your seed,'* a phrase
characteristic of P.

10. את כל נפש החיה. The adj. alone defined, the
noun being regarded as sufficiently definite through the preceding כל; cf. on 1, 21.

מכל יוצאי ' *all whatever;*' מן denoting the *genus ex quo,* the general to which the particular partitively belongs, as in 6, 2. 7, 22 ; Ewald, § 278 c. ל, as in 23, 10 לכל באי='*with respect to,*' etc.; cf. Lev. 16, 21. 11, 42 ; Ewald, § 310 a (ל with a generalizing and particularizing force).

13. נתתי. '*I set,*' as in 1, 29 הנה נתתי ; cf. Driver, § 14 a; Ewald, § 135 c.

14. בעננִי ענן. Inf. Pi‘el with the prep. ב, and suffix of the 1st pers. sing. נ is pointed with ־ַ, as the doubling of the letter has fallen away ; cf. Ges., § 10. 2. Rem.; the more regular form of the inf. Pi‘el would be בְּעַנְּנִי:

עֵנֵן is a denom. of עָנָן. Render, '*when I cloud my clouds;*' the apodosis begins with ver. 15, ונראתה being a continuation of the inf.; see Ges., § 132. 3. Rem. 2 ; Driver, § 118.

18. היצאים. Here the participle must be rendered as past, '*those who went out,*' equivalent to אשר יצאו, but neater ; cf. Ges., § 134. 2 c; Driver, § 135. 1 ; so 13, 7 ואז ישב ; 19, 1 ישב '*sat,*' or '*was sitting;*' 37, 7. 41, 1–3. 42, 23.

19.. ומאלה נפצה כל הארץ. '*And out of these was the whole earth overspread.*' נפצה is a lightened form of the 3rd pers. fem. perf., Nif‘. sing. of פוץ=פצץ ; cf. 1 Sam. 13, 11. Is. 33, 3 (נפצו) ; Ewald, § 193 c (who compares נְסַבָּה from סבב ; נָקְטָה from קטט ; נָבְקָה from בקק) ; Ges., § 67, note 11.

20. ויחל נח ... ויטע. Render, '*And Noah the husbandman began and planted.*' So most moderns ; cf. Ges., § 142. 4 with 3 a. Some, however (Tuch, Kn.), appealing to Ewald, § 298 b (cf. M. R., § 43 a) and 1 Sam. 3, 2 החלו כהות—which is scarcely parallel—render, '*And Noah began to be a husbandman, and planted;*' but this would require איש אדמה instead of איש האדמה ; cf. 25, 27 איש שדה (for M. R.'s explanation, § 76 b. Rem. a, is hardly satisfactory), and what is noticeable

in the narrative is, not that Noah began to be a husbandman,
but that he began the cultivation of the vine.

21. וַיֵּשְׁתְּ. The imperf. apoc. Qal of שתה without a helping vowel; see Ges., § 75. Rem. 3 c and § 28. 4; Stade, §§ 70 a.
2. 2, 101 c, 489 b.

אָהֳלֹה is the older form for אָהֳלוֹ. The ה is preserved in
Arabic, and on the Moabite stone, e. g. l. 5 בה ובארצה=
בּוֹ וּבְאַרְצוֹ; l. 7 וּבְבֵיתֹה ובביתה=בה; other examples in lines
9. 10. 19. 25. אהלה always has a Kri, אהלו; cf. Ges., § 91. 1.
Rem. 2. הֹ- for וֹ- occurs, however, elsewhere in the O. T.,
and is by no means confined to the oldest books.

22. חם may be called the father of Canaan here with
reference to ver. 25.

וַיַּגֵּד, sc. '*it*;' see Ges., § 121. 6. Rem. 2; cf. 38, 17.

23. הַשִּׂמְלָה. '*The upper garment*,' also used (e. g. by the
poor) as a covering by night; cf. Ex. 22, 26. Deut. 24, 13.

24. מִיֵּינוֹ '*from his wine*,' i. e. his intoxication which the
wine had caused, as in 1 Sam. 1, 14. 25, 37.

בְּנוֹ הַקָּטָן, i. e. '*his younger son*,' not '*his youngest*,' as
Japhet was the youngest of the three; cf. 5, 32. 10, 1. 2. 6.
21. הקטן grammatically can be either comparative or superlative; cf. 1, 16 and the note there.

25. עֶבֶד עֲבָדִים = '*servant of servants*,' i. e. '*meanest servant*;' cf. שִׁיר הַשִּׁירִים '*song of songs*,' '*choicest song*;' see Ges.,
§ 119. 2. Rem.; M. R., § 81 a. Canaan is made Shem and
Japhet's servant. As Noah's son Ham sinned against him,
so shall he (Ham) be punished through his own son Canaan,
by the curse laid upon him by Noah. The settlements of
Canaan on the islands and coasts of Asia Minor were at an
early date overcome by the Japhetic races (Di.).

26. לָמוֹ is poetical for לָהֶם, as often; cf. Stade, § 345 c,

note 1; Ges., § 103.2, foot-note 2. Shem is not blessed directly, but the God of Shem (Deut. 33, 20), i.e. Shem is blessed through his God, the highest possible form of blessing. If God is to be blessed for His goodness, which is implied in blessing Him, how great must be the happiness of those who are under His protection and enjoy His favour.

27. '*May God spread out Japhet far, and may he dwell in the tents of Shem.*' Onq. and others (Baumg., etc.) take God as the subject to יִשְׁכֹּן; but the change of subject is awkward, and we should in this case rather expect וְהוּא יִשְׁכֹּן. Some again (Ges., Schr.) take שֵׁם as meaning '*repute;*' cf. 6, 4 אַנְשֵׁי שֵׁם; but this is not suitable to the context, and Japhet could not at that date have had any opportunity of acquiring fame. Dwelling in the tents of Shem does not mean conquest, but points to the friendly relations that should exist between the Semitic and Japhetic races; the latter participating in the honour paid the former, and sharing the religious privileges enjoyed by them.

10.

In chapter 5 we had a list of the descendants of Adam, containing ten generations, and ending with Noah. In chapter 10 we have a continuation of the list found in chapter 5, viz. a genealogical table of the sons of Noah, and the various peoples that sprang from them. In the first verse we find the sons of Noah given in the same order as in 5, 32; but in verse 2—in accordance with the custom observed in the book of Genesis, to first notice the side branches of the family tree, in order to prepare the way for mentioning the chief line—we have the order, Japhet, Ham, Shem; Ham standing next to Shem, being, through Canaan, Mizraim, and Cush, more closely allied to him than Japhet was. It should be observed in these תולדות that the list of nations is by no means complete. We find no mention made of nations of a more modern origin, such as Moabites, Edomites, Ishmaelites, Keturaeans, nor of some nations, such as the Rephaim and Amalekites, who were of very ancient descent; also we find no allusion to the Chinese and the other Mongolian races of Eastern Asia, to the Indians or Eranians, probably because they were entirely unknown in Palestine at the time of the narrator. ' In general the notice embraces the peoples who were grouped round the basin of the Mediterranean and its vicinity, the peoples of the so-called Caucasian race' (Di.). The nations mentioned in this table are regarded as the individuals of a large family, as sons, grandsons, and great-grandsons, of a common father, e. g. just as Shem, Ham, and Japhet are Noah's sons, so the Chittim and Dodanim in ver. 4 are the grandsons of Japhet; cf. ver. 6, Mizraim as the son of Ham; ver. 13, Ludim as the son of Mizraim; and (ver. 16) the similar use of the patronymics (the Amorite and Jebusite being spoken of as the children of Canaan; compare vers. 17. 18).

The table falls into three chief divisions, viz. I. 2-5. The Descendants of Japhet, the Northern Races. II. 6-20. The Descendants of Ham, the Southern Races. III. 21-31. The Descendants of Shem, the Central Races. The list is repeated with some variations in 1 Chr. 1, 4-23. For a list of works bearing on this chapter, see Dillmann's *Commentary*. p. 161. In the following notes—which are not intended to form a complete commentary on the chapter—Dillmann has been chiefly followed, and for fuller information his notes and the works there cited should be consulted.

1. תולדות. Cf. the note on 2, 4.

ויפת. ו with pretonic qameç, see on 1, 2.

2–5. The Descendants of Japhet.

2. גמר. LXX, Γαμέρ, mentioned again in Ez. 38, 6 (LXX, Γομέρ), as an ally of Gog of Magog. 'Usually, since the time of Calmet, supposed to be the *Cimmerii* (Κιμμέριοι, Hom. *Od.*, xi. 14), who inhabited the Tauric Chersonese, were driven out in the seventh century by the Scythians, and overran the Lydian kingdom in Asia Minor; finally they disappeared, but traces of their existence are still extant in names of places.' Others (Kiepert, Lagarde) consider that גמר is Cappadocia, called by the Armenians *Gamir* (Pl.). Josephus, *Ant.*, i. 6. 1, considers that גמר = the Γαλάται, who were formerly called Γομαρεῖς, in Northern Phrygia. Bochart also decides for Phrygia. Saadiah explains גמר by الترك 'the Turks.' The name is found in the Assyrian inscriptions, '*Gimirrai*=*those who belong to the people* (Ass. *land*) *of Gimir;*' see Schr., *K.A.T.*², p. 80.

מגוג. 'The second son of Japhet must be sought for between Gomer and Media. In Ez. 38, 2. 6. 15. 39, 2 Magog appears as a remote and warlike people in the far North, having Tubal and Meschek under them, and to whom Gomer and the House of Togarma have attached themselves.' Josephus l. c. and Hieron., *Quaest.* ed. Lagarde, p. 14, explain מגוג as '*the Scythians*,' the people of lake Maeotis and the Caucasus, and this view is the one commonly adopted since the time of Bochart.

מדי. '*The Medes*,' elsewhere mentioned in the O. T., viz. 2 Kings 17, 6. 18, 11. Jer. 25, 25. 51, 11. 28. Is. 13, 17 f. 21, 2. The name is found on the Assyrian inscriptions, '*Madai*' ('*Ma-da-ai*'); see Schrader, *K.A.T.*², p. 80.

יון. '*The Ionians*' ('Ιάονες, 'Ιάϝονες), in the whole of the

East, up to India, the name for the Greeks; also found on
the Assyrian inscriptions of Sargon II and Sanherib '*Javnai*'
('*Ja-av-naai*'), Schr., *K. A. T.*[2], p. 81. They are frequently
mentioned in the O. T., e. g. Joel 4, 6. Ez. 27, 13. Is. 66, 19.
Dan. 8, 21. 10, 20. 11, 2.

תובל ומשך. 'Always (except Is. 66, 19, Mass. text, and
Ps. 120, 5) joined together. In Ez. 32, 26 they are mentioned
as having suffered severe reverses, in Ez. 27, 13 (together
with Javan, possibly from Gen. 10, 2) as connected by trade
with the Tyrians, whom they supplied with slaves and vessels
of brass. In Ez. 38, 2 f. 39, 1 they are spoken of as forming
the flower of the army of the Scythian king Gog, in Is. 66, 19,
LXX, as distant peoples. They are usually identified with
the *Tibareni* and *Moschi*, who inhabited the hill country on
the south-east of the Black Sea, the *Moschi* between the
sources of the Phasis and Cyrus, the *Tibareni* east of the
Thermodon, in Pontus. In the Assyrian inscriptions (see
Schrader, *K. A. T.*[2], p. 82 ff.) their territory extended further
south, the "*Tabali*" ("*Tibareni*") up to Cilicia and the "*Muski*"
("*Moschi*") north-eastwards of the *Tabali*. Josephus, *Ant.* l.c.,
explains תובל as the *Iberians* in the Caucasus land, and משך
as Μάζακα in Cappadocia (being deceived by the similarity in
sound).'

תירס is mentioned nowhere else, but must, according to
its position, be looked for either east of משך, or in the
west, and more towards the south than משך. Since Josephus
תירס has been usually identified with the *Thracians*, but Di.
questions the suitability of this identification, as תירס = the
Thracians would be already included in the Gomer group.
Other conjectures are Τύρης, Τύρας, i. e. the Dniester with the
people dwelling on it, the Τυρῖται (Her. iv. 51); the Τυρσηνοί
(Tuch, Nöld., Di.), who belonged to the *Pelasgi*, and who made

themselves by their acts of piracy a terror to the islands and
coasts of the Aegean Sea between Greece and Asia Minor
(Her. i. 57. 94; Thuc. iv. 109); see Tuch, p. 171.

3. The sons of Gomer.

אשכנז, 'the first son of Gomer, is mentioned in Jer. 51,
27 together with Ararat and Minni, i.e. with North-eastern
and South-eastern Armenia.' Josephus explains by 'Ρηγῖνες,
who are otherwise unknown. The Ber. Rabba gives Asia;
and the Jews of the Middle Ages, Germany. 'As the ending
az in (phryg.) Armenian forms patronymics, and as *Askanians*,
according to several authorities, settled in Mysia, Bithynia,
and Phrygia, whose name at a later date still attached to a
lake, river, and village [*Il.* ii. 862 ff., xiii. 793, etc.], this old
Askanian people must be understood,' Di. In Jeremiah the
Western Armenians are intended, i.e. the *Askanians*, who had
emigrated from Phrygia into Western Armenia, and Tuch,
Ges., and Schr. consider this to be the case in the present
passage.

ריפת, in 1 Chr. 1, 6 דיפת. Josephus explains by *Riphcans*,
i.e. *Paphlagonians*, which Bochart seeks to support by comparing *Rhebas*, a river of Bithynia, which falls into the Black
Sea near Paphlagonia; so Lag., Di. Kn., however, prefers the
view that ריפת=the fabulous ὄρη 'Ριπαῖα, which were regarded
by the ancients as the boundary of the northern side of the
earth. Del. regards the name 'as not yet deciphered with
certainty.' Saadiah and the modern Jews apply ריפת fancifully to France. The LXX have 'Ριφάθ here and in 1 Chr. l.c.

תגרמה, mentioned in Ez. 38, 6 together with Gomer,
in the army of Gog; and in Ez. 27, 14 after Javan, Tubal,
and Meshek, as supplying horses and mules for the Tyrian
traders: both times called in Ez. בית תגרמה. Josephus

understood תגרמה to mean the *Phrygians*. But as the *Phrygians* are already included in אשכנז, the view that "ת= *the Armenians*, is to be preferred; 'according to the oldest sense of the word, Western Armenia,' Di. With this identification, Phrygia, Paphlagonia, and Western Armenia naturally follow one another in the direction from west to east. The LXX have the name slightly altered, Θοργαμά; Codex A, Θεργαμά; cf. Lagarde, *Gen. Graece*, p. 34.

4. The sons of Javan.

אלישה, mentioned in Ez. 27, 7, '*the coastlands of Elishah*,' whence purple was obtained. Josephus thinks that אלישה means the *Aeolians*. The Targ. of Jonathan here takes it to = *Hellas*. Others, *Elis* (Boch.). But Di. objects, firstly, that שה—for the Greek nom. ending *s*—is inconceivable, and secondly, that Greece and the Greeks are already included in Javan. He suggests *Italy* and *Sicily*, citing the Targ. to Ez. l.c. מְדִינַת אִיטַלְיָא. If we take Javan as the *Ionian* Greeks (esp. in Asia Minor), Elishah might well denote some branch of *Dorian* or *Achaean* Greeks. Upon this view, however, what the name corresponds to, remains to be explained.

תרשיש is frequently mentioned in the O. T. Josephus thinks *Tarsus* in Cilicia is intended, but the more generally accepted view is that *Tartessus* in Spain is meant, which was celebrated in the east for its abundance of silver, and carried on an extensive trade with Tyre (cf. Herod. i. 163, iv. 152; Is. 23). 'Not the town as a Phoenician colony (Stade), but the land and people is intended,' Di. *Tartessus* embraced the coastland from Gibraltar to the mouth of the Baetis or Guadalquiver. The Tarshish navy, mentioned in the book of Kings (1 Kings 10, 22. 22, 49), was not a navy that was intended to traffic with Tarshish, but is a term for large vessels, just as we speak of East or West-Indiamen; cf. Ges., *Thes.*, p. 1315.

כתים. *Cyprus* and its inhabitants, where was an old town Κίττιον, the modern Larnaka (Schrader), which Josephus mentions in his explanation of the name. The Assyrian name of the island was '*Jatnâna*' or '*Atnâna;*' see Schr., *K. A. T.²*, p. 85 f. The name seems at a later date to have included other islands and coastlands; cf. Jer. 2, 10. Ez. 27, 6 כתים איי. Dan. 11, 30.

דדנים. So the Targ., Pesh., and Vulg.; but the LXX and Sam. give רדנים, as 1 Chr. 1, 7. The reading רדנים is generally accepted as the correct one, as דדנים cannot be suitably explained. Conjectural explanations that have been offered are *Dodona*, the seat of the famous oracle in Epirus, which would be unsuitable here; or דדנים = the Δάρδανοι; Targ. Jon. לִרְדַנְיָא, Jer. Targ. דּוֹדַנְיָא, i.e. the *Trojans*. With the other reading רדנים Bochart explains the word as meaning the *Rhone*, and the people dwelling near it: more probable, however, is the explanation by which רדנים = *Rhodes*, or in a more general sense the *Rhodian Islands*, i.e. the islands of the Aegean Sea. In Ez. 27, 15 the LXX give for דדנים, Ῥόδιοι.

5. 'In ver. 20 and ver. 31 we find at the conclusion of the list אלה בני חם and אלה בני שם respectively; and we should expect here אלה בני יפת. As מאלה cannot refer to בני יפת in ver. 2, but to בני יון ver. 4 (since Magog, Media, etc. cannot be spoken of as populating the sea coasts), and as, moreover, בארצתם does not agree with איי הגוים, these three words (אלה בני יפת) must be inserted before בארצתם, without its being, on account of this, necessary to strike out ... מאלה הגוים as a gloss,' Di. This emendation, proposed by Ilgen, is adopted also by Ewald, and apparently accepted by Del.

Render, '*From these have the sea-lands of the peoples separated themselves. (These are the sons of Japhet) in their lands, each according to his language, according to their families, by their peoples.*'   אִיִּים denotes regularly '*the islands and coastlands*' of the Mediterranean.

On בְּ = '*by, according to,*' see on 7, 21; and cf. ver. 20 and ver. 31 of this chapter.

6-20. THE DESCENDANTS OF HAM.

6. כּוּשׁ, 'called by the ancient Egyptians "*Kaš, Kiš, Keš, Kesi,*" and used as the name of a people of a reddish-brown colour, between Egypt and Abyssinia, viz. in the East between the Nile and the sea.'   In the O. T. Cush seems to have had a wider and narrower signification.   In 2, 13 and here it has a wider meaning, and is used to denote the southern limit of the known world, including the inhabitants of the coastland of Southern Arabia.   From Isaiah's time and onwards it was used with a more limited signification, as the special name of the state situated at the foot of mount *Barkal*, viz. *Ethiopia.* כּוּשׁ is found on the Assyrian inscriptions ('*Kusi*') as the name of Ethiopia; see Schr., *K. A. T.*[2], p. 86. 'It is uncertain whether the "*Kaṣṣi*" of the inscriptions, the Κοσσαῖοι in Susiania, and to the north of Susiania, the Κισσίων χώρη, represent the same name of a people as *Kuš, Keš*, and thus bear testimony to an extension and emigration on the part of the Cushites,' Di.

מִצְרַיִם. *Egypt.* Assyr. '*Muṣur, Muṣru, Miṣir,*' Schr., *K. A. T.*[2], p. 89. The dual form of the word in Hebrew probably is used with reference to the two parts of Egypt, upper and lower, which are always mentioned on the oldest Egyptian monuments when the whole of Egypt is spoken of.

It is, however, used in Hebrew where Lower Egypt is meant, Upper Egypt being expressly excluded, e. g. Is. 11, 11. Jer. 44, 1. 15. Various etymologies have been suggested for the name. Bochart thinks that מצר = '*walling in*,' and Egypt would then = the land *that is shut off* or *walled in*; but this opinion of Bochart's rests on the use of the name in Is. 37, 35. 19, 6. Another derivation (Ges. in the *Thes.*, p. 815) is from מצר which occurs in Aram., Assyr., and Arab. = '*a limit, province*,' so מצרים = '*the two lands*.'

פוט. This name occurs frequently in the O. T. In Nah. 3, 9 פוט is mentioned with Cush, Mizraim, and Lubim; in Jer. 46, 9 in the Egyptian army, together with Cush and Ludim; cf. Ez. 30, 5. In Ez. 27, 10 the soldiers of פוט are found among the Tyrian soldiers, together with those of Persia and Lud; and again in Ez. 38, 5 פוט occurs with Persia and Cush in Gog's army. In the LXX, Is. 66, 19 (Mass. text פול), it is spoken of as a distant nation of the west. The LXX in Jer. and Ez. translate it by Λίβυες, so Josephus: and this is the view generally adopted. Knobel (*Völkertafel*, p. 296) points out that the Coptic name for Libya was *Phaiat*. Ptol. iv. 1. 3, Pliny v. 1 mention a river Φθούθ or *Fut* in Libya.

כנען (from כנע '*to be low, depressed*') = '*the low land*,' as opposed to the high lands of Aramea. This, however, Di. disputes, and regards כנען as the original name of the low land by the sea and the Jordan, which was afterwards extended to all the country west of the Jordan. Canaan embraced all this district, exclusive of Philistia, but inclusive of Phoenicia. It is remarkable that כנען — though the language of the land was Semitic — should be found among the sons of Ham. Perhaps this was due to a sense of their different origin; it being more or less certain that they were emigrants from the south, from the neighbourhood of the Persian Gulf (see Di., p. 170, and the authorities he cites in favour of the view of the southern origin of the Canaanites, viz. Her. i. 1, vii. 89; Justin. xviii. 3; Strabo i. 2. 35, xvi. 3. 4; Dion. per. 906; compare *The Book of Jubilees*, c. 10; see also Schröder, *Phoen. Gram.*, p. 4). The Assyrians do not seem to have been acquainted with the name Canaan, their name for the land being usually '*mat Aḥarri,*' '*the Westland;*' see Schrader, *K.A.T.*², p. 90 ff.

7. The sons of Cush.

סְבָא is mentioned in Ps. 72, 10 together with שְׁבָא, as a distant land in the south. In Is. 43, 3. 45, 14 it is spoken of together with Egypt and Cush; and in 45, 14 the סבאים are described as being very tall. Since Josephus (*Ant.*, ii. 10. 2), סבא has usually been identified with *Meroë;* and possibly this identification is supported by a comparison of Is. 45, 14 with 18, 2. 7 (Her. iii. 20. 114). Di., however, prefers to identify סבא with a branch of the Cushites, dwelling on the Arabian sea, on the east of Napata; and he supposes that remains of this proper name are to be found in *Asta-soba* and *Soba*, the capital of the Christian kingdom of *Senaar* in the Middle Ages. His reason for objecting to the identification given by Josephus is that the kingdom of Cush, which reached to the southern island of Meroë, was neither known to the Egyptians, nor called in the O.T. סבא.

חֲוִילָה. Cf. on 2, 11. Di. supposes that a trace of this people is to be found in the name Κόλπος Αὐαλίτης or Ἀβαλίτης, and the people Ἀβαλῖται, on the African coast near the Straits of Bab-el-Mandeb. This would suit the order of the enumeration. In ver. 29 חוילה is mentioned among the sons of

Joqtan on the Persian Gulf; and we must either suppose that there was more than one חוילה, or that a great Cushite people were scattered over the east and south coast of Arabia, who also had penetrated to the west coast of north-eastern Africa, and there left traces of their name. Possibly, as Tuch suggests, the difference is due to two different accounts.

וסבתה. Josephus, *Ant.*, i. 6. 2, explains by Ἀστάβαροι, i.e. the inhabitants of *Astaboras*, now *Atbara*, in Abyssinia, which Gesenius in the *Thes.* approves. More general is the view held by Tuch and Del., and accepted by Di., that סבתא is to be connected with the old Arabian town Σάβ-βαθα or *Sabota*, the capital of the *Chatramotitae*, which had sixty temples, and was a great emporium of the frankincense trade.

רעמה, LXX, Ῥεγμά, cf. on 4, 18, is mentioned in Ez. 27, 22 in connection with שבא, as a trading people, who supplied the Tyrians with spices, precious stones, and gold. Tuch and others identify רעמה with Ῥῆγμα or Ῥέγμα, mentioned by Ptolemy and Steph. Byz., a town with a harbour on the Arabian side of the Persian Gulf. Di. prefers to identify it with the רעמה of the Sabean inscriptions, in the neighbourhood of מען *Me'in*, north of *Marib*.

וסבתכא is unknown. Those who consider that רעמה is situated on the Persian Gulf compare Σαμυδάκη, a seaport town and river in Carmania; so Bochart. The Targ. of Jon. here, and the Targ. to Chron., give זנגאי, i.e. *Zingis*, on the east coast of Africa.

The sons of Ra'ma.

שבא. '*The Sabeans*,' often mentioned in the O. T. as a distant land and people, whose great wealth in gold, precious stones, frankincense, and cassia, was brought, partly by themselves, and partly by others, to the north. They dwelt in southern Arabia, the capital of their empire being *Mariaba* or *Saba*.

דדן, mentioned in 25, 3 among the descendants of Keturah. Possibly there were two different accounts of their origin, both of which have been employed by the narrator. In Ez. 38, 13 דדן is mentioned together with שבא, as a most important trading nation, and in Ez. 27, 20 as supplying Tyre with costly carpets. In Is. 21, 13 the caravans of Dedan are mentioned, and in Jer. 25, 23. 49, 8 it is spoken of together with the Edomites and other desert tribes of Arabia. In Ez. 25, 13 דדן is the tribe on the frontier of Edom. 'Since Bochart, the Cushite דדן has usually been placed on the Persian Gulf, and a trace of the name is supposed to have been found in *Daden* (دادن, Syr. ܕܕܢ?; see Ges., *Thes.*), one of the Bahrein Islands, and the Keturaean Dedanites are distinguished from those of Cush; traces of the former being perhaps extant in the ruins of *Daidán*, west of Têmâ, south-east of Aila, in northern Ḥiǵâz,' Di. דדן occurs in Halevy's *Sab. Inscriptions*, and Di. remarks that the original Dedan must be sought for further south than on the Persian Gulf. After the exile the Dedanites disappeared, their place being taken by the Gerrheans (on the west of the Persian Gulf). On this word and שבא in the Assyr. inscrip., see Schrader, *K. A. T.*², pp. 92, 145 ff.

8. יָלַד. P would use הוליד; so in 6, 10.

נמרד. LXX, Νεβρώδ. Found once again in Micah 5, 5. Its derivation is uncertain; some derive it from מרד 'to revolt;' so נמרד 'rebeller,' *H. W. B.*, 9th ed. The name has not yet been discovered in the Assyrian inscriptions. The Assyriologists identify the Nimrod of the Bible with the Babylonian hero *Iṣtubar;* see Schrader, *K. A. T.*²,

p. 92 ; and Haupt quoted by Schrader, l. c., believes that the name can mean, as an old Babylonian gentilic, '*he who is of Marad*,' *Marad* (also *Amarad*) being a town of central Babylonia.

גבור='*a mighty man*,' cf. Ps. 52, 3; a powerful ruler, who, by his courage, activity, and the terror he inspired, reduced all around him, either voluntarily or involuntarily, to sub-mission, 'Del.;' cf. ver. 10.

9. Nimrod was also distinguished as a mighty huntsman. גבור ציד='*a hero in* (lit. *of*) *the chase*.'

לפני יהוה (cf. Jon. 3, 3 לאלהים; τῷ Θεῷ, Acts 7, 20). The expression is doubtless taken from the mouth of the people, and denotes that he was exceptionally mighty, a person whom God himself must regard as *sui generis*. Onq. has גִּבַּר תַּקִּיף='*a mighty hero*;' LXX, γίγας κυνηγὸς ἐναντίον Κυρίου τοῦ Θεοῦ.

על כן יאמר. This formula is also used elsewhere in citing what was well known as a proverb, e. g. Num. 21, 14; cf. 1 Sam. 10, 12 with 19, 24, also Gen. 22, 14.

10. בבל. Cf. 11, 9.

ארך. LXX, 'Ορέχ. The Targg. of Jon. and Jer., also Ephrem Syrus and Jerome, take this to be *Edessa* (in Syriac ܐܘܪܗܝ), but incorrectly, as Edessa is a Mesopotamian, not a Babylonian town. Bochart and others identify it with *Arecca*, on the lower Tigris, on the frontier of Susiania. More probably it is 'Ορχοή, mentioned by Ptol. v. 20. 7; the modern *Warka*, on the left bank of the lower Euphrates, south-east of Babylon. Its name on the inscriptions is '*Arku*' or '*Urku*,' interpreted by Oppert as meaning '*Moon-town*;' see Schrader, *K.A.T.*[2], p. 94 f.

אכד. LXX, 'Αρχάδ. The site of אכד is unknown. Knobel

explains it by Ἀκκήτη, a district north of Babylon. Akkad occurs frequently in the inscriptions as the name of a Babylonian people and land, but its position cannot be determined; all that can be said is that it must be sought for in northern Babylonia; see Schrader, *K.A. T.*[2], p. 95. The Targg. of Jon. and Jer. explain it as *Nisibis*, and this explanation is adopted for the Pesh. ܢܨܒܝ here, by Ephrem Syrus and Bar Hebraeus.

כַלְנֵה. LXX, Χαλάννη. In Amos 6, 2 it has the form כַּלְנֵה, and in Is. 10, 9 כַּלְנוֹ. It has not yet been found in the Assyrian inscriptions. The Targ. Ps.-Jon. and Targ. Jer., also Ephrem, Jerome, etc., identify it with *Ctesiphon Seleucia*, on the Tigris. G. Rawlinson (*Anc. Mon.*, i. p. 20), cited by Di., thinks it is *Nippur* (Niffer), following the Talmud.

בְאֶרֶץ שִׁנְעָר. *Shin'ar* is Babylonia proper, exclusive of Mesopotamia, the Bab. *Iráq* of the Arabs. Shin'ar is now commonly understood to be a dialectic variation of the Bab. Assyrian '*Sumer;*' '*Sumer*' being the name of the southern portion of Babylonia, the northern part being *Akkad*. The Hebrews would then have applied the original name of south Babylonia to all Babylonia; see Schrader, *K.A. T.*[2], p. 118. Onq. has בְּאַרְעָא דְבָבֶל '*in the land of Babel.*' The word occurs besides in Josh. 7, 21. Is. 11, 11. Dan. 1, 2. Zech. 5, 11.

11. Render, '*From that land he went forth to Asshur,*' etc. This translation is not only demanded by ver. 22, where Asshur is enumerated among the sons of Shem, but by ver. 10, אַשּׁוּר here, being opposed to Shinar in that verse. The versions, however, except Targ. Jon., take אַשּׁוּר as subject, as though it were the name of a person, which is never the case in the O. T. אַשּׁוּר is here taken in its geographical sense, and denotes the district on the east bank of the Tigris, as the site of the cities assigned to it shews; cf. 2, 14.

אַשּׁוּר is the acc. of motion towards, without the ending
ה‍ָ‍; cf. 35, 1. 3. 43, 15. Ex. 4, 19, and constantly; see
Ges., § 118. 1; M. R., § 41 a.

נִינְוֵה. LXX, Νινευί, Assyrian 'Ninua,' also 'Nina,' on the
east bank of the Tigris, now Kujundschik.

רחבת עיר = lit. '*streets of a city*,' or '*wide places of a
city*;' unless it be preferred to regard the two words as in
apposition. The LXX have τὴν Ῥοωβὼθ πόλιν. Probably
רחבת עיר is distinct from רחבות הנהר in 36, 37, though it has
been conjectured that the two are identical, and that it is
Rahaba on the Euphrates; see Tuch, p. 189. Di. supposes
that, according to its name, it formed the suburb to some
larger city whose position is unknown; so Del. in his
Paradies, p. 261, comparing '*Ri(rê)-bit ir Ni-na-a*' in
the inscription of Asarhaddon (i. 53), etc.; see Schrader,
*K. A. T.*², p. 101, who agrees with the view held by
Di.

כלח was formerly identified with Καλαχηνή of Strabo,
חֲלַח, whither (according to 2 Kings 17, 6. 18, 11) a portion
of the ten tribes was carried away captive by Shalmaneser.
More probably it is the same as *Kalhu* of the inscriptions,
built about 1300 by Shalmaneser I, and refounded by Asur-
nâṣirhabal (883–859), and raised to the position of a royal
residence (see Schrader, *K. A. T.*², p. 98). *Kalhu* occupied
the site of the present village and hill of *Nimrud*, in the
most southern angle of the triangle formed by the Tigris
and Zâb; see Di., p. 176. It is distinct from חלח mentioned above.

12. רסן, LXX, Δασή, cf. Lag., *Gen. Graece*, p. 36, is only
mentioned here, and is not found on the inscriptions; but as
it lies between Nineveh and Kelach, it is to be sought for
between *Kujundschik* and *Nimrud*. Prof. Sayce identifies it

with *Rêṣ-ẹni*, i.e. ראֹשׁ עִין; see *Academy*, May 1, 1880, and Schrader, *K.A.T.²*, p. 100.

הוא העיר הגדולה cannot refer to רסן alone, as nothing further is known of the large city of Resen; and from its position between Nineveh and Kelach, it must be regarded as insignificant. We must therefore refer it either to the four cities, or to Nineveh, together with the other three; Nineveh being regarded as forming with the other three a great city; cf. Jon. 1, 2. 3, 2. 4, 11.

13. The sons of Mizraim.

לוּדים, 1 Chron. 1, 11 לודיים Ktb. We find the לודים (in Jer. 46, 10. Ez. 27, 10. 30, 5) mentioned as bow men in the army of the Egyptians, or Tyrians; in Jer. and Ez. 30, 5, with Cush and Phut; in Ez. 27, 10, with Persia and Phut; and in Is. 66, 19, among the most distant people. In Is. l.c. and the two passages in Ez., the sing. form לוּד is used. They are identified by Hitzig with the *Libyans;* by Movers (*Phoen.*, ii. 1. 377 ff.) with the Berber tribe of *Lewála* dwelling on the Syrtes; by Knobel with the Egyptised portion of the Semitic לוּד (cf. ver. 22), who had settled in north-eastern Egypt. All these identifications are precarious. A people of western lower Egypt, or on its borders, seems to be required to explain לוּדים. לוּד in ver. 22 is different from the לודים here mentioned; cf. further, Di. and Tuch on this verse.

ענמים. LXX, 'Ενεμετιείμ, uncertain. Pesh. has ܢܥܡܝ, which Tuch emends to ܠܢܥܡܝܢ. Kn. and Bunsen connect it with '*emhit*,' i.e. '*north*,' and explain it as North Egypt. Ebers explains ענמים as = '*an-aamu*,' the wandering herds-men who had settled on the Bucolic or Phatmetic arm of the Nile, where there was pasture for their cattle.

להבים. LXX, Λαβιείμ—probably identical with the לובים in Nah. 3, 9. 2 Chron. 12, 3. 16, 8. Dan. 11, 43—are the

Libyans, old Egyptian '*Tahennu*' ('*Thihenu*'), also '*Lebu*' or '*Rebu*.' Wright compares for the interchange of ה and ו, לודים, Sam. להדים; בוש, Syr. ܒܘܫ; רוין, Syr. ܪܘܝܢ. 'The name here is to be understood of the Libyans on the borders of Egypt,' Di.

נפתחים. LXX (Tisch. and Lag.) omit, but Walton's text has Νεφθαλείμ. Pesh. ܢܦܬܘܚܝܡ, ܀ for ܀. Bochart identifies נפתחים with Νέφθυς, in Plut. *de Isid.*, p. 96, the most northern portion of Egypt on the sea-shore. More probable is the identification proposed by Ebers, '*na-ptah*,'=οἱ τοῦ Φθᾶ, i. e. *those belonging to Ptah* or *Hephaestus*, the Memphitic Egyptians.

14. פתרסים, derived from פתרס, which (see Is. 11, 11. Jer. 44, 1. 15. Ez. 29, 14. 30, 14) signifies Upper Egypt (Thebais).

כסלחים. LXX, Χασμωνιείμ; cf. Lag., *Gen. Graece*, p. 36. Since Bochart's time, usually identified with the *Colchians* on the Black Sea, because these (according to Herodotus, Strabo, and others) were descendants of the Egyptians. Knobel thinks that the dry and salty strip of land stretching from the eastern mouth of the Nile along the sea up to the southern frontier of Palestine, with lake Sirbonis and mount Casius, is intended. But this identification is doubtful; see Di. here.

אשר יצאו משם פלשתים. If כסלחים are the *Colchians*, this notice is senseless, and then we must assume that here and in 1 Chron. 1, 12 the words are out of place, and should come after כפתרים. Del. keeps the present order of the text, and distinguishes between Philistines who came from the כסלחים, and Philistines who came from כפתר; but in Deut. 2, 23. Amos 9, 7. Jer. 47, 4, the Philistines are spoken of as coming from כפתור, and no mention is made of any such

double origin. Di. prefers to assume that the immigration of
the Philistines was not made directly from Crete, but came
by the way of the Egyptian sea coast; see on כסלחים. The
versions follow the order of the Mass. text. פלשׁתים = probably
'*emigrants*' or '*strangers*,' from פלשׁ, Eth. *falasa*, '*to wander*.'
פלשׁת, *Philistia*, is called Παλαιστίνη by Josephus, and this
name afterwards was used as the name of the whole land
of Canaan. In Assyrian it is '*Palastav*' or '*Pilista;*' see
Schrader, *K. A. T.*[2], p. 102 f.

כפתרים. Not the *Cappadocians*, as LXX in Deut. 2, 23.
Amos 9, 7; Vulg. (everywhere else, but here '*Caphtorim*'),
Targg. Onq., Ps.-Jon., and Jer., and Pesh.; but more
probably *Crete;* not only because such an important island
would scarcely be omitted in this table of nations, but also
because *Kaftor* in Jer. 47, 4 is expressly mentioned as an אי,
and the Philistines in 1 Sam. 30, 14. Zeph. 2, 5. Ez. 25, 16,
etc. are called כרתים: cf. Tac., *Hist.* v. 2, who indirectly
testifies to the origin of the Philistines from Crete; see Del.,
p. 248 f.

15. The descendants of Canaan.

צידון, the first-born, prop. '*the fisher-town*' (from צַיָד), the
oldest settlement of the Canaanites, and the only one of all
the Phoenician towns known to Homer. In Josh. 11, 8.
19, 28 it is called צידון רבה. Even when Tyre had gained
a reputation, the Phoenicians were still called Sidonians;
Josh. 13, 6. 1 Kings 11, 5. 16, 31. The absence of any
mention of Tyre in the table is noticeable.

חת. 'The form חת (without יִ , although חתים elsewhere
is common) points to the name of a people of wide range,'
Di. חת = the '*Cheta*' of the Egyptian monuments and
'*Hatti*' of the Assyrian inscriptions, the chief people in Syria

between the middle Euphrates and Orontes, who were gradually forced back by the Arameans or absorbed by them. Their chief city was Kadesh on the Orontes. In 1 Kings 10, 29. 2 Kings 7, 6 Hittite kings are mentioned in Syria; see further, Di.; Sayce in the *Trans. of the Soc. of Bib. Arch.*, vii. 2. 248 ff.; Cheyne, *Enc. Brit.* s.v.; Wright, *Empire of the Hittites.*

16. היבוסי. '*The Jebusites*,' who dwelt in and around Jebus, afterwards called Jerusalem.

האמרי. '*The Amorites*,' who dwelt in the hill country of Ephraim and Judah, and spread out far into the south; the most powerful and warlike of all the Canaanitish tribes. The Canaanites in general are sometimes called Amorites. Deut. 3, 9 is cited by Di. as '*eine Probe ihrer Sprache*,' 'a sample of their language.' The name may possibly = '*those who dwell on high ground*,' from אָמִיר=אֱמֹר, Is. 17, 9, '*top*,' '*height*.'

גרגשי. '*The Girgashites*,' their position is uncertain, possibly they must be sought for in the west Jordan land; cf. Josh. 24, 11. They are mentioned again in 15, 21.

17. החוי. '*The Hivites*.' חוי possibly = '*those who live in town-communities (Stadtgemeinden)*, חַוֹּת,' Di.; cf. 34, 2. Josh. 9. Later they are found in the Lebanon and Hermon district, perhaps driven thither by the Israelites; Josh. 11, 3. Judg. 3, 3. 2 Sam. 24, 7.

The פרזי, i.e. '*Perizzites*,' '*those who dwell in open villages*,' פרזות, who are mentioned in 13, 7. 15, 20, are not found in this table; see Di., p. 180.

הערקי are the Phoenicians of Ἄρκη (Talm. ארקים דלבנן, Del.), at the foot of mount Lebanon, about five hours north of Tripolis, the birth-place of the emperor Alexander Severus.

Ἄρκη has been rediscovered in the modern *Tell Arqa* and village *Arqa*. LXX, Ἀρουκαῖος. In Assyrian '*Ar-ḳá*;' see Schrader, *K.A.T.*[2], p. 104.

הַסִּינִי. '*The Phoenicians of Sin.*' Hieron., *Quaest.* ed. Lag., p. 17, mentions a town *Sin*, not far from *Arqa*. Breydenbach (see Di., p. 181) in 1483 found a village *Syn*, half a mile from the river *Arqa*.

18. הָאַרְוָדִי. LXX, Ἀράδιοι. '*The Aradians,*' mentioned in Ez. 27, 8. 11 as the sailors and warriors of the Tyrians, are the inhabitants of Ἄραδος, a Phoenician city built on a rocky island north of Tripolis, according to Strabo, by exiles from Sidon. Arvad is frequently found on the Assyrian inscriptions '*Ar-va-da*;' see Schrader, *K.A. T.*[2], p. 104 f.

הַצְּמָרִי. '*The Phoenicians of Simyra,*' south of Aradus, north of Tripolis, mentioned by Strabo. In Assyrian '*Ṣi-mir-ra*;' see Schrader, *K.A.T.*[2], p. 105.

הַחֲמָתִי. '*The inhabitants of Hamath,*' later name '*Epiphania,*' on the Orontes, often mentioned in the O. T., and Assyrian inscriptions up to Sargon's time, '*mat Hamatti*;' see Schrader, *K.A. T.*[2], p. 105 f.

נָפֹצוּ is Nif. of פוץ; there is no necessity to take it with Ewald from פצץ.

הַכְּנַעֲנִי, used here and ver. 19 in its narrower sense, excluding the Phoenicians and Syrians.

20. בֹּאֲכָה *scriptio plena*, for בֹּאֲךָ; בֹּאֲכָה here, ver. 30, 13, 10. 25, 18, is to be taken as an adv. acc. for the fuller עַד בֹּאֲךָ, 19, 22, lit. '*as thou comest*;' cf. on 13, 10.

גְּרָרָה. '*Gerar,*' in Philistia, it was more towards the south than Gaza. On the ה of motion towards, see Ges., § 90. 2; Dav., § 17. 3.

עַזָּה. '*Gaza,*' the southernmost frontier stronghold in

Philistia. In Assyrian (*ir*) *Ha-zi-ti*; Schr., *K.A.T.*[2], p. 107. On the ע = *g*, see 4, 18.

סדמה ועמרה ואדמה וצבים, the four cities of the plain, mentioned with Bela in 14, 2. They probably occupied the ground now covered by the southern portion of the Dead Sea; see Di., p. 222.

לשׁע. Hieron. and Targ. Jer. identify it with *Callirrhoe*, on the east side of the Dead Sea, in the *Wady Zerqa Ma'in*, celebrated afterwards for its hot springs. But Di. objects to this identification, as Callirrhoe lies too far north; and points out, that according to the analogy of the preceding verse, a town on this side of the Dead Sea or of the Ghor is required.

21–31. THE DESCENDANTS OF SHEM.

21. ולשׁם . . . גם הוא; see the note on 4, 26.

עבר; see the note on 14, 13.

אחי יפת הגדול. Render, '*The elder brother of Japhet.*' The rendering '*Brother of Japhet, the elder,*' adopted by the LXX, Symm., Massoretes, Rashi, and others, is refuted by the fact that the limitation of גדול to the age would only then be sufficiently indicated if the text ran בן נח הגדול (9, 24. 27, 1. 15. 42). הגדול without בן or אח cannot = '*natu major.*' On הגדול, as comparative (or superlative), see on 9, 24. Shem was the eldest son, Ham the second (cf. vers. 1. 6. 21), and Japhet the youngest; cf. 9, 24.

22. עילם = '*Elam*' and '*the Elamites,*' the land and people on the east of the lower Tigris, south of Assyria and Media, north of the Persian Gulf; nearly corresponding to the more modern *Susiana* and *Elymais*. 'עילם neither here nor elsewhere in the O. T. included Persia or all the land up

to India,' Di. In Assyrian '*Ilam*' or '*Ilamti;*' see Schrader, *K. A. T.*[2], p. 111 f.

אַשּׁוּר. '*Assyria and the Assyrians,*' 'for the most part on the eastern side of the central Tigris, between Armenia, Susiana, and Media; its extent cannot be accurately defined; so called after its old capital and deity *Aṣur;*' see Schrader, *K. A. T.*[2], p. 112 f., also p. 35. The Assyrians (as their inscriptions testify) spoke a Semitic language.

אַרְפַּכְשַׁד, since Bochart's time usually explained by Ἀῤῥαπαχῖτις (Ptol. vi. 1. 2), the hill country of the upper Zab (east of Carduchia or Gordyene). Neuville cited by Di., p. 183, understands by אַרְפַּכְשַׁד '*the Accadians;*' and Del. *the Babylonians* (*Par.* 255 f.): both very doubtful. Schrader, *K. A. T.*[2], p. 112 f., rejects the identification with Ἀῤῥαπαχῖτις, Assyrian '*Arbaḫa,*' and thinks that the land of the Chaldees (in the O. T. *Kasdim*), i.e. Babylonia, is most probably intended. Di., p. 184, thinks that the view that בַּשְׂדִּים = כשׂד, and that אַרף is a word = '*boundary, province*' (Arab.) is more suitable. 'That the Hebrews were acquainted with Chaldeans outside Babylonia is certain from 22, 22. Job 1, 17 ' (Di.).

לוּד. '*The Lydians*' and '*Lydia;*' probably the Lydians of Asia Minor; but Di. rejects this limitation, and remarks that 'a more eastern position must be accepted; or the territory between Lydia and the eastern Semitic land (Caria, Lycia, Pamphylia, and Cilicia)—in so far as it is not included in אֲרָם—must be regarded as embraced in the term לוּד, as the coast lands of Asia Minor within the Taurus naturally belong to Shem.'

אֲרָם. 'Rather the name of a people than a land, and with a wider meaning than Syria, so that when it is more accurately spoken of, some addition is made to the name, as

ארם נהרים, ארם דמשׁק. ארם = the peoples of Syria and
Mesopotamia, up to the upper plains of the Tigris and the
valley-land within the Taurus, which was at a later date
considered as belonging to Armenia. The expl. of the
name as '*Highland*' is very doubtful. In Assyrian '*Aramu*,'
'*Arumu*,' and '*Arimu;*' see Schrader, *K. A. T.*[2], p. 115 f.

23. The sons of Aram[1].

עוּץ is mentioned in 22, 21 as the first son of Nahor; in
36, 28 as a son of Dishan (דִישָׁן); in Job 1, 1 as a people
north-east of Edom. In Jer. 25, 20 kings of the land of Uz
are spoken of, and in Lam. 4, 21 Edomites are mentioned as
dwelling in the land of Uz. According to Josephus, *Ant.*,
i. 6. 4, Uz founded Trachonitis and Damascus. 'All this
points to a people who were widely scattered in southern
Syria and the Wilderness, viz. in the neighbourhood of
Hauran and Damascus,' Di.

חוּל is uncertain. Josephus, *Ant.*, i. 6. 4, gives חוּל as the
founder of Armenia. Bochart refers it to Χολοβοτήνη in
Armenia. It is usually identified (see Di., p. 185) with Hule
(الحولة); a name that still attaches itself to lake Merom in
Galilee and the marshy land around it, but also to a district
between Emesa and Tripolis. A district '*Ḥuli*(*j*)*a*' near
mount Masius is mentioned in the Assyrian inscriptions; see
Del., *Par.*, p. 259.

גֶתֶר is unknown. Josephus l. c. mentions נתר as the
founder of the Bactrians. Jerome supposes נתר to be *the
Carians*. Clericus takes it to be '*Karthara*' on the Tigris;
see Tuch, p. 204.

מַשׁ. Heb.-Sam. משׁא; LXX, Μοσόχ, 1 Chron. 1, 17 מֶשֶׁךְ;
cf. Ps. 120, 5. Josephus l. c. explains by Μησαναῖοι, at the mouths

---

[1] These words are wanting in 1 Chron. 1, 17.

of the Euphrates and Tigris (Syr. مَسِم). More probable is
Bochart's identification with Mons Masius, north of Nisibis.

24. The descendants of Arpachshad.

שֶׁלַח and עֵבֶר the son of שֶׁלַח, also found in 11, 12. 14.

25. יֻלַּד. On the passive, see 4, 18.

פֶּלֶג, the same individual is mentioned in 11, 18.

נִפְלְגָה הָאָרֶץ. '*The earth was divided*,' i.e. the popula-
tion of the earth; possibly to be referred to 11, 1–9; cf. Ps.
55, 10; or it may refer to some partition of the soil amongst
distinct nations, in which case we should expect to find חלק. פלג
may have been used here on account of the proper name פלג.

יָקְטָן. '*Joqtan.*' 'Joqtan, from the notices in the Bible, was
regarded by the Arab genealogists under the name " Qaḥṭán,"
as the ancestor of the genuine Arabs in Arabia proper, from
whom the old prehistoric inhabitants, as *Ad*, *Thamud*,
Gadis, etc. on the one hand, and the Ishmaelites of the north
(Gen. 25, 12 ff.) on the other, were distinguished,' Di. The
name ' *Qaḥṭan* ' is still preserved as the name of a district in
northern Yemen, and as the name of a tribe.

26. אַלְמוֹדָד. 'With the Arabic article *al*, the oldest
testimony to which is this word,' Di.; cf. Josh. 15, 30
אֶלְתּוֹלַד. According to *H. W. B.*, 9th ed., p. 40, אלנבישׁ,
אלמגים, אלקום are other instances of the Arabic article
in Hebrew words[1]. The identification of this name is
uncertain. Bochart connects it with the Ἀλλουμαιῶται of
Ptolemy in the midst of Yemen. Tuch corrects it into

---

[1] D. H. Müller, cited *H. W. B.*, p. 975, denies that אל in אלמדד is the
Arabic article, as the southern Arabians did not know of this article;
he also thinks that א has nothing to do with *Murád*, but is either =
אל+מודד ' *God (is) a loving one;* ' or = אלם+ודד ' *Il loves.*' Cf. also
Di., *Comm.*, 5th ed., p. 196, who has somewhat modified his former view.

אלמודד, i.e. مُرَاد, grandson of Sabas, who, with his tribe, inhabited the hill country of Yemen, near زبيد. Welsted (see Di., p. 186) mentions a town *Mádudi* in Ḥaḍramaut.

שׁלף is uncertain. 'Bochart compares the Σαλαπηνοί of Ptolemy, vi. 7. 23; Knobel, a district *Salfie* (سلفية in Niebuhr, *Arab.*, p. 247), south-westward of *Ṣan'á;* Osiander, *Sulaf* or *Salif*, the name of a tribe in Yemen,' Di., p. 186.

חצרמות, rediscovered on the Sabean inscriptions as חצרמות, the 'Αδραμῖται or Χατραμωτῖται of Ptolemy, the inhabitants of Ḥaḍramaut (حَضْرَمَوْت), the name of a district east of Yemen on the sea coast. The name is preserved at the present day.

ירח is uncertain. 'As the word means "*moon*" in Heb., Sab., and Geez, Bochart conjectured the بني هِلال "*sons of the new moon*" or *Alilaei* in northern Yemen; Michaelis, the *moon-coast* and *moon-mountain*, غبّ القمر or جبل in eastern Ḥaḍramaut,' Di.

27. הדורם, Heb.-Sam. אדורם, is unknown. The 'Αδραμῖται of Ptolemy, or the *Atramitae* of Pliny, have been suggested, but they belong to חצרמות.

אוזל, Heb.-Sam. איזל, LXX, Αἰζήλ (Lagarde, Αἰβήλ, so Tisch.'s text), according to Arab tradition, was the old name of the capital of Yemen, called, since the Ethiopic occupation in the fifth century A. D., *Ṣan'á* (صنعاء).

דקלה is unknown. Perhaps='*a palm-bearing district*' (Arab. دَقَل '*a palm tree*'). Bochart identified it with the *Minaei* of Pliny and Strabo.

28. עובל, 1 Chron. 1, 22 עיבל, so Heb.-Sam., Vulg. '*Ebal*,' LXX, Γεβάλ and Εὐάλ, is unknown.

אבימאל is unknown.

שׁבא, see ver. 7. '*The Sabeans*,' here as the descendants

of Joqtan, among the Arabs; in 25, 3, among the descendants of Abraham, as the son of יקשן. 'In this verse the people and land of this name in south-western Arabia are intended, with the capital *Mariaba* or *Saba*,' Schrader, *K. A. T.*[2], p. 118.

29. אופר is mentioned, from Solomon's time onwards, as the land whence the fleet of Hiram and Solomon, after a three years' voyage, brought gold, precious stones, sandal-wood, silver, ivory, apes, and peacocks (1 Kings 9, 28. 10, 11. 22. 2 Chron. 8, 18. 9, 10), and whose gold became proverbial as fine gold (Ps. 45, 10. Job 22, 24. 28, 16. Is. 13, 12. 1 Chron. 29, 4). Its position has been disputed, but as it is mentioned among the sons of Joqtan it must be sought for in Arabia. Thus the identifications with *Supara* on the coast of Malabar, *Sofála* on the east coast of Africa, opposite Madagascar, and *Abhíra* on the coast east of the Indus Delta, are untenable. On the Arabian coast, however, no suitable place with which Ophir can be identified is at present known; see Di., p. 187.

חוילה. Cf. ver. 7. 'It seems probable from 25, 18. 1 Sam. 15, 7, cf. Gen. 2, 11, that there was a חוילה in north-west Arabia, on the Persian Gulf. The Χαυλοταῖοι of Strabo would suit this, and a *Huwaíla* in Bahrein on the coast is mentioned by Niebuhr, *Arab.*, p. 342,' Di.

יובב is unknown. Bochart compares the Ἰωβαρῖται of Ptol. vi. 7. 24 (which he emends to Ἰωβαβῖται) on the coast of the Indian Ocean.

30. משא is uncertain. Bochart, Μοῖζα, a seaport town within the Bab-el-Mandeb; Knobel, *Bischa*, in northern Ye-men; Tuch and others, *Mesene*, a district at the head of the Persian Gulf.

סְפָרָה הַר הַקֶּדֶם. Render, '*Towards Sephar, towards the mountain of the east.*' הַר הַקֶּדֶם cannot be predicate of the sentence on account of its position, nor in apposition to סְפָרה, because nothing is known of a mountain bearing this name. סְפָר 'is usually taken for Σάπφαρα, *Saphar*, capital of the king of the Sabaites and Homerites, in the south-western corner of Arabia, which is well known to Arabic writers as an old and important town (ظفار); to be distinguished from *Saphar* (ظفار), a town of the same name,—also of great age and importance,—situated in eastern Ḥaḍramaut on the sea coast,' Di.

הַר הַקֶּדֶם is the Arabian hill country (*Negd*), which extends from the foregoing limit far towards the east. According to Knobel, the mountain range between Ḥaḍramaut and Mahra.

11.

1. וַיְהִי. The imperf. with waw conv. commencing the narrative, the chapter being loosely connected with the preceding one; cf. Ges., § 129. 1.

כָל הָאָרֶץ שָׂפָה וְגוּ". '*The whole earth was one tongue.*' The predicate in Hebrew, as in Arabic, is often a substantive, where in our idiom an adj. is used, or some such phrase as '*consists of*,' '*contains*.' This construction is commonly used in designating the material out of which an object is made, and in specifying weights or measures, etc.; but an extension of this usage is also often found in Hebrew, 'when terms other than material attributes are treated similarly;' Driver, § 189; Ewald, § 296 b; Ges., § 106. 1. Rem. 2; cf. 2 Sam. 17, 3 כָל הָעָם יִהְיֶה שָׁלוֹם; Job 3, 4 הַיּוֹם הַהוּא יְהִי חֹשֶׁךְ; Is. 19, 11, and often.

שָׂפָה=lit. '*lip,*' then '*language;*' so in Is. 19, 18 שְׂפַת כְּנַעַן;

33, 19 עמקי שפה; cf. Ez. 3, 5. P uses לשון in this sense, 10, 5. 20. 31; cf. Deut. 28, 49.

דברים אחדים = lit. '*single words*,' i. e. '*the same*' or '*similar words*.' The use of אחדים in the phrase ימים אחדים 27, 44. 29, 20. Dan. 11, 20, meaning '*single*,' i. e. '*a few days*,' is different from its use here.

2. נסע does not only mean '*to break up the camp*,' but '*to strike the tents and move onward on the journey*.'

מקדם. Not '*from the east*,' but as 13, 11 '*eastwards*' (cf. M. R., § 49. Rem. d. 12, 8), i. e. 'from the standpoint of the author, who was in Palestine, and to whom the Mesopotamians were בני קדם' (29, 1), Di.

בקעה, prop. '*a split*' or '*cleft*,' but according to the usage of the language, '*a plain lying in a broad valley*,' '*a valley plain*;' cf. the Syriac ܦܩܥܬܐ '*campus patens*.' The distinction between geographical synonyms should be noted; see Stanley, *Sinai and Palestine*, App., § 5, where the בקעות mentioned in the Old Testament are enumerated.

בארץ שנער. Cf. on 10, 10.

3. איש אל רעהו. '*One to the other*.' On this mode of expressing the reciprocal relation, see Ges., § 124. 2. Rem. 4: M. R., § 72. 3. Rem. a; cf. § 94 c. Rem. a.

הבה is properly imper. with ה cohort. (Ges., § 48. 5; Stade, § 592 c) from the root יהב '*to give*,' which, though common in Aramaic and Arabic (وهب), is confined in Heb. to the imper. sing. and plural. הבה sing. sometimes has the force of an interjection, so here, '*up*,' '*come on*;' A. V. '*go to*,' so vers. 4. 7. Ex. 1, 10. For the form, cf. Ges., § 69. 2. Rem. 2. Other verbal forms used as interjections are ראה '*see!*' לכה '*come!*' cf. Stade, § 380.

נלבנה. '*Let us bake*,' the imperf. with ה cohort., to

express the intention with greater energy; cf. Ges., §§ 48. 3, 128. 1; Dav., § 23. 1, 2; M. R., § 9; Driver, § 49 β. The verb לבן is a denominative from לְבֵנָה.

לבנים ' *bricks,*' perhaps so called as being baked white by the heat of the sun. The word occurs in Assyr. under the form *libittu,* cstr. state *libnat,* Schrader, *K. A. T.*², p. 121.

לשׂרפה. Dat. of the product; cf. 2, 22. Amos 5, 8, lit. '*into what is burnt,*' i. e. '*bricks.*' Render, '*And let us burn them into bricks.*' The bricks here mentioned were different from those made of a mixture of straw and clay, Ex. 1, 14. 5, 7.

4. וראשׂו בשׂמים. Render, ' *With its top in the heavens.*' The clause is a simple circumstantial one; cf. Driver, § 159; Ewald, § 341 a; so Is. 6, 6 ובידו רצפה; Zech. 2, 5 ובידו חבל מדה. In Deut. 1, 28 we have the word ערים qualified by בצורות בשׂמים '*fortified in the heavens,*' i.e. '*with high and lofty fortifications;*' cf. Dan. 4, 8. 17.

נעשׂה לנו שׂם, lit. '*let us make us a name,*' i. e. '*let us gain an honourable name;*' so Is. 63, 12. Jer. 32, 20. פן נפוץ refers to both halves of the first part of the verse. They had a double object in view, to found a city, and gain for them-selves an honourable name; the city being a common place of assembly for all, and so a means of keeping them to-gether and preventing their being scattered over the earth. Others connect פן נפוץ closely with שׂם, and take that word in the sense of '*monument*'=Arab. سِمَة, as in 2 Sam. 8, 13. This however is doubtful, and here unsuitable.

פן נפוץ. LXX, πρὸ τοῦ διασπαρῆναι ἡμᾶς, so Vulg. '*ante-quam dividamur,*' apparently taking פ as though it were לפני. Frankel, *Einf.,* p. 47, sees here a reference to the Haggada, which narrates that the descendants of Noah frequently dis-

regarded the warning given them to send out colonies; cf.
Josephus, *Ant.*, i. c. 4, §§ 1–3.

6. '*Behold one people (are they), and one language have they
all.*'   The A. V. '*The people is one,*' is scarcely correct, as
that would be rather אחד העם.   The A.V.R. renders, '*Behold
they are one people,*' etc.

החלם is inf. cstr. Hif'il of חלל, with the ה pointed with
pathach instead of a composite sheva, on account of the
following guttural ח; cf. Stade, § 80. 2 b; Ges., § 67. Rem. 6;
Ewald, § 199 a.   So Esth. 6, 13 הַתְחִלּוֹתָ; Is. 9, 13 הַחְתִּתָ.

וזה החלם וגו׳ =lit. '*and this is their beginning to do,*' i. e.
'*merely the commencement of their plan.*'

יבצר =lit. '*will be cut off,*' i. e. '*they will not be debarred
from it;*' so once besides, Job 42, 2 לא יבצר ממך מזמה.

יזמו is a lightened form of יָזֹמּוּ from זמם; so נָבְלָה, ver. 7,
for נָבְלָה; cf. 9, 19, and Ges., § 67. Rem. 11; Stade, § 521 a, β,
who explains the form in question as formed after the analogy
of the third pers. pl. perf., instead of יָזֹמּוּ or יִזְמּוּ; cf. Ewald,
§ 193 c.

7. נבלה.   See note on ver. 6; and on the first pers. pl.,
see on 1, 26.   The word was probably chosen with reference
to the name בָּבֶל.

אשר, expressing the result rather than the aim, =' *so that,*'
not '*that;*' cf. Ex. 20, 26. Deut. 4, 10. 40; contrast Gen. 3.
22, where we have פן introducing the negative final clause :
see M. R., § 164 b; Ewald, § 337 b. 2.

איש שפת רעהו.   Cf. on ver. 3.   שמע =not merely '*to
hear,*' but '*to understand,*' as in Is. 33, 19. Deut. 28, 49.

8. ויחדלו לבנת.   After verbs of '*ceasing,*' '*hastening,*'

etc., two constructions are usually possible ; either the inf. cstr. with לְ as here, or the inf. cstr. alone ; cf. Ges., § 142. 2 ; Ewald, § 285. 1. With חדל, מִן may be used, see Ex. 23, 5. 1 Kings 15, 21.

9. עַל כֵּן קָרָא. '*Therefore they called its name Babel*,' i. e. '*they, people called.*' On the impersonal use of the third pers. perf. masc. sing. (= lit. '*one called*'), cf. Ges., § 137. 3 a ; M. R., § 123. 2.

בָּבֶל, according to the etymology given in the text, is from בלל. בבל must then be regarded as contracted from בַּלְבֵּל ; cf. קִיקָלוֹן from קִלְקָלוֹן; עֲזָאזֵל for עֲזַלְזֵל; see Ewald, § 158 c ; Stade, § 124 a ; cf. also the Syriac ܒܽܘܠܒܳܠܐ '*confusion of speech*;' Arab. بَلْبَلَ. This is the Hebrew explanation of the name. For the Babylonian it had another meaning, which is probably the correct one. Some (Eich., Winer) derive it from *Báb Bel*, باب بل '*gate*,' i. e. '*court of Bel*;' following the ancients, see Steph. of Byzant. ; compare the Aramaic and Talmudic ܒܳܒܐ, בבא = '*gate*,' also the names of the Talmud Tracts בבא קמא '*the front gate*;' בבא בתרא '*the back gate*;' בבא מציעא '*the middle gate*;' others, from בית, בל = בבל, so Tuch, comparing for the contraction בעשתרה, Josh. 21, 27 = בית עשתרה '*Temple of Ashtoreth*,' and the Phoen. בת עתר = בעתר '*Temple of 'Ather*;' *Inscr. Melitensis*, 5, l. 4 ; Schröd., *Phoen. Gramm.*, p. 235 ; cf. p. 108 ; and the Syriac ܟܐܦܐ = ܟܐܦܐ ; see further, Tuch, p. 221. The name as given on the Assyrian inscriptions is *Báb-Il* = '*Gate of God*,' which is certainly the most probable meaning ; cf. Schr., *K. A. T.*², p. 127 ff. ; Del., *Par.*, p. 212 ff. ; so most moderns.

In the following verses, 10–32, we have a genealogical table carrying on the history of the patriarchs from Shem to Abram—the founder of the house of Israel—and his two brothers, Nahor and Haran. This table is in many respects very similar to the one found in chap. 5. In both ten generations are given, Abram closing the list here, and Noah in chap. 5. In both lists the ages of the persons mentioned are considerably higher than those usually reached. Here, as well as chap. 5, we find the length of each person's life reckoned, both from his own birth to the birth of his first son, and from that event to his death. The LXX and the Samaritan deviate in their methods of reckoning the years here, as well as in the earlier chapter, as may be seen from the following table taken from Dillmann, p. 196.

	HEBREW TEXT.			LXX TEXT.			SAMARITAN TEXT.		
	The years before the birth of the first son.	The remaining years of the life.	Total years of life.	The years before the birth of the first son.	The remaining years of the life.	Total years of life.	The years before the birth of the first son.	The remaining years of the life.	Total years of life.
Shem ...	100	500	600	100	500	600	100	500	600
Arpachshad	35	403	438	135	(430) 400	(565) 535	135	303	438
Kainan ...	...	...	...	130	330	460	...	...	...
Shelach ...	30	403	433	130	330	460	130	303	433
Eber ...	34	430	464	134	(370) 270	(504) 404	134	270	404
Peleg ...	30	209	239	130	209	339	130	109	239
Reu ...	32	207	239	132	207	339	132	107	239
Serug ...	30	200	230	130	200	330	130	100	230
Nahor ...	29	119	148	(79) 179	(129) 125	(208) 304	79	69	148
Terach ...	70	(135)	(205)	70	(135)	(205)	70	(75)	(145)

In both chapters the Hebrew text has most probably preserved the more correct lists, though the Samaritan is perhaps the most consistent of the three tables. The Samaritan list never allows the son to be older than the father; so the numbers, e. g. in the cases of Terach and Eber, have to be lowered in order to carry out this rule. With the single exception of Terach, the Sam. text increases the number of years before the birth of the first son, and in all cases, except that of Shem, decreases the number of years which each person lived after the birth of the first son. The Sam. text in the third column agrees with the Hebrew, with the exception of the cases of Eber and Terach. The LXX text, having a large number of variants, is more or less uncertain. Like the Sam. text, seventy years seem to have been the limit before which no children were begotten, and with the exception of Shem,—where all three texts are the same, and Naḥor, where one hundred and fifty years are added, with a variant, seventy-nine,—the LXX add one hundred years to the number each person lived before the birth of the first son. In the second column the readings are uncertain, but sometimes the numbers are lower than the corresponding numbers in the Heb. text. In the third column, the LXX have always higher numbers than the Hebrew, except in the cases of Eber (reading doubtful, variant 504) and Terach; the LXX in the latter case agreeing with the Heb. text. The years of Kainan's life are only given in the LXX text.

The object of this table, as of that in chap. 5, was probably twofold, to give some account of the period from the flood to Abram's birth, a period treated as uneventful, and to draw attention to the gradual decline in the number of years reached by each patriarch.

10. וַיּוֹלֶד is the imperf. Hif'. with waw conv. from יָלַד.

28. עַל פְּנֵי תֶרַח. '*Coram eo*,' i. e. so that he witnessed it, '*during his life-time;*' compare Num. 3, 4. Deut. 21, 16 (Dillmann).

אוּר כַּשְׂדִּים occurs again ver. 31. 15, 7. Neh. 9, 7, but not elsewhere. The LXX have χώρα τῶν Χαλδαίων (Acts 7, 4 ἐκ γῆς Χαλδαίων), χώρα possibly having arisen from a reading הוּר (but the article is against this), unless we suppose that the reading χώρα has arisen out of χωρ, and was then supplied with the article, and so ἐν τῇ χώρᾳ. Kn. takes אוּר as = הוּר '*mountain*,' but this is very doubtful. Oppert in the *Hist. des Emp. de Chaldée*, etc., explains אוּר כַּשְׂדִּים as meaning '*Land (Ur) of the two (Kas) waters (Dim)*,' i. e. Mesopotamia, the name being old Turanian. Since J. D. Michaelis, אוּר has usually been identified with the castle of Ur, lying within the Persian frontier, and six days' journey north of Hatra, mentioned by Amm. Marc. xxv. 8. But the Ur mentioned by Marcellinus was first founded by the Persians or Parthians (Del.), and being in an unfruitful and barren district would hardly be a suitable place for Abram, the shepherd-prince. Besides, כַּשְׂדִּים points rather to the land about the lower Euphrates than to Mesopotamia, and most of the ancients (e. g. Eupolemus in Euseb., *praep. evang.*, Del., p. 275) pre-suppose that Ur was in Babylonia (Chaldea or Shinar). Another identification is that proposed by Sir Henry and Prof. George Rawlinson, Ur being אֶרֶךְ (which occurs only in 10, 10), i. e. the present Warka, on the left bank of the lower Euphrates; the name being explained by them as meaning '*the moon city*,' after the Arab. قمر. This view has been adopted by Loftus, *Trav.*, p. 126. The view most current among modern expositors is that אוּר is El-Mugheir, a little south of Warka, on the right bank of the Euphrates, where ruins are still to be found. The name אוּר is found on the inscriptions in the form *Uru* (i. e. '*town*,' viz. '*moon-town*'), one of the oldest of the Babylonian royal towns in Sumer; see Schrader, *K. A. T.*², p. 129 ff.; Del., *Par.*, pp. 200, 226. כשׂדים would then be an addition due to the Jews, and not part of the native name (Di.).

The identification with Mugheir, though adopted by many moderns, is perhaps not to be regarded as quite certain. Di. contends in favour of a site in north Babylonia, whence he supposes the Chaldeans of south Babylonia to have emigrated. The Casdim were the inhabitants of south Babylonia and Babylon; they are not mentioned in the Bible or on the monuments before the time of Isaiah (see 23, 13). The name in a wider sense might possibly have included Mesopotamia. The origin of the Casdim is obscure, but they seem to have been a tribe which from small beginnings gradually acquired supremacy over south Babylonia and the capital; cf. Sayce, *Ency. Brit.*, art. *Babylonia.* The Talmud, *Baba Bathra*, 91, places Ur Casdim in the neighbourhood of Babylon. Ur Casdim has also been identified,—but without any great probability,—with Edessa (in Syr. ܐܘܪܗܝ), by Hitzig. The Syrian Christians boast of Edessa as being the Ur Casdim of Abraham; see further, Di., p. 200. The old interpretation current among the Jews (also found in the Qoran, Sur. 21) takes אוּר as meaning fire, and narrates that Abraham confessed the true God, and denied the gods of Nimrod, so he was cast into the fire, but saved in a miraculous manner by God. Hier. probably had this in view when he translated Neh. 9, 7, '*eduxisti eum de igne Chaldaeorum;*' see Del., p. 275 and his note 74.

30. וָלַד, only here and as Kṭib in 2 Sam. 6, 23 for יֶלֶד,

the original וֹ of the root, which still exists in Arabic وَلَدَ, وَلَدَ,
and reappears in the Hif. and Nif. of the verb in Hebrew,
is here preserved.

31. וַיֵּצְאוּ אִתָּם. ' *They went out with them,*' i. e. perhaps
' *They (the other members of the family) went out with them
(Terach,*' etc.).   אתם cannot be rendered ' *with one another,*'
as this is against grammar, the suffix never being reciprocal.
To make Terach and Abraham the subject to ויצאו, and
understand Lot and Sarai, under אִתָּם (Rashi, Del.), is very
harsh, and there is nothing in the Heb. text to support it.
Ewald (J. B., x. 28) supposes that some words designating
the other members of the family have fallen out.   The LXX
read the text וַיּוֹצֵא אֹתָם, ἐξήγαγεν αὐτούς, i.e. Terach, perhaps
to avoid the difficulty; so Sam., Vulg., Luth.   The Syr. reads
וַיֵּצֵא אִתָּם, Terach being again the subject, ܘܢܦܩ ܥܡܗܘܢ (so
Ilgen, Vater, Ols.).

הָרָן, Assyr. *Harran*, Syr. ܚܪܢ, Arab. حَرَّان, Gk. Κάρραι,
Lat. *Carrae*, was situated in north-west Mesopotamia, south-
east of Edessa, about twenty-six Roman miles distant from it.

12.

1. וַיֹּאמֶר. A. V. wrongly, ' *Now the Lord had said,*' more
correctly A. V. R., ' *Now the Lord said,*' the passage being
like Judg. 17, 1. 1 Sam. 9, 1; a new narrative is commenced,
amplifying the preceding one which is regarded as a whole,
the association of the two being in *thought*, not in *time*.
Whether the imperf. with waw conv. can denote a pluperfect
is very doubtful; the question is fully discussed, Driver,
§ 76. Obs., where it is pointed out that there is not sufficient
evidence to justify the adoption of a pluperfect rendering
in the place of the simple past.

לֶךְ לְךָ 'get thee,' the dat. adds an element of feeling to the bald לְךָ, implying a reference to, or a regard for, the person addressed. The dative is often found similarly after verbs of motion, e.g. Deut. 1, 7. 40. 5, 27, etc.; see Ges., § 154. 3 e; Ewald, § 315 a.

מֵאַרְצֶךָ, probably Haran; cf. ver. 4 with 24, 4. 7. 38. In Acts 7, 2 מֵאַרְצֶךָ is taken as Ur-Casdim; so Hupfeld.

אַרְאֶךָ for אַרְאֶנְךָ. Impf. Hif. of ראה with נ demons.; the verb ראה and other verbs ל"ה frequently use the strengthened form of the suffix; cf. Stade, §§ 576 c, 127 b; Ges., § 58. 4; Dav., § 31. 5.

2. וְאֶעֶשְׂךָ is imperf. with weak waw. The imperf. in this case is jussive, so וְאֶעֶשְׂךָ = lit. 'and let me make,' but as this is dependent on the command, 'get thee out,' in ver. 1, it comes to mean, 'that I may make.' Thus the impf. with weak waw is often used to express the *purpose* or *design* of a preceding act, which it does more neatly than when לְמַעַן or בַּעֲבוּר followed by the imperf. is used; cf. Driver, § 60; Ges., § 128. 1 c; M. R., §. 10; Ewald, § 347 a. The other two verbs וַאֲבָרֶכְךָ and וַאֲגַדְּלָה (note the voluntative form used here; in the case of the two first verbs it could not be employed) fall under the same rule.

וֶהְיֵה, pointed according to Ges., § 63. Rem. 5; Stade, § 592 d. Here the imperative with waw is used where a voluntative with weak waw would be expected, to express the intention or purpose with greater energy; cf. 20, 7 וֶחְיֵה; 2 Sam. 21, 3 וּבָרְכוּ; Driver, § 65; Ges., § 130. 2; M.R., § 10; Ewald, § 347 a.

בְּרָכָה. 'And be a blessing,' LXX, καὶ ἔσῃ εὐλογημένος (cf. Ps. 21, 7. Is. 19, 24), God will bless him, and men will bless him, in that they will use his name as a formula of blessing, cf. 3, Zech. 8, 13; he himself too will be a source of blessing to others; cf. ver. 3 a.

3. וּמְקַלֶּלְךָ. LXX, Pesh., Vulg., Sam., read the pl. וּמְקַלְלֶיךָ. The Mass. reading is the better one, 'God does not expect that *many* will so far forget themselves as to curse him' (Di.).

וְנִבְרְכוּ. LXX, ἐνευλογηθήσονται ἐν σοί; Sir. 44, 21. Acts 3, 25. Gal. 3, 8; so Onq. and Vulg., rendering as a passive, '*shall be blessed:*' it is interpreted in the N. T. as meaning that in Christ all the nations should be blessed. The Nif'. would then be passive, as in 18, 18. 28, 14. But in 22, 18. 26, 4, we find the reflex. Hithp'. וְהִתְבָּרְכוּ, which can scarcely be taken as passive, but must = '*all peoples shall bless themselves with thy seed,*' i. e. wish that they may be as blessed as Israel; cf. 48, 20. Jer. 29, 22. Is. 65, 16; the Nif'al is also taken as a reflexive here by Del., Di., and most moderns, after Rashi. Di. remarks that it would not be unreasonable to expect the Pu'al in these passages if the passive sense were intended. Tuch slightly alters the meaning, and renders both Hithp'. and Nif'. '*to call oneself happy,*' i. e. '*to regard oneself as blessed,*' which is perhaps not impossible, but at least for the Hithp'. improbable.

5. רְכוּשׁ = '*moveable property.*' LXX, τὰ ὑπάρχοντα.

הַנֶּפֶשׁ אֲשֶׁר עָשׂוּ. '*The souls which they had gotten in H.*' הנפש is used collectively. The meaning of these words is not the persons whom they had begotten (Luth.), but the slaves they had acquired during their sojourn in Harran. עשו occurs again in this sense in 31, 1. Deut. 8, 18. נפש as in נפשות ביתו, 36, 6; נפש אדם, Ez. 27, 13, etc.; cf. a similar use of ψυχή, 1 Macc. 10, 33. Rev. 18, 13. רכש and רכוש are characteristic of P, נפש in this sense is also common in P, so 17, 14. 36, 6. 46, 15. 18. 22. 25, and often. Onq. renders, וְאַף נַפְשָׁתָא דִּשַׁעֲבִּידוּ לְאוֹרַיְתָא בְּחָרָן. '*And also the souls which they had subjected to the law in Harran,'* possibly, as Tuch suggests, to avoid the suspicion that strangers accompanied Abram to Canaan; cf. also Frankel, *Einf.*, p. 48, who traces in the rendering of the LXX the influence of the Midrash.

6. מקום שכם. '*To the district of Shechem.'* מקום as in Ex. 3, 8 אל מקום הבנעני. Shechem is the modern Nablous (نابلس), one of the best known towns of Mid-Canaan, in the hill country of Ephraim, situated between mount Ephraim and mount Gerizim. Its Roman name was Flavia Neapolis.

עד אלון מורה. '*To the terebinth of Moreh.'* Di. '*The terebinth of the teacher.'* אלון מרה is probably to be explained, according to Deut. 11, 30 אלוני מרה, as a terebinth grove, where in ancient times the priests who were seers or prophets had their dwelling, and gave instruction and information to those who resorted to them. The fact that Jacob (35, 4) buried the idols and amulets at Shechem, and that Joshua—after the address to the tribes at Shechem, previous to his death, wherein the covenant between them and God was renewed—raised a stone there as a testimony (Josh. 24, 26), is not without significance, as pointing to the religious character belonging to the locality. Perhaps, as Di. suggests, this grove at Shechem is the same as the terebinth of the Wizards, Judg. 9, 37.

אֵלוֹן, to which אֵילָה and אֵיל belong, was probably '*the terebinth,'* while אַלּה, and prob. also אַלָּה (Josh. 24, 26), was '*the oak.'* The terebinth, being less common than the oak, was more suitable for marking out any spot (Di.). The LXX translate אֵלָה, and (sometimes) אַלּוֹן, by δρῦς, and the Massoretic pointing varies, e. g. cf. Josh. 19, 33 and Judg. 4, 11. In Aramaic ܐܝܠܢ means a tree in general (cf. δρῦς and *tree*), and it is possible that איל and אלון might be used of other great trees (Ges., *Th.*, 51 a). The Targg. of Onq. and Ps.-Jon. render אלון by מֵישְׁרֵי '*plain*,' which the Vulg. '*convallis illus-tris*' and A. V. follow (A. V. R. has '*oak*,' marg. *terebinth*). From this, perhaps, we may infer that they were acquainted with the idolatrous sense of אלון, for they often render בעל in the same way. Syr. has ‏ܒܒܠܘܢܐ ܕܡܡܪܐ‎ '*at the oak of Mamre*,' so also Saadiah.

מוֹרֶה. LXX render by ὑψηλός, Vulg. '*illustris*,' prob. taking מוֹרֶה as though it were מָרְאֶה (a confusion between the sound of the two words).

הכנעני אז בארץ. אָז points to a time when the Canaanites should not be in the land as rulers of the same, this notice was perhaps inserted with reference to the promise made in ver. 7.

הכנעני has the article, 'a generic word being used col-lectively to denote all the individuals belonging to it,' Ges., § 109. 1; Ewald, § 277 c.

8. ויט אהלה. אהלה, ה for ו, the older and original form of the suffix, is found sporadically throughout the O. T. The *ô* arose by contraction from *ahu, au*, but the ה was retained in writing, and is constantly found on the Moabite stone ; cf. Stade, § 345 b; Ges., § 91. 1. Rem. 2; and the note on 9, 21.

מים '*on the west*,' the Mediterranean sea forming the western boundary of Palestine. This use of ים (cf. נגב in ver. 9) as marking a point of the compass is purely Palestinian.

בית אל ... מקדם is a simple circ. clause, without any connecting particle; cf. 1 Sam. 26, 13. Gen. 32, 12; Driver, § 161.

הָעָי. '*Ai*,' lit. '*the stone heap*,' *par excellence*; cf. for the article thus used with a pr. name, Ges., § 109. 3; M. R., § 66. Rem. a.

9. הלוֹך ונסוע, cf. on 8, 3.

הנגבה. Cf. ver. 8. '*Towards the south.*' LXX, ἐν τῇ ἐρήμῳ; Aq. better, νότονδε; Symm. εἰς νότον. נֶגֶב = '*dryness, dry land*,' with the art., is the name of the southern portion of the territory of the Hebrews. Frankel, *Einf.*, p. 5, alters the LXX reading into εἰς τὴν ἔρημον, as in 13, 1, and cites this passage as an instance of good rendering on the part of the LXX translators, the desert forming the boundary between Egypt and Canaan.

10. וירד. ירד is the usual word in the O. T. for a journey from the high land of Canaan into the valley of the Nile, e.g. Is. 31, 1; עלה for the journey from Egypt to Palestine; cf. 13, 1. 44, 23. 24. 46, 4.

11. הקריב לבוא, lit. '*drew near to come*,' i.e. '*came near*;' cf. Ges., § 142. 2; cf. on 11, 8.

יפת מראה. The adj. in the cstr. state is defined by a following genitive; cf. נקי כפים '*with clean hands*,' lit. '*clean of hands*;' אנמי נפש '*sorrowful in spirit*;' ערל שפתים '*uncircumcised of lips*,' Ges., § 112. 2; M. R., § 80. 2 b; Ewald, § 288 c. 3. Render, '*That thou art fair to look at.*'

12. ואתך יחיו. אתך, by being placed first, varies the two clauses, and is more emphatic.

13. אמרי נא אחתי את. כי is omitted in the *oratio indirecta*, as in 41, 15. Is. 48, 8. Hos. 7, 2; Ges., § 155. 4 c; Ewald, § 338 a; M. R., § 162.

למען ייטב . . . וחיתה. The perfect with waw conv., after an imperf. with למען; cf. 18, 19 למען אשר יצוה . . . ושמרו, Is. 28, 13 למען ילכו וכשלו; cf. Driver, § 115 (p. 160); M. R., § 24. 2 a.

15. וַיְהַלֲלוּ is pointed with a comp. shewa, the dagesh in the first ל being omitted, by Ges., § 10. 2. Rem.; Stade, § 136. 2 (who cites ל as one of the consonants that frequently give up their doubling when pointed with shewa). The shewa is here composite instead of simple, by Stade, § 105, i.e. ḥâṭêph-pathach is used instead of a simple shewa after a vowel with Metheg, when two similar sounds follow one another, so עֹרְרִים Ps. 8, 3, גֹּוָחַיָּ Is. 53, 7, הַרֲרֵי Ps. 87, 1.

בֵּית פַּרְעֹה is acc. of place, in answer to the question '*whither?*' see Ges., § 118. 1; M. R., § 41 a; Ewald, § 281 d.

פַּרְעֹה, formerly explained (e. g. Ges. in *Thes.*, p. 1129) from Josephus, *Ant.*, viii. 6. 2, as a Hebraised form of the Coptic word Π-ΟΥΡΟ *pi-ouro* (*phouro*), '*the king*' (Del.), is now generally explained (by Lauth, Brugsch, etc.) from a notice in Horapollo, i. 62 (οἶκος μέγας), as *per-aa* or *pher-ao*='*the great house.*' It remained the usual title of the Egyptian kings up to the time of the Persian conquest. Ebers, *Egypt. und die B. M.*, p. 263, compares the modern title of the Turkish government, '*The Sublime Porte.*' The title פַּרְעֹה is often found on the oldest monuments, Ebers, p. 264. Ebers (p. 262), after remarking that the courtiers of the Egyptian king appeared to have shewn great zeal in procuring beautiful women for the harem of their master, narrates, from the *Papyrus d'Orbiney*, that a lock of hair belonging to a beautiful woman was found in Pharaoh's linen, and shewn to his lettered men, who brought it to their master, saying, '*This is a lock of hair of a daughter (of the god) Ra-Harmachu. The sap of that god is in it.*' Pharaoh gave himself no rest until he had discovered this beauty, who at once received the name of '*Favourite.*'

16. The presents Abram received from Pharaoh are else-

where mentioned as forming the riches of a nomad prince;
cf. 24, 35. 32, 15. Job 1, 3. 42, 12.

וַיְהִי לוֹ, lit. '*and there was to him,*' i. e. *he had;* for the
singular, cf. Ges., § 147.

17. פַּרְעֹה נְגָעִים . . . וַיְנַגַּע.   נגע, Qal='*to touch,*' Pi'el,
intens. '*to touch heavily,*' '*smite.*' A verb in Hebrew is frequently followed by a noun, derived from it, in the acc.; cf.
Ges., § 138. Rem. 1; M. R., § 36.   נָגַע and נֶגַע are often used
in this connection, e. g. 2 Kings 15, 5. 1 Sam. 6, 9. Job 19,
21 (both with יד). Ex. 11, 1.

18. לָמָה.   On the pointing here and ver. 19, cf. Ges.,
§ 102. 2 d; Stade, § 372 b.

19. Render, '*Why didst thou say, She is my sister, so that I
took her to be my wife* (i. e. *and so lead me to take her*')? The
second idea being really a consequence of the first, the waw
conv. may be rendered, '*so that* or *and so;*' see Driver, § 74 a,
and cf. 20, 12. 23, 20.

20. וַיְצַו עָלָיו '*commanded concerning him;*' cf. Num. 8,
22. 2 Sam. 14, 8.

וַיְשַׁלְּחוּ '*and they brought him on his way;*' cf. the N. T.
προπέμπειν, Acts 15, 3. 21, 5.

13.

2. בְּמִקְנֶה בַּכֶּסֶף וּבַזָּהָב.   The article is generic, being
used with different materials which are generally known; cf.
Ges., § 109. 3 b; M. R., § 68. Di. suggests that the Massoretes possibly had the particular wealth acquired by Abram
in Egypt in their mind, and so inserted the article.

3. לְמַסָּעָיו '*by his stations*' (stationenweise), implying
that he proceeded gradually, adapting his speed to the
requirements of the flocks and herds he had with him; cf.

Ex. 17, 1, where LXX render κατὰ παρεμβολὰς αὐτῶν, Ex. 40. 36. Num. 33, 2. The מסעים are the مراحل '*day-journeys.*' by which they still reckon at the present time in the east (Tuch). The LXX (καὶ ἐπορεύθη ὅθεν ἦλθεν) and Vulg. (*re-versus est per iter, quo venerat*) take the מסעים as the places Abram had halted at on his journey down to Egypt, but this is not so suitable. ל with the pl. is used distributively here, as in Ps. 73, 14 לבקרים '*morning-wise;*' Job 7, 18; see Ewald, § 217 d, a; M. R., § 51. 5, who explains the usage somewhat differently from Ewald.

ועד ביתאל. When the two prepositions '*from . . . to*' are both expressed, a ו '*and*' is generally inserted before the second. '*From the south to Bethel,*' lit. '*from the south and (then further) to Bethel;*' cf. M. R., § 49. 1 b.

5. אֹהָלִים for אֲהָלִים, explained by Ges., § 23. 3, 2 ; § 93. 1. Rem. 3, as a Syriasm. Stade, § 109, cf. § 327 b. 3, explains the lengthening of the ḥâṭêph qameç into ḥolem before the guttural ה as due to the influence of the counter-tone (Gegenton): other instances are פֻּעֲלוֹ instead of פֻּעֳלוֹ; אָהֳלַי. The change is less frequent with ḥâṭêph qameç than qameç ḥâṭûph.

6. ולא נשא אתם. Cf. 36, 7 לא יכלה ארץ מגוריהם לשאת אתם. נשא, the verb comes first, and is put in the nearer gender, the masc., though the subj. הארץ is fem.; cf. Ges., § 147 a; M. R., § 133; Ewald, § 339 c. 1.

לשבת. ישב in this connection is characteristic of P, so ver. 12. 36, 7. 37, 1, also נשא.

7. יֹשֵׁב. .Cf. 9, 18. The plural is more usual when the predicate follows a compound subject; cf. on 8, 22 and Prov. 27, 9. 2 Sam. 20, 10. Neh. 6, 12; Ewald, § 339 c. 2; Ges., § 148. 2; M. R., § 138. The second noun holds a more

subordinate position than the first, the waw being almost 'with' (waw of association), 'the Canaanite with the P.' On פרזי, cf. 10, 17.

8. אנשים אחים, in apposition; cf. 9, 5, and the note there. Num. 32, 14. 2 Sam. 4, 2. אחים='relatives,' not to be taken strictly in the sense 'brothers;' cf. 29, 12. 14, 16.

9. 'Is not all the land before thee? pray separate thyself from me, if towards the left, then I will go to the right, and if towards the right, then I will go to the left.' The hyp. sentence is similar in form to ואם מעט ואוסיפה לך, 2 Sam. 12, 8. The simple waw introducing the apod. is very rare; cf. Driver, § 136 β*; M. R., § 165. השמאל and הימין are acc. of place; cf. on 12, 15; תִּפָּרֵד being understood with each.

הימין and השמאיל are denominatives from ימין and שמאל respectively; on the quad. form of the latter, see Ges., § 56; Stade, § 627. Onq. renders שמאל by לְצִיפּוּנָא 'to the north,' and יָמִין by לְדָרוֹמָא 'to the south.' In Arabic أَشْأَم, IV conj.,= 'to go to Syria' (اَلشَّأْم), and أَيْمَنَ, IV conj.,='to go to Yemen' (اَلْيَمَن), lit. 'to go to the left and right,' respectively; see other similar instances in Wright, Arab. Gram., i. p. 36.

מעלי 'from my presence,' 25, 6. Ex. 10, 28.

10. ככר הירדן recurs 1 Kings 7, 46. Cf. in the N. T. Matt. 3, 5. Luke 3, 3 ἡ περίχωρος τοῦ Ἰορδάνου; more frequently we find merely הככר, 19, 17. 25. 28. Deut. 34, 3. 2 Sam. 18, 23. The district (prop. circle) of the Jordan was the land on both sides of the Jordan, from lake Tiberias to the Dead Sea, called by Josephus τὸ μέγα πεδίον, Bell. Jud., iv. 8. 2. The valley of Siddim, 14, 3, also belonged to the ככר.

מֹשׁקה='well watered,' lit. 'a well-watered place;' it occurs again Ez. 45, 15 משקה ישראל; cf. Is. 58, 11 כגן רוה.

כְּגַן יהוה, probably referring to the garden of Eden, 2, 8. LXX, ὡς ὁ παράδεισος τοῦ Θεοῦ; Pesh. ‏ܐܝܟ ܦܪܕܝܣܐ‎. Del. and Schumann, however, regard יהוה as used in a superlative sense, and render, '*as a beautiful garden;*' cf. 10, 9 and the note there, 1, 2. This rendering, however, is not so natural as the other. In Is. 51, 3 we have גן יהוה, and in Ez. 36, 35 גן עדן, used in comparisons.

כְּאֶרֶץ מצרים is added to tone down the previous גן עדן, the comparison with the garden of Eden being a somewhat too lofty conception.

בֹּאֲכָה. '*On the way to,*' lit. '*as thou comest;*' for the second pers. sing. used impersonally, cf. Ges., § 137. 3 c; M. R., § 123. 4. The second pers. thus used occurs chiefly in this phrase. The form of the suff. כה־ is merely an orthographic variation for the more usual ך־, e. g. 19, 22.

צֹעַר. LXX, Ζόγορα, also called בֶּלַע, 14, 2. A small town, generally regarded as situated on the south-east end of the Dead Sea. Tristram, however (*Land of Moab*), and Grove (*Bible Dict.*, Smith) adduce reasons for thinking it was on the north of the Dead Sea; cp. Cheyne on Is. 15, 5. Wetzstein in Del., *Comm.*, p. 564, adopts the first view, and places Zoar in the *Gôr eṣ Ṣáfia*, on the south-east of the Dead Sea. Pesh. reads צען, ‏ܕܡܨܪܝܢ ܦܢܐ‎, which Ebers, p. 272, accepts as the real reading. With this reading, which however is not necessary, באכה צער would refer to ארץ מצרים alone, and not to the whole sentence.

12. וַיֶּאֱהַל. This verb is a denom. from אהל '*a tent,*' = '*to tent,*' i.e. '*to wander about nomad fashion,*' hence, perhaps, the pl. בְּעָרֵי. Render, '*Moved with his tents towards Sodom.*'

13. הַחַטָּאִים '*sinners,*' i.e. '*habitual sinners,*' different from חֹטְאִים '*people sinning,*' not necessarily as a habit; cf. Ges., § 84. 6; also Ryssel, *De Eloh. Pent. sermone*, p. 40.

ליהוה ‘ *towards*,’ i. e. ‘ *against Yahweh*.’ Cf. 20, 6. 39, 9.
14ᵇ. Cf. 28, 14 ימה וקדמה וצפנה ונגבה.

15. אתגנה is impf. Qal of נְתַן, with the suffix strengthened by נ *demonstrativum*; see note on 12, 1. אַרְאֶךָ, notice the *casus pendens*, here marked as the acc. by את, כי את כל הארץ ‘ *For all the land . . . I will give it;*’ cf. Driver, § 197. 6 and 21, 13.

16. אשר אם יוכל, either I. ‘ *so that, if any one can number*,’ etc.; cf. 11, 7. 22, 14. 24, 3, so Syr. ܠܐ, Del.; or II. Tuch, ‘ *quem* [*pulverem*] *si, quis*,’ אשר referring to עפר in the first half of the verse, and עָפָר being repeated in the second half, where we would rather expect אתו. Tuch compares 50, 13 (= 49, 30), (where, however, אֵת rather means ‘ *with*’), and Ewald, § 331 c. 3, cites Jer. 31, 32. Num. 26, 64, which are apparently quite regular. The LXX have simply εἰ δύναταί τις, not translating אשר. Perhaps, however, it is simplest to regard אשר as in Deut. 3, 24. 1 Kings 3, 12. 13, as a link which cannot be literally translated.

<h3 style="text-align:center">14.</h3>

1. בימי אמרפל וגו׳. The four kings’ names are all genitives after the construct state בימי. Hebrew prefers, as a rule, to repeat the construct state before each genitive ; cf. Ges., § 114. 1; M. R., § 75 c; Ryssel (*De Eloh. Pent. sermone*, p. 61). The four kings, the subject to עשו in ver. 2, are not given again, as they can easily be inferred from ver. 1; cf. Ewald, § 303 b. 1; 9, 6 כי בצלם אלהים עשה ‘ *For in God’s image, He* (*God*),’ etc., Esth. 2, 21. The renderings of the LXX, ἐν τῇ βασιλείᾳ τῇ Ἀμαρφὰλ βασιλέως Σεναάρ, and Vulg. ‘ *factum est in illo tempore ut*,’ are probably merely intended to explain the meaning of the verse, and do not of necessity presuppose any variant. Clericus’ emendation,

inserting אברם before אמרפל, adopted by Ewald in his *Komp. der Gen.*, p. 221, is not necessary.

The meanings of the names in this verse are obscure. אמרפל, cf. Schrader, *K. A. T.*[2], p. 135, has not yet been discovered on the inscriptions. Bohlen explains it from the Sansk. *amarapâla* (*guardian of the immortal*), which is doubtful (Di. hat hier keine Stelle). אריוך is perhaps the Akkadian *Êri-aku*, '*Servant of the moon-god*' (*aku*). Cf. Del., *Par.*, p. 224. Formerly it was explained from the Sansk. *âryaka, venerabilis*, so Ges., Boh.; cf. Judith 1, 6 Εἰριὼχ ὁ βασιλεὺς 'Ελυμαίων; Dan. 2, 14 אַרְיוֹךְ רַב טַבָּחַיָּא '*A. chief of the executioners.*' אלסר is identified with תְּלַשָּׂר, Is. 37, 12, by Targ. Ps.-Jon.; with Pontus, by Symm. and Vulg.; with Artemita, in south Assyria, by Kn.; with Kal'ah Sirgat, by Sayce. More recently (e. g. by Rawl., Del., Sch.) with the old Babylonian town Larsam, south-east of Uruk. All very doubtful. כדרלעמר, LXX Χοδολλογομόρ (notice the γ=ע, and cf. on 4, 18). On the Assyr. inscriptions several kings of Elam have names compounded with *Kudur*. In the inscriptions the name of a deity *Lagamar* has been found. The name would perhaps = *Crown of Lagamar;* cf. Schr., *K. A. T.*[2], p. 136 ff. תדעל, LXX Θαργάλ, uncertain. Lenor. makes it = Akk. *tar-gal*, '*great Son.*' גוים, not a nom. appel. as A. V., '*King of nations*,' so Onq., for this rendering is too indefinite, and gives no suitable sense without some further name to define it; but a proper name, compared variously with the '*circuit* ("*Galil*") *of the nations*' (Is. 8, 23), Pamphylia (Symm.), and איי הגוים 10, 5 (Ges., Nöld.). Others, as Lenor., connect it with the *Guti, Kuti* that are frequently found in the inscriptions; cf. Lenor., *La lang. prim.*, p. 361; Di., p. 222. A. V. R. has '*Goiim*,' marg. '*nations.*'

2. The proper names in this verse are even more uncertain than those in ver. 1, the readings being possibly corrupt;

cf. the LXX text with the Hebrew. These five towns were, with the exception of Zoar, according to the narrative in chap. 19, destroyed.

3. חברו אל. A pregnant construction; cf. ver. 15. Render, '*Came allied to the valley of Siddim;*' cf. Josh. 10, 6 כי נקבצו אלינו '*for they have gathered together* [*and come*] *unto us.*' Other instances of preg. cstr. are to be found in Ewald, § 282 c; Ges., § 141.

עמק השדים. '*Valley of Siddim,*' i. e. '*Valley of the level fields,*' so Onq. מֵישַׁר חַקְלַיָא; Aq., Symm., Theod. κοιλὰς τῶν ἀλσῶν, so Vulg. The Pesh. takes השׂדים, as = '*the inhabitants of Sodom,*' and renders ܒܕܡܣܓܐ ܘܐܬܡܣܥܪ. Others connect it with the Arabic سِدّ '*stony ground.*' LXX have here φάραγξ ἡ ἁλυκή, and in ver. 9 κοιλὰς ἡ ἁλυκή. On עמק, see Stanley, *Sinai and Palestine*, App., § 1.

ים המלח. יָם with qameç is the construct state. *H. W. B.*, 9th ed., has 'יָם *m. cstr.* יָם־, *more rarely* יָם,' which requires qualification. יַם, with pathach and maqqeph, occurs as cstr. state twenty-three times, and always of the Red Sea (יַם־סוּף). יָם with qameç occurs as construct state twenty-four times, seventeen times *without* maqqeph, and seven times with maqqeph, but never of the Red Sea.

4. שתים עשרה שנה, acc. of time, in answer to the question '*how long?*'

ושלש עשרה, acc. of time, in answer to the question '*when?*' cf. Ges., § 118. 2 a and b; M. R., § 42 a and b; Ewald, § 300 a. When a *particular* point of time is mentioned, the preps. ב, ל, or כ are used; so Ols. and Nöld. prefer the reading of the Sam. here, viz. ובשלש—cf. M. R., § 42 b—as being more correct; see the next verse.

5. הרפאים. '*The Refa'im,*' or '*sons of the Rafa,*' i. e.

'*Giants*,' so LXX and Syr. here. Partly the name of the original inhabitants of Canaan, in the western and eastern Jordan-land, whose territory was promised Abram's descendants, 15, 20; partly a special name of the giants in Bashan, as here and Deut. 3, 11. Josh. 13, 12. The last traces of them in the O. T. are in 2 Sam. 21, 15 ff. ילידי הרפה, where they are spoken of among the Philistines at the time of David.

עשתרת קרנים, also simply עשתרת, Deut. 1, 4, and בית עשתרת=בעשתרה, Josh. 21, 27, was one of the principal towns of Bashan, identified with the present Tel 'Aṣterâ, two and a half hours from Nawâ, nearly between Nawâ and M'zârîb; it is situated on a hill in a rich meadow-land, well watered, and many ruins are still to be found (Ritter in Di., p. 223). Wetzstein, however, prefers to identify it with Bosra, one hour and three quarters from Edrei, where ruins have been found. The name means '*The two-horned Ashtoreth*,' who, as the goddess of the moon, was represented with two horns. The name עשתרת occurs frequently in Phoenician inscriptions, e. g. Eṣmunazar inscription, line 17, בת לבעל צדן ובת לעשתרת (cf. Schröder, *Phoen. Gramm.*, p. 225) '*a house for the Baal of Sidon, and a house for Astarte.*' The town was probably so called as being devoted to the worship of Ashtoreth.

ואת הזוזים בהם, possibly identical, as Ges. supposed, with the זמזמים, Deut. 2, 20, the name given by the Ammonites to the רפאים who formerly dwelt in their land. LXX have here, ἔθνη ἰσχυρὰ ἅμα αὐτοῖς, reading בָּהֶם and (?) עַוִּים: so Syr. Onq. has תַּקִּיפַיָּא, and gives for בָּהֶם, דִּבְהָמְתָא '*who were in Hamta* (?).' It is quite uncertain where הם was. Tuch conjectures that Ham was perhaps the old name of the capital Rabbath Ammon.

האימים, perhaps '*the terrible ones.*' The giant aborigines of the land of Moab; cf. Deut. 2, 10. 11, where they are expressly mentioned as the original inhabitants of Moab.

בְּשָׁוֵה קריתים = '*in the plain (of) Kiryathaim.*' שָׁוֵה is found only once again, in ver. 17, both vowels being unchangeable. In Num. 32, 37. Josh. 13, 19 the town Kiryathaim is mentioned as belonging to the Reubenites; in Jer. 48, 23. Ezek. 25, 9 to the Moabites; it was situated, according to the Onomas., four hours south-west of Medeba. The ruins are called at the present day Karêyât (south-west of Makaur (Machaerus) and south of mount Attârûs). קריתים = '*double town.*'

6. וְאֶת הַהֹרִי. The original inhabitants of Edom, Deut. 2, 12. 22.

בהררם ' *on their mountain,*' for בְּהָרָם. LXX, ἐν τοῖς ὄρεσι; so Sam. reading בהררי, cstr. pl. On the pointing, compare on 12, 15 (and add to the instances there, צָלֲלוּ and גָּלֲלוּ); הָרֲרִי and the other forms of הר, which resolve the doubled letter, and write it instead twice, are found in poetry and higher prose, as Deut. 8, 9 : other instances of a doubled letter being written twice, instead of having a dagesh, are חֲנֻנְכֶם, inf. cstr. of חנן, Is. 30, 18 ; מדדו for מדו, from מדד, Ez. 43, 10 ; עֲמָמִים = עַמִּים, Neh. 9, 22. 24 [cf. the regular emph. pl. in Chaldee עַמְמַיָּא]; and in poetry, Judg. 5, 14.

עַד אֵיל פָּארָן = '*to the terebinth of P.;*' cf. on 12, 6. אֵיל פארן is possibly identical with the well-known port Elath, on the Elanitic gulf, variously called אֵילַת, אֵילָה, or אֵילוֹת, in the O. T., which were perhaps abbreviated names of more modern origin, for the full name אֵיל פארן.

7. עֵין מִשְׁפָּט. '*Well of judgment,*' i.e. a place where decisions were given to disputants, perhaps the seat of a temple or oracle; cf. the other name קָדֵשׁ. The position of *Qadesh,* so often mentioned in the Pentateuch, is still un-

certain. Three identifications are given by Di., p. 225 :
I. that it is to be sought for in '*Ain el Weibeh*, near the
Araba, 30° 42′ lat. (Robinson). II. Identified by Prof. E. H.
Palmer and others with *Ain Qudeis*, south of Elusa, four and
a half hours east-south-east of the Well of Hagar. See also
Trumbull (*Kadesh Barnea*, 1884). III. Identical with *Qâdûs*,
about eleven kilometers north of mount Mâdara, in the
neighbourhood of the Wady-el-Yemen, one day's journey
from Hebron (Wetzstein, in Del., *Gen.*⁴, p. 574).

חַצְצֹן תָּמָר. Cf. 2 Chron. 20, 2, where it is explained
by היא עין גדי ' *En-gedi*,' on the west side of the Dead Sea,
noted for its palm trees. Knobel prefers to identify it with
עיר התמרים, Judg. 1, 16, or תָּמָר, Ez. 47, 19. 48, 28 (as Engedi
lay too far north), on the south-east border of the Holy Land,
the modern Kurnub (Di.). The name perhaps means '*Palm
rows*,' or '*cutting of Palms*,' but this is not certain.

10. בָּאֱרֹת בֶּאֱרֹת חֵמָר, lit. '*pits, pits of asphalt*,' i. e.
'*full of asphalt pits*.' On the repetition of the noun to
express plurality, cf. Ges., § 108. 4 ; Ewald, § 313 a ; M. R.,
§ 72. 2. בֶּאֱרֹת בֶּאֱרֹת חֵמָר. The first two nouns are both
construct states to the genitive חֵמָר ; the first of the two
being an instance of the so-called *suspended construct state*,
cf. Ps. 78, 9 נוֹשְׁקֵי רוֹמֵי קָשֶׁת, the second noun explaining
the first, which is in the construct state, its proper genitive
being קָשֶׁת ; so נַהֲרֵי נַחֲלֵי דְּבַשׁ, Job 20, 17, נחלי explaining נהרי,
the נהרי being really cstr. state before the genitive דבש ; cf.
Ewald, § 289 c ; M. R., § 73, note a. 4 ; Ges., § 116. 5.

וְעֵמֶק הַשִּׂדִּים בֶּאֱרֹת וגו״. Note the form of the
predicate in Hebrew. In English we say, ' *The valley of
Siddim was full of slime pits*,' i. e. we have to use some term
such as, *consist of, contains*, or the like, to express the relation
between the subject and the predicate. In Hebrew the pre-

dicate is expressed by the simple noun. '*The valley of Siddim was slime pits.*' Cf. Ex. 9, 31 השערה אביב והפשתה; Ps. 23, 5 כוסי רויה; see Driver, § 188. 2; Ges., § 106. 1. Rem. 2; Ewald, § 296 b.

חמר is '*asphalt*' or '*bitumen*,' found in the neighbourhood of the Dead Sea and of Babylon. The Babylonians used it as mortar; cf. 11, 3.

מלך סדם ועמרה. LXX, βασιλεὺς Σοδόμων καὶ βασιλεὺς Γομόρρας, so Syriac and Sam., reading מלך סדם ומלך עמרה, which would be the more correct expression; cf. on ver. 1. The second מלך might have slipped out by homoioteleuton.

ויפלו שמה. Rather the followers of the kings, for the king of Sodom (ver. 17) at least escaped.

הֶרָה. הַר, with the acc. ending ה, implying motion towards, '*mountainwards.*' The form is pointed with —ֶ instead of —ַ, because the short a (pathach) before a guttural with long a (qameç) is changed into é (seghol); cf. הֶחָכָם for הַחָכָם, Ewald, §§ 70 a, 71. הֶרָה, however, seems to be the only instance of this with ר. Delitzsch compares סֶלָה for סַלָּה, the doubling being resolved, and the —ַ changed into —ֶ; cf. his *Commentary on the Psalms*, 4th ed., p. 83.

11. רכֹש. LXX, τὴν ἵππον, reading the word as though it were רֶכֶש.

13. ויבא הפליט. '*And the fugitive came,*' i.e. 'the fugitive or escaped one, who in such cases is wont to come,' see esp. Ez. 24, 26. 33, 21. 22. Or it may be taken as a collective. On the article with פליט, cf. Ewald, § 277 a; Ges., § 109. Rem. 1 c; M. R., § 68; cf. המגיד, 2 Sam. 15, 13.

העברי. '*The Hebrew.*' עברי means '*one who has come* מעבר (*from the other side of*) *a river.*' This name was given to the Israelites by the Canaanites; the name being Hebrew,

the people who gave it them must have spoken the same
language as they did. It is only used in O. T. to or by
foreigners, or when the Hebrews are mentioned in opposition
to other nations. The name Israelite was, on the other hand,
a patronymic, and the national name used by the people
themselves. The river from beyond which the Hebrews
came is, according to some, the Euphrates; so most commentators. Reuss and Stade prefer the Jordan, on the
ground that the Hebrews on their return from Egypt spent
some time in the land east of Jordan, leaving the Canaanites
in possession of that on the west, which, however, does not
seem very conclusive against the general view. LXX render
it here τῷ περάτῃ, Vulg. '*Transeuphratensis.*' Another explanation is that עברי is a patronymic from עבר, mentioned as
an ancestor of Abram, 10, 24. 11, 14. 15. Num. 24, 24.

באלני ממרא. Cf. on 12, 6. The terebinth grove being
named after the Amorite Mamre, who possibly owned or
planted it.

והם בעלי ברית אברם. '*They being confederates of
Abram's,*' notice the circ. clause. The text literally translated
is, '*And they (were) owners of a covenant with A.;*' בעל being
used to form an adjective here, as in 37, 19 בעל החלמות=
'*dreamer;*' 49, 23 בעלי חצים='*bow-men* (lit. *arrow-men*);' בעל
שער='*hairy,*' 2 Kings 1, 8; בעל כנף='*winged,*' Prov. 1, 17,
etc. Cf. Ges., § 106. 2 a; M. R., § 79. 6 d. We have a similar
expression to בעלי ברית in Neh. 6, 18, viz. בַּעֲלֵי שְׁבוּעָה. The
phrase בעל ברית occurs nowhere else. In Judg. 8, 33. 9, 4
it is a proper name.

14. וירק is the imperf. apoc. Hif'. of רוק='*to empty out,*'
e. g. arrows from a quiver, or a sword from the sheath, Ex. 15, 9.
Lev. 26, 33. Ps. 35, 3; but only in this passage and Ps. 18,

43 with a personal object.   Render, '*Let loose.*'   LXX have ἠρίθμησε, '*mustered*,' reading וירק as though it were וַיָּרֶק, which the Heb.-Sam. has, and which seems to have been the reading of the Sam. text, which has ᴎᴧᴦ '*recensuit*,' and the Vulg. '*numeravit*.'

חניכיו ילידי ביתו.   חניכיו='*his tried ones;*' cf. the Arab. خَنِيك='*experienced*.'   LXX, τοὺς ἰδίους, who were ילידי ביתו '*home-born slaves*,' as opposed to מקנת כסף, 17, 12. 23, who were purchased slaves (or גֵּר, Ex. 23, 12); cf. the similar phrases, בן־בית, 15, 3 ; בן־אמה, Ex. 23, 12.

חניך only occurs here.

דן, i. e. Laish, on the north-east frontier of Canaan, which in the time of the Judges received the name of Dan, Josh. 19, 47. Judg. 18, 29.

15. ויחלק עליהם, lit. '*he divided himself against them,*' i. e. '*he divided his forces and came against them;*' cf. Job 1, 17. 1 Sam. 11, 11, for a similar manœuvre.   For the *cstr. praegnans* cf. on ver. 3.

חובה is on the left, i. e. north of Damascus, identified by Wetzstein with Ḥoba, twenty hours north of Damascus, in the neighbourhood of Ḥimṣ and Tadmor; cf. Del., *Gen.*[4], p. 561.

17. עמק שוה הוא עמק וגו׳—mentioned again 2 Sam. 18, 18, as the place where Absalom set up his monument—is hardly identical with שוה קריתים ver. 5, as it is now mentioned as though it were not previously known, and its position not far from Salem is against this identification, cf. ver. 18. It is usually—following Josephus, notice *Ant.*, vii. 10. 3, that Absalom's pillar was two stadia distant from Jerusalem— supposed to be in the neighbourhood of Jerusalem.

18. שלם.   Generally taken as Jerusalem, so Del., Kn.,

Targg., Hieron. (*Quaest.*), Joseph., etc. Others, Roed. in Ges., *Thes.*, and Tuch, identify it with the Σαλείμ of John 3, 23, cf. Judith 4, 4, which, according to Eusebius and Jerome, was eight Roman miles south of Scythopolis. In Ps. 76, 3 Salem is certainly Jerusalem. The objections to its being Jerusalem are: I. That this city lay too far south. II. That its old name was Jebus; cf. Judg. 19, 10. III. That Ps. 76, 3 is late, and the שלם there is a late poetical abbreviation of ירושלם. But as Del., p. 306, shews, Jerusalem would not necessarily be too far out of the way—whether Abram returned down the Jordan valley to Sodom, or took his way home through Samaria to Hebron—for the king of Sodom to come and meet him from the south-east, and Melchisedek out of Jerusalem. Further, the facts (I) that in Josh. 10, 1 there is a king of Jerusalem bearing the name אדני צדק, which is very similar to מלכיצדק, and (II) that the comparison of David, Ps. 110, 4, with Melchisedek would be far more suitable if he were king of Jerusalem, favour the identification with Jerusalem. The other two objections are not conclusive: it is quite uncertain that שלם is a poetical abbreviation of ירושלם, and that the old name of Jerusalem was Jebus is not of necessity fatal, as the name שלם might have been intentionally chosen with some hidden significance, just like מוריה 22, 2.

כהן לאל עליון = not '*the priest*,' as A.V., but '*a priest of God most high*,' so A.V.R.; see Ges., § 115. 2 a. כהן אל ע"י (which, as a proper name (cf. אל שדי), has no article) might mean '*the priest*,' or '*a priest*;' but to avoid this ambiguity of meaning, the construction with the prep. ל, instead of the construct state, is chosen; cf. M.R., § 76 b; Ewald, § 292 a. 2. עליון in the O.T. when joined with יהוה, or אל, never has the article.

19. לְאֵל עֶלְיוֹן . . . בָּרוּךְ 'blessed by God,' לְ after the passive denotes the agent; cf. 25, 21. Ex. 12, 16. Ges., § 143. 2; Ewald, § 295 c; M. R., § 51. 3. Rem. a.

קָנָה combines the double idea of *creating* and *possessing*. קנה is cstr. state, followed by two genitives; cf. M. R., § 75 c. Rem. a. Possibly the two words, heaven and earth, were conceived of as really forming one idea = '*the world*,' and so construed as though one word stood; cf. on ver. 1.

The phrase קנה שמים וארץ is only found in this chapter.

19[b] to 20[a] are poetical in form. Notice קָנָה for בָּרָא or עָשָׂה, צָרֶיךָ for אֹיְבֶיךָ, and מִגֵּן, which occurs twice again, Hos. 11, 8. Prov. 4, 9; all poetical words, though צרים is also found in prose writings; also the poetical sounding אל עליון.

22. הֲרִמֹתִי יָדִי. '*I lift up my hand*,' i. e. '*I have, just at the moment of speaking, lifted up*;' the perfect is used for the immediate past; cf. Driver, § 10; M. R., § 2. 1; the meaning being, I swear by Yahweh, etc.; cf. Ex. 6, 8. Num. 14, 30. Deut. 32, 40 כי אשא אל שמים ידי (of God, always נשא יד, Del.); Dan. 12, 7 וירם ימינו ושמאלו אל השמים; see also Ex. 17, 16.

23. אִם. The negative particle אִם is often used in the oath-formulae. The oath-formula would run in full somewhat as follows: '*I swear, if I do so and so, may God*,' etc.; then the second portion being omitted, the first part came to have a negative force, so אם = *I will not*, and אם לא = *I will* (Num. 14, 28). Render, '*I lift up my hand . . . that I will not take from a thread even to a shoe latchet, of all which is thine*,' i. e. 'I will not even take the most trifling thing for myself.' On this use of אם, see Ges., § 155. 2 f. N. B.; Ewald, § 356 a; M. R., § 168 β.

24. Render, '*Nought for me, only that which the young men have eaten, and the portion of the men who went*

with me: 'Aner, 'Eschol, and Mamre, let them take their portion.' Note the *casus pendens* ענר אשכל וממרא: cf. 3, 12.

15.

1. שכרך הרבה מאד=' *Thy reward shall be very great.*' שכרך ונו״ can scarcely be taken as a second predicate to אנכי, as this would rather require ו, and God cannot be regarded as Himself the reward.

הַרְבֵּה, inf. abs. Hif‘. of רבה, see on 3, 16. This inf. (properly a subst.), which is generally used as an adverb, is here regarded as an adj., and used as a predicate; cf. מְעַט, used quite similarly in 47, 9 מעט ורעים היו ימי שני חיי; and תְּמוֹל in Job 8, 9 כי תמול אנחנו; Ewald, § 296 d; Ges., § 131. 2. The Sam. has a correction אַרְבֶּה, which is easier.

2. ואנכי הולך ערירי. Circ. clause. Render,'*Seeing that I am going to die childless.*' הלך '*e vita decedere;*' cf. 25, 32. Ps. 39, 14. 2 Chron. 21, 20.

ערירי, lit.='*bare, naked,*' but restricted by usage to one who has no children; cf. Jer. 22, 30. Lev. 20, 20. 21 (all).

ובן משק ביתי=' *and the son of the possession of my household,*'=*my heir.* משק from מֹשֶׁק,=מֹשֵׁךְ=' *to draw, to hold, grasp*' (the form being perhaps chosen on account of its similarity in sound to דמשק) = '*possession;*' cf. מֶמְשָׁק, Zeph. 2, 9.

בן משק=יורש in ver. 3, the construction being the same as in בעל ברית 14, 13, which compare. Theod., Vulg. render בן משק '*son of the manager,*' i. e. '*of the steward,*' משק being from שׁקק, with the meaning, '*to go about busily,*' cf. מֶמֶר from מרר; which is possible, but forced and un-suitable. The other VSS. vary. The LXX have ὁ δὲ υἱὸς Μασὲκ τῆς οἰκογενοῦς μου (their rendering of בן ביתי in the next verse is ὁ δὲ οἰκογενής μου), τῆς οἰκογενοῦς being either a mistake for οἰκίας, or υἱὸς is a gloss, and the word should be οἰκογενής; see Frankel, *Einf.*, p. 17. Onq. has וּבַר פַּרְנָסָא הָדֵין דִּבְבֵיתִי הוּא דַּמַּסְקָאָה אֱלִיעֶזֶר '*this nourisher who is in my house, he is the Damascene, Eliezer.*' The Syriac has ܐܠܝܥܙܪ ܕܪܡܣܩܝܐ '*Eliezer the Damascene, the child of my house, he will be my heir.*' Aq. has ὁ υἱὸς τοῦ ποτίζοντος οἰκιάν μου, connecting משק with מַשְׁקֶה '*a cup-bearer.*'

הוא דמשק אליעזר cannot be rendered with the Syriac ܐܠܝܥܙܪ ܕܪܡܣܩܝܐ '*Eliezer the Damascene*' (so A. V., but A. V. R. '*Dammesek Eliezer*'), for this would either be אליעזר הדמשקי, or אליעזר בן דמשק, or אליעזר איש דמשק. Hos. 12, 8, which Gesenius cites in favour of this rendering, is not conclusive, the more correct rendering there being '*Canaan!*
in his hand are deceitful balances;' see Dr. Cheyne's *Hosea*, Cambridge, 1884, p. 115. Besides, בן ביתי in the next verse is not compatible with this explanation, see on 14, 14. Ewald, § 286 c, renders דמשק אליעזר '*Damascus of Eliezer,*' i. e. the city of Damascus, regarded as a community with which Eliezer was associated; cf. גבעת שאול. A view which is possible, but somewhat forced; Eliezer himself might be called בן משק, but hardly Damascus. The LXX and Vulg. translate the two words as one proper name, '*Dammesek Eliezer,*' which is contrary to usage, men never having double names. Del. considers אליעזר as in apposition to דמשק, but one would hardly explain the name of a town by that of a person. Hitzig and Tuch reject הוא דמשק as a gloss; but this weakens the sentence, and, as Di. remarks, leaves the choice of the rare word משק unexplained. Di., adopting Ewald's construction, explains as follows: '*These words could be well explained if Eliezer not only had a prominent position in Abram's household, but also was closely connected with Damascus;*

then we might expect, failing other heirs, that Abram's property would in time fall to him, and return with him to Damascus when he went back thither. We certainly do not read of any such relationship between Damascus and Eliezer, but then this is the only passage where Eliezer is mentioned, and the Damascenes still in Greek times boasted of their connection with Abram' (cf. Del., p. 311).

3. הן לי לא נתתה. Observe the emphatic position of לִי.

4. הוא is inserted for emphasis, as in 3, 12 הוא נתנה לי, which compare.

6. והאמן ביהוה. The perf. with waw conv. would here be quite out of place. It could hardly be frequentative, as believing in a person cannot be conceived of as a frequentative act. Like the other instances in 21, 25. 28, 6. 38, 5—cf. Driver, § 133. (2)—this is probably not a perfect with waw conv., but a case of the perfect with simple waw, where an imperf. with waw conversive would be expected.

ויחשבה לו וגו׳. Verbs of *considering* are either construed as here, with two accusatives, or with one acc. and the prep. ל; see M. R., § 45. 5 with § 51. 1 end; cf. 38, 15. 50, 20. In Ps. 106, 31 we have ותחשב לו לצדקה; and the LXX of this passage, καὶ ἐλογίσθη αὐτῷ εἰς δικαιοσύνην (as though they read ל here), is quoted three times in the N. T., Rom. 4, 3. Gal. 3, 6. James 2, 23.

8. בַּמָּה. The pathach is not the article, but the preps. כ, ב, ל before many short pronouns are pointed with long *a* (cf. Ewald, § 243 b; Ges., § 102. 2 d), but with מה the union is still closer, the vowel being doubled and the long *a* shortened into short *a*; see also Stade, § 134 f.; cf. בַּמָּה.

9. מְשֻׁלָּשׁ, not '*threefold*,' i.e. '*three of each kind*,' as Onq. and Rashi, but '*three years old*.' This is the only passage

where it occurs in this sense, but doubtless the LXX are right in reading it in 1 Sam. 1, 24 (בפר משלש for בפרים שלשה).

10. איש בתרו לקראת רעהו=' *each piece over against the other;*' cf. on 9, 5 איש אחיו, and the use of אשה of inanimate things in Ex. 26, 3. 5. Ez. 1, 9. 3, 13.

ואת הצפר לא בתר. ' *But the birds he did not divide.*' צפור is collective, as in Ps. 8, 9.

בֶּתֶר, a rare word; cf. Jer. 34, 18 f., possibly an allusion to this passage.

11. הָעֵיט. The generic use of the article, as in 14, 13, which compare.

הפגרים ' *the carcases,*' always used of dead bodies in Hebrew. In Syriac ܦܓܪܐ is used of a body, whether living or dead; cf. Bernstein, *Lex. Syr.,* p. 390 b. So פגר in Chaldee; cf. Levy, *Chald. W. B.,* p. 254 b sub voce.

וישב אתם. Hif'. of נשב. ' *And he scared them away,*' lit. ' *blew them away.*' The LXX read the consonants as וַיֵּשֶׁב אֹתָם συνεκάθισεν αὐτοῖς.

12. ויהי השמש לבוא. Render, ' *And it came to pass, when the sun was about to set.*' The ויהי does not here, combined with לבא, form the predicate to השמש, but stands alone. השמש לבא being a complete sentence in itself; לבא, the inf. cstr. with ל, being used as a periphrastic future; cf. Hos. 9, 13 ואפרים להוציא להורג ' *and Ephraim is for bringing forth,*' etc., Is. 10, 32 בנוב לעמד ' *in Nob is he for tarrying;*' Josh. 2, 5 ויהי השער לסגר ' *and it came to pass, the gate being about to be shut;*' cf. Driver, § 204 [cf. also § 165], where numerous instances are cited, and Ewald, § 217 d. b. Ges., § 132. note 1, and M. R., § 113, combine the היה with the inf. cstr., which, here at any rate, is quite unnecessary.

תרדמה '*a deep sleep.*' LXX here, and 2, 21, ἔκστασις, '*a trance.*'

והנה אימה חשכה גדלה. Render, '*And a very terrible darkness,*' lit. '*a terror, great darkness.*' חשׁבה גדלה being an explanatory apposition to אימה.

נפלת. The participle is more graphic than the perfect נפלה would be.

13. בארץ לא להם. '*In a land not theirs;*' cf. Hab. 1, 6 לרשׁת משׁכנות לא לו; Prov. 26, 17 על ריב לא לו. The relative, which here would stand in the nominative, being omitted, the antecedent being indefinite; M. R., § 159 a; Ges., § 123. 3 a; Ewald, § 332 a. 1; see also Wright, *Arab. Gram.*, ii. p. 343, the construction in Arabic being the same as in Hebrew.

ועבדום. '*And they (the Hebrews) shall serve them (the strangers=the Egyptians).*' LXX, καὶ δουλώσουσιν αὐτούς, cited Acts 7, 7, '*and they shall enslave them,*' which would require ועבדו בם; cf. Ex. 1, 14. Jer. 22, 13. עבד with the acc. is δουλεύω; in Hif., or Qal with ב, δουλόω.

14. '*The nation which they shall serve am I judging,*' Driver, § 135. 3. The participle as *futurum instans;* cf. on 6, 17.

16. ודור רביעי. '*In the fourth generation.*' LXX freely, τετάρτῃ δὲ γενεᾷ. The construction strictly is (Ewald, § 279 d), '*And as a fourth generation, they shall return;*' as in Deut. 4, 27. Zech. 2, 8. Jer. 31, 8; acc. of the complement.

17. '*And it came to pass, the sun having gone down.*' השׁמשׁ באה, being a circ. clause, by Driver, § 165, ויהי does not belong to באה, which is accented on the penult., and is thus *perfect* (see Driver, foot-note, p. 21), and so incapable of being combined with ויהי as predicate. Ryssel, *De Eloh. Pent. sermone,* p. 59, is surely in error when he speaks of באה as

participle ('ubi in participio באה nihil nisi notio diuturnitatis inest'). The ordinary editions and that of Baer have the accent on the penult.

וְעֲלָטָה הָיָה. The subject in the feminine is followed by the predicate in the masculine. Perhaps, as Müller suggests (M. R., § 39. Rem. a), עלטה was regarded as acc. after היה, '*and there became darkness* (i. e. *it turned to a darkness*);' see also Ges., § 147. Rem. 2.

18. כרת . . . ברית, lit. '*to cut a covenant*' = ὅρκια τέμνειν, *foedera icere;* on the difference between כרת ברית and הקים ברית, see on 9, 9.

נתתי '*I give,*' lit. '*I have given;*' the act is regarded as so certain of its fulfilment that it is looked upon as already accomplished; hence the use of the perfect in promises, contracts, etc.; see M. R., § 3. 1 a; Ges., § 126. 4; Dav., § 46. 2. 3; Driver, § 14; cf. 1, 29. 9, 2. 3.

מנהר מצרים. The southern boundary of the promised land is elsewhere (Num. 34, 5. Josh. 15, 4. Is. 27, 12) the נחל מצרים, the modern Wady el-'Arish, and this has led Knobel to identify the נהר מצרים of this verse with the נחל מצרים. But even if נהר can be used of smaller rivers and canals (2 Kings 5, 12. Job 14, 11. 28, 11. Ez. 1, 3. 3, 15), it seems more natural to identify the נהר מצרים here with the Nile or eastern arm of the Nile. In the time of David and Solomon (1 Kings 5, 1. 8, 65) the kingdom under their rule reached from the Euphrates to the Egyptian frontier.

עד . . . נהר פרת. Cf. Ex. 23, 31. Deut. 1, 7. Josh. 1, 4. Is. 27, 12. Notice the difference of idiom. In English we say '*the river Euphrates,*' while in Hebrew we find '*the river of Euphrates;*' cf. M. R., § 79. 1; Ewald, § 287 e. b, who compares the German '*Rheinfluss.*'

16.

1. הָגָר, probably a Semitic name=‘*flight*’ (Arabic مجر ‘*to flee*,’ مَجَرَة ‘*flight*’), and scarcely, as she was an Egyptian, her real name. Perhaps, as Del. suggests, she was given to Sarai by Pharaoh, cf. 12, 16; and according to this the Midrash explains the name fancifully, as=הא אינרא ‘*behold, a reward.*’ The Arab nomad tribe הגרים, Ps. 83, 7, derive their name from הגר.

2. מִלֶּדֶת, lit. ‘*away from bearing*,’ i.e. ‘*so that I cannot bring forth*;’ cf. 18, 25 מעשׂת; 23, 6 מקבר מתך; 27, 1 מראת, etc.

אִבָּנֶה as in 30, 3; cf. Ruth 4, 11. Ex. 1, 21. Deut. 25, 9, etc.

3. עֶשֶׂר שָׁנִים לָשֶׁבֶת. ל in the place of the genitive, as in 7, 11 (and regularly in dates, Ex. 16, 1. 19, 1, etc.) שֵׁשׁ מאות שָׁנָה לְחַיֵּי נח; cf. the note there.

4. וַתֵּקַל, cf. 1 Sam. 1, 6 f., is the imperf. Qal (intrans.) of a verb ע״ע with —; cf. יִמַּר, יֵרַד, etc.; Ges., § 67. Rem. 3; Stade, § 510 g. The two forms of the imperf. are, I. יִסֹּב, with the ב doubled when it ceases to be final. II. יָסֵב trans. (intrans. יִסַּב), with the ס doubled. In תֵּקַל the doubling has been given up, and compensation made by lengthening the — into —, as is usual with gutturals; cf. תֵּרַע, יֵחַת, יֵהַם.

5. חֲמָסִי. ‘*The wrong done to me.*’ Obj. genitive; cf. on 9, 2. LXX, ἀδικοῦμαι ἐκ σοῦ; Vulg. ‘*inique agis contra me.*’

וּבֵינֶיךָ. The point over the second yod (Mass. note, בתרא י׳ על נקוד *point on the last yod*) probably marks it as superfluous, because the form elsewhere is בֵּינְךָ, in pause בֵּינֶךָ; cf. 17, 2. 7. The other passages where points are found over words in Genesis are, 18, 9. 19, 33. 33, 4. 37, 12.

7. וַיְמִצָאֶהָ (cf. 1 Chron. 20, 2) is the companion form of וַיִּמְצָאֶהָ, which, however, does not occur in this verb; cf. וַיַּכִּירָהּ, 37, 33; וַתִּתְנֶהָ, 2 Chron. 20, 7; the imperf. taking the affix of the third pers. fem. sing. either in the form הָ‎‑ or קָ‎‑.

עַל עֵין הַמַּיִם, probably the well-known fountain on the way to שׁוּר; hence the article.

בְדרך שׁוּר. 'On the way to Shur;' cf. 3, 24 דרך עץ החיים.

שׁוּר must have been somewhere on the frontier between Palestine and Egypt. Josephus, *Ant.*, vi. 7, 3, erroneously supposed that שׁוּר was Pelusium, which is סִין. Saadiah holds that שׁוּר was Gifâr, جفار. ' The Arab. geographers understand by the wilderness of Gifâr (as distinct from the wilderness of the children of Israel, or Paran), the desert strip of land—which required five or six days' journey to traverse—bounded on the east by the desert of Paran, between Rafia in Philistia, up to lake Tennis (Menzaleh), and from thence to Qulzum or Suez; in a word, the western declivity of the desert of Paran towards Egypt' (Dillmann). The name probably means ' *wall.*'

8. אֵי מִזֶּה בָאת, more frequently the imperfect was used in questions after למה, מאין, etc., as being less outspoken and more courteous than the perfect. The perfect would= ' *Whence hast thou come?*' the imperf. ' *Whence art thou coming?*' or ' *Whence mayest thou be coming?*' Cf. Driver, § 39 γ; 42. 7.

אֵי מִזֶּה. Cf. Ges., § 150. Rem. 5; Ewald, § 326 a. מאין=simply ' *whence,*' with a verb or substantive, see Gen. 42, 7. Num. 11, 13. אֵי מִזֶּה is used similarly, but admits of being joined with a substantive, as 2 Sam. 15, 2 אֵי מִזֶּה עִיר אַתָּה; Jon. 1, 8 וְאֵי מִזֶּה עַם אַתָּה; but this is not frequent.

זה אי = '*where*,' but is used rather of things (e. g. with מקום, דרך, בית) than persons; for which איפה is the common word, as in 37, 16.

11. הרה is a fem. adj.; cf. 2 Sam. 11, 5 הרה אנכי; the masc. would be הָרֶה, like כָּלֶה, יָפֶה (fem. pl. כָּלוֹת, Deut. 28, 32).

יֹלַדְתְּ. The participle fem. We have here the ground form of יֹלֶדֶת, which has remained unchanged, and not passed over into the segholate form יֹלֶדֶת. This ground form re-appears before the suffixes, e. g. יֹלַדְתְּךָ, יֹלַדְתִּי, etc.; cf. Dav., § 29, esp. p. 73. 2; Ges., § 94. 2. Ewald, § 188 b, supposes that as this form is only found when the second pers. is spoken about, the word was so pointed on account of its similarity with the second pers. fem. sing. It occurs again Judg. 13, 5. 7, but in Is. 7, 14, with the third pers., the pointing is יֹלֶדֶת.

וְקָרָאת. Here the mother names the child, as in 4, 1. 25. 19, 37 f., etc.; in P the father, so 5, 3. 16, 15. 17, 19, etc. וקראת is pointed in Baer and Del. edition וְקָרָאתְ, in the common editions וְקָרָאת. The second pers. sing. fem. is, in verbs ל״א, usually pointed *without* the shewa; cf. Ewald, § 195 b, who mentions the two ways of pointing, and cites הָיִיתְ as well.

12. פרא אדם. '*A wild ass of a man*,' i. e. a man like the wild ass, who lives in the desert, wanders about at will, and cannot be tamed; cf. Job 39, 5. פֶּרֶא is the onager, Arab. فَرَأ, *asinus ferus;* Assyr. *purivu.* The construction is the same as in Prov. 21, 20 כסיל אדם; Is. 29, 19 אביוני אדם; and probably Is. 9, 5 פלא יועץ, 'the subordinated noun describing merely the relation of the individual [part] to the whole [genus]; the figurative to the actual,' Ewald, § 287 g; cf. M. R., § 79. 2. Rem. a; Ges., § 113.

עַל פְּנֵי Tuch renders '*east of*,' referring to Ishmael's geographical position; cf. 25, 18. 23, 19, but this is unnatural and forced. The text apparently means, Ishmael shall live close to his brethren, before their face, but shall not be on friendly terms with them. This meaning seems to suit יחו בכל ויד כל בו better.

13. אתה אל ראי='*thou art the God of seeing*,' i. e. '*the all-seeing God*.' Tuch explains, 'the God who appears, manifests himself;' but this does not suit the explanation which follows in the second half of the verse.

כי אמרה וגו'. '*For she said, Have I even here looked after Him that seeth me?*' i. e. Have I even here in the wilderness, where I should not expect to see God, seen Him. *He* saw her, but *she* did not see Him; but after He had gone, she perceived that He had been there.

רָאִי is a substantive; out of pause pointed רְאִי, in pause רֹאִי; cf. Job 33, 21 מֵרֹאִי; Nah. 3, 6 כְּרֹאִי (both Baer and Del.); 1 Sam. 16, 12 רֹאִי='*vision*,' '*seeing*.' Cf. צְרִי, pausal form of צֳרִי, Ez. 27, 17; חֹלִי, pausal form of חֳלִי, Deut. 7, 15. ראי at the end of the verse, pointed רֹאִי, and Job 7, 8 רֹאִי (both Baer and Del.; ordinary editions have רָאִי; cf. Del., *Gen.*, p. 321), is the participle act. of ראה, with the suffix of the *noun=my seer*, just as דְּבָרִי=*my word*, differing from רֹאֵנִי, where the suffix is a verbal one and would='*he who* or *one who sees me*.' The LXX erroneously take אֶל־רֳאִי as אֶל רֹאִי, and render ὁ Θεὸς ὁ ἐπιδών με, and paraphrase the second half of the verse with καὶ γὰρ ἐνώπιον εἶδον ὀφθέντα μοι. Syr. has,

='*thou art God in a vision, for she said, Lo, indeed a vision I have seen, after that He hath seen me;*' taking

ראי in *a* as a substantive, and paraphrasing *b*. Onq. has a paraphrase, אַתְּ הוּא אֱלָהָא חָיֵי כּוֹלָא אֲרֵי אָנָא שָׁרֵיתִי חַזְיָא בָּתַר דְּאִתְגְּלִי לִי '*thou art God, seeing everything ; for she said, Here indeed I begin seeing* (=*living*, so some moderns, Tuch, etc., a sense ראה does not bear), *after He revealed Himself to me.*'   The Vulg., with '*Profecto hic vidi posteriora videntis me*,' takes אחרי, like אַחֲרֵי in Ex. 33, 23 ; cf. 2 Sam. 2, 23 בְּאַחֲרֵי החנית.

14. '*Therefore they called the well, well of the Living one, who sees me*' (lit. *my seer*, see above).   קרא is third pers. used impersonally (cf. 11, 9)='*Man nannte den Brunnen.*'   The rend. '*Well of the living-one-of seeing*,' רֹאִי as pausal form of רֹאִי (see above), i. e. '*where one sees God and remains alive*,' requires a reading לְחִי רֹאִי, which is unnecessary, and presupposes a compound (Wortcomposition), which is impossible in Hebrew (Di.).   Wellhausen, *Hist. of Israel*, Eng. transl., p. 326, proposes to emend the text thus, הנם אלהים ראיתי ואחי אחרי ראי '*have I seen* [*God and remained alive*] *after* [*my*] *vision?*' cf. for the popular belief that one who sees God died, 19, 17. Ex. 3, 6. 19, 21.   Mich. emends בְּאֵר לְחִי רְאִי '*well of the jawbone* (i. e. *rock?* Judg. 15, 19) *of vision.*'   With the naming of the well, cf. 22, 14. 28, 19. 32, 31.

The position of the Hagar-well is uncertain, see some identifications that have been proposed in Del., *Gen.*[4], p. 321 f., who decides for its position on the road from Beersheba, along the ' Gebel-es-Sûr, which stretches from north to south.

בֶּרֶד, position unknown.

17.

1. אֵל שַׁדַּי . אֵל. The oldest and most general name of God, and restricted as a rule to Yahweh, but occasionally

used of other gods. The word is most common in poetry, elsewhere always with some qualifying word, such as עֶלְיוֹן, זוּר, or as here שַׁדַּי: it only takes the suffix of the first person אֵלִי. On אֵל, see Appendix II.

שַׁדַּי, according to P the name of God revealed to the Patriarchs (see Di., *Exodus*, p. 54), 28, 3. 35, 11 (cf. 43, 14). 48, 3 (cf. 49, 25). Ex. 6, 3 (in all these passages, except 49, 25, with אֵל). In poetry and the poetical style (Ruth 1, 21) we find שַׁדַּי alone, it is very often found in Job. Explained by the Rabbins as = דַּי (דַּי) · שֶׁ 'he who is sufficient,' 'the all-sufficient,' but such compounded names are not found in Hebrew; so Aq., Symm., and Theod. Roediger in Ges., *Thes.*, supposes that שַׁדַּי, which never has the article, is a plural form with the suffix of the first pers., like אֲדוֹנָי, Ges., § 121. 6. Rem. 4; but אֲדוֹנָי is the only clear instance of this. Del. supposes the ending ־ַי is an adjectival ending, as in זַכַּי (Ζακχαῖος), חַגַּי, יְשִׁישַׁי; but this would presuppose a noun שַׁד 'power,' which does not exist: and the adjectival suffix ־ַי is only found in a few proper names, and may admit of another explanation. Gesenius took it to be a *pluralis majest.*, but it is doubtful whether a plural ending ־ַי exists. Most moderns take it as an intensive adjective formed from שַׁדַּי = שָׂדֶה, with the pathach preserved, as in שָׂדַי = שָׂדֶה, and the proper name שָׂרַי, Ewald, § 155 c. The form is thus similar to the nominal formation קַטֵּל; cf. דַּנִּי, חַלָּשׁ, with — instead of —; possibly, as Wright suggests, pointed thus by the Massoretes in accordance with the Rabbinical etymology of the word. The LXX render it always in Genesis by a pronoun, here ὁ θεός σου; cf. 49, 25 and Ex. 6, 3 (αὐτῶν), but elsewhere (often in Job) they have sometimes παντοκράτωρ, sometimes ἱκανός. The Vulg. has 'omnipotens' here.

לִפְנֵי='*before me*,' i. e. under my eyes, in consciousness of my presence, 24, 40. Is. 38, 3; different from התהלך את, 5, 22. 6, 9.

2. בְמאד מאד. Cf. on 7, 19.

4. '*As for me, behold my covenant is with thee, and thou shalt become a father of a multitude of nations*.' אֲנִי is prefixed, as in 6, 17. 9, 9, for emphasis; it is opposed to וְאַתָּה, in ver. 9.

והיית לאב. והיית, perf. with waw conv., though no imperfect precedes; compare the companion construction of waw conv. with the imperf. when no perfect precedes. So 26, 22 ופרינו; Ex. 6, 6 והוצאתי; Driver, § 119 a.

אב, cstr. state for אֲבִי, is chosen on account of the name Abraham. This form is also found in proper names, e. g. אבנר, אבשלום, but not so frequently as the longer form אבי.

המון גוים. המון is used here instead of the more usual קהל, 28, 3. 35, 11, on account of the etymology of אברהם, suggested by the writer in ver. 5.

5. ולא יקרא . . . את שמך. The acc. after the passive verb as in 4, 18, which compare.

אַבְרָם, אברהם='*exalted father*;' not identical with אבירם, where the י is the suffix of the first person, the name meaning, '*my father is high*.' Di. offers an alternative explanation, '*Father of Raham* or *Ram*,' i. e. '*the Height*.' The etymology of the second name אברהם given in the text is really no etymology, but merely a play on the words; cf. the etymologies given for נח, קין; the name being changed into Abraham, because thus pronounced, an assonance was produced between the הם of המון and אברהם. אברהם does not = *Father of a multitude*. The etymology is quite unknown. Di. suggests that it may be a different—perhaps older—perhaps more Aramaic pronunciation of אברם, since with רום, ראם and רהם could be interchanged. A word רהם,='*multitude*,' does not exist; the connection with the Arabic word رَهَام, mentioned by the Arabic lexicographers, being very precarious.

אב המון ... נתתיך. נתן, with two accusatives, in the sense '*to make any one anything*,' Ges., § 139. 2; M. R., § 45, 5; so 1 Kings 14, 7. 16, 2. Jer. 1, 5. The other construction with ל in place of the second acc. is equally common; cf. ver. 6. 48, 4. Is. 49, 6, etc.

7. לדרתם = '*throughout their generations*' (successively); the plural suffix is used, זרע being taken collectively. למשפחותם would be '*throughout their families*' (contemporaneously). Formulae of this kind are common in P; so 8, 19. 10, 5. 20. 31. 32. 13, 3.

להיות לך ... אחריך, i. e. Abraham's descendants will stand in a close relationship to God as His servants, and be under His protection. He will protect and specially favour them, they will serve and worship Him as their God, Ex. 6, 7. Deut. 26, 17.

8. אחזה, מגורים, and ארץ כנען are all marks of P. Also the phrase, '*Thou and thy seed after thee*,' vers. 7–10.

10. המול לכם כל זכר. הִמּוֹל is inf. abs. Nif. of מלל or מול; cf. Ges., § 67. Rem. 5. The infinitive abs. being emphatically prefixed to indicate a command; cf. Ewald, § 328 c; M. R., § 106. 1 c; cf. Ex. 20, 8. Render, '*Every male to be circumcised*,' i. e. '*let every male be circumcised*.' Ges., § 131. 4 b. γ, prefers taking the inf. abs. as an imperative.

11. וּנְמַלְתֶּם is Nif. of מלל for נְמַלּוֹתָם; a root נמל does not exist; cf. תֵּמְנוּ, Num. 17, 28, for תַּמּוֹנוּ; הֵטַלְתָּ, where one

would expect הַטִּילוֹת, Ewald, § 234 e; Ges., § 67. Rem. 11;
cf. on 11, 6. The perf. with waw consec. is in continuation
of the imperative, which is implied in the last verse in the
inf. abs. הִמּוֹל, Driver, § 112 (cf., however, § 113. 1, where it
is explained on the analogy of Is. 5, 5).

בשׂר is acc. of respect, as in 3, 15, which compare. See
also 1 Kings 15, 23 חלה את רגליו.

12. יִמּוֹל is imperf. Nif'. of מלל (for יִמַּל, the regular form,
Job 14, 2); cf. תִּדֹּמִי, Jer. 48, 2, as though they were from
verbs ו״ע; cf. Ges., § 67. Rem. 5; Stade, § 504 e, who apparently regards יִמּוֹל as from a verb מול.

ובן שמנת ימים. 'Every male, when eight days old, shall
be circumcised for you throughout your generations.' בן שמנת
ימים is a secondary predicate; cf. Is. 65, 20 כי הנער בן
מאה שנה ימות; Job 15, 7 הראישון אדם תולד; cf. Driver,
§ 161. 3.

בן נכר, a mark of P; so ver. 27. Ex. 12, 43. Lev. 22, 25.
מקנה and כל זכר are also characteristic of P.

13. The repetition after ver. 12 is in the legal style of
this writer (P); cf. 26 f.

14. 'The uncircumcised male who shall not be circumcised as
to the flesh of his foreskin—that soul shall be cut off from his
people, my covenant he has violated.' The subject is placed
first for emphasis, as a casus pendens, and taken up by
הנפש ההוא, instead of by a pronoun; cf. M. R., § 132 a;
Driver, § 197. Obs. 2; Ex. 12, 15 and 17, 12.

עמים = 'fellow-tribesmen.' A peculiar use, found chiefly
in one or two stereotyped phrases.

ונכרתה. Being cut off from one's fellow-tribesmen is
probably to be explained of sudden removal by God, rather
than death inflicted by man; cf. Di., p. 245 et sq.; Del.,

p. 326. Tuch explains it as=מות יומת, but if this were here intended, it would probably have been added; cf. Ex. 31, 14.

ונכרתה is perf. with waw consec., after a *casus pendens;* cf. Ex. 12, 15 והאיש אשר ... כי כל אכל , ונכרתה; Deut. 17, 12 ; cf. Driver, § 123 a. ונכרתה הנפש יעשה ... ומת האיש ההוא; ההיא is a phrase characteristic of P; so Ex. 12, 15. 19. Lev. 7, 20 ff. Num. 9, 13.

הֻפַר. Pausal form for הֻפַּר, so הֵתַז, Is. 18, 5; Ewald, § 93 a. 2; Stade, § 393 b. β; Ges., § 29. 4, c. note.

15. שָׂרַי. The name שרה,='*princess*,' being the feminine form of שַׂר. The meaning of שָׂרַי is not so clear; the LXX have Σάρα; so סִינַי Σινâ. Possibly the name שרי was an older form of the name שרה (with ﮯ fem.=ה‍ָ), (Di.). The ending ‍ַי is hardly an adjectival ending; cf. on שָׁדַי, ver. 1. Another explanation is that שָׂרַי is from שָׂרָה, 32, 29; and so ='*the contentious, disputing one;*' cf. שָׂרַי=שָׂרָה, which is quite possible, but cannot be regarded as certain. Other explanations are that שׂרי='*the merry one*,' שׂרה '*one that makes merry, delights* (*erfreuende*),' from سَرّ, which Di. says violates both the laws of sound and form; or from the Arabic سَرُوَ سَرِيَ سَرَا '*generosus fuit*,' so '*the liberal, generous one.*'

17. הֲלְבֶן. ה interrog. pointed with dag., acc. to Ges., § 100. 4; Dav., § 49. 2.

ואם שרה הבת. The repetition of the interrog. ה of the first member, after the ואם of the second member of a double interrogative clause, is uncommon [this seems to be the only instance]; cf. M. R., § 145; Ewald, § 324 c.

18. לוּ ישמעאל יחיה=' *if Ishmael may live before thee*,' and as no apodosis follows, '*would that Ishmael might live;*' cf. Driver, § 142; M. R., § 147; Ewald, § 329 b; Ges., § 136. 2.

לו is also followed (exceptionally) by the imperative, 23, 13, or jussive, 30, 34.

19. ילדת . . . וקראת. The participle used as future, followed by the perf. with waw consecutive; so 6, 17. 48, 4; Driver, § 113. 1. The accent on וקראת is not thrown forward on to the last syllable by the waw conv., in accordance with the rule, that in the perfect Qal of verbs ל״א and ל״ה the waw conv. does not cause the accent to move forward, Driver, § 110. 4; cf. והיית, ver. 4.

20. ולישמעאל. 'And with regard to I.;' cf. 19, 21 אשר חלם נם לדבר הזה 'also with regard to this matter;' 42, 9 להם 'which he dreamt about them;' cf. M. R., § 51. 5. Rem. b; Ges., § 154. 3 e.

ברכתי . . . והפריתי, the perfect with waw conv., after a prophetic perfect; so Deut. 15, 6 ברכך . . . והעבטת; Num. 24, 17 דרך כוכב . . . וקם, Is. 2, 11. 43, 14; cf. Driver, § 113. 1 ad fin.; M. R., § 24. 2 b. Rem. b; Ewald, § 342 b. 2.

נשיאם. נשיא is almost confined to P in the Pent. and Josh.

ונתתיו לגוי גדול; cf. 48, 4 ונתתיך לקהל עמים, both in P.

23. וימל is imperf. Qal of מלל or מול, the form with waw conv. and retrogression of the tone being the same in both verbs.

בעצם היום הזה. Cf. on 7, 13.

24. בהמלו is either reflexive, 'in his circumcising himself,' i.e. 'when he circumcised himself,' or better passive (see ver. 25, where Ishmael could hardly circumcise himself), 'in his being circumcised,' i.e. 'when he was circumcised.'

26. נמול 'is the Nif'. of מול, formed from the form מלל,' Ewald, § 140 a; see also Ges., § 72. Rem. 9; Stade, § 397 b, γ;

cf. נָחַת from חתת, נָחַר from חרר. Stade and Ges. both regard it, however, as the Nif'al proper of מוּל, comparing נֵעוֹר from עוּר.

18.

1. וְהוּא יֹשֵׁב פֶּתַח וגו״. Circ. clause, '*While he was sitting at the door of the tent.*' LXX excellently, καθημένου αὐτοῦ. פתח וגו״ is acc. of place, in answer to the question '*where?*' Ges., § 118. 1 b; M. R., § 41 b.

כחם היום, LXX μεσημβρίας; cf. 1 Sam. 11, 9 בחם השמש; Neh. 7, 3 עד חם השמש; see also on 3, 8 לרוח היום='*at even.*' חם היום='*the heat of the day,*' i. e. noon.

2. יִשְׁתַּחוּ, in pause יִשְׁתָּחוּ, is the apocopated imperf. of הִשְׁתַּחֲוָה, a rare Hithpalel form, from שׁחה '*to bow,*' formed by a repetition of the third radical; cf. מטחוים in 21, 16. יִשְׁתַּחוּ is for יִשְׁתַּחְוְ, analogous to the segholate form שָׁחוּ for שָׁחְו; cf. Ges., § 75. Rem. 18; Stade, § 502 a.

אַרְצָה = '*to the ground,*' lit. '*earthwards,*' ה (as the position of the tone shews) being the ה of motion.

3. אֲדֹנָי is marked by the Massoretes קרש '*holy,*' i. e. that God is here intended; cf. the Mass. note on 19, 2, and Ges., § 121. 6. Rem. 4; Stade, § 359 e. The Sam. read the word אֲדוֹנַי '*my lords,*' as is clear from the use of the plural suffixes in בעיניכם for בעיניך, and עבדכם for עבדך, and the plural תעברו for תעבר. Dathe and Tiele correct the text into אֲדוֹנַי; so Di., who points out that in this verse Abraham addresses one of the three men whom he, possibly, recognised as the leader of the party (contrast ver. 4, where all are addressed). Di. further considers that Abraham, in the course of the conversation, first discovers the divine character of his guests (13), for if he had perceived it at once, the honour he paid them would really be no honour, and the offering of food

and drink without meaning; further, it would have been no trial of Abraham's faith, had he known that it was Yahweh who conversed with him. Tuch, Knobel, and Del. follow the Massoretic punctuation.

אִם נָא מָצָאתִי. נָא is added to shew the precative nature of the entire sentence; cf. 30, 27. 33, 10. So Ges. in *Th.*, p. 834 b, 'si—quod opto magis quam sumere audeo—gratiam inveni.'

4. '*Let there be taken a little water, and wash your feet, and rest yourself under the tree.*' The feet were washed before every meal; cf. 19, 2. 24, 32, Luke 7, 44.

תַחַת הָעֵץ '*under the tree.*' It is not necessary to take הָעֵץ collectively, as three people could very well sit down under one tree.

5. וְאָקְחָה. The doubling may fall away from a letter pointed with sheva, provided it be not one of the aspirates בּ, גּ, דּ, כּ, פּ, תּ, in which case the doubling is usually (but not always) retained; cf. Ges., § 20. 3 b; Dav., § 7. 4, foot-note. Accurate texts mark the omission by placing Raphe (ˉ) over the letter whose doubling is given up; cf. Stade, § 41. Render, '*And let me take a morsel of bread.*' פַּת לֶחֶם '*a morsel of bread;*' cf. Judg. 19, 5; a modest way of describing the rich meal he will set before them (Di.).

כִּי עַל כֵּן = '*quandoquidem,*' Ewald, § 353 a; '*for as much as,*' the reason being adduced the second time by the demonstrative '*therefore*' after the relative [conjunction]; cf. Ges., § 155. 2 d.

6. הָאֹהֱלָה is accented on the penult., as the locative ה does not take the accent, and אֹהֶל is a seg. noun: cf. Ges. § 90. 2 a; Dav., § 17, 3. In B. and D. there is a misprint here (see *Jesaias*, p. v, note): read הָאֹהֱלָה. So חֲרִישָׁה, נֹגְבָה (13, 14).

"מַהֲרִי שָׁלֹשׁ וגו׳. '*Bring quickly three measures of meal;*'
מַהֲרִי, lit. '*hasten*.' מהר with the acc. is rare, so 1 Kings
22, 9. Is. 5, 19.

קמח is the acc., '*three measures in meal,*' or '*as to meal,*'
the acc. perhaps being an acc. of respect; cf. Ges., § 118. 3.
M. R., § 71. 4, regards קמח as in apposition, so apparently
Ewald, § 287 i; cf. Ex. 9, 8 מלא חפניכם פיח; Ruth 2, 17
איפה שְׂעוֹרִים.

סלת is in apposition to קמח, defining it more closely,
'*meal, fine flour.*' Three seahs of meal made an ephah,
something over an English bushel. The large quantity was
probably intended as a mark of distinction; cf. 43, 34. 1 Sam.
9, 22 f.

עֻגוֹת. ג without dagesh; cf. B. and D., *Gen.*, p. 77.
The cakes were small round cakes, baked in the hot ashes,
so called from their round form. Greek ἐγκρυφίαι, which
word the LXX use here.

9. אֵלָיו, the points above the word probably point to a
various reading לו; cf. on 16, 5.

10. כָּעֵת חיה = '*next spring;*' explained, ver. 14, by
למועד; in 2 Kings 4, 16. 17 we have the fuller phrase למועד
הזה כעת חיה. LXX have κατὰ τὸν καιρὸν τοῦτον (from ver. 14)
εἰς ὥρας, i. e. '*about this time next year.*' The phrase literally
translated = '*about the time when it revives,*' i. e. '*when this time
lives again;*' cf. Ges. in *Th.*, p. 470. חיה does not qualify
עת, which has the article, but is predicate; cf. Ex. 9, 18
כָּעֵת מָחָר '*about the time when it is to-morrow.*' In 17, 21 we
have the time stated more clearly, למעד הזה בשנה האחרת;
cf. 1 Sam. 1, 20 לתקופות הימים.

וְהוּא אַחֲרָיו. '*It (the door) being behind him (the
speaker*);' so the Massoretic text. The LXX, οὖσα ὄπισθεν αὐτοῦ,
took הוא here as הִוא, cf. on 2, 12, and referred it to Sarah.

11. באים בימים =‘*well on in days.*’ So 24, 1; Josh. 13,
1, etc.; cf. προβεβηκότες ἐν ταῖς ἡμέραις in Luke 1, 7.

חדל, as ver. 11 is a circumstantial sentence, explanatory
of what takes place in ver. 12, חדל must be translated ‘*there
had ceased.*’

12. ‘*And Sarah laughed within herself, saying, After I have
grown old, shall I have pleasure, my lord being old?*’ LXX,
ἐγέλασε δὲ Σάρρα ἐν ἑαυτῇ, λέγουσα, Οὔπω μέν μοι γέγονεν ἕως τοῦ
νῦν. ὁ δὲ κύριός μου πρεσβύτερος; leaving אחרי untranslated, and
apparently taking בִלְתִי = בִלָתִי, and עֶדְנָה = עֶדְנָה = עֶדְ־הֵנָּה.
Contrast the explanation of P in 17, 17.

14. היפלא מיהוה דבר. ‘*Is anything too hard* (lit.
wonderful, extraordinary) *for Yahweh?*’ cf. Jer. 32, 17 לא
יפלא ממך כל דבר, and ver. 27 הממני יפלא כל דבר; Deut.
17, 8 כי יפלא ממך דבר.

מֵיְהוָֹה. י pointed with shewa: so B. and D. Ordinary
texts have מֵיהוָֹה, without shewa. The shewa is inserted
according to the Massoretic note, quoted by Del. in his
Commentary, p. 551 משֹה מפיק וכלב מכנים, i.e. ‘*Moses leads
(Israel) out, and Caleb leads them in,*’ which is the Massoretic
way of saying that the letters ה, שׁ, מ make the א of ארני—
the vowels of which are always in the text placed under יהוה—
heard; while after the letters בּ, לָ, כֹ, the א is not sounded
as a consonant, e.g. בַּאדוֹנָי = בֵּיהוָֹה for בֵּאדֹנָי; the latter
part of the rule holds good for ו. So וַאדוֹנָי=וַיְהוָֹה for וַאֲדוֹנִי;
cf. Ges., § 23. 2; Stade, § 112 b. note (who gives instances,
e.g. Mic. 4, 13. Neh. 8, 10. Gen. 40, 1 (cf. B. and D.'s
editions here), where ⸗ does not become ⸗).

15. לא כי צחקת ‘*nay, for* (i.e. *but*) *thou didst laugh,*’
לא כי, as in 19, 2. 42, 12.

16. ואברהם הלך עמם לשלחם ‘*while Abraham*

went with them to bring them on their way,' circ. clause, as in vers. 12 and 18; cf. Driver, § 159 ; M. R., § 152.

לְשַׁלְּחָם. Cf. on 12, 20.

17-19. *'And Yahweh said (i.e. to Himself), Shall I hide from Abraham what I am going to do, (18) seeing that Abraham will surely become a great and powerful nation, and all the nations of the earth will bless themselves in him? (19) For I have chosen him, to the end that he may charge his sons, and his house after him, and that they may observe Yahweh's way, by doing righteousness and right ; so that Yahweh may bring upon Abraham that which He hath promised concerning him.'*

17. הַמֲכַסֶּה, the participle preceding the subject, as in Num. 11, 29. Ez. 9, 8 ; see Driver, § 135. 4.

18. הָיוֹ יִהְיֶה. הָיוֹ is for הָיֹה, the Ḥolem quiescing in a Waw, instead of a He ; cf. 26, 28 רָאוֹ ; Is. 22, 13 שָׁתוֹ ; see Ges., § 75. Rem. 2 ; Stade, § 623 a.

וְנִבְרְכוּ. Cf. on 12, 3.

19. יְדַעְתִּיו. Cf. Amos 3, 2. Hos. 13, 5, ידע here, and in the two passages cited, = *'to know a person thoroughly,'* and so, after becoming well acquainted with him, *'to choose or select him,'* almost = בחר ; cf. a similar use of προγινώσκειν, Rom. 8, 29.

לְמַעַן אֲשֶׁר, stronger than כִּי, = *'eo consilio ut,'* *'with the intention of,'* *'to the end that,'* A.V.R., always introduces the intention ; so Lev. 17, 5. Deut. 3, 4. Jer. 42, 6 ; Ewald, § 337 b ; Ges., § 155. 2 e.   A.V. is incorrect, למען always = *ut.*

לְמַעַן אֲשֶׁר יְצַוֶּה . . . וְשָׁמְרוּ. Cf. on 12, 13.

The LXX have ᾔδειν γὰρ ὅτι συντάξει, misunderstanding the text ; so Syriac and Vulg.

20. '*And Yahweh said, The cry concerning Sodom and Gomorrha, it is indeed great; and their sin, it is indeed very heavy.*'

זעקת is *gen. object.*, as in 9, 2. 16, 5, which compare.

זעקת and חטאתם are *casus abs.* רבה has the accent on the penult., and so is third pers. perf. from רבב. Wellhausen renders, '*It is a report about Sodom and Gomorrha, that their sin is great, that it is very heavy;*' ו before חטאתם being struck out; which Di. rejects on the grounds that זעקה does not mean '*a report,*' and that God would not listen to a report.

כי = '*indeed*' or '*it is the case that,*' as in Is. 7, 9. Ps. 118, 10; cf. Ewald, § 330 b; unless it is assumed, with Lagarde and Olshausen, that שמעתי has fallen out at the beginning of the sentence. The LXX omit כי.

21. '*I will indeed go down, that I may see whether they have altogether done according to the cry concerning them, that has come up to me.*'

הבאה is pointed by the Massoretes as perfect, with the article; cf. Ewald, § 331 b; Ges., § 109. Rem. As this usage is rare outside the later books of the Bible, Ewald, l. c., and Di. reject it here, and point as a participle. M. R., § 92. Rem. a, points out (citing cases, e.g. 1 Kings 11, 9 and Gen. 12, 7) that the Massora itself varies in this point. The participle here is more natural, and only involves a change in the position of the accent, from the penult. to the last syllable; so 46, 27.

עשׂו כלה, separated by the accents, so to be taken alone, כלה = '*omnino,*' as in Ex. 11, 1 כשלחו כלה גרש יגרש אתכם. In other passages עשׂה כלה means '*to utterly destroy;*' cf. Nah. 1, 8. Zeph. 1, 18.

22. ‏ואברהם עודנו עמד לפני יהוה‎. According to
a tradition found as early as the Mechilta (on Ex. 15, 7) and
often repeated, this verse originally ran ‏ויהוה עודנו עמד לפני‎
‏אברהם‎, but was altered as too anthropomorphic; ‏עמד לפני‎
having the notion of serving. But 19, 27 is against this, and
all the versions follow the text as we now have it, and read
‏לפני יהוה‎. This and similar corrections, called *Tiqqune
Sopherim*, are not to be regarded as real various readings, but
merely as changes proposed by the Massoretes, to avoid
expressing anything in the text that was repugnant to them;
cf. Strack, *Proleg. Crit.*, p. 87. Geiger, *Urschrift*, p. 331,
considers that ‏יהוה עודנו עמד לפני אברהם‎ is the real reading,
citing the Talmud and Midrash in support of his view.
There are eighteen such passages in the O. T., but only this
one in Genesis. Cf. further, Strack, l.c., who cites authorities;
also Bleek's *Introduction*, 4th ed. [Wellhausen], p. 624. The
eighteen instances are given in Levy's *Chald. W. B. über
die Targ.*, ii. p. 553 b; the larger Massora, on Num. 1, 1;
and in the *Dikduke Ha-t*^e*amim*, edit. Baer and Strack,
Leipzig, 1879, § 57.

24. ‏ולא תשא למקום‎. ‏נשא ל‎, sc. ‏עון‎ or ‏פשע‎=' *to take
away the sin for any one,*' so ' *to forgive.*'

25. ' *Far be it from Thee to do according to this thing, to slay
the righteous with the wicked, and that the righteous should be
as the wicked, far be it from Thee; shall the Judge of all the
earth not execute judgment?*'

‏להמית . . . והיה‎, the cstr. inf. breaking off into a
perfect with waw conv.: the perfect is used here, as a possible
case is stated, and not a fact; in which case we should find
the imperf. with waw conv., as in 39, 18 ‏ואקרא . . . כהרימי‎;
cf. Driver, § 118 (see the preceding section); Ges., § 132.

Rem. 2 : so 27, 45 וישכח . . . עד שוב, Ex. 1, 16 . . . בילדכן וראיתן, 2 Sam. 13, 28 ואמרתי . . . כטוב.

חללה = 'profanum (lit. *in profanum*), *nefas tibi sit.*' Del. compares the Targ.-Talmud חלין הוא לך ' *it is unholy for thee.*' The ה is not the feminine ending, as the word is accented on the penult. ; cf. 44, 7 חלילה לעבדיך.

מעשׂת, מן as in 16, 2, which compare.

27. עפר ואפר. Notice the alliteration, and cf. תהו ובהו, 1, 2. נע ונד, 4, 14. הוד והדר, Ps. 21, 6.

28. יחסרון, with the fuller ending ון-, preserved in Aramaic, and in classical Arabic (as the ordinary form) ; but only occasionally found in Hebrew ; cf. Ges., § 47. 3. Rem. 4 ; Stade, § 521 a, a. See on 3, 3.

חסר being one of the verbs of *abounding* and *wanting*, takes the acc.; cf. Ges., § 138. 3 b; Ewald, § 283 b.

30. אל נא יחר לאדני וגו׳. ' *O let not my Lord be angry, and let me speak.*' יַחַר is apoc. from יֶחֱרֶה; the jussive is here used in asking permission; cf. M. R., § 8. 2 ; Ges., § 127. 3 b; Driver, § 49 β; so the cohortative ואדברה : cf. 33, 14. 50, 5.

19.

1. שׁני המלאכים = not as A. V. ' *two angels,*' but ' *two of the angels,*' i.e. two of the three mentioned in 18, 2. On the construction, cf. Ges., § 120. 1 a; M. R., § 96 b.

ולוט ישׁב. Circ. clause, as in 18, 1; cf. also on 9, 18. Render, ' *While Lot was sitting in the gate.*' The city gate in the east was usually a vaulted entrance, with large recesses on either side; here business matters were settled, and the affairs of the town and all public matters discussed and arranged; cf. 23, 10. 13. 34, 20. Deut. 21, 19.

2. הִנֵּה נָא, with short *e* (Seghol) (only here; cf. Ewald, § 91 d) and *dagesh forte conj.*, is unique.

אֲדֹנַי is marked by the Massoretes נ״ בפתח וחול (i. e. '*נ pointed with pathach and profane*,' i. e. '*not used of God*').

סורו נא וגו״. It was regarded as a neglect of the duties of hospitality to allow strangers to spend the night in the street; cf. Judg. 19, 15, and contrast with this inhospitality, 24, 25. Ex. 2, 20. Judg. 13, 15. 'The modern Arabs consider it a privilege to lodge strangers who may come to them, and often disputes arise as to who shall have this honour.' Kn. cited by Di.

והיׁשכמתם. הׁשבים prop.='*to shoulder* or *place on the shoulders*,' i. e. to put one's baggage on the beasts of burden, which was done early in the morning, so '*to rise early, to resume the journey*.' The verb is a denom. from ׁשכם '*a shoulder*,' or rather '*the portion of the back between the shoulders*,' where any burden would be carried.

לֹא, with emphatic or euphonic dagesh; an unusual use of dagesh, generally considered to be for the purpose of securing a clear and distinct pronunciation of the consonant: cf. Stade, § 40 b, c; Ges., § 20. 2 a. Rem. 2; so קומו צאו, ver. 14; ויאמרו לֹא, 1 Sam. 8, 19; cf. Ex. 12, 31. Deut. 2, 24. It is only found in accurate editions and MSS. See also Del., *Commentary on Ps.* 94, 12, 4th ed.

3. מִׁשתה, prop. '*a drinking feast*,' then generally '*a meal or banquet*;' cf. 21, 8. 26, 30.

מצות = '*sweet* or *unsoured*,' i. e. '*unleavened cakes*' (from מצץ '*to lap, suck*'), and so more quickly prepared.

4. טרם וגו״; cf. on 2, 5. Render, '*They had not yet gone to sleep, when the men of the city, the men of Sodom, surrounded the house, both young and old, all the people in a body.*'

נָסַבּוּ is third perf. pl. Nif‘. of סבב = נִסְבְּבוּ. Nif‘al being originally Naf‘al; the pathach being thinned down into ḥireq; cf. Dav., § 25. Rem. a; Ges., § 51. 1; and compare the Arabic vii form اِنْقَتَلَ (in-qatala) and such Heb. forms as נֶעֶשָׂה, נוֹשַׁב = נַוְשַׁב (Dav., § 9. 1. Rem. b; Ges., § 24. 2 b); Wright, *Gram. Arab.*, i. p. 42. נַסְבַּב becomes נַסַּב, and the pathach under the nun, standing in an open syllable before the tone, becomes tone-long qameç: cf. Stade, § 86. 3; Dav., § 6. 2 b; see also Ges., § 27. 2 a.

מִקָּצֶה = lit. '*from the end*,' i.e. including the whole, so in Jer. 51, 31. Cf. Judg. 18, 2. 1 Kings 12, 31 (not '*of the lowest*,' but '*of the whole body of the people*').

5. הַלַּיְלָה = '*to-night*,' '*this night*,' the article, as in הַיּוֹם, הַשָּׁנָה, has a demonstrative force: Ges., § 109. Rem.; Ewald, § 277 a. 3. So in 30, 15.

6. פֶּתַח . . . דֶּלֶת. דֶּלֶת = '*the door of the house*.' פֶּתַח = '*the entrance (gate)*.'

7. אֶחָי = '*my friends;*' cf. 29, 4. Judg. 19, 23.

8. אֵל for אֵלֶּה is found eight times in the Pentateuch and once besides (1 Chron. 20, 8), and always (except Chron. l. c.) with the article; see Ges., § 34; Dav., § 13. Rem. a; Stade, § 171 b. It is commonly explained as an archaism, but this is very doubtful.

9. גֶּשׁ־הָלְאָה. So in correct editions; the ordinary editions have הָלְאָה, with metheg, which is wrongly placed, as the tone is on the penult. LXX, Ἀπόστα ἐκεῖ. Vulg. '*recede illuc;*' cf. Is. 49, 20 גְּשָׁה־לִּי '*stand away*.' Render, '*Stand back*.'

שָׁפוֹט . . . וַיִּאמְרוּ הָאֶחָד. '*This one came in to sojourn and goes on playing the judge;*' cf. 31, 15 וַיֹּאכַל גַּם אָכֹל אֶת כַּסְפֵּנוּ

'*and goes on to eat up our silver ;*' Job 10, 8 וַתְּבַלְּעֵנִי '*and yet thou goest on to swallow me up;*' cf. Driver, § 79, 'The action or its results continuing into the writer's present;' also Ewald, §§ 231 b, 342 a. 1 a.

שָׁפוֹט. When the inf. abs. *follows* the finite verb, it generally denotes a continued or lasting action; cf. Ges., § 131. 3 b; Ewald, § 280 b.

הָאֶחָד. The הָ is the article, *not* the ה interrogative.

11. בסנורים '*with blindness ;*' not absolute blindness, but temporary loss of sight; the word only occurs once again, 2 Kings 6, 18. Elsewhere we find עִוָּרוֹן, Zech. 12, 4. Deut. 28, 28. סנורים is from סַנְוֵר [Safel of נור (نَوَّرَ)] = '*to make blind,*' which occurs in Aramaic; cited by Levy, *Chald. W. B. sub voce*, as occurring in Num. 16, 14 Targ. Ps.-Jon. (תסנוור). The article is according to Ges., § 109. 3. Rem. 1 c. LXX, ἀορασία; Onq. שַׁבְרִירַיָּא '*fatuitas ;*' Syr. ‍ '*illusiones.*'

מקטן ועד גדול. Cf. 1 Sam. 5, 9. 30, 2 ; lit. = '*from a little one even unto a great one,*' i.e. '*all,*' every one being regarded as either small or great, so the two extremes would embrace all persons. Cf. further, Dietrich, *Abhand. zur hebr. Gram.,* p. 206, who gives a list of other expressions for '*all,*' '*nobody ;*' cf. Ex. 11, 5.

מִן . . . וְעַד, as in 14, 23, and often.

12. עֹד מִי לְךָ פֹה = '*Who hast thou still here?*' i.e. '*hast thou any more belonging to thee in Sodom besides those in thy house ?*'

חָתָן, perhaps collective = '*sons-in-law ;*' but the singular without the suffix is strange, as one would expect חֲתָנֶיךָ, which the Syr. has, ‍. Di. conjectures that ובני was

inserted between יך and חתנ, as no mention is made elsewhere of sons which Lot had before the destruction.

13. כי משחתים אנחנו. The participle is used of
future time, with the subject following, as in 3, 5, which
compare.

צעקתם = ' *the cry concerning them ;*' cf. on 18, 20.

את פני יהוה as in ver. 27. 33, 18. Ex. 34, 23. 1 Sam.
1, 22. Ps. 16, 10.

14. לקחי ' *who were to take,*' ' *the takers of his daughters ;*'
so Ewald, § 335 b, better than (LXX, Targ. Ps.-Jon., Kimchi,
Del.) '*who had taken,*' which would be more naturally expressed
by אשר and the perf.; and Lot would scarcely leave his
married daughters in Sodom without calling them away.

קומו צאו. צ with emphatic dag. (see on ver. 2), to
ensure the clear pronunciation of the צ between the two
u-sounds.

היה כ . . . = ' *to appear as,*' for which there is no proper
word in Hebrew ; cf. 27, 12. 40, 10.

15. Render, ' *And when the morning dawned, the angels
urged Lot, saying, Take thy wife and thy two daughters that are
with thee, lest thou be swept away in the punishment of the city.*'

וכמו השחר עלה . כמו = כאשר is rare and poetical,
Is. 26, 18. Ps. 58, 8 ; cf. M. R., § 60 ; Ewald, § 337 c.

ויאיצו is imperf. Hif'. of אוץ. The waw conv. is used
after a time determination : so 22, 4 ביום השלישי וישא אברהם,
1 Sam. 21, 6 בצאתי ויהיו, Josh. 22, 7 ויברכם . . . כי שלחם ;
cf. Driver, § 127 b.

הנמצאת, lit. ' *who are found,*' i.e. who are with thee in
thy house ; cf. 1 Sam. 13, 15. 21, 4. The participle may
often be rendered by the present, as in 4, 10. 16, 8. 37, 16,
etc. הנמצאת probably refers to את אשתך as well as to
ואת שתי בנותיך.

פֶּן תִּסָּפֶה. כפה = '*to be snatched off, carried away;*' so
1 Sam. 12, 25. Num. 16, 26.

עון = '*punishment;*' cf. 4, 13.

16. וַיִתְמַהְמַהּ, imperf. Hithpalpal of מהה; cf. יתמרמר
from מרר, Dan. 8, 7; Stade, § 503.

בחמלת יהוה = '*through Yahweh's sparing him,*' i. e.
'*because Yahweh spared him,*' the subject of the inf. construct
following in the genitive; cf. M. R., § 117; Ges., § 133. 2:
also Ps. 133, 1 שֶׁבֶת אחים, Is. 47, 9 בעצמת חבריך. The inf.
cstr. חמלת has the fem. cstr. ending; here intentionally, as
בחמלה יהוה could not be taken as construct state with a
following genitive. The inf. with fem. ending ה is common,
especially in particular words, viz. שִׂנְאָה, יִרְאָה, אַהֲבָה, occasionally we find חָזְקָה, דִּבְקָה, דְּבָקָה, הַאֲבָה, קִרְבָה; cf. Stade, p. 339;
Ges., § 45. 1. Rem. b.

17. אל תביט. The jussive form תַּבֵּט would rather be
expected after אל, but cf. Ps. 121, 3 אַל־יָנוּם, 1 Sam. 25, 25
אַל יָשִׂים; cf. Driver, § 47; Ges., § 127. 3 c.

18. אֲדֹנָי, noted by the Massoretes קדש; אלהם does not
of necessity imply that Lot did not recognise that Yahweh
was speaking with him, and that אֲדֹנָי = '*my lords,*' pausal
form of אֲדֹנַי; as in ver. 19 we find singular suffixes. The
Syr. and Saadiah regard אדני as חול, but the LXX, Onq.,
Vulg., and Sam. follow the Massoretes; so Del.

19. פֶּן־תִּדְבָּקַנִי. Imperf. with the so-called union vowel
pathach instead of tsere; cf. 29, 32 יֶאֱהָבַנִי; see Ges., § 60.
Rem. 2; Stade, § 636 b, who cites 1 Kings 2, 24 וַיּוֹשִׁיבַנִי,
Is. 56, 3 יַבְדִּילַנִי, Job 9, 18 יַשְׂבִּעֵנִי.

וְרַמַתִּי. ו with pretonic qameç, the tone is not thrown
forward, because the word is in pause; see Driver, § 110, 2.
מַתִּי = מַתִּי. The perf. with waw conv., as in 3, 22, which
compare.

22. צוער, probably one hour south-east of the Dead Sea, in that portion of the Araba which is now called Ghor eṣ Ṣâfia. In 14, 2. 8 its older name is given, בלע; cf. Wetz. in Del. *Gen.*, p. 564, and Di., p. 256, who remarks that the name was still in existence at the time of the Crusades (Segor; cf. LXX, Σηγώρ); the Arab geographers call it Soghar or Zoghar, and the Dead Sea, the Sea of Zoghar. Grove, however, in Smith's *Dict. of the Bible*, art. *Zoar*, brings forward evidence in favour of a site for Zoar on the north of the Dead Sea.

23. [1] הששמש . . . צערה. ' *The sun had risen over the earth when Lot came to Zoar;*' cf. 44, 3. 4 . . . הם יצאו העיר והוא יצא ועבדיו באו 24 ,3 .Judg ,ויוסף אמר; also 38, 25. Judg. 18, 3. Time or place determinations are generally subordinated to the main clause in a sentence; here and in the other instances cited, the time determination is co-ordinate, and placed first for emphasis; cf. Driver, § 169.

24. מאת יהוה מן השמים, the fire and brimstone are described as proceeding both *from Yahweh* and *out of heaven*, מן השמים and מאת יהוה; cf. 2 Kings 1, 12. Job 1, 16. Di. comparing Mic. 5, 6 supposes that מאת יהוה, like the Greek ἐκ Διός, was an archaic expression, similar in meaning to מן השמים, by which it is explained; cf. Ewald, *Hist. of Israel* (*Eng. Trans.*), ii. p. 157.

מאת = παρά with the genitive. מן = ἐκ.

25. ויהפך. מהפכה is a technical word, always used of the destruction of Sodom and Gomorrha (to which there is at least an allusion even in Is. 1, 7), just as מַבּוּל is always used of the great Deluge.

---

[1] Baer and Delitzsch's reading צֶרָה should be corrected into צֹעֲרָה: see *Jesaias*, p. v, note.

26. מֵאַחֲרָיו '*from behind him*,' i.e. Lot; she was follow-ing Lot, and out of curiosity turned her face away from him.

28. עָלָה is pluperfect, 'The smoke had begun to ascend before Abraham looked.'

כְּקִיטֹר הַכִּבְשָׁן. Cf. Ex. 19, 18: '*Like the smoke of a smelting furnace.*' כבשן = '*a smelting oven.*' תנור '*a baking oven.*'

29. בַּהֲפֹךְ אֶת הֶעָרִים. The inf. cstr. always governs its *object* in the accusative; cf. M. R., § 116; Ges., § 133. 1.

30. בַּמְּעָרָה. '*In the cave;*' either the generic article, as in 14, 13. 15, 11, or possibly a particular cave was meant, which the narrator could speak of as '*the cave;*' cf. 16, 7.

33. תִּשְׁקֶיןָ. *Scriptio defectiva* for תַּשְׁקֶינָה; cf. Ges., § 47. Rem. 3. This defective form is found occasionally, but by no means uniformly, in the Pent. It occurs also elsewhere, e.g. in Ezekiel תִּהְיֶיןָ four times, with the full form also four times.

בְּלַיְלָה הוּא. הוּא without the article—which would be expected, as לַיְלָה is defined—as being in itself definite; cf. 30, 16. 32, 23. 1 Sam. 19, 10 (all): see Ges., § 111. 2 b; M. R., § 85. Rem. c. This is a very rare variation for the more usual בְּלַיְלָה הַהוּא.

וּבְקוּמָהּ with a point on the ו; cf. ver. 35 בְּקֻמָהּ. Possibly the point refers to a various reading בְּקֻמָהּ, as in ver. 35. Hieron., *Quaest.*, ed. Lag., p. 30 (Appendix to the *Genesis Graece*), says: 'Denique Hebraei quod sequitur *et nesciuit cum dormisset cum ea et cum surrexisset ab eo* adpungunt desuper quasi incredibile et quod rerum natura non capiat coire quempiam nescientem;' cf. Strack, p. 88.

34. מִמָּחֳרָת. The ending ת, in this word is quite unique, and apparently without analogy; cf. Stade, § 308 d; Ges., § 80. Rem. 2 b, classes it among nouns with the bare fem.

ending ת֞, e.g. Canaanitish names of towns, cf. בַּעֲלָת, אֶפְרָת, חֲמָת, and other names such as תִּמְנָע, prob. abbreviated for תִּמְנָתָה, also נַחֲלָת, prob. for נַחֲלָתִי; cf. Stade, l. c. Olshausen, *Grammar*, § 38 c, explains the form by contraction out of מֵאָחֳרָה. Another explanation (cf. Levy, *Chald. W. B.*, i. p. 330) is that it is contracted out of יוֹם אַחֵר; cf. the Aramaic word יוֹמָחֳרָא=יוֹם חֲרָא.

36. מֵאֲבִיהֶן. מִן is used intentionally instead of לְ (38, 18 b), on account of the etymology in ver. 37; cf. vers. 32, 34.

37. מוֹאָב. LXX add the explanation, λέγουσα, Ἐκ τοῦ πατρός μου, i.e. מֵאָב '*from the father*' (like קַיִן, נֹחַ, not a strict etymology): another explanation is that the word is compounded of מֹ for מַי '*water*,'=מוֹי in Aramaic (cf. Is. 25, 10, and the prop. name מה דבא, Moab. Stone, l. 8=Biblical מֵי דִבֹא, see Schlottmann, *Siegessäule Mesa's*, Halle, 1870, p. 41; and מוֹפַעַת, Ktb., Jer. 48, 21; Kri, מֵיפַעַת (cf. 1 Chron. 6, 64), a town of the Levites, in the territory of Reuben, which afterwards belonged to Moab), and אָב, the meaning being then '*semen patris*.'

38. בֶּן־עַמִּי='*son of my people*,' after which the LXX insert, λέγουσα, Υἱὸς γένους μου. עַמּוֹן='*belonging to the people*' (abs. then concrete) bears the same relation to עַם as אַגְמוֹן to אֲגַם (Del.).

20.

1. אַרְצָה הַנֶּגֶב. '*To the land of the south*.' ה locative and the construct state; cf. Ges., § 90. 2 a; Stade, § 342 d: so Ex. 4, 20 אַרְצָה מִצְרַיִם; Gen. 43, 17 בֵּיתָה יוֹסֵף; Deut. 4, 41 מִזְרָחָה שָׁמֶשׁ; other instances in Genesis are (?) 24, 67. 28, 2. 46, 1.

גְּרָר, probably three hours south-east of Gaza, where

N

Rowlands found ruins bearing the name Chirbet-el-Gerâr;
on a broad and deep torrent, Ġurf-el-Ġerar, flowing from the
south-east; cf. Del., p. 344; Di., p. 262.

2. אֶל־שָׂרָה = '*concerning Sarah:*' so ver. 13 אמרי לי;
32, 30 לשׁמי; cf. Ob. 1, 1. Ps. 3, 3; see Ewald, § 217 c;
Ges., § 154. 3 e.

3. וְהוא בעלת בעל '*she being married;*' so Deut. 22,
22 אשׁה בעלת בעל; cf. Is. 62, 5.

4. הגוי גם צדיק. גם (emphasizing the following צדיק)=
ὅμως; cf. Ewald, § 354 a; Ges., § 155. 2 a: so ver. 5 והיא
ואחשׁך גם אנכי 6 ver. ,גם הוא.

6. מחטוֹ for מחטא, written according to the sound. Cf.
2 Kings 13, 6 הֶחֱטִי; Jer. 32, 35 החטי. The Kri gives the
ordinary form מחטא. Cf. Stade, § 143 e. 2, who regards it as
a mistake, like רָאוֹ for רָאה, יָצְתִי for יָצָאתִי, both written according to their pronunciation. Ges., § 75. 21 c, takes
חטו as an instance of a verb ל״א following the form of a verb
ל״ה, which is hardly correct, as then the form would be הַטוֹת.

לא נתתיך לנגע = '*I did not allow thee*' etc. '*To let,*' or
'*allow,*' is always expressed thus in Heb.; so 31, 7 ולא נתנו
אלהים להרע; Judg. 1, 34 כי לא נתנו לרדת; see Ges., § 142. 2.
foot-note 1.

7. נביא, as under God's protection; cf. Ps. 105, 15. נָבִיא
possibly comes from a root נבא = '*to express,*' '*announce*' (so
quite commonly in Assyrian). The original meaning of נביא
is *active*, not *passive*, '*the announcer, speaker,*' i. e. of God, or
of divine mysteries: the form being an intensive form of the
part. act.; cf. the Arabic نَبِيّ or نَبِيّ, a noun of the form
نَعِيل, with an active meaning like the Heb. חסיל. Cf. Wright,
Arab. Gram., i. p. 151, and Fleischer in Del., *Gen.⁴*, p. 551.
Bleck (*Einleitung⁴*, p. 306) thinks that נבא may be connected

with נבע='*ebullire*,' and so '*to pour forth words*,' '*to speak*,' נביא='*speaker*.' This however is doubtful, as נבא does not actually occur with the meaning '*gush up*.' See a good note on נביא in Robertson Smith (*Prophets*, p. 389 f.).

ותחיה. Cf. on 12, 2.

ואם אינך משיב. '*And if thou art not going to restore*;' the affirmative form would be אם ישך משיב; cf. 43, 5 ואם אינך משלח, neg.; and ver. 4 אם ישך משלח, affirmative. אין and יש are often used thus in hypothetical sentences.

9. מעשים אשר לא יעשו='*deeds which ought not to be done*;' cf. 4, 2 ואתה תמשל בו '*thou shouldest rule over him*;' 34, 7 וכן לא יעשה '*so it should not be done*;' Ex. 10, 26 מה נעבד '*how we ought to serve*;' see Driver, § 39 a; M.R., 7. 2 b.

10. מה ראית='*what hadst thou in view?*' so ראה in Ps. 66, 18 און אם ראיתי.

11. כי אמרתי, supply עשיתי from עשית in ver. 10 '(*I did it*) *because I thought*;' cf. 27, 20. 31, 31. Ex. 1, 19.

רק. Knobel and Del. render (I) '*surely*;' cf. Num. 20, 19 רק לשטף מים רבים; Ps. 32, 6 רק אין דבר. (II) Di. prefers to translate '*only*,' '*at least*,' not considering the two passages above cited decisive.

אין יראת . . . והרגוני. '*There is no fear of God in this place, and they will kill me*;' cf. 2 Sam. 14, 7 וכבו '*and they will quench*;' Gen. 34, 30 ואני מתי מספר ונאספו עלי.

12. '*And she is also really my sister, the daughter of my father, only not the daughter of my mother, so she became my wife*;' cf. on 12, 19. Such marriages, though prevalent among other nations, e. g. in Canaan, Assyria, Persia, Egypt, Arabia, were forbidden in the Levitical law, Lev. 18, 9. 11. 20, 17. Deut. 27, 22. From this passage it would seem that they were customary also among the Hebrews in pre-Mosaic times.

13. אלהים . . . התעו, marked by the Massoretes קרש, to shew that the true God is meant, although the verb is plural; possibly the plural here is used because Abraham was conversing with a heathen. Cf. 35, 7, where probably the angels are included under אלהים; see Ewald, § 318 a; Ges., § 146. 2. note. The Heb.-Samaritan text here, and 35, 7, read the singular. The later books of the Bible also avoid the plural; cf. Neh. 9, 18 with Ex. 32, 4.

16. אלף כסף = '*a thousand shekels of silver.*' שֶׁקֶל omitted (cf. 8, 5) by Ges., § 120. 4, 2.

The thousand shekels of silver could hardly be the value of the presents given to Abraham, ver. 14, for such a valuation of these gifts is here quite out of place; besides the present here mentioned is given to Abraham for Sarah, and on account of the insult she had suffered; whilst the one in ver. 14 was for Abraham himself.

הוא refers to the gift, not to Abraham; as in the latter case, no reason would be assigned for giving the thousand shekels.

לכל אשר אתך. The simplest way of taking these words seems to be Dillmann's. '*It is for thee, a covering of the eyes for all those who are with thee.*' לכל, introducing those whose eyes are to be covered, and לך being *dat. comm.* Del. renders, '*See, this may be unto thee a covering of the eyes* (i. e. a propitiation which makes *thee* blind to what has happened, and *this* as though it had not happened; cf. 32, 21) *to all who are in thy neighbourhood* (a propitiation, in regard to their mistress who had been insulted).' The propitiation being made first to Sarah, and then to those who were with her. But this would rather require וּלְכָל, which LXX read καὶ πάσαις. Knobel and Tuch adopt another rendering,

'*With regard to all that which has befallen thee;*' which is
forced and unnatural.

ואת כל is separated from אתך by the accents, and connected with ונכחת.   Render, '*And among all* (or "*in the
judgment of all,*" cf. Is. 59, 12) *so art thou justified.*' ואת כל
is taken by Tuch in close connection with אתך '*for all which
has happened (with) unto thee and (with) unto all.*' But ואת כל can
hardly mean this, and nothing had happened את כל '*with all.*'

ונכחת probably ought to be pointed וְנֹכַחְתְּ, which is
the usual form of the second pers. fem. perf. in a ל guttural
verb, as the ו is difficult before anything but a second perf.
To take the form נכחת as second perf., comparing לָקַחַתְּ,
30, 15, is unsafe, as לקחת there is probably infinitive.   Del.
takes נכחת as participle fem. standing for ונכחת את, and
renders, '*and with all justified,*' viz. '*thou standest justified.*'
The Mass. points seem to intend ונכחת as perf. third pers.
fem., which is pointed without shewa under the ת, to distinguish it from the second pers. fem. perf., which has shewa.
The rendering would then be, '*And with regard to all—so it
is settled;*' but then the feminine would not be necessary.

הוכיח='*to procure right for any one,*' so '*to justify, set
right;*' cf. Is. 11, 3. 4.   נכחת may here be either pass. of
הוכיח, with an acc. of the thing, Job 13, 15. 19, 5='*to
represent as right;*' or passive of הוכיח ל, Job 16, 21 '*to procure right for.*'   Ges. renders ונכחת '*and she stood reproved,*'
which is possible, but unsuitable, as Abimelech is not re-
proaching Sarah.   It is possible that the sentence is corrupt.

כסות עינים; cf. כפר פנים in 32, 21. Job 9, 24 פני שפטיה
יכסה, and כסה, Ps. 85, 3, of covering sin; כפר, Jer. 18, 23,
of atoning, lit. covering, guilt; cf. also 1 Sam. 12, 3 ואעלים
עיני בו (if the Mass. text is correct here, but see LXX, and

Thenius in loc.). The rendering of כסות by '*veil*' is unsuitable, and not supported by 12, 14. 24, 16. 29, 16. 17,
compared with 24, 65; as it is not certain from these passages
that women wore veils first when they were engaged (Tuch).
Besides, a thousand shekels would be rather a high price
to give for a veil, about £100. LXX have ταῦτα ἔσται σοι εἰς
τιμὴν τοῦ προσώπου σου, καὶ πάσαις ταῖς μετὰ σοῦ, καὶ πάντα
ἀλήθευσον: πάντα ἀλήθευσον being, perhaps, a guess on the
part of the translator, who misunderstood the original. Onq.
has: הָא הוּא לִיךְ כְּסוּת דִיקַר חֲלַף דִשְׁלַחְתִּית דְּבָרְתִּיךְ וַחֲזֵית יָתִיךְ וְיַת
אִיתוֹכָחַת דְאָמַרְתְּ מָא כָּל וְעַל דְעֵימִּיךְ כָּל ' *Behold, it is unto thee
for a covering of glory, because I sent (and) took thee, and saw
thee, and all that is with thee, and concerning all that thou hast
spoken, thou hast proved thyself right.*' The Syriac has:

'*Behold, I give a thousand of silver to thy brother, and behold
it is also given to thee, because thou hast covered the eyes of all
those who are with me, and concerning everything, thou hast
reproved me.*' Vulg. '*Ecce mille argenteos dedi fratri tuo ; hoc
erit tibi in velamen oculorum ad omnes qui tecum sunt, et quo-
cumque perrexeris: mementoque te deprehensam.*'

17. ואמהתיו possibly='*concubines ;*' שפחה then being
'*maid-servants.*'

וילדו='*they bare,*' masc. for fem.; cf. 30, 39; or as ילד is
also used of the male, e.g. Zech. 13, 3. Hos. 9, 16 '*they
begat,*' Abimelech being included in the subject.

21.

1. פקד. P uses זכר, not פקד; so 8, 1. 19, 29.

2. זקנים = '*old age.*' So—always in the plural—חיים

'*life;*' נְעוּרִים '*youth*' (all nouns denoting space of time); cf. שָׁמַיִם, צַוָּארִים, nouns denoting extension of space; see Ges., § 108. 2 a; Ewald, § 179 a; cf. § 178 a, b; Stade, § 324 b.

3. הַנּוֹלַד־לוֹ.   Participle Nif'. of יָלַד, with the qameç shortened into pathach, on account of the following maqqef. Others take it as perf. Nif'. with the article אֲשֶׁר נוֹלַד=הַנּוֹלַד; cf. on 18, 21.

יִצְחָק.   Other nouns (mostly proper names) formed after the analogy of the imperfect Qal are יַעֲקֹב, יִדְלָף, 22, 22, יְהוָה=יַהֲוֶה, יִבְשָׂם, יִדְבָּשׁ, according to the pointing usually adopted by modern scholars (see App. II).   יְקוּם and יְשִׁימָה (in בֵּית הַיְשִׁימוֹת) are abstract nouns of this form; cf. also יוֹנָה='*a dove*,' יַחְמוּר '*a stag;*' see Stade, § 259 a.

5. בְּהִוָּלֶד לוֹ.   On the construction, cf. on 4, 18.   בְּהִוָּלֶד is accented on the penult. to avoid the concurrence of two tone-syllables, this shortens the tsere in the last syllable into seghol; see Ges., § 29. 3 b; cf. on 4, 17.   Two tone-syllables may however come together, if the first word is separated from the second, by a distinctive accent.

6. '*And Sarah said, Laughter hath God prepared for me, every one who hears will laugh at me.*'

יִצְחַק לִי.   צחק with לְ='*to laugh at*' (as is clearly shown by Job 5, 22. 39, 7. 18. 22. Ps. 59, 9), here rather in astonishment than in derision.   A. V. '*will laugh with me;*' so VSS., but incorrectly.

יִצְחַק, with shewa resolved into hateph pathach; so even where no guttural follows, as Jer. 22, 15 הֲתִמְלֹךְ; Gen. 2, 12. 23.

7. מִי מִלֵּל וגו׳.   Render, '*Who could have said to Abraham?*'   '*The perfect is used in questions to express astonish-

ment at what appears to the speaker in the highest degree improbable,' Driver, § 19; cf. 1 Sam. 26, 9 ונקה . . . מי שלח;
Num. 23, 10 מי מנה עפר; Gen. 18, 12 היתה לי עדנה; see also
Ges., § 126. 5 a; M. R., § 3. 2. note a. LXX have ἀναγγελεῖ,
'*who shall say.*' Tuch renders, '*who says,*' which would rather
be יַגִּיד or יְמַלֵּל, admitting, however, that the perfect in interrogative sentences usually refers to a past act.

מלל is only found in Hebrew three times again, viz. in
Ps. 106, 2. Job 8, 2 and 33, 3. It is a common word in
Aramaic for the Heb. דִּבֶּר.

היניקה בנים. '*Sarah will suckle children:*' היניקה is
prophetic perfect, Driver, § 14; Ges., § 126. 4; M. R., § 3.
1 b; cf. Num. 24, 17 דרך כוכב; Is. 5, 13 לכן גלה עמי; Jer. 2,
26 כן הובישׁ בית ישׂראל; and often.

בנים is generic plural, as in Ex. 21, 22 . . . כי ינצו אנשׁים
ויצאו ילדיה; Is. 37, 3 כי באו בנים וגו׳.

8. ויגמל, pausal form, Ges., § 51. Rem. 2; Stade, § 504 b,
who gives other instances, viz. וַיָּאנַשׁ, וַיֹּאמַר, וַיִּנָּפַשׁ, וַיָּחָנַק.

9. מְצַחֵק. So Baer and Delitzsch, who compare Ex.
32, 6 לְצַחֵק, Deut. 32, 11 יְרַחֵף, where the ordinary editions
point (as they do here) with tsere; see Stade, § 88. 3 a.
מצחק (LXX παίζοντα, with the gloss μετὰ Ἰσαὰκ τοῦ υἱοῦ αὐτῆς;
so Vulg. '*ludentem cum Isaac filio suo*')='*playing, sporting;*'
cf. Ex. 32, 6. Judg. 16, 25: צחק in the Pi'el being always
used in a good sense. A. V. here and 39, 14 render צחק
by '*to mock;*' so Kimchi and some moderns, e. g. Baumgarten, Keil. Cf. Gal. 4, 29, where the apostle speaks of
Isaac and Ishmael, ὁ κατὰ σάρκα γεννηθεὶς ἐδίωκε τὸν κατὰ πνεῦμα.

11. על אודת = lit. '*on account of the circumstances,*' then
simply, '*on account of;*' 'a rare and antiquated form of expression' (Di.).

12. יִקְרָא לְךָ‎; cf. 48, 16 וַיִּקְרָא בָהֶם שְׁמִי‎. Render, ' *In*
(or *through*) *Isaac will a seed be called for thee,*' i. e. ' in the
line of Isaac will those descendants from thee come, who
shall bear thy name, and as such be heirs of the divine
promise, viz. the Israelites, who were the offspring of
Abraham, chosen by God,' Kn. in Dillmann ; cf. Rom. 9, 7.
Heb. 11, 18 ; see also 17, 21.

13. Construction as in 47, 21. 13, 15 ; cf. note on 13, 15,
also Ges., § 145. 2.

14. וְחֵמַת מַיִם‎. חֵמַת‎, cstr. state of חֵמֶת‎, a word which
only occurs in this chapter, perhaps so pointed (Tuch) to
distinguish it from חֵמָה‎ ' *anger.*'

שָׂם‎ is perfect, ' *he placed it,*' i. e. the skin of water. The
clause is a circumstantial clause, appended without any connecting particle ; cf. 44, 12 הֵחֵל‎ ; 48, 14 שִׂכֵּל‎ ; Judg. 6, 19
שָׂם‎ ; Driver, § 163 ; Ewald, § 346 a ; M. R., § 153.

וְאֶת הַיֶּלֶד‎ is acc. after וַיִּתֵּן‎, not שָׂם‎, which at any rate
would not suit the present narrative. LXX seem to have
read וַיָּשֶׂם עַל שִׁכְמָהּ אֶת הַיֶּלֶד‎, καὶ ἐπέθηκεν ἐπὶ τὸν ὦμον αὐτῆς τὸ
παιδίον, but badly, as Ishmael, cf. 17, 25, would be about
fourteen years old. Vulg. better, ' *tollens panem et utrem aquae,*
imposuit scapulae ejus, tradiditque puerum.'

וַתֵּתַע‎ is imperf. Qal apoc. from תעה‎. יִתְעֶה=יִתְעְ‎, then
with a helping vowel יִתַע‎, and lengthening hireq into tsere,
יִתֵּע‎ ; cf. Ges., § 75. Rem. 3 ; Driver, p. 60. foot-note 2 (where
the analogy between the apocopated forms of verbs ל״ה‎ and
the segholate nouns is noticed); Stade, § 545 d ; cf. § 489 b.

בְּמִדְבַּר בְּאֵר שֶׁבַע‎, i. e. the southern frontier of Canaan.

16. לָהּ‎ is ethic dative ; common with verbs of motion, esp.
in the imperative ; cf. לֶךְ לְךָ‎, 12, 1. 22, 2 ; לְכוּ לָכֶם‎, Josh. 22,
4 ; see M. R., § 51. 3. Rem. a. 3 ; Ewald, § 315 a.

הרחק וגו״=' *about a bow-shot off*,' lit. ' *distant like the shooters with the bow.*' הרחק is inf. abs.='*making far;*' cf. Ex. 33, 7. Josh. 3, 16; see Ewald, § 280 a; used here as an adverb (Ges., § 100. 2 d)='*at a distance.*'

מטחוי is participle plural, cstr. state, Pilel from טחה; cf. Ges., § 75. Rem. 18; Stade, § 155 b; also § 279, the word only occurs here.

אראה במות. ראה with ב, as in 44, 34; see Ges., § 154. 3 a. ad fin.

17. באשר הוא=אשר במקום, 2 Sam. 15, 21. Jer. 22, 12, and often.

18. החזיקי את ידך בו, lit.='*make fast thy hand on him,*' i.e.'take hold of him,'which is more commonly expressed without יד, החזיק ב.

19. באר מים ' *a spring of water.*' באר='*a spring,*' בור ' *a cistern for rain-water.*'

וַתַּשְׁקְ is apoc. imperf. Hif'. of שקה, without a helping vowel; cf. on ver. 15: so ותבך, ver. 16, apoc. imperf. Qal of בכה.

20. ויהי רבה קשת. Three renderings are given: (I) '*And he became, as he grew up, an archer;*' cf. Job 39, 4 (N.B. רבה=' *to become great,*' ' *gross werden;*' ורבו כמו רבו בבר Zech. 10, 8 יחלמו בניהם ירבו בבר; רבב='*to be great,*' '*gross sein*'); so Hieron., which is not necessarily excluded by ויגדל. (II) Del. renders, '*And he became a shooter, (viz.) a bow-man,*' קֶשֶׁת being a closer definition of רבה, and רבב=רבה (cf. 49, 23) and רמה (cf. Jer. 4, 29. Ps. 78, 9); cf. 13, 8. 1 Kings 1, 1; see Ges., § 113. (III) '*And he was growing up an archer,*' i.e. became every day a more skilful bow-man; cf. on 4, 17, which perhaps is not quite so natural as I or II. LXX render ἐγένετο δὲ τοξότης, but whether they read the text

רֹבֶה קַשָּׁת or קַשָּׁת, passing over רֹבֶה, is quite uncertain. The
Vulg. takes רבה='*juvenis*,' '*factusque est juvenis sagittarius.*'
Onq. has וַהֲוָה רָבְיָא קַשָּׁתָא, which probably ought to be
rendered, '*And the youth became an archer*' (רָבְיָא being
Onqelos' translation of הנער or הילד in vers. 8, 14, 15, 16, 17);
cf. Levy, *Chald. W. B.*, ii. pp. 395, 400. Di. adopts the
reading of Kn. רֹבֶה קַשָּׁת '*a shooter of the bow*,' '*a bow-man*;'
cf. the rendering of the LXX: but there seems to be no real
reason for altering the text. A passage somewhat similar to
this is 1 Kings 5, 29 נֹשֵׂא סַבָּל. The Itureans and Kedarenes,
both descendants of Ishmael, cf. 25, 13. 15, were celebrated
as bow-men; cf. Is. 21, 17.

21. במדבר פארן. The desert-plateau lying between the
Sinaitic peninsula, Idumea, and Canaan, bounded on the
south by Gebel-el-Fêh, west and north-west by Shur, north
by the wilderness of Sin, on the east by the Arábah and the
Elanitic Gulf.

22–34.

22. LXX have here and ver. 32, καὶ 'Οχοζὰθ ὁ νυμφαγωγὸς
αὐτοῦ, probably a gloss which has crept in from 26, 26.

23. '*And now swear unto me by God here, that thou wilt not
lie unto me or my offspring or offshoot.*'

הנה is not '*these things*,' but '*here*;' cf. 15, 16: properly
'*hither*' (German, *hier, hierher*).

ולניני ולנכדי, only Job 18, 19. Is. 14, 22: notice the
alliteration, and cf. on 18, 27. The two words always stand
together='*proles et soboles.*'

25. והוכח. Di. explains this on the ground that this
conversation took place before the actual swearing, but one
does not quite see why the writer should have used a perfect

with waw (apparently weak waw, as waw consecutive seems quite out of place here) to express this, and not the perfect separated from the waw by some intervening word; Driver, § 76. Obs.   The perfect here seems to be the same as והאמין in 15, 6; cf. the note there.

באר המים, on the article, cf. on 16, 7.

26. לא ... וגם ... לא ... וגם = 'neither ... nor;' cf. Num. 23, 25 גם קב לא תקבנו גם ברך לא תברכנו.

29. לְבַדְּנָה (for the form לְבַדְּהֶן=(לְבַדְּהֶן); cf. the rare forms כֻּלָּנָה, 42, 36; Prov. 31, 29, and כֻּלְהֵנָה, 1 Kings 7, 37; הנה, which as a separate pronoun is pointed הֵנָּה, being affixed; cf. Ges., § 91. 1. Rem. 2; Stade, § 352 b.

הֵנָּה, not 'here,' but as in 25, 16. Zech. 1, 9. 4, 5; cf. Driver, § 201. 3; Ges., § 121. 2, where the pronoun is described as a sort of substitute for the copula.

30. כי את שבע. כי, like the ὅτι recitantis in Greek, introduces the words of the speaker.

תהיה לי לעדה. תהיה does not refer to כבשׂות, but to the whole transaction, 'it shall be for a witness;' cf. Job 4, 5. Mic. 1, 9.

The number seven had for the ancients a special significance as the sacred number; cf. Ex. 37, 23. Lev. 4, 6; so solemn oaths were attested, either by the presence of seven witnesses (Her. iii. 8) or by the slaughter of seven animals, as here; cf. the word נִשְׁבַּע 'to swear,' probably a denom. from שֶׁבַע 'seven'='to use or call seven' (sich besiebenen), so the name באר שבע may mean 'well of seven,' or 'well of an oath,' שבע= שבועה; cf. the proper names יהושבע, אלישבע.

31. באר שבע is the modern Bir-es-Seba' (بير السبع), twelve hours distant from Hebron. Ruins are still to be seen

there, in the neighbourhood of which are two cisterns of excellent water.

33. אשל = 'tamarisk,' Arab. أَثْل. The renderings of the VSS., LXX ἄρουρα, Aq. δενδρών, Sym. φυτεία, Onq. נִיצְבָּא, were perhaps intentionally adopted for the same reason as מֵישָׁרָא in 12, 6 for אלון; see the note there, ad fin.

22.

2. את יחידך 'thine only one.' LXX τὸν ἀγαπητόν; cf. Prov. 4, 3, LXX. According to Frankel, *Einfluss*, p. 7, the rendering of the LXX was intentional, as Abraham had another son Ishmael. Isaac is called a בן יחיד, as the son of Abraham by his own wife Sarah, not as the only remaining son after Ishmael was sent away; all through the narrative Isaac and Ishmael are regarded by the writer as standing in a different relation to Abraham; cf. chap. 21 with chap. 16.

ארץ המריה. '*To the district of Moriah;*' cf. Num. 32, 1. Josh. 8, 1. 10, 41, where ארץ occurs again in the sense of '*district.*' מריה with the article (cf. העי '*Ai,*' הירדן '*Jordan,*' הלבנן '*Lebanon*') is the name of the hill on which in later times the temple stood, 2 Chron. 3, 1. Jos., *Ant.*, i. 13. 1 f. This is the view usually adopted by modern expositors, as Del., Di., but is not without difficulties; Moriah was the later name for the Temple hill; the common name in use at an earlier period being Sion, and the whole district around the hill being called 'the district of Moriah,' would presuppose that it was a well-known name. Tuch prefers the view that מריה here = the מורה in 12, 6, near Shechem, called Judg. 7, 1 גבעת המורה, on the ground of the LXX reading εἰς τὴν γῆν τὴν ὑψηλήν, and in 12, 6 τὴν δρῦν τὴν ὑψηλήν. But this Moreh was a place of no significance in the history of Israel, and too far from Beersheba to be reached in three days. Further, no great stress can be laid on the reading of the LXX either here or in 12, 6, their translation being probably a mere guess, as it can hardly be a rendering of the Hebrew text. The VSS. render variously, and throw no light on the question. Vulg. has '*terram visionis.*' Onq. לְאַרַע פּוּלְחָנָא '*land of worship.*' Syr. ܐܪܥ האמורי = ܠܘܟܐ ܕܐܡܘ̈ܪܝܐ, cf. their rendering of 2 Chron. 3, 1, '*land of the Amorites;*' also Geiger, *Urschrift*, p. 278.

הַמֹּרִיָּה. The derivation is unknown, but seems to have been connected by a *play* with ראה; cf. vers. 8 and 14. For derivations of the word that have been suggested, cf. Ges., *Thes.*, p. 819, also a note by Prof. Cheyne in the American Journal, *Hebraica*, April, 1885, p. 252. It cannot mean '*shown of Jah,*' which would be מָרְאֵיָה (cf. מַעֲשֵׂיָה).

4. בַּיּוֹם הַשְּׁלִישִׁי is connected by the LXX with וַיֵּלֶךְ in ver. 3, but incorrectly.

וַיִּשָּׂא is the imperf. with waw consec. after a time determination; cf. on 19, 15.

5. נֵלְכָה. Cohortative, expressing the intention more strongly than the simple imperf.; cf. Driver, § 49 a.

כֹּה has here a local force, as Gen. 31, 37 (rare).

7. הִנֵּנִי, also pointed הִנְנִי, and in pause הִנֵּנִי; cf. Dav., § 49; Ges., § 100. 5; Stade, § 380. The suffix is a verbal suffix here with the nun demonstrative; cf. Stade, § 359 b. 4.

8. אֱלֹהִים יִרְאֶה לּוֹ = '*God will provide him*' etc.; cf. 41, 33 וְעַתָּה יֵרֶא פַּרְעֹה; 1 Sam. 16, 1 כִּי רָאִיתִי בְּבָנָיו לִי, 17 רְאוּ נָא לִי אִישׁ.

12. '*And He said, Stretch not forth thine hand to the boy, and do not do anything to him; for now I know that thou art*

a fearer of God (cf. note on 4, 14); *for thou hast not withheld thy son, thine only one, from me.*'

ולא חשכת is almost=כי לא חשכת, which would be more emphatic: ‍ו‍ here expresses a consequence ; see M.R., § 148 c ; cf. its use in the waw conv. in 20, 12, '*and so she became my wife ;*' 23, 20 ; Driver, § 74.

מאומה from מאום '*a spot,*' '*a dot,*' then '*anything ;*' cf. the French *point.*

13. אַחַר. Sam., LXX, Targums, Pesh., forty-two Codices (Tuch and Wright) read אחד, i. e. '*a single ram,*' rams in ordinary cases going about in flocks (Tuch), which is preferred by some, e. g. Ewald, but which is not so probable, for אחד looks like an emendation of אחר, and אחר explains how it was that Abraham did not see the ram before. Geiger, *Urschrift,* p. 244, reads אֶחָר, regarding Isaac as the one lamb (das Opferlamm), and the ram caught in the thicket as '*the other :*' and thinks, that as this view was objectionable, the reading was corrected into אחד, which was again changed into אַחַר. This however is improbable. אחר is not *temporal,* but *local*='*behind ;*' cf. Ps. 68, 26 ; so תחת, as an adv., 49, 25, and a prep.: על, as an adv., 2 Sam. 23, 1, and a prep.

נֶאֱחַז. Perf., so Baer and Del., '*it was caught ;*' another reading is נֶאֱחָז, participle, '*caught ;*' so Theile.

בַּסְּבַך. So Baer and Del.; cf. וְזָהַב, 2, 12. Ordinary editions point בַּסְּבַךְ. Render, '*In a thicket.*'

14. יהוה יראה='*Yahweh sees,*' i. e. '*provides ;*' cf. ver. 8 ; so LXX, Κύριος εἶδεν.

אשר וגו'. '*So that* (cf. 13, 16) *it is said* (i. e. "*people are in the habit of saying*"), *In the mountain of the Lord provision shall be made.*'

יראה,='*provision shall be made*,' suits the context best; although the Nif'al has not elsewhere this meaning. Some render, '*On the mountain of Yahweh He* (*Yahweh*) *appears;*' but this is very awkward, and the point to be explained is not so much Yahweh's appearance (there was no real vision, only a voice from heaven) as the providing of a substitute, ver. 8. Di. renders according to Ewald (§ 332 d), '*On the mountain where Yahweh is seen,*' lit. '*On the mountain of Yahweh's appearing;*' cf. Hos. 1, 2. Ps. 4, 8, which however gives no suitable sense; as one cannot regard it as a proverb to say, '*On the mountain where Yahweh appeared,*' we should rather expect הר יי׳׳ יראה '*the mountain where Yahweh appeared:*' in either case the sentence is very incomplete. The sense '*provision shall be made*' seems least objectionable; as the Qal clearly means '*to provide,*' the Nif'al may be regarded as its passive, though no other instance of this use can be cited. The LXX, ἐν τῷ ὄρει Κύριος ὤφθη, would require בְּהַר יהוה יֵרָאֶה. The text would be easier of explanation if יֵרָאֶה at the end of the verse were pointed יִרְאֶה; so Vulgate.

16. כי introduces the contents of the oath; cf. 2 Sam. 3, 35. Jer. 22, 24.

17. וירש. The imperf. with simple waw used as a jussive, '*And may thy seed possess the gate of thy enemies;*' cf. 27, 29. 9, 27. 17, 2 ; Driver, § 134 : the ordinary construction would be the perfect with waw consec. וְיָרַשׁ ; cf. ver. 18, here possibly the imperf. with simple waw was chosen intentionally. וְיִרַשׁ would='*and thy seed shall,*' in continuation of ארבה.

20-24. A short notice of the families of Abraham's relatives in Mesopotamia, Nahor and Bethuel. It is probably inserted here, as Ribqah, Isaac's wife, was the daughter of Bethuel,

Nahor's son, Ribqah being specially noticed in ver. 23. The families here mentioned can only be partially identified.

21. עוץ. Cf. 10, 23, probably to be taken in a more limited sense here (Di.).

בוז is mentioned in Jer. 25, 23, together with Dedân and Têma, and so must be sought for in the neighbourhood of Edom. Elihu, Job's fourth adversary, was a Buzite, Job 32, 2. Del., *Par.*, p. 307, compares the land *Bâzu* mentioned in Asarhaddon's inscriptions.

קמואל אבי ארם. קמואל is otherwise unknown. In 10, 22 ארם is the son of Shem. Perhaps ארם here, as Di. suggests, was the name of a single people, ארם in 10, 22 being the name of a nation in a wider sense.

22. כשד. It is uncertain whether כשד is to be considered as the ancestor of the whole family of the כשדים, or of one tribe of the same, perhaps those who robbed Job of his camels, Job 1, 17 (Kn.).

חזו is very uncertain; the Arab geographers (cf. Di., p. 278) mention a خَزُ in Mesopotamia, between Nisibis and Râs 'Ain. An Assyrian *Chazu* is found on the inscriptions (cf. Del., *Par.*, p. 306 f.), but its position is uncertain.

פלדש is unknown; ידלף is also unknown; בתואל is unknown as the name of a place; in 25, 20. 28, 5 it is the proper name of a person.

24. ופילגשו, *casus pendens*, the narrative being resumed by waw conv., '*And his concubine, whose name was R'uma, she bare;*' cf. 30, 30. Is. 44, 12. Jer. 6, 19. Job 36, 7; Ewald, § 334 b; Driver, § 127 a; M. R., § 132 c.

פילגשו. פִּילֶגֶשׁ, also פִּלֶגֶשׁ, perhaps from פָּלַג '*to divide;*' the concubine dividing the married pair; for the שׁ added, cf.

the word חַרְמֵשׁ from חרם: the word has passed over from
the Semitic into Greek and Latin, πάλλαξ, *pellex*.

טבח, גחב, and תחשׁ are all equally unknown; מעכה
a town and district at the foot of mount Hermon, not far from
Geshur; cf. Deut. 3, 14. Josh. 12, 5. 2 Sam. 10, 6.

23.

1. שְׂנִי חיי שׂרה. The phrase שׁני חיי פ״ is only found
(in the Pent.) in P; so 25, 7. 47, 9. 28.

2. קרית ארבע. '*Arba city*,' so called perhaps from
Arba, one of the giants who formed the original inhabitants
of the land; cf. Josh. 14, 15. 15, 13. 21, 11. Others (Ewald,
etc.) explain it as='*Four town*,' which is improbable, and
contrary to Josh. 14, 15. 15, 13. In ver. 19 Mamre is identified with Hebron, and in 35, 27 the town is thrice named,
Mamre, Kiryath Arba, and Hebron; so that Mamre was
either another name of Hebron, or must have formed a portion of it, or have belonged to it. The LXX have an addition in their text, ἥ ἐστιν ἐν τῷ κοιλώματι, perhaps a marginal
gloss, occasioned by 37, 14 הברון מעמק. The Sam. also
insert אל עמק between ארבע and הוא.

לבכתה, with כף זעירא, '*small Caph*:' there seems to be
no reason for כ being written smaller than the other letters
here, see another instance 2, 4, and the note there; cf.
Strack, *Proleg.*, p. 92, who does not, however, mention this
passage or 2, 4.

3. מתו '*his dead*:' of common gender here, as in Lev.
21, 11. Num. 6, 6; contrast Zech. 11, 9 המתה '*the dying
one.*' The distinction of gender in the case of a dead person
being less regarded than in that of a living person (Del.);
cf. Ges., § 107. 1. note; M. R., § 62.

אל בני חת. בני חת is only found in P: in 14, 13 they are called Amorites, and in Judg. 1, 10 Canaanites.

4. Family graves were not uncommon among the people of high rank; cf. Judg. 8, 32. 2 Sam. 2, 32. 1 Kings 13, 30, and Is. 22, 16, where Shebna the scribe hews out of the rock a sepulchre for himself.

התושב is characteristic of P.

6. As לאמר לו is a very unusual phrase (לאמר אליהם is found once, Lev. 11, 1), Hitzig's conjecture לוּ שְׁמָעֵנוּ—which is adopted by most commentators, and brings the text here in accordance with ver. 13—seems preferable. So in ver. 15 we must read לוּ אֲדוֹנִי. לוּ then, here and ver. 13, will be followed by the imperative (cf. 17, 18 with the imperf.; 30, 34 with the jussive); cf. Ges., § 136. 2, '*Pray hear us.*' ' In accordance with the politeness which both parties endeavour to shew (Di.).' LXX and Sam. understand לו as = לֹא; then the text ought to be inverted אדני שמענו, as in ver. 11.

נשיא אלהים=' *a prince of God,*' i. e. belonging to God, under God's protection, and blessed by Him, or ' *a mighty prince;*' cf. Ps. 36, 7. 80, 11.

במבחר קברינו, lit.=' *in the choice of our sepulchres,*' i. e. ' *in our choicest sepulchre,*' cf. Is. 22, 7 מבחר עמקיך. The usual order of the words is here abandoned, the noun expressing the quality preceding, instead of following, the noun which it qualifies; cf. Ges., § 106. 1. Rem. 1.

יִכְלָא=יִכְלֶה, a verb ל״א following the conjugation of a verb ל״ה; cf. Ges., § 75. Rem. 21 c; Stade, § 143 e, note 1 a.

מקבר מתך; cf. on 16, 2 מלדת.

8. אם יש את נפשכם, lit.=' *if it is with your soul,*' i. e. ' *if it be your intention;*' cf. 2 Kings 10, 15. Job 10, 13. 23, 14.

9. הַמַּכְפֵּלָה. LXX, τὸ σπήλαιον τὸ διπλοῦν, Vulg. 'speluncam duplicem,' i.e. a cave with two entrances or two compartments, from the root כפל; but—as may be seen from vers. 17. 19 and 49, 30—המכפלה is a proper name.

בבסף מלא = 'for full money,' i.e. for its full value in money; cf. 1 Chron. 21, 22 תנה לי מקום הגרן . . . בכסף מלא, 24 לא כי קנה אקנה בכסף מלא.

10. לכל באי שער וגו'. Cf. on 9, 10 and Ewald, § 310 a. באי וגו' is the shorter form for באים ויוצאים. Render, ' With regard to all those entering the gate of his city,' i.e. ' his fellow-citizens.'

11. לא אדני שמעני. 'Nay, my lord, hear me.' Hitzig and Maurer read לא as לּוֹא=לּי; cf. vers. 13. 15, and see 1 Sam. 14, 30. 2 Sam. 18, 12, which is unnecessary, as לא suits the context better, Ephron refusing at first to receive anything for the field till Abraham presses it upon him. The same politeness and apparent unwillingness to sell anything, but rather to give it, still prevails in the east; cf. Del., Com., 4th ed., p. 553.

נתתי is perfect of certitude, often used in contracts or promises; cf. Ruth 4, 3 מברה נעמי ' No'omi is selling,' 1 Kings 3, 13 כי נתתי במדבר ; Is. 43, 20 גם אשר לא שאלת נתתי לך מים; cf. Driver, § 13; M. R., § 3. 1 a; Dav., § 46. 2. 3.

13. 'And he spake unto Ephron in the ears of the people of the land, saying, If only thou—pray hear me—I give the money for the field, take it from me, that I may bury my dead there.' The optative sentence beginning with אם is broken off, and continued with וֹל and the imperative. Olshausen supposes that some words have dropped out of the text after אתה. Hitzig ingeniously renders אִם אַתָּה, as perfect Qal of אות ' if thou art willing,' which is quite suitable; but the Qal of

אות occurs nowhere else, the verb being only found in the Nif'al; cf. 34, 15. LXX have ἐπειδὴ πρὸς ἐμοῦ εἶ, i. e. probably לי for לו; comp. 29, 34. 31, 5 (Driver).

15. Cf. on ver. 6. The LXX and Sam. have also read לא here.

16. עבר לסחר. '*Current with the merchants;*' the art. is according to Ges., § 109. 1; M. R., § 68; cf. the shorter phrase in 2 Kings 12, 5 כסף עבר '*current money,*' i. e. such as the merchants would accept. 'People had at that time no coins stamped by the State, but only bits of metal—which came into use through the requirements of trade—of a fixed weight, and possibly with the weight marked on them; these pieces were weighed to avoid any fraud,' Knobel, cited by Di., p. 281.

17. ויקם. '*So the field was ensured to Abraham;*' cf. Driver, § 74 a; M. R., § 18. Rem. a. קום in this sense occurs again in Lev. 25, 30. 27, 14. 17. 19. This use of קום is peculiar to P.

לפני ממרא=' *before,*' i. e. '*east of;*' so על פני in ver. 19; cf. 16, 12.

18. בכל באי וגו״. ב corresponds to ל in ver. 10; it is distributive here, as in 7, 21, which compare.

19. שדה המכפלה. מכפלה is only found in P; so again 25, 9. 49, 30. 50, 13.

ממרא הוא חברון. Observe that P never mentions the אלוני ממרא (13, 18. 14, 13. 18, 1), but calls the place ממרא; so 25, 9. 35, 27. 49, 30. 50, 13.

24.

2. זקן ביתו=' *the old one of his house,*' i. e. '*the oldest;*' so 42, 13 הקטן '*the young one,*' i. e. '*the youngest one;*' 2 Chron. 21, 17 קטן בניו '*his youngest son;*' cf. M. R.,

§ 81 b; Ges., § 119. 2. Probably Eliezer is the servant here intended. The Targ. Ps.-Jon. mentions him here expressly by name. Each large household had a servant of this sort; cf. Joseph in 39, 4. 22, also 43, 16. 44, 1 אשר על ביתו. At a later period the office was one of the important posts at court; cf. 1 Kings 4, 6. Is. 22, 15.

שׂים נא ידך תחת ירכי = '*place thy hand under my thigh*,' i.e. swear to me; cf. 47, 29, which is the only other passage where this mode of swearing is mentioned. Some (Tuch, Del.) see a reference to circumcision in these words. Others (Di.) explain—from 46, 25. Ex. 1, 5. Judg. 8, 30—the words symbolically, as invoking his descendants to maintain the oath and avenge any infraction of it; cf. Di., p. 284, who cites an instance of a similar form of oath among the Be-douins in Egypt; also the following extract from the *Journals of Expeditions in North-west and West Australia*, by George Grey, vol. ii, p. 342, London, 1841: 'Genesis, chap. 24, ver. 9,' after quoting the verse from the A. V. the writer continues, 'this is exactly the form that is observed in south-western Australia, when the natives swear amity to one another, or pledge themselves to aid one another in avenging a death. One native remains seated on the ground with his heels tucked under him in the eastern manner; the one who is about to narrate a death to him approaches slowly and with averted face, and seats himself cross-legged upon the thighs of the other; they are thus placed thigh to thigh, and squeezing their bodies together they place breast to breast— both then avert their faces, their eyes frequently fill with tears—no single word is spoken, and the one who is seated uppermost *places his hands under the thighs of his friend;* having remained thus seated for a minute or two, he rises up and withdraws to a little distance without speaking, but an inviolate pledge to avenge the death has by this ceremony passed between the two[1].' Ibn Ezra in his commentary on the passage has the following: שׁים נא ידך תחת ירכי. יש אמר רמז למילה ואילו היה כן היה נשבע בברית המילה לא בשם והקרוב אלי שׁהיה משפט בימים ההם לשׁום אדם ידו תחת ירך מי שׁהוא ברשׁותו והטעם אם אתה ברשׁותי שׁים נא ידך תחת ירכי והאדון יושׁב והירך על היד כטעם הנה ידי תחת רשׁותך לעשׁות רצונך וזה המשׁפט עדיין הוא בארץ הודו. ' *Some say this refers to circumcision; but if this were so, he would have sworn by the covenant of circumcision, and not by Jehovah. What appears most probable to me, is that it was a custom in those days for a man to place his hand under the thigh of him in whose service he was: the meaning would then be, " if thou art in my service, place thy hand, I pray, under my thigh;" the master would thus be sitting with his thigh on the (servant's) hand; the meaning being, " behold, my hand is under thy authority to do thy will;" and this custom still exists in India.'*

4. כִי='*but*,' after the negative; cf. Is. 48, 2 ; see Ewald, § 354 a (who compares the German *sondern* (not *aber*) after *nicht*), Ges., § 155. 1 e, ad fin. Fifteen MSS. and the Heb.-Sam. Codex read כִּי־אָם.

לִבְנִי לִיצחק. When the pr. name follows, the preposition must be repeated ; when it precedes, it only stands with the pr. name; cf. 22, 20 לִנחור אחיך ; see M. R., § 71. 1. Rem. a.

5. הֶהָשֵׁב. ה pointed with seghol before the guttural with qameç, Ges., § 100. 4 ; Dav., § 49. 2 d.

7. '*The God of the heavens who took me . . . may He (emphatic) send His angel before thee, and mayest thou,'* etc.

---

[1] For this reference I am indebted to Prof. Driver, who kindly sent me a note he had received on this verse from Dr. Tylor, the Reader in Anthropology at Oxford.

יִשְׁלַח . . . , וְלָקַחְתָּ. The perfect with waw conv. after the imperfect as a jussive; cf. 1, 14. 28, 3. 43, 14. 47, 29, and often; see Driver, § 113. 2 a, cf. § 111; M. R., § 24 b.

8. וְאִם לֹא תֹאבֶה . . . , וְנִקִּיתָ. 'But if she does not consent, then thou art free.' נִקִּיתָ for נָקִיתָ, Ges., § 75. Rem. 7: the tone does not advance with ו conv. as the verb is a ל״ה verb; cf. Stade, § 470 b. note.

מִשְּׁבֻעָתִי זֹאת. זֹאת without the article as regularly after a word with a pronom. affix; see Ewald, § 293 a; Ges., § 111. 2 b.

לֹא תֵשֵׁב. Cf. the note on 4, 12.

9. אֲדֹנָיו is *pluralis excellentiae*, referring to Abraham; see Ewald, § 178 b; Ges., § 108. 2 b; cf. Stade, § 324 a; so 40, 1 לַאֲדֹנֵיהֶם לְמֶלֶךְ, of Pharaoh; 42, 30 אֲדֹנֵי הָאָרֶץ, of Joseph.

10. כָּל טוּב אֲדֹנָיו. LXX, ἀπὸ πάντων τῶν ἀγαθῶν; so 45, 18 וְכָל טוּב אֶרֶץ מִצְרַיִם; 2 Kings 8, 9 אֶת טוּב אֶרֶץ דַּמֶּשֶׂק.

אֲרַם נַהֲרַיִם. 'Aram of the two rivers,' i.e. Mesopotamia, Deut. 23, 5. Judg. 3, 8. The two rivers are usually identified with the Euphrates and Tigris. Halévy, cited by Di., p. 285, takes them to be the Euphrates and Chrysorrhoas. Di. himself thinks that the Euphrates and Chaboras (חָבוֹר) are the two rivers intended.

11. אֶל בְּאֵר הַמָּיִם, i.e. the fountain that is usually to be found near a town; cf. Ex. 2, 15; see Ewald, § 277 a.

12. הַקְרֵה נָא. 'Pray cause it to meet me;' cf. 9, 22 for the omission of the acc., and the note there; see also 27, 20 כִּי הִקְרָה יְהוָה אֱלֹהֶיךָ לְפָנָי.

14. '*May it be that the damsel to whom I shall say, Pray*

*let down thy pitcher that I may drink, and she answer, Drink,
and I will also water thy camels; (may it be that) her thou
hast adjudged to thy servant Isaac, and thereby I shall know
that thou hast shewn my master kindness.'*

וְהָיָה is the perf. with waw conv., where no imperf.
precedes, used as a precative or mild imperative; cf. 47, 23
וירעתם את האדמה; Deut. 7, 9 וידעת; Driver, § 119 d.

וְאמרה . . . אשר אמר. ואמרה is perf. with waw
conv. after an imperf. with אשר; cf. ver. 43, where the relative is avoided; so Lev. 21, 10 אשר יוצק . . . ומלא; Is. 56, 4
אשר ישמרו ובחרו; Judg. 1, 12. 1 Sam. 17, 26; see Driver, § 115.

הנער . . . אשקה is a *casus pendens*, resumed in אֹתָהּ,
which stands before its verb for emphasis; cf. 28, 13. 26, 15;
Driver, § 197. 1.   The text is to be pointed הַנַּעַר, this word
being of common gender in the Pentateuch, also in Ruth 2,
21; cf. Ges., § 107. 1. note; Ewald, § 175 b; Stade, § 309 d,
who regards נער as 'a remnant of an older period of the
language, when the feminine ending did not exist.' The Kri
directs the ordinary form to be read.

בָהּ is not '*through her*,' Ribqah, but '*thereby;*' cf. 15, 8.

15. '*And it came to pass before he had done speaking, that,
behold, R. was coming out,*' etc. טרם כלה, the perf. after טרם is
very rare (Driver, p. 38. foot-note), contrast ver. 45 טרם
אכלה. The perfect after טרם is found again, 1 Sam. 3, 7
טרם ידע את יי" (if the punctuation is right), but immediately
afterwards וטרם יגלה; cf. בטרם, Ps. 90, 2 בטרם ילדו; Prov. 8,
25 בטרם הרים הטבעו; see Ewald, § 337. 3 c.

וכדה על שכמה. '*With her pitcher on her shoulder,*'
circ. clause.

16. טבת מראה. Cf. 12, 11 יפת מראה, and the note there.

בתולה='*a virgin*,' from בתל '*secludere*,' the maiden who

lives in seclusion in her parents' home. עלמה from עלם, Arab. غَلِمَ ' *to be strong,*' '*fully ripe,*'= the maiden who had reached a marriageable age, *puella nubilis.* In עלמה stress is laid on the fact that the maiden is of a marriageable age, in בתולה that she is a virgin; so here we have the addition ואיש לא ידעה.

19. עד אם כלו לשתת. ' *Until they shall have finished drinking,*' כלו being a future perfect; so עד אם דברתי, ver. 33. Is. 30, 17 עד אם נותרתם כתרן; and with the fuller phrase, עד אשר אם עשיתי, Gen. 28, 15 עד אשר אם; Num. 32, 17 עד אשר אם הביאנם; see Driver, § 17; M. R., § 3. 2; Ges., § 126. 5 c.

21. והאיש משתאה לה מחריש. ' *And the man was watching her in silence.*'

משתאה is the construct state before the preposition לה; cf. הוסי בו, Ps. 2, 12; יושבי בארץ, Is. 9, 1; משחרי לטרף, Job 24, 5; see Ewald, § 289 b; Ges., § 116. 1.

מחריש defines משתאה more clearly; cf. Num. 16, 27 בהנות ידיהם ורגליהם מקצצים היו מלקטים; Judg. 1, 7 יצאו נצבים; Jer. 41, 6 ויצא . . . הלך . . . ובכה; cf. Ewald, § 341 b. 3.

22. נזם is ' *a nose ring;*' cf. ver. 47, where על אפה is added; here the Sam. have וישם על אפה after משקלו, which Di. considers the original reading.

בקע is ' *a half-shekel,*' it occurs once again, Ex. 38, 26.

עשרה. שקל must be understood here, as in 20, 16.

23. בית אביך is acc. of place, as in 12, 15, which compare.

27. אנכי בדרך נחני וגו״. ' *As for me, in the way hath Y. guided me.*' אנכי, *casus pendens;* cf. 17, 4; see Driver, § 197. 4; M. R., § 129.

בדרך, i. e. without any mistakes, straight to the house of Bethuel; cf. ver. 48 בדרך אמת.

28. לבית אמה, i. e. to the female members of Bethuel's family. Ribqah, as a בתולה, would live apart from the men, among the females of the family.

29[b]. וירץ לבן . . . אל העין. Di. regards this half-verse as out of place here [er greift in unerträglicher (durch ver. 10 nicht zu rechtfertigender) Weise dem ver. 30 vor], having been placed here, instead of after ver. 30[a] (before ויבא), by a copyist's mistake. Knobel regards it as a duplette (i. e. the same thing narrated twice over); or in ver. 30, ויבא may be explained by Driver, § 76 γ, as giving a more detailed account of Laban's running.

30. כראת את הנזם. On the inf. cstr. without a subject, cf. M. R., §§ 111 b, 117; Ewald, § 304 a; 25, 26 בלדת אתם; 1 Sam. 18, 19 בעת תת את מרב; 2 Sam. 17, 19 באמר אלי כל היום. The Sam. read the more correct form כראתו 'when he saw.'

הנה עמד. הנה, placed before the participle, as in 38, 24 וגם הנה הרה; Is. 29, 8 והנה אכל, to arrest the attention and give more liveliness to the narrative; cf. Ewald, § 306 d; Driver, § 135. 3. Obs. 1.

31. '*And he said, Come in, blessed of the Lord, why dost thou stand without, seeing I have prepared my house, and a place for the camels?*' cf. ver. 56; Josh. 17, 14 ואני עם רב '*seeing I am a great people;*' Judg. 3, 26 והוא עבר '*he having passed;*' see Driver, § 160; M. R., § 152.

32. Laban is probably the subject to ויפתח and ויתן, as one can hardly suppose that Abraham's servant would be so inhospitably treated that he had to unsaddle his own camels. It would be easier if the text ran ויבא (instead of

וַיָּבֹא), which Dathe and Olsh. prefer, but this again would require אֶת הָאִישׁ instead of הָאִישׁ.

33. The Ktb. is וַיָּישֶׂם '*he* (*Laban*) *set*,' imperf. Qal of שׂוּם=יישׂם; cf. 50, 26 ויישׂם without Kri. The Kri here reads וַיֻּישַׂם '*and there was placed*,' impf. Hof‘al of שׂוּם, with pathach not qameç; see Baer and Del., *Genesis*, p. 77; Stade, § 500 γ, reads here וַיִּישֵׂם, the ordinary imperf. Qal of שׂוּם. Ewald, § 131 d, considers that the û of the passive here, 50, 26 and Ex. 30, 32 (ייסך from סוּך), has been sharpened into î.

38. אִם לֹא, prop.='*if not*,' after a negative '*but*;' cf. (possibly) Ez. 3, 6 אִם לֹא אֲלֵיהֶם שְׁלַחְתִּיךָ; cf. Ges., § 155. 2 f. אִם לֹא . . . תֵלֵךְ . . . וְלָקַחְתָּ, so Ez. 20, 33 f. לֹא . . . אֶמְלֹךְ . . . וְהוֹצֵאתִי . . . וְקִבַּצְתִּי; see Driver, § 115.

42–43. אִם יֶשְׁךָ . . . מַצְלִיחַ . . . וֹ . . . וְהָיָה; cf. Lev. 3, 7 אִם יֶשְׁךָ מוֹשִׁיעַ . . . . ; Judg. 6, 36 f. כְּשֵׁב הוּא מַקְרִיב . . . וְהִקְרִיב . . . וְיָדַעְתִּי; hypothetical sentences with a participle, with or without יֵשׁ or אֵין in the protasis, and the perfect with waw conv. in the apodosis; see Driver, § 137 a; Ewald, § 355 b. 1; M. R., § 166. 2; cf. ver. 49, where an imperative takes the place of the perfect with waw conv. in the apodosis.

46. וָאֶשְׁאַת· The short form of the first pers. sing. imperf. in ל"ה verbs is not quite so frequent as the long. Böttcher, cited by Prof. Driver (*Tenses*, p. 89. note), mentions forty-nine instances of the short form, and fifty-three of the long. In the other persons, on the contrary, the full form is very exceptional.

48. וָאֶשְׁתַּחֲוֶה here, and וָאֲצַוֶּה, Deut. 1, 16. 18, are the only instances of the first pers. with ה‑ in the Pentateuch; cf. Driver, p. 89. foot-note.

בְּדֶרֶךְ אֱמֶת '*in the right way*;' cf. ver. 27.

49. '*And now, if ye are going to deal kindly and straight-*

*forwardly with my master, tell me ; and if not, tell me ; that I
may turn to the right hand, or the left;'* cf. ver. 42 f. and the
authorities there cited.

55. ימים או עשור, lit.=‘*days or ten,*’ i.e. ‘*a week or
ten days;*’ cf. 4, 3 ויהי מקץ ימים; LXX, ἡμέρας ὡσεὶ δέκα. The
Syr. has ܬ݁ܰ ‘*a month in days,*’ Sam. ימים או חדש;
possibly, as Di. suggests, חדש has fallen out before ימים;
cf. 29, 14. עשור=*decas*, ‘*a space of ten days.*’

56. ויהוה הצליח דרכי. ‘*Seeing Yahweh hath pros-
pered my way;*’ cf. ver. 31.

57. ונשאלה את פיה. ‘*And let us ask her, herself,*’
lit. ‘*ask her mouth,*’ i.e. let her speak for herself; cf. Josh.
9, 14 ופי לא שאלו; ואת פי יהוה לא שאלו; Is. 30, 2.

62. ‘*Now Isaac had come;*’ בא is pluperf., accounting
for Isaac's presence when Ribqah arrived; cf. Driver, § 76.
Obs.

בא מבוא באר usually would mean, ‘*had come from
coming to the well,*’ etc., i.e. had returned from a journey
thither. But לֶכֶת is the more suitable word for a journey,
and what one would rather expect to find noticed is, where
he had come to, or where he was. Del. takes מבוא as a
correlative of לָבֹא, 35, 16, or לְבֹא, Num. 13, 21 and often,
and says ‘בא מבוא says more than בָּא מִבְּאֵר (Lagarde's
emendation for בָּא מִבֹּא בְאֵר), that he had come to the well,
but was not settled there, and now had come back from his
journey thither,’ which is much the same as the view first
mentioned. Houbigant reads מֵעָם for מבוא, Lagarde מִבְּאֵר;
but one does not see why the place where he came from
should be noted. Ewald, § 136 h, renders, ‘*er war eben
gekommen nach*’ (*he had just come to*), but how this can be got
out of the Heb. text is not quite clear. Di. offers two

solutions of the question; either (I) to strike out מבוא, or
(II) to read מדבר from the Samaritan and LXX, במדבר;
the meaning being in the second case, '*Isaac had come to the
wilderness of Beer-laḥayroi, for he lived in the south*' (circ.
clause, as in 19, 1).

63. לשׂוח variously rendered: I. '*To meditate,*' either over
his approaching marriage (Del.), or on matters connected
with his flocks (Tuch); so LXX, ἀδολεσχῆσαι, Vulg. '*ad
meditandum in agro;*' לְשִׂיחַ=לְשִׂיחַ in Ps. 119, 148; cf. 77, 4. 7.
II. The Targg. Sam. etc. render, '*to pray;*' cf. Ps. 102, 1
שִׂיחוֹ, with תפלה in the parallel member of the verse. III. Aq.
ὁμιλῆσαι and Sym. λαλῆσαι take לשׂוח as = '*to talk.*' IV. Knobel
and Ewald render, '*to wail* or *lament,*' comparing שִׂיחַ in Ps.
55, 3. 18. Job 7, 11, etc. (see ver. 67). V. Bött., *Neue Heb. Aehr.*,
renders, '*to fetch brushwood:*' the verb being a denom. from
שִׂיחַ, but this denom. cannot be proved to exist from other passages; cf. Ibn Ezra, ללכת בין השׂיחים '*to walk between the
shrubs.*' VI. Ges. reads לְשׂוט; cf. the Syr., which has
ܟܡܢܐ܂ܟܟܡ '*to walk,*' and ver. 65 ההלך בשׂדה. The renderings
I and IV seem better than the others, perhaps IV (cf.
ver. 67) fitting into the context a little better than I.

לפנות ערב, i.e. when the Oriental used to go out;
cf. 3, 8 לרוח היום.

64. ותפל מעל הגמל; so 2 Kings 5, 21 ויפל מעל המרכבה.
In Judg. 1, 14 (=Josh. 15, 18) we find צנח '*to spring quickly
from the camel.*' LXX here κατεπήδησεν.

65. מי האישׁ הלזה. '*Who is yonder man?*' cf. Ges.,
§ 34. Rem. 2; Dav., § 13; Stade, § 172 b. הלזה = the Arabic
الَّذِي = *who, which;* it occurs again, 37, 19.

67. האהלה שׂרה. אהל with the article and ה of
motion. The presence of the article before the noun, which

should be in the construct state, is explained by Ewald, § 290 d, Ges., § 110. 2 b, as a loose co-ordination of the two words, instead of the second being subordinate to the first; cf. Josh. 7, 21. Di. regards שרה אמו as inexplicable, and considers that they are a gloss to bring about a closer connection with chap. 23.

25.

1. אשה, not in the sense Sarah was, but a concubine; cf. ver. 6, where she is called a פלגש, and 1 Chron. 1, 32.

קטורה, pr. name = '*incense*.'

2. Many of the following tribes cannot be identified with certainty, as they have either disappeared at an early date, or become merged into other tribes. The genealogy occurs again in 1 Chron. 1, 32 ff. in an abbreviated form.

Keturah bare Abraham six sons (five if we regard מדן and מדין as one and the same).

זמרן, perhaps from זְמֵר, a species of '*antelope*.' Knobel compares זמרן with Ζαβράμ, the royal town of the Κιναιδο-κολπῖται, on the west of Mecca, on the Red Sea, mentioned in Ptol. vi. 7, 5, but whether they are identical is uncertain. Grotius and Del. consider the Zamareni of Pliny vi. 32 as more probable.

יקשן is identified by Tuch with יָקְטָן (10, 26); by Ewald with כּוּשָׁן, Hab. 3, 7; by Knobel with the Κασσανῖται of Ptol. vi. 7, 6, south of the Kinaedokolpites, on the Red Sea, but these are the Gassanides (cf. Del. here and Di.).

מדין and מדן, the best known of the sons of Keturah. מדינים and מדנים occur again in 37, 28. 36 as names of the same people, so that probably מדן and מדין are but different forms of the same name. The Midianites are often mentioned in the O. T.; in 37, 28. 36 they are spoken of as carrying on trade with Egypt. In Ex. 2 and 18 we find them dwelling in the Sinaitic peninsula, and in Num. 22, 4. 7. 25, 6. 17 f. 31, 1 ff. they are mentioned among Israel's enemies in the land east of the Jordan. In the time of the Judges (cf. Judg. 6 ff.) hordes of Midianites overran Palestine. They are also mentioned in Is. 60, 6 as a trading people. Their territory on the east of the Elanitic Gulf stretched from the neighbourhood of Sinai northwards to the territory of the Moabites; see further, Di., p. 291 f.

ישבק is unknown.

שוח is mentioned in Job 2, 11 as a tribe in the neighbourhood of the land of עוץ, but otherwise unknown. Del., *Par.*, p. 297 f., compares the Assyrian *Suchu*, on the right bank of the Euphrates, between the mouth of the Beliḥ and Chabor; Di., the Σαύη of Ptol. v. 19; cf. Di., l. c. Others (*H. W. B.*, 9th ed.) connect it with the Arab tribe سياحة, east of Aila.

3. On שבא and דדן, see 10, 7. Probably the northern branches of these two great Arab tribes are here meant, the genealogy in these verses being more limited in range than that in chap. 10 (Di.). Of the sons of Dedan nothing further is known; see conjectures in Di., p. 292; Del., p. 37².

4. עיפה occurs again in Is. 60, 6, mentioned with Midian as rich in camels, and as bringing gold and incense from Sheba. Del., *Par.*, p. 304, compares the *Ḥajápá* of the inscriptions. The other names do not occur elsewhere; see Di. l. c. for conjectures about them.

8. ושבע. Sam., LXX, ושבע ימים as in 35, 29.

ויאסף אל עמיו. '*And was gathered to his people;*' cf.

the synonymous expressions, בוא אל אבותיך, 15, 15; נאסף אל
אבותיו, Judg. 2, 10; and שכב עם אבותיך, Deut. 31, 16.   The
phrase נאסף אל עמיו is peculiar to P; so in 35, 29. 49, 33, etc.

10. השדה is in apposition to שדה עפרן in ver. 9.

שמה=not 'thither,' but, in a weaker sense, 'there;' so
Jer. 18, 2 אשר קטרו שם; ושמה אשמיעך את דברי 2 Kings 23, 8
שמה הכהנים; see Ges., § 90. 2 b.

13. בשמתם לתולדתם. 'With their names, according
to their genealogies.'   The two words are to be taken closely
together.

נבית the best known and most important of the descendants of Ishmael, '*the Nabatheans.*'   The Nabatheans dwelt
in Arabia Petrea.   In Is. 60, 7 they are mentioned with
Kedar; the two names also being found together on
the Assyrian inscriptions of Assurbanipal (Schr., *K. A. T.*[2],
p. 147).   Probably they are identical with the Nabataei
and Cedrei, mentioned together by Pliny, v. 12.   The
only other notices about נבית in the O. T. are that Esau
(28, 9. 36, 3) married Mahalath (called, 36, 3, Basemath),
the sister of Nebayoth, and Is. l. c., that they were rich in
cattle; see further, Di., p. 294.

קדר. '*The Kedarenes.*'   A nomad tribe in the Syro-
Arabian desert; they are frequently mentioned in the O. T.
in the time of the kings.   In Is. 21, 16 f. Jer. 49, 28 they
are mentioned as skilled bow-men; Song of Songs 1, 5, as
dwelling in black tents, but Is. 42, 11. Jer. 49, 31, in open
villages.   In Is. 60, 7. Jer. 49, 32 they are spoken of as rich
in camels and flocks; and in Ez. 27, 21 as trading with
Tyre.   The Rabbis use the name קדר for Arabia in general,
לשון קדר being the Arabic language.

אדבאל and מבשם are unknown names.

14. מִשְׁמָע is unknown.

דּוּמָה is probably different from the Duma of Is. 21, 11 and Josh. 15, 52. Wetzstein identifies דומה here with the Duma in East Haurân. Di. and Del. consider it to be the Δούμαθα of Steph. Byz., Domata of Pliny, vi. 32, the modern دومة الجندل = 'the rocky Duma,' in the lowest-lying district of the Syrian Nufûd land; the so-called Gôf (Del.), on the borders of Syria and Arabia.

מַשָּׂא, usually connected with the Μασανοί of Ptol. v. 19. 2, north-east of Duma. In Asurbanipal's inscriptions, Mas'u is found together with Nabaitai and Ḳidri (Schr., K. G. F., p. 102; K. A. T.², p. 148 f.).

15. חֲדַד is unknown. Baer and Del. read חדר, Theile חדר, with the marg. note, בכפרים אחרים חדד, i. e. 'in other copies חדר;' so 1 Chron. 1, 30, Sam., Joseph. The Massora mentions the reading here as being חדר, not חדר; cf. Baer and Del., Gen., p. 77 f.

תֵּימָא is identified by Wetzstein with Taimâ, three-quarters of an hour from Duma, in the Haurân; by Knobel with Θαμοί, Ptol. vi. 7. 17, on the Persian Gulf, or the Banu Taim (بنو تيم) also on the Persian Gulf; by Di. and Del. with תימא, a tribe mentioned in Jer. 25, 23. Job 6, 19, as traders (cf. Is. 21, 14)= تَيْمَاء, on the border of the Neǵd and the Syrian wilderness; also found on the inscriptions, together with the Mas'ai (Schr., K. G. F., p. 262 f.).

יְטוּר and נָפִישׁ are mentioned (1 Chron. 5, 18 ff.) as neighbours of the tribes east of the Jordan, who made war against them and partially subdued them; נפיש is otherwise unknown. יטור, 'the Itureans,' dwelt in the hill country of Lebanon and Haurân, according to Strabo; cf. Luke 3, 1.

קֵדְמָה, not mentioned elsewhere.

16. בחצריהם ובטירתם. '*In their villages, and in their encampments*,' i. e. who dwelt partly in unwalled villages (Lev. 25, 31. Is. 42, 11) and partly in moveable camps (Num. 31, 10. Ez. 25, 4). טירה is from טור, and means '*a camp*,' the tents being pitched in the form of a circle; cf. the modern دُوَّار (Burckh., *Bed.* 26, cited by Di., p. 297). LXX, ἐν ταῖς σκηναῖς αὐτῶν, καὶ ἐν ταῖς ἐπαύλεσιν αὐτῶν.

לאמתם. '*According to their tribes*.' אמה occurs again in Num. 25, 15, and—as here—is used of an Arab tribe: the word is more an Arabic than a Hebrew word, and its use here and Num. 25, 15 is perhaps, as Di. suggests, intentional. Ryssel, *De Eloh. Pent. sermone*, p. 71, says of אמה, 'quae vox ad sermonem populi Midianitici spectat (eodem sensu dictum atque apud Scotos *clan*, apud Arabes *gum*=قَوْم).'

18. חוילה. See 10, 29. It is not the Indian Ḥavila, but the land of the Χαυλοταῖοι (cf. خَوَيْلَة in Niebuhr, *Beschreibung von Arabien*, p. 342: Del.) of Strabo, xvi. 4. 2, between the Nabatheans and the Agroeans. Thus the Ishmaelites spread themselves over the country between the Persian Gulf to the wilderness of Shur, on the confines of Egypt.

שׁור . . . על פני מצרים. See on 16, 7.

באכה אשׁורה. '*In the direction of Ashur*.' באכה, cf. on 13, 10. אשׁורה is explained by Del. as meaning 'up to the lands under the Assyrian rule (bis nach den Länden assyrischer Herrschaft).' Nöldeke (*Unters.*, p. 26) considers that אשׁורה is the name of an Egyptian place, which has been corrupted in the Heb. text. According to Hupfeld it has arisen out of באכה שׁורה (1 Sam. 15, 7) by corruption. Wel. and Del. (*Par.*, p. 131) think that it is an instance of dittography for עד שׁור.

עַל פְּנֵי =‘ *east of;*’ cf. 16, 12.

נפל =‘ *settled;*’ in 16, 12 שׁכן is used of Ishmael; cf.
Judg. 7, 12 וכל בני קדם נפלים בעמק.

19–34.

20. פדן ארם=שׂדה ארם in Hos. 12, 13, ‘*Mesopotamia.*’
‘פדן in Aramaic=“*a yoke,*” and in Arabic (where it is a
Nabathean foreign word, *Gawaliqi*, 112. 2) = “*ploughing
oxen,*” and then their “*plough,*” so a fixed measure of land,
like *jugum, jugerum* (Lane, p. 2353), and is regarded by
Lagarde (*Proph. Chald.*, p. xliii) as Persian. But II. Raw.,
62. 33, *padanu* (which as *padánu* means elsewhere, according to Schrader, *K. A. T.*², p. 612, “*way, path*”) is equivalent
to *ginú* (*garden*) and *iklu* (*field*), (compare Del., *Par.*, p.
135), and so it might have meant “*field*” or “*plain*” in
Assyrian (cf. فَدَن “ *depression, plain,*” Ges., *Thes.*, p. 1092),’
Di. It is most probable that שׂדה ארם in Hos. l. c. is the
Hebrew translation of the word. In 24, 10 we have ארם
נהרים for פדן ארם (P). The LXX and Vulg. render it
Mesopotamia Syriae or *Mesopotamia;* cf. the *campos Meso-
potamiae* in Curt. iii. 2. 3; v. 1. 15. From this it by no
means follows that the two ideas are completely identical,
still less that Paddan Aram was the district round Ḥarran.
‘Still it is worth noticing that the name פדן (cf. 48, 7)
attaches to a place *Faddán*, and a *Tell Faddán*, in the neighbourhood of Ḥarran, which Jâqût still knows of (Chwolsohn,
Ssab., i. 304; *Marás.*, ii. 337). That the neighbourhood of
Edessa and Ḥarran is a plain surrounded by mountains is
evident from Edrisi p. Jaub. ii. 153; Wilh. of Tyrus, 10. 29.
Buck, *Mesopotamia*, 111,’ (Kn. in Di.)   פדן ארם is only
found in P as the name of Mesopotamia; so 28, 2. 6 f. 31, 18.
33, 18. 35, 9. 26. 46, 15.

21. ‏ויעתר לו יהוה‏, lit. '*suffered himself to be prayed to*,' i.e. '*hearkened to him*.' The Nif'al *tolerativum*; cf. Is. 53, 7 ‏והוא נענה‏; and Cheyne's crit. note, ad loc.

22. ‏ויתרצצו‏ is imperf. Hithpo'. of ‏רצץ‏; see Ges., § 55. 1; Stade, § 532 a. γ; cf. ‏יתגדדו‏ from ‏גדד‏, ‏יתהללו‏ from ‏הלל‏.

‏אם כן למה זה וגו׳‏ = '*if thus, why am I?*' i.e. '*if it be thus, why do I live?*' cf. ‏למה לי חיים‏ in 27, 46; so the Syriac. The LXX, εἰ οὕτω [μοι μέλλει γίνεσθαι], ἵνα τί μοι τοῦτο; and so Vulg.; hence it has been rendered, '*if it be so, why am I thus?*' i.e. pregnant; but ‏זֶה‏ cannot be predicate, as the LXX have taken it; ‏זֶה‏ merely strengthens the ‏למה‏, as in 18, 13.

23. (α) '*Two nations are in thy womb,*
    (β) *And two peoples shall separate themselves from thy lap:*
    (α) *And one people shall overpower the other,*
    (β) *And the elder shall serve the younger.*'

The answer given to Ribqah's prayer is poetical in form. ‏רב‏ and ‏צעיר‏ in prose would require the article; cf. Ewald, § 294 a.

‏לאם מלאם‏. On ‏מן‏ used in comparison, cf. Ges., § 119. 1; M. R., § 49. 2.

24. ‏וימלאו ימיה‏. '*And her days were full;*' so 29, 21. 50, 3.

‏תומם‏ is contracted from ‏תְּאֹמִים‏.

25. ‏אדמוני‏, probably referring to the colour of his skin, rather than the hair; cf. David in 1 Sam. 16, 12. 17, 42. 19, 13.

‏עשׂו‏. '*Esau*' = '*hairy one*.'

26. ‏יעקב‏ the author takes from ‏עָקַב‏, a denom. of ‏עָקֵב‏ '*heel,*' = '*heel-holder;*' cf. Hos. 12, 4. Reuss, *Gesch. des A. T.*, p. 52, explains Jacob as = '*successor*.' In 27, 36 another explanation is given; see the note there.

בלרת אתם; cf. on 24, 30.

27. ידע ציד. 'ציד is acc. after ידע, not gen., for then ידַע would be necessary,' Wright: the form ידַע, however, does not occur in the O. T. Cf. 2 Chron. 2, 11 ידֵעַ שֹׂכל וּבינה; Ps. 44, 22 ידַע תעלומות לב, which are parallel to this passage. The pl. cstr. is used in 1 Kings 9, 27. Amos 5, 16.

איש שדה='*a field man,*' one who spends his time in the fields hunting; but איש האדמה, 9, 20,='*an agriculturist.*'

איש תם. '*A quiet, domestic man.*' '*An upright man*' does not suit the context here, and hardly fits in with the later accounts of Jacob's dealings with his brother. Elsewhere תם always='*upright,*' except Ex. 26, 24. תם is here the German '*fromm,*' which also means *ruhig (quiet),* thus 'ein frommes Pferd,' *a quiet horse.*

אהָלִים for אֱהָלִים; see Ges., § 23. 3. Rem. 2; Stade, § 109.

28. כי ציד בפיו. '*For venison was in his mouth,*' i.e. was according to his taste; cf. 27, 5. 7.

30. מן האדם האדם הזה. '*From the red (stuff), this red stuff;*' the words האדם הזה being epexegetical; cf. M. R., § 72. 3.

31. מכרה כיום. '*Sell now first of all*' etc.; see M. R., § 56. 2. Rem. a, who points out the different shades of meaning in כיום and כְּהַיום.

32. הנה אנכי הולך למות. '*Behold, I am going to die,*' i.e. Esau's life was a dangerous one, and he might meet his death at any moment. Tuch prefers the rendering, '*I am at the point of death,*' i.e. from hunger, which is not so natural (so A. V. and A. V. R.), and would be better expressed by הנני מת.

26

3. את ׳כל הארצת האל, i. e. Canaan and the adjoining districts, ארצת being used of the different portions of what was afterwards the land of Israel, as in 1 Chron. 13, 2. 2 Chron. 11, 23. האל, cf. note on 19, 8.

7. לאשתו = '*concerning his wife;*' cf. 32, 30 למה זה תשאל לשמי '*why dost thou then ask about my name?*' 43, 7 שאול שאל האיש לנו ולמולדתנו '*the man asked indeed about us and about our birth-place.*'

8. מיצחק את רבקה. '*Sporting with R.*' צחק את = צחק עם, of mutual playing or caressing, and so distinct from צחק ב, where the action is not mutual; see 39, 14 (Luzz. cited by Del.).

10. כמעט שכב אחד העם וגו״. '*One of the people might have lain with her, and so thou hadst brought*' etc., lit. '*almost had one of the people;*' cf. Ps. 119, 87 כמעט כלוני בארץ; Prov. 5, 14 כמעט הייתי. והבאת is the perf. with waw conv., after כמעט; cf. Driver, § 115, p. 160: the tone being thrown forward on to the last syllable. Del., p. 385, explains the position of the tone on והבאת as due to the ע following, which would otherwise be scarcely audible, comparing Is. 11, 2 וְנָחָה (where, however, the tone on the last syllable may be due to the waw conv.; cf. Driver, § 110. 5). See also ver. 22 רבו עליה, and cf. Ewald, §§ 63 c, 193 b.

12. מאה שערים. '*A hundred measures,*' '*a hundred-fold.*' שער in Biblical Hebrew does not occur again in this sense. In Aramaic and the language of the Mishna, שֵׁעֵר, Pa'el of שָׁעַר = '*to reckon, estimate*' (cf. Targ. Onq. here,

עַל חַד מְאָה בְּדְשַׁעֲרוּהִי = '*the hundredfold of that which they had estimated it (the field)*;' cf. Levy, *Chald. W. B.*, ii. p. 504), and שַׂערא subst. = '*interest, price;*' see Levy, l. c., and cf. the Arabic سِعْر '*pretium annonae.*' LXX and Syr. incorrectly read שְׂעֹרים '*barley.*' 'A hundred measures' would imply that the harvest was very abundant. The neighbourhood of Gerar was very fruitful, and at the present day the Arabs have grain magazines at Nuttâr Abu Sumâr, a little north-west of Elusa; Rob., *Pal.*, i. p. 562.

13. הלוך וגדל. Cf. the note on 8, 3. גדל, the participle, here takes the place of the more common inf. abs.; so Judg. 4, 24 וַתֵּלֶךְ יד בני ישראל הלוך וְקָשָׁה; 2 Sam. 16, 5. 18, 25 וילך; הלוך וקרב; cf. Ewald, § 280 b; M. R., § 108. וְגָדֵל, however, may be perfect, cf. Josh. 6, 13. Is. 31, 5; see Ges., § 131. 3. Rem. 3.

14. עבדה occurs once again in Job 1, 3; cf. the N. T. θεραπεία, Matt. 24, 45, and see Ges., *Thes.*, sub voce.

15. סתמום . . . וימלאום. Notice the masc. suffixes referring to feminine nouns; so ver. 18. 31, 9. 32, 16. 33, 13. 41, 23; see Ewald, § 249 b; Ges., § 121. 6. Rem. 1.

וימלאום with double acc., according to Ges., § 139. 2; M. R., § 45. 2.

18. בימי אברהם. LXX, οἱ παῖδες; so Sam. and Vulg., reading עבדי, possibly from עבדי יצחק in ver. 19.

ויסתמום is imperf. with waw conv. in continuation of חפרו.

19. מים חיים. '*Living*, i. e. *flowing water*,' as contrasted with still water; so Lev. 14, 5. Jer. 2, 13.

20. עֵשֶׂק = '*strife;*' the word only occurs here.

21. שטנה = '*hostility.*'

22. רחבות=' *wide spaces.*' Probably the modern Ruḥaibe, about three hours south-east of Elusa, eight hours south of Beersheba, where remains of fountains are still to be found: cf. Robins, i. p. 289 ff.

כי, not =ὅτι *recitativum*, but as in 29, 32. 33. Ex. 3, 12, affirmative, '*surely*,' '*indeed.*'

ופרינו is perf. with waw conv. without a preceding imperf.; cf. 17, 4; Driver, § 119 a; M. R., § 24. 2 b.

26. ואחזת מרעהו. אחזת is a pr. n. with the fem. ending ת‗, like גָּלְיַת, בְּשֹׁמַת, ver. 34; מְחֲלַת, 28, 9: so LXX, Syr., Vulg., Saad. Onq., who renders וְסִיעַת רַחְמוֹהִי, Berl. (some texts מֵרַחֲמוֹהִי), seems to have taken אחזת as fem. cons. state of אחזה, in the sense of '*a troop*,' '*crowd*,' a meaning אחזה never has: and מרעהו as compounded of מן and רע (if we follow the reading מֵרֲחֲמוֹהִי, and not Berliner's רֲחְמוֹהִי). מרעהו, only here in the Pentateuch, ='*friend*,' '*confidant*,' one who advised him, and rendered him other services; cf. 1 Kings 4, 5. 1 Chron. 27, 33. מֵרֵעֵהוּ has a firm unchange-able tsere in the first syllable. The LXX translate מרעהו by νυμφαγωγός; supposing that to be the capacity in which he acted as his '*friend*;' cf. Judg. 14, 20, LXX. Translate,'*With Ahuzzath, his counsellor.*'

27. ואתם וגו׳. Render, '*Seeing that* (or *since*) *ye hated me, and sent me away from you.*'

28. רָאוֹ, inf. abs. Qal of ראה for רָאֹה; so שָׁתוֹ, Is. 22, 13; and see Ges., § 75. Rem. 2.

אלה = here a compact ratified by a solemn oath; so Deut. 29, 11. Ez. 16, 59.

29. תעשה is pointed with tsere, instead of seghol, under

the ה; so in three other places, Josh. 7, 9. 2 Sam. 13, 12. Jer. 40, 16 (Kri). In the last two instances and here, 'in order to avoid, by emphasizing the final sound of the first word, any confusion in sound with the initial sound of the next' (Del.). Cf. also Ges., § 75. Rem. 17; Stade, § 143 e. Rem. 3, who gives other instances, e. g. Josh. 9, 24 וַתַּעֲשֶׂה; Lev. 5, 9 יִמָּצֶה; Nah. 1, 3 יְנַקֶּה (but not Baer and Del. in their edition, who point יְנַקֶּה with seghol).

רק טוב. 'Only good,' 'nothing but good;' cf. 6, 5 רק רע; Deut. 28, 33 רק עשוק ורצוץ.

31. איש לאחיו. Cf. the note on 13, 11.

33. שבעה = 'oath.' The author takes it as equivalent to שְׁבֻעָה. The word is a ἅπαξ λεγόμ. In 21, 31 another account of the origin of the name Beersheba is given.

34. Cf. 36, 2 foll.

35. וַתִּהְיֶין scriptio defectiva, for וַתִּהְיֶינָה; cf. 19, 33 וַתִּשְׁקֶין; 27, 1 וַתִּכְהֶין.

מרת רוח, cf. Prov. 14, 10 מרת נפשו, = 'bitterness of spirit.' LXX, ἦσαν ἐρίζουσαι, but incorrectly; so Onq. וַהֲוָאָה מְסָרְבָן וּמַרְגְּזָן = 'they were disobedient and provoking to anger' etc.; taking it from מָרָה = 'to rebel.'

27.

1. מראת = lit. 'away from seeing,' i. e. 'so that he could not see;' cf. 23, 6 and the note on 16, 2.

3. תליך. תְּלִי, a ἅπαξ λεγόμ., is from תָּלָה 'to hang;' just as כְּלִי is from כָּלָה, דְּלִי from דָּלָה. The LXX, Vulg., Targ. Ps.-Jon., Ibn Ezra, etc. render 'quiver.' Onq., Pesh., Rashi, 'sword.' The former rendering is preferable, being more in

accordance with the context (bow and quiver are more naturally mentioned together than bow and sword); cf. Is. 7, 24. 2 Kings 13, 15: and the root תלה, '*to hang*,' suits the rendering '*quiver*' better than '*sword*;' as a sword would be girded on, while a quiver was hung on the shoulders. תליך = the later word אשפה, which occurs first in Is. 22, 6.

צידה. The Ktb. is צֵידָה, feminine of צַיִד; being what is called by the Arab grammarians a *nomen unitatis*, meaning '*a single head of game*;' while ציד would be '*game*' in general; cf. Wright, *Arab. Gram.*, i. § 246; see also Ges., § 107. 3 e; Ewald, § 176 a. The Kri is צַיִד (ה יתיר, ה *is redundant*), which was probably chosen by the Massoretes, as צידה usually means '*provisions for a journey*,' e. g. 42, 25. 45, 21; or they might have pointed it צַיִד here, as this word stands again so pointed in vers. 5, 7, 33. צידה, '*a single head of game*,' is quite suitable here—as Isaac would not require more—and is in no wise against vers. 5, 7, 33.

4. והביאה לי ואכלה. '*And bring it to me, and let me eat*,' i. e. '*and bring it to me that I may eat*;' see Driver, § 60; Dav., § 23, p. 61; Ges., § 128. 1 c.

5. להביא. LXX read לאביו, τῷ πατρὶ αὐτοῦ; but להביא is justified by vers. 4 and 7.

6. אל יעקב בנה. '*To Jacob her son*,' i. e. her favourite child, Esau being the father's favourite; cf. 25, 28. The LXX, however, have τὸν υἱὸν αὐτῆς τὸν ἐλάσσω, reading בנה הקטן, cf. vers. 15, 42, perhaps on account of Esau's being called בנו הגדול in ver. 1; cf. ver. 42.

8. לאשר אני מצוה אתך = '*in regard to that which I am charging thee*;' so 17, 20 ולישמעאל '*and with regard to Ishmael*;' cf. M. R., § 51. 5. Rem. b.   אשר includes the demonstrative pronoun; cf. Ges., § 123. 2.

9. גְּדָיֵי. So לְחָיֵי: the pretonic ◌ָ in the construct state is unusual; cf. Stade, § 332 d. 2; Ewald, § 212 b.

וְאֶעֱשֶׂה אֹתָם מַטְעַמִּים. 'That I may make them [into] dainty dishes.' עָשָׂה with a double acc., according to Ges., § 139. 2; M. R., § 45. 5.

12. 'Perchance my father will feel me, and I shall be as one that mocks in his sight,' etc.; cf. Driver, § 115.

מְתַעְתֵּעַ is part. Pilpel, from תעע; cf. Ges., § 55. 4; Stade, § 281. תעע, like the Arab. نَغَثَ, means 'to stammer,' 'stutter,' and then 'to mock;' cf. לוּץ and לָעַג.

13. קִלְלָתְךָ. 'Thy curse,' i. e. the curse that shall come upon thee; cf. the note on 9, 2.

15. הַחֲמֻדֹת=lit. 'costlinesses,' 'costly things,' 'desiderabilia,' so בִּגְדֵי must be understood before it. Esau's best clothes are intended, which he wore on any festive occasions; cf. Judg. 14, 12 ff.

20. מַה זֶּה מִהַרְתָּ לִמְצֹא. 'How then hast thou found it so quickly?' lit. 'how then hast thou made haste to find it?' cf. Ges., § 142. 2; M. R., § 113. מִהַרְתָּ corresponds to the adverb in English.

24. וַיֹּאמֶר is really in point of time before וַיְבָרֲכֵהוּ in ver. 23. In ver. 23 the transaction is briefly described by the single word וַיְבָרֲכֵהוּ, the particulars of the blessing being added by ו conv.; cf. Driver, § 75 β; so in 37, 6. 42, 21 ff. 45, 21–24. 48, 17.

אַתָּה זֶה בְּנִי עֵשָׂו. 'Thou art then my son Esau,' = 'art thou then my son Esau?' An interrogative sentence without the interrogative particle ה; cf. 2 Kings 20, 9. Job 38, 18; Ewald, § 324 a; Ges., § 153. 1. זֶה is added to give emphasis to the question.

26. וְיֵשְׁתְּ. Cf. on 2, 12.

27ᵇ–29 are the words of the blessing. The blessing is poetical in form : observe the parallelism in the verses, and the poetical words and forms, e. g. רָאָה for הִנֵּה, שְׁמַנֵּי הָאָרֶץ, הֱוֵה for הָיָה, לְאֻמִּים, גְּבִיר.

> 27ᵇ. ‘ *Behold, the smell of my son is as the smell of a field which Yahweh has blessed:*
>
> 28. (α) *And may God give thee of the dew of the heavens, and of the fatnesses of the earth,*
>
> (β) *And abundance of corn and wine.*
>
> 29. (α) *May nations serve thee, and peoples bow down to thee; Be a prince over thy brethren, and may thy mother's sons bow down to thee :*
>
> (β) *Cursed be those that curse thee, And blessed be those that bless thee.’*

28. מִשְׁמַנֵּי, the שׁ is undageshed (cf. מִשְׁתִּים, Jon. 4, 11 ; מִגְּבוּרָתָם, Ez. 32, 30), as it is pointed with shewa. The word is compounded of מִן partitive, and שְׁמַנֵּי, corresponding to מִטַּל just before. שְׁמַנֵּי is plural cstr. from שָׁמָן, like קְטַנִּים from קָטָן, גְּמַלִּים from גָּמָל, not from שָׁמֵן. The A. V. takes it as pl. of מִשְׁמָן, but the sense and the parallelism are against this. On כְּ part., see on 4, 3, and cf. 28, 11. 30, 14. Cf. the rendering of the A. V. R. in these verses. On the great fertility of the land of Canaan, cf. Ex. 3, 8. The dew is here mentioned instead of the rain ; as in summer, in Palestine, there is very little rain, and the dew takes its place ; cf. 49, 25. Deut. 33, 13. Hos. 14, 6. Zech. 8, 12.

תִּירֹשׁ from יָרֹשׁ ‘ *to take possession;*’ so called as taking possession of the head or mind; cf. Hos. 4, 11.

29. וְיִשְׁתַּחוּ Ktb.; Kri וְיִשְׁתַּחֲוּ. The Kri is preferable, as the plural precedes (יַעַבְדוּךָ). The Ktb. is possibly—as in 43, 28—an incorrect way of writing the word. The sing. might perhaps stand by Ewald, § 316 a; Ges., § 147 a.

הֱוֵה for הֱיֵה. The verb הָוָה for הָיָה is North Palestinian and late; cf. the Aramaic הֲוָה and ﻮﻫ. The imper. occurs again in Is. 16, 4 and Job 37, 6 (with א for ה).

לְאָחִיךָ . . . בְּנִי אִמְּךָ; cf. Ps. 50, 20, where they are again rhythmically interchanged.

אָרוּר . . . בָּרוּךְ. The singular for plural; cf. Ex. 31, 14 מְחַלְלֶיהָ מוֹת יוּמָת; Lev. 19, 8 וְאֹכְלָיו עֲוֹנוֹ יִשָּׂא; Num. 24, 9 מְבָרֲכֶיךָ בָרוּךְ וְאֹרֲרֶיךָ אָרוּר; see Ewald, § 319 a; Ges., § 146. 4; M. R., § 135. 4 b.

30. אַךְ יָצֹא יָצָא יַעֲקֹב. '*Jacob having only just gone out*,' circ. clause; cf. Josh. 4, 18 נִתְּקוּ כַּפּוֹת רַגְלֵי הַכֹּהֲנִים '*the soles of the feet of the priest having been withdrawn;*' 2 Kings 12, 7ᵇ לֹא חִזְּקוּ הַכֹּהֲנִים אֶת בֶּדֶק הַבַּיִת '*the priests not having repaired the breach in the house;*' see Driver, § 165; Ewald, § 341 c.

31. וַיֹּאכַל is imperf. with weak waw in a jussive sense; so וַיִּשְׁתַּחוּ, ver. 29; see Driver, § 134.

33. וַיֶּחֱרַד . . . חֲרָדָה וְגוֹ״, so ver. 34 וַיִּצְעַק צְעָקָה וְגוֹ״; the verb being followed by a substantive derived from it in the acc.; cf. Matt. 2, 10, and see Ges., § 138. 1. Rem. 1.

מִי אֵפוֹא הוּא הַצָּד= '*who then is he, the one that hunted?*' cf. Ps. 24, 10 מִי הוּא זֶה מֶלֶךְ הַכָּבוֹד '*who then is this one—the king of glory?*' Zech. 1, 9 מָה הֵמָּה אֵלֶּה '*what are they— these?*' מִי אֵפוֹא הוּא anticipating the subject; see Driver, § 201. 2; Ewald, § 325 a.

הַצָּד צַיִד וַיָּבֵא. '*Who hunted game and brought it;*' cf. 35, 3 . . . וַיְהִי; 49, 17 וַיִּפֹּל . . . הָעֹנֶה אֹתִי; הַנֹּשֵׁךְ . . . וַיִּפֹּל. The participle breaks off into the *imperf.* with *waw consec.;* a fact being stated, not a possibility, in which case we should find the *perf.* with *waw consec.;* cf. Driver, § 117; M. R., § 15; Ges., § 134. 2. Rem. 2.

34. ‏וַיִּצְעַק . . . כִּשְׁמֹעַ‏ is either to be explained as 19, 15 by Driver, § 127 b, the imperf. with waw conv. after a time-determination, or the word ‏וַיְהִי‏ must be supplied with the LXX, Sam.; so Tuch, Di. ‏ויהי‏ might easily have fallen out after ‏יהיה‏ at the end of ver. 33. Hitzig emends as follows (his emendation being accepted by Geiger, *Urschrift*, p. 377), ‏וַיְהִי : בָּרוּךְ גם ואברכהו‏.

‏ברכני גם אני‏. Cf. 4, 26 ‏לְשֵׁת גם הוּא‏; Num. 14, 32 ‏וּפגריכם אתם‏; see Ges., § 121. 3; Ewald, § 311 a; M. R., § 72. 1 and Rem. a.

36. ‘*Is it that they have called his name Jacob? for he hath supplanted me now twice,*’ etc.; cf. 29, 15 ‏הכי אחי אתה‏. LXX, δικαίως ἐκλήθη; Vulg. ‘*juste vocatum est nomen ejus;*’ cf. M. R., § 143. Rem. b; Ewald, § 324 b, who remarks that ‏הכי‏ ‘is used when the reason is unknown’=the Lat. *numquid*, Ger. *etwa*. In 25, 26 another explanation of the name is given.

‏זה פעמים‏; cf. Ges., § 122. 2. note; M. R., § 91.

37. ‏סמכתיו‏, with a double acc.; see Ps. 51, 14 ‏ורוח נדיבה תסמכני‏; so ‏סעד‏, Judg. 19, 5 ‏סעד לבך פת לחם‏; cf. Ewald, § 283 b (2).

‏לְכָה‏, *scriptio plena* for ‏לְךָ‏, only occurs here in the Pentateuch; cf. ‏איכה‏ in 3, 9 for ‏איך‏.

38. ‏הַבְרָכָה‏, see on 34, 31.

39. ‏מִשְׁמַנֵּי‏, not ‏מ‏ partitive as the A.V. margin, nor cstr. plural of ‏מִשְׁמָן‏ as A.V. and M. R., § 136. Rem. a; cf. ver. 28, because ‏מטל‏ in the second half of the verse is against this, but privative (so most modern scholars). ‘*Away from the fatnesses;*’ cf. vers. 37, 40. Render,

‘*Far from the fatnesses of the earth be thy dwelling-place,*
And far from the dew of heaven from above.’

Other instances of ‏מִן‏ privative are Num. 15, 24 ‏מעיני העדה‏

'*out of sight of the congregation;*' Prov. 20, 3 מריב '*away from strife;*' Job 11, 15 מאום '*without blemish.*'

The sterility of Edom is here contrasted with the fertility of Palestine; so ver. 40,

> '*And by thy sword shalt thou live, and thy brother shalt thou serve;*
>
> *And it will be, when thou rebellest, that thou wilt break his yoke from off thy neck.*'

40. על חרבך, i. e. the sword is conceived of as the means of procuring the necessities of life, or as the basis on which Esau's life will rest; cf. על in Deut. 8, 3 על הלחם לבדו; Is. 38, 16 עליהם יחיו.

תריד. The root רוד occurs four times in the Old Test., twice in Qal, Jer. 2, 31. Hos. 12, 1, and twice in Hif'., here and Ps. 55, 3. רוד is the Arab. راد, conj. I. '*to go to and fro;*' II. '*to desire, long for;*' III. '*to strive after, wish.*' In Hebrew the root means '*to wander about unrestrained,*' a meaning which suits Hos. and Jer., loc. cit.; Judah being described (Hos. 12, 1 עד רד) as still wandering about with regard to God, i. e. independently, of his own free will, withdrawing himself from God; so Jer. 2, 31 רדנו '*we have wandered about,*' i. e. abandoned God. In Ps. 55, 3 אריד בשיחי (where the Hif'il is used) the meaning is slightly different, '*I wander to and fro in my meditation,*' '*I am tossed about by anxiety and care.*' Del. and Kn. render here, '*when thou roamest about,*' but this is unsuitable, as a yoke would not be broken by roaming about, nor could a person under a yoke be well conceived of as roaming about at will. כאשר in this case would be like Num. 27, 14. Tuch renders, '*when thou rebellest*' (cf. Jer. and Hos., l. c.), to which Di. objects that every one who is under a yoke rebels, but does not get free; but this is not

conclusive against Tuch's rendering. Di. prefers the rendering, '*when thou strivest;*' cf. زار, IV, the meaning being,
'when thou, though in bondage, strivest to become free, thou
shalt break off the yoke from thy neck, and attain thy desire.'
The A.V. renders, '*when thou shalt have dominion*' (so Kimchi;
cf. Ges., *Thes.*, p. 1269 a), as though תריד were from רדה,
but this is tautological. Other renderings are, '*when thou
shall wish;*' '*when thou shall bewail,*' both extremely doubtful.
The Versions seem to have misunderstood the word. Onq.
renders it by "כַּד יְעִיבְּרוּן בְּנוֹהִי וגו' *when his sons transgress*'
etc., probably a paraphrase. Syr. has ܘܐܠ ܬܬܘܒ '*and if thou
repentest;*' but how they get this out of תריד is not clear.
LXX have ἡνίκα ἐὰν καθέλῃς, probably connecting it with ירד,
Hif'. הוריד. The Vulg. has a free paraphrase, '*tempusque
veniet cum excutias, et solvas jugum ejus,*' etc. The Heb.-Sam.
has תאדר, Nif'. of אדר ('*when thou becomest great*'), for תריד,
so the Book of Jubilees (Di.). The best rendering seems
to be either Tuch's or Dillmann's. The A.V.R. renders, '*break
loose.*' For the fulfilment of the blessing, cf. 2 Kings 8, 20 ff.
16, 6.

41. **יקרבו ימי אבל אבי**. Render, '*The days of mourning for my father,*' etc., i.e. Isaac would soon die; cf. ver. 4
and ver. 7, and then Esau contemplated taking vengeance on
Jacob; אָבִי being obj. genit. Others, e.g. Luther, Kalisch,
render as genit. of the subject, '*days of grief for my father,*'
i.e. Isaac would grieve when he heard of Jacob's death.
But the genitive after אבל is always obj. genit.

42. '*And they told* (lit. *it was told*) *Ribqah the words of
Esau;*' on the construction, cf. the note on 4, 18.

מתנחם. '*Will revenge himself upon thee,*' lit. '*procure for
himself satisfaction, or ease* (viz. by taking revenge);' cf. the
Nif'. אנחם in Is. 1, 24.

44. יָמִים אֲחָדִים. '*A few days*,' lit. '*some days*;' cf. 29, 20 כְּיָמִים אֲחָדִים; Dan. 11, 20 וּבְיָמִים אֲחָדִים. 'Ribqah mentions a short time in order to persuade Jacob more easily,' Di.

45. עַד שׁוּב . . . וְשָׁכַח. '*Until thy brother's anger turn . . . and he forget*;' cf. 18, 25 וְהָיָה . . . לְהָמִית, and the note there.

גַם שְׁנֵיכֶם; cf. Prov. 17, 15. They would both perish, as the murderer would (9, 6) be put to death.

28.

2. פַּדֶּנָה אֲרָם. The construct state with ה local; cf. on 20, 1. The syllable הָ— is pointed with orthophonic Ga‘ya (cf. Ges., § 16, 3), so that its sound may be kept distinct from that of the following א in אֲרָם; cf. 44, 2 גְּבִיעַ הַכֶּסֶף; 11, 25 תִּשַׁע־עֶשְׂרֵה (Baer and Del. ed.); see also Stade, § 56. פַּדֶּנָה = פַּדַּנָה; cf. סֶלָה = סֵלָה; and see Del. on Ps. 3, *Comment.*, 4th ed., p. 83.

3. יְבָרֵךְ אֹתְךָ . . . וְהָיִיתָ. The perf. with waw consecutive, after the imperf. as a jussive; cf. on 1, 14.

5. Cf. Hos. 12, 13 וַיִּבְרַח יַעֲקֹב שְׂדֵה אֲרָם.

6. וְשִׁלַּח. We should expect here וַיְּשַׁלַּח; no adequate reason can be given for the use of the perfect with waw here, where the imperf. with waw cons. would be expected: possibly the present reading has arisen through י having dropped out between ו and שׁ. See Driver, § 133. Di. explains it on account of its being dependent on כִּי, but this would require the waw conv. with the imperf. when another perfect had preceded, as already וַיִּשְׁמַע in ver. 7.

בברכו . . . ויצו. The imperf. with waw conv. continuing an inf. cstr., a fact being stated; cf. Driver, § 118 ad fin. So 39, 18 ואקרא . . . כהרימי; see also Ges., § 132. 3. Rem. 2.

9. מחלת. In 36, 3 בָּשְׂמַת (cf. the note there) is the name of the daughter of Ishmael whom Esau married.

על נשיו = 'in addition to his wives,' i. e. the wives mentioned 26, 34; so 31, 50 נשים על בנותי.

Verse 9 forms the apodosis to ver. 6; וישמע, ver. 7, being dependent on וירא, ver. 6, and וירא, ver. 8, resuming the וירא of ver. 6.

11. ויפגע במקום. מקום with the article = 'the place,' i. e. the place that was suitable for passing the night.

מאבני המקום. 'Some of the stones;' מִן partitive as in 4, 3.

מראשתיו = 'at his head.' מְרַאֲשׁוֹתָיו for מְרַאֲשׁתָיו; cf. מְתַלְּעוֹתָיו for מַלְתְּעֹתָיו. The plural is the plural used to mark extension of space (as here) or time; see Ges., § 108. 2 a; Stade, § 313 b. The feminine plural being used, according to Stade, § 322 c ('single things in which a definite quality appears'), מראשות = 'that which is at the head,' just as מרגלות = 'that which is at the feet;' cf. מטעמות and מעדנות 'dainties;' נפלאות 'wondrous deeds.'

12. סֻלָּם from סלל, with the ending ם–ָ, as in אוּלָם from אֻגל, כְּנָם; cf. Stade, § 293; Ges., § 87. 1 d. This ending is more frequent in proper names, e. g. בִּלְעָם, עֵדְלָם, אֲחְלָם, מִרְיָם, עַמְרָם. סלם is a ἅπαξ λεγόμ.

וראשו . . . השמימה. 'With its top reaching heavenwards;' cf. 11, 4, and see Driver, § 159.

13. נצב עליו. 'Standing on it' (the ladder). LXX, ἐπ' αὐτῆς; so Vulg., Syriac, Del. Tuch and Di. render, 'standing

by him' (Jacob), which perhaps is better (cf. 18, 2), as one does not see why it should be said that Yahweh stood on the ladder, while the thought, 'Yahweh stood by Jacob,' is more natural; and if עליו referred to סלם, we should expect לו, or ליעקב, after ויאמר.

14. וָקֵדְמָה . . . וָנֶגְבָּה; cf. on 1, 2.

15. עד אשר אם וגו״. '*Until that I shall have done,*' lit. '*until that when;*' cf. on 24, 19 and Num. 32, 17 עד אשר אם; Is. 6, 11 עד אשר אם שאו ערים הביאנם.

16. ואנכי לא ידעתי = '*without my knowing it,*' circ. cl.; cf. Driver, § 160; see on 24, 31.

17. מה נורא. '*How dreadful!*' cf. Ps. 8, 2 מה אדיר '*how glorious!*' Num. 24, 5 מה טבו אהליך '*how goodly are thy tents,*' etc.; see M. R., § 93. Rem. c.

20-22. The apodosis commences with והיה יהוה לי at the end of ver. 21. Render, '*If God be with me, and keep me on this journey which I am going, and give me bread to eat, and raiment to wear, and I return safe and sound to my father's house, then shall Yahweh be my God, and this stone,*' etc.; so LXX, Pesh., Vulg., Di., Del.; and this division is more natural than that proposed by Tuch, who commences the apodosis with ver. 22. Cf. Driver, § 115, on the perfect with waw conv. after an imperf. with אִם.

29.

1. The LXX add after ארצה בני קדם, πρὸς Λάβαν τὸν υἱὸν Βαθουὴλ τοῦ Σύρου, ἀδελφὸν δέ 'Ρεβέκκας, μητρὸς 'Ιακὼβ καὶ 'Ησαῦ, probably a gloss to harmonise this passage with 28, 5; the expression ארצה בני קדם for Mesopotamia—which is only found here—being in itself more or less indefinite.

2. *'And he looked up, and behold a well in the field, and behold there, three flocks of sheep were lying by it; for out of that well they used to water the flocks,'* etc. 3. *'And all the flocks used to be gathered thither, and they used to roll away the stone from off the mouth of the well, and water the sheep, and bring back the stone upon the mouth of the well to its place.'*

Observe the tenses, which are instructive. The participle רבצים, '*were lying*,' describing the condition at the particular occasion, the frequentative imperfect ישקו, and this followed by four perfects with waw conversive, והשקו, ונללו, ונאספו, והשיבו, describing what used habitually to be done ; cf. Driver, §§ 31; 113. 4 β; M. R., § 25; Ges., §§ 127. 4 b; 126. 6 d.

2. והאבן גדולה. *'And the stone on the mouth of the well was great,'* lit. *'and the stone was great on the mouth of the well;'* גדולה without the article, and therefore predicate; so in ver. 7 הן עוד היום גדול; cf. Ges., § 110. 3 (misprinted 4 in the 1880 ed.); Dav., § 11. Rule 2 ; M. R., § 125.

והאבן גדולה על פי הבאר, i.e. 'the stone on the mouth of the well,' etc., which in the more common construction would be וגדולה האבן אשר על פי הבאר; cf. Mic. 6, 12 ולשונם רמיה בפיהם.

With these two verses cf. 24, 11 ff. Ex. 2, 16 ff. (where, however, the tenses are different, a *single* occasion only being described).

4. אחי = '*my friends!*' cf. 19, 7.

6. באה = '*is coming*,' participle not perfect; in ver. 9 בָּאה is accented on the penult., and is therefore the perfect.

7. לא עת האסף המקנה. *'It is not time for the cattle to be gathered together,'* lit. *'it is not the time of the being gathered together of the cattle,'* i.e. for the cattle to be collected and put up for the night. On the construction of the inf.

cstr. with a subj. following and a construct state preceding,
cf. Ges., §§ 132. 1 b; 133. 2; M. R., §§ 111, 118.

8. כל העדרים. The LXX have πάντας τοὺς ποιμένας,
reading כָּל־הָרֹעִים, an easier reading than that of the text; so
the Sam. here and ver. 3.

עד אשר יאספו ... וגללו ... והשקינו. The impf.
continued by the pft. with waw conv., as in Ex. 23, 30 עד
אשר יאשמו ובקשו פני ;Hos. 5, 15 אשר תפרה ונחלת את הארץ,
and often; cf. Driver, p. 161.

9. עודנו מדבר ... ורחל באה. Cf. on 38, 25.

אשר לאביה. אשר ל to express the genitive, as in 40, 5
לצאן אשר לעבדיך ;47, 4 המשקה והאפה אשר למלך מצרים; see
Ges., § 115. 1; M. R., § 83.

11. וישק יעקב. נִשֵּׁק (ver. 13) Pi'el = 'to kiss fondly,' or
'cover with kisses,' as distinguished from the Qal נָשַׁק (here)
'to kiss;' cf. φιλέω and καταφιλέω in Greek.

13. את שמע יעקב. LXX, τὸ ὄνομα Ἰακώβ; so LXX in
Num. 14, 15. 1 Kings 10, 1, possibly confusing שמע with שֵׁם,
which was very similar in sound.

14. חדש ימים. 'A month, days,' i.e. a whole month; cf.
41, 1 שנתים ימים 'two years;' Num. 11, 20 חדש ימים : ימים
being loosely subordinated to חדש; see Driver, § 192. 1;
Ewald, § 287 h; Ges., § 118. 3; M. R., § 71. 4.

15. הכי אחי וגו″. Cf. 27, 36. 'Art thou, as a brother, to
serve me for nothing ?' lit. 'is it the case that thou art my brother,
and shouldest serve me for nothing ?' cf. the Vulg. 'num quia
frater meus es, gratis servies mihi ?' On ועבדתני, perf. with
waw conv. after כִּי, without an imperf. preceding, cf. Driver,
§ 123 γ.

17. ועיני לאה רכות. The predicate in the plural with
the subject in the dual, as the dual in Hebrew only occurs in

a few nouns, never in the verb or adj. (contrast the Arabic);
see M. R., § 134; Ges., § 146. 5.

רכות. ‘*Weak*,’ lit. ‘*tender*,’ neither bright nor clear. So
LXX and Syr. But Onq. and Saadiah take רכות as meaning
‘*beautiful*,’ as though Leah had fine eyes, but otherwise was
not so handsome as Rachel. Good eyes were considered by
the Orientals one of the essentials of beauty; cf. Song of
Songs 4, 1. 1 Sam. 16, 12.

18. שבע שנים. Jacob wished to purchase his wife by
seven years’ service without hire, the seven years’ service
taking the place of the ordinary price (מהר) paid the wife’s
relatives before marriage; cf. 24, 53. 34, 12. Hos. 3, 2.
1 Sam. 18, 23 ff.

19. טוב תתי וגו״. ‘*It is better for me to give her to thee,
than for me to give her to another man ;*’ cf. Ex. 14, 12 כי טוב לנו
טוב לשבת על פנת גג Prov. 21. 9 ; עבד את מצרים ממתנו במדבר
מאשת מדונים; so ver. 19.

לאיש אחר, i. e. a stranger; cf. Jer. 6, 12. 8, 10. At the
present day in Arabia the cousin is preferred as a husband
to a stranger; cf. Lane, *Manners and Customs*, vol. i, p. 167.

21. הבה את אשתי. הבה is accented on the last syllable,
on account of the light consonant א in את, that both ה and א
may have their full sound.

22. משתה, i. e. the wedding banquet; cf. Judg. 14, 12.
Tobit 11, 19.

23. The bride was brought to her husband veiled (cf. 24,
65), and so the deception practised by Laban could easily be
accomplished.

26. לא יעשה וגו״=‘*it is not customary in our land*,’ lit.
‘*it is not wont thus to be done ;*’ cf. 34, 7 ובן לא יעשה; 2 Sam.
13, 12 כי לא יעשה כן בישראל.

27. שֶׁבַע זֹאת. The wedding festivities usually lasted a week; cf. Judg. and Tobit, l.c.

וּנְתְנָה, i.e. Laban and his relatives; cf. 24, 50. The LXX and Sam. read וָאתֵן.

30. גַם אֶל רָחֵל. גַם = '*also*;' the second גם in גם את רחל may either emphasize Rachel only (see Ges., § 155. 2 a), or may be taken with מן = '*etiam*,' '*still more than*,' which is perhaps a little forced. Di. condemns both ways as against the usage of the language, and following the LXX and Vulg., rejects the second גם. Knobel takes the second גם with ויאהב, i.e. did not only go in to her, but also loved her: but this would require ויאהב גם אהב; cf. 31, 15. 46, 4.

ויאהב ... מלאה. On the comparative, cf. M.R., § 49. 2; Ges., § 119. 1.

31. שְׂנוּאָה, not absolutely '*hated*,' but relatively '*less loved*;' cf. Deut. 21, 15. Matt. 6, 24.

32. אמרה כי. כי as in 26, 22; cf. the note there; so ver. 33.

ראה ... בעניי. ב ... ראה = '*to look upon with compassion*;' so 1 Sam. 1, 11 אם ראה תראה בעני אמתך; Ps. 106, 44 וירא בצר להם.

יאהבני; cf. 19, 19 and the note there.

33. שמעון = '*hearing*.'

34. ילוה ... אלי. '*Will become attached to me*;' cf. Num. 18, 2. 4. לוי as though = '*attachment*' or '*dependent*.'

קרא. As the mother in the case of the other three sons, Simeon, Reuben, and Judah, gives them their names, so probably the reading of the LXX, ἐκάλεσε (not ἐκλήθη), Syr. ‎ܦ‎ = קראה, is correct. קרא would = '*one called him*,' '*people called him*.'

35. יהודה = 'praise,' 'a subject of praise.'   A Hof'al derivative; cf. Ps. 28, 7. 45, 18. Neh. 11, 17, where the ה of the Hif'. of ידה (ודה) is irregularly retained.

30.

1. מתה; cf. on 29, 6.

2. התחת אלהים אנכי.   'Am I in God's stead?' i. e. am I all powerful, so that I might give you children? so again 50, 19 (אני); cf. 2 Kings 5, 7 האלהים אני להמית ולהחיות.

3. על ברכי; so 50, 23 על ברכי יוסף; cf. Job 3, 12.   Rachel follows Sarah's example (16, 2), and gives her maid Bilhah to Jacob, so that she might rear up her (Bilhah's) child as her own, and in some measure escape the reproach of childlessness.

6. דָנַנִּי with the tone-syllable doubled; so תְּבַעֲתַנִּי, Job 7, 14; cf. Stade, § 71. 3.

דן = 'judge.'   God heard Rachel's prayer, and decided (דין) according to her wish.

8. נפתולי אלהים = lit. 'struggles of God,' i. e. struggles or wrestlings for God's favour; cf. ver. 6. 29, 31. 30, 2.   The A.V. renders, 'with great wrestlings,' i. e. for the husband's love: but the sisters were never rivals for the husband's love (cf. 29, 33 and ver. 15 of this chapter), as Rachel was always the favourite wife of Jacob.   נפתולי is a ἅπαξ λεγόμ. and the only noun of this form; see Stade, § 251.   נפתלי = 'one obtained by struggling' (?).   Di. *Kampfmann* ('*man of combat*' or '*struggling*').

11. בְּגָד = the Kri בא גד 'good fortune comes;' so Onq. and the Syriac (ܐܬܐ 'my fortune cometh'): but this reading of the Kri is unnecessary.   The Ktb. בגד, pointed בְּגָד (LXX, ἐν τύχῃ; Vulg. 'feliciter')—the pausal form of גַּד— yields a good sense, 'I am in luck;' cf. באשרי, ver. 13.   גד

(cf. Is. 6₅, 11, where it is the Babylonian god of good fortune, identified with Bel, and later with the planet Jupiter) was the name of an old Phoenician and Canaanitish god.   Traces of the name are still preserved in the proper name בעל גד, Josh. 11, 17, and the Phoenician proper names גרנעם, נדעת; see Euting, *Sechs Phönizische Inschriften aus Idalion*, p. 14 (1875). The Ktb. might be read בְּגָד, and explained by Ges., § 102. 2 c, the ב being pointed with pretonic qameç; the meaning being, as above, '*I am in luck.*' But this is improbable.

The A.V. (but not the A.V. R., see Prof. Driver's paper on the Revised Version in *The Expositor*, July, 1885) and Gr. Ven. (ἥκει στράτευμα) give גד the meaning of גדוד; cf. 49, 19. But גד never means '*a troop*,' and 49, 19 is not decisive on the meaning here.

13. בְּאָשְׁרִי='*In my prosperity!*' i.e. I am in luck; cf. ver. 11.

כִּי אִשְּׁרוּנִי. '*For the daughters are sure to call me lucky;*' cf. Is. 11, 9 כי מלאה הארץ דעה; Jer. 25, 14 כי עבדו בם.   The perfect of certitude or prophetic perfect; cf. Driver, § 14 β; M. R., § 3. 1; Ges., § 126. 4; Dav., § 46. 2. 3.

אָשֵׁר = '*the lucky one;*' cf. אשרה ? '*the goddess of good fortune.*'

14. דודאים is pl. of דּוּדַי; cf. לְלָאֹת, from an obsolete singular לוּלָי, יִ־ of the singular being softened into א in the plural; so חֲלִי, pl. חֲלָאִים; צְבִי, pl. צְבָאוֹת and צְבָאִים; פְּתִי, pl. פְּתָאִים¹; cf. Stade, §§ 122. 301 a. דודאים = '*love apples,*' i.e. the fruit of the *Mandragora vernalis*, or mandrake, of a yellow colour, and similar in shape to an apple; found in Palestine, especially in Galilee. There seem to have been two kinds of דודאים, the *Mandragora vernalis* and *autumnalis* (Song of Songs 7, 14), unless we suppose with Tuch that in

---

¹ But cf. Baer and Del., *Liber Psalmorum*, Lipsiae, 1880, p. 115.

this passage the fruit is intended (at the time of the wheat harvest, i. e. May to June), while in Song of Songs the blossom is meant (cf. the LXX rendering in Song of Songs, οἱ μανδραγόραι, with their translation here, μῆλα μανδραγορῶν). On the supposed efficacy of the דודאים as love potions, see Tuch, p. 385 f., and the authorities cited by him.

15. '*Is thy taking away my husband a little thing, and (art thou) for taking away the love apples of my son too?*' cf. Esth. 7, 8 הגם לכבוש את המלכה ; 2 Chron. 19, 2 הלרשע לעזר. ולקחת is not perf. as Tuch, but inf. cstr. used as a periphrastic future; see Driver, § 204; also Ges., § 132. 3. Rem. 1. Di. remarks that 'the inf. ולקחת ("*and to take*" = "*and thou will take*"?) expresses the intention more forcibly than the more natural construction with the perfect וְלָקַחַתְּ; see 20, 16.'

16. שׂכר שׂכרתיך, i. e. by giving Rachel some of the love apples.

בלילה הוא ; cf. 19, 33 and the note there.

18. יששכר. The reading given in Baer and Del.'s edition is pointed יִשָּׂשכָר, with the Kri *perpetuum* יִשָּׂכָר, i. e. wherever יששכר occurs in the O. T. it is always pointed יִשָּׂכָר, as though there were no second שׂ: this is the reading of Ben Asher (the Tiberian or Occidental punctuation). Ben Naftali reads יִשְׂשָׂכָר (the Babylonian or Oriental punctuation); cf. Baer and Del., *Gen.*, p. 84. On the readings of Ben Asher and Ben Naftali, see Bleek-Wellhausen, *Einl.*, pp. 563, 614 f.; Bleek, *Introduction*, Eng. trans., ii. p. 463; Strack, *Proleg.*, p. 36 f., *De codicibus Orient. et Occident.* Ben Asher's reading יִשָּׂכָר is perhaps a derivative from the Nif'al of שׂכר = '*got for hire*' (Wright); so apparently the LXX, 'Ισσάχαρ; Vulg. *Issachar;* Syr. ; Saad. ; Josephus, ἐκ μίσθου γενόμενος. The reading of Ben Naftali, יִשְׂשָׂכָר, is the same as that of Ben Asher, but

written differently. Some think that Ben Naftali read יִשָּׂשְׂכָר
('affert proemium') = יִשָּׂא שָׂכָר; see Baer and Del., loc. cit., 'At
certe de Ben Naf. falluntur.' Mose ben Mocha read יֵשׁ־שָׂכָר
'est proemium,' after Jer. 31, 16. 2 Chron. 15, 7.

20. זבדני and יזבלני are both ἅπαξ λεγόμ.

זבלון (of the same form as יְשׁוּרוֹן) = 'habitation.' In this
verse two explanations of the name are given, (a) זבד ... זבדני
'presented me with a goodly present,' and (b) זבל [1] יזבלני (זבל with
the acc. like שׁכן and גור) ' will dwell with me,' probably being
derived from different documents; so ver. 24.

21. דינה = 'vindicatio;' the daughter's name is here given,
as necessary to explain chap. 34. Jacob's daughters are elsewhere presupposed (46, 7. 37, 35), but not mentioned by name.

24. יוסף explained from ver. 23 אסף אלהים את חרפתי,
as though it were יאסף = ' taker away,' i. e. of my reproach
of childlessness. In 24[b] the name is explained differently,
יוסף יי" לי בן אחר ' may Yahweh add to me another son,'
so = ' multiplier;' see on ver. 20, and cf. 35, 18.

27. אם נא מצאתי וגו". 'If now I have found favour in
thine eyes,—I have observed the omens, and Yahweh has blessed
me for thy sake.' The apodosis to אם נא מצאתי וגו" is suppressed; the apodosis would perhaps run אל נא תעבר מעלי,
as in 18, 3. The words cannot be translated ' Would that I
had found favour in thy eyes' (Ges. in Thes.), as this would require the imperf., not the perfect; cf. Ps. 81, 9. 139, 19. נחשתי;
see on 44, 15. The LXX have οἰωνισάμην ἄν, making נחשתי into
the apodosis to אם מצאתי. The A.V. renders, 'I have learned
by experience,' following the Vulgate 'experimento didici.'

---

[1] In Assyrian the root zabal = ' to bear,' ' lift up;' it is possible,
therefore, that יזבלני should be rendered, ' will lift me up,' i. e. ' honour
me;' see Cheyne's crit. note on Is. 63, 15; Del., Heb. Lang., p. 38 f.;
and his Prolegomena (Leipzig, 1886), p. 62.

28. עָלָי = lit. '*upon me.*' עַל because it will be as a burden to him; cf. 34, 12.

29. '*Thou knowest how I have served thee, and what thy cattle has become with me.*' אֵת אֲשֶׁר עֲבַדְתִּיךְ and אֵת אֲשֶׁר הָיָה ׳וגו are both accusatives after יָדַעְתָּ. אַתָּה is emphatic, '*thou* with whom I have been in service shouldest know.' אִתִּי '*with me,*' i. e. under my care.

30. וַיִּפְרֹץ. Waw conv., as in Ex. 9, 21, which compare.

לְרַגְלִי, lit. '*at my steps,*' i. e. wherever I went; cf. Is. 41, 2 צֶדֶק יִקְרָאֵהוּ לְרַגְלוֹ '*whom righteousness meeteth wherever he goeth;*' Job 18, 11 וְהֵפִיצֻהוּ לְרַגְלָיו.

גַּם אָנֹכִי. Emphatic, '*I too.*' You have been prosperous, when shall I begin prospering?

31. אֲשׁוּבָה אֶרְעֶה. '*I will again feed;*' so 26, 18 וַיָּשָׁב יִצְחָק וַיַּחְפֹּר '*and Isaac dug again.*' Two verbs to express one idea, where in English an adverb is used; so Ps. 7, 13 יָשׁוּב ... יִלְטֹשׁ '*will again sharpen;*' see Ges., § 142. 3 b; M. R., § 30 a.

32–43. These twelve verses are very obscure, possibly corrupt. In ver. 31, Jacob, in answer to Laban's request to tell him what reward he desires, replies that Laban is to give him nothing if he will accede to a proposal he has to make. In ver. 32, Jacob proposes to go through Laban's flock, and separate the particoloured and black sheep, and all the particoloured goats. The normal colour of the goats is black, or at least dark-brown; that of the sheep, on the contrary, white; see Song of Songs 1, 2. 6, 6. Dan. 7, 9; cf. Song of Songs 1, 5. The greater number of the sheep and goats would naturally be of normal colour, white and black respectively. Jacob proposes that the abnormal cattle shall be his hire. Laban, vers. 34–36, consents to Jacob's proposal, and separates the normal and abnormal coloured sheep and goats, and sends the latter off, under the charge of his sons, three days' journey distant from the remainder of his flock of normal coloured animals, left in Jacob's charge. Jacob, in order that the animals left with him may bring forth a greater number of abnormal coloured offspring than they would usually produce, has recourse to the stratagem of the peeled rods in the drinking-troughs (37–39). Ver. 40 seems to contain a second contrivance on the part of Jacob to increase his flock, but the text is very obscure and almost certainly corrupt (see the note there). Vers. 41, 42 either contain a third stratagem, or refer to the previous two (the frequentative tenses perhaps supporting the latter view), 41, 42 being a more detailed account of the contrivance practised in vers. 38, 39.

32. הַיּוֹם seems to imply that the cattle separated *that day*, if of abnormal colour, were to belong to Jacob; but against this is firstly ver. 31, where Jacob declines any hire, and secondly vers. 35, 36^b, where Laban, not Jacob, separates and drives off the abnormal coloured cattle, which seem, according to ver. 32, to belong to Jacob, but here are apparently regarded as Laban's. To avoid this difficulty, some, e.g. Tuch, suppose that Jacob's hire is to be the abnormal coloured cattle that would be born, cf. ver. 37 ff.; but nothing is said of this in ver. 32, and it is questionable whether וְהָיָה שְׂכָרִי would fit in with this view. Di. proposes to alter the accentuation of ver. 32, and point the first טָלוּא with *Athnach;* then the meaning would be '*every black sheep among the sheep, and spotted and patched among the goats, shall be my hire,*' i.e. you are to give me nothing now, but the abnormal coloured cattle born after the division, in ver. 32, has taken place will be

mine; cf. מחר, ver. 33. This seems the simplest solution of the difficulties.

הסר is inf. abs. Others prefer taking הסר as imperative, addressed to לבן, which suits ver. 35, but not אעבר. נקד וטלוא '*spotted and patched.*' טלוא is not found again outside this chapter, except in Ez. 16, 16, pl. fem. טְלָאוֹת. והיה שׂכרי '*and (these) shall be my hire,*' i.e. the sheep and goats of abnormal colour that shall be born after the division mentioned in this verse has been carried out; see above. שׂה is used here of both sheep and goats, being further defined by כשׂבים and עזים. Ver. 35 is a more minute description of this verse. The LXX have παρελθέτω, reading the easier reading יַעֲבֹר כָּל־; Vulg. '*gyra omnes greges tuos*' (עבר בכל), both regarding הסר as imper.

כשׂבים. A form peculiar to the Pent., for which we find elsewhere כבשׂים.

33. וענתה בי צדקתי. Mühlau and Volck (Ges., *H. W. B.*, 9th ed.) render here and 1 Sam. 12, 3, '*bear witness for me;*' but as ענה ..., ב always elsewhere means '*to bear witness against,*' and as this meaning is not unsuitable in 1 Sam. 12, 3, it is preferable to follow Del. and render '*my righteousness shall testify against me,*' i.e. I shall be self-condemned (Wright).

ביום מחר = '*hereafter;*' cf. Ex. 13, 14. Deut. 6, 20. Josh. 4, 6.

כי תבא ... לפניך. '*When thou comest about my hire, before thee,*' i.e. when thou comest to inspect the cattle (my hire) which will be before thee; or לפניך may be connected with וענתה בי צדקתי, in the sense '*my righteousness will testify against me ... before thee;*' but the position of לפניך, at some distance from וענתה בי צדקתי, is against this.

וחום‎ = ‏חום‎ ‏ואיננו‎, as the black sheep, being Jacob's hire, could not be regarded as stolen.

35. ‏יָסַר‎, imperf. Hif., not Qal, although the apocopated imperf. third pers. masc. sing. Qal and Hif. are the same, the context alone deciding the conjugation intended. Laban is here the subject, as is clear from ‏בניו‎ at the end of the verse, and ‏בינו ובין יעקב‎ in the next verse. The cattle left with Jacob were of normal colour, white sheep and dark-coloured goats.

36. ‏בינו‎ ' *between him.*' LXX and Sam. ‏בינם‎ (‏ביניהם‎) ' *between them,*' i. e. his sons.

37. ‏מִקֵל‎ doubtless collective, hence the fem. (as ‏בהן‎, cf. Jer. 4, 29[b], shews); elsewhere it is masculine.

‏לבנה‎ = ' *Styrax*' (*Styrax officinalis*). Arabic لُبْنَى. The noun ‏לבנה‎ is of the same form as ‏פִּשְׁתָּה‎, ‏אִשָּׁה‎, ‏ה‎ﹷ = 'ﹷ (cf. the Arabic name ending in ئ = 'ﹷ, and see Stade, § 301 b), from ‏לבן‎, so called on account of the milk-like gum that flows from it when its bark is cut. Others, following the Vulg. here and the LXX in Hos. 4, 13, render '*poplar ;*' so A.V. here.

‏לוז‎ = ' *almond.*' Arabic لُوْز, Aram. ‏ܠܘܙܐ‎. Del. remarks that ‏לוז‎ is the more Aramaic-Arabic word for ‏שָׁקֵד‎.

‏ערמון‎ = ' *plane tree*' (*Platanus orientalis*), from ‏ערם‎ ' *to strip,*' so called because the bark peels off from year to year, and the tree becomes as it were naked.

‏מחשׂף‎ = ‏חשׂף‎, inf. abs. ' *exposing the white ;*' one of the very few instances in Hebrew of an abstract form with the force of an infinitive ; so ‏מִקְרָא‎, ‏מַפַּע‎ (as inf. cstr.) from ‏נָסַע‎, ‏מצוה‎ (Neh. 12, 45, with acc.); cf. Ewald, § 239 a. In Aramaic the inf. of the first conjugation (=Qal) is formed by prefixing ‏מ‎.

38. רהטים, rare and Aramaising, here explained by
שקתות מים.

שׁקתות is pl. of שֹׁקֶת, like אֲמָרוֹת, Ps. 12, 7, from אֹמֶר;
cf. Stade, § 187 b; Ewald, § 212 b, who cites סֻבְכֵי from סֹבֶךְ.

לנכח ' *over against.*'

ויחמנה from חמם, instead of וַתֵּחַמְנָה, as 1 Sam. 6, 12
וַיִּשַׁרְנָה; Dan. 8, 22 יַעֲמֹדְנָה (all). In Arabic the third fem.
pl. form is يَقْتُلْنَ, and in Aramaic יִקְטְלָן; see Ges., § 47. 3.
Rem. 3; Stade, § 534. 1. *H. W. B.*, 9th ed., gives the root
as יחם, not חמם, ויחמנה = וַיֵּחַמְנָה; cf. יֵשֵׁב from יָשַׁב. If it is
from חָמַם it follows the analogy of יֵרַד, יֵמַר.

39. וַיֶּחֱמוּ, plural masc., because the male animals are
included. יחמו is either imperf. from חמם = יֵחַמּוּ, or imperf.
Qal of יָחַם, for יֶחֱמוּ or יֵחַמּוּ; cf. Judg. 5, 28 אֶחֱרוּ for אֶחֱרוּ;
Ps. 51, 7 יֶחֱמַתְנִי for יֵחֲמַתְנִי: see Ges., §§ 64. 3. Rem. 3; 67.
5. Rem.; cf. Stade, § 523 d, who regards יֶחֱמוּ as lightened
from יֵחַמּוּ, for יֶהֱמוּ, after the analogy of verbs ל״ה.

אל המקלות. Cf. 24, 11 אל באר המים ' *at the well of
water.*'

עקדים = ' *striped.*'

40. והכשבים are the particoloured animals, goats and
sheep; these Jacob separated from the normally coloured
animals in Laban's flock. He then turns Laban's normal
coloured animals in the direction of the כשבים, so that they
might have these before their eyes. But these abnormal
coloured animals belong to Jacob, according to his agreement with Laban, and so cannot be spoken of as עקר וכל חום
בצאן לבן. If the text were emended as follows, the difficulty
would disappear, ויתן פני צאן לבן אל עקר וכל חום בצאנו, i. e.
' *he set the face of Laban's flock towards what was striped and
(towards) everything dark in his own flock.*' לבן has fallen out

of its place after צאן, which then received the article, and the waw of בצאנו disappeared before the waw of וַיָּשֶׁת. Knobel emends by reading כל עקד, with Onq., Ps.-Jon., and takes פני for לפני 'before,' as Ex. 23, 15. Ps. 42, 3; but then Jacob's dark and particoloured cattle are described as Laban's. Wright adopts Knobel's emendation, but avoids the above-mentioned difficulty by deleting לבן and reading בצאן. לבן might certainly have crept in, from the צאן לבן in the next line. Del. retains the text, and supposes that after the first separation, ver. 32, the normal and abnormal coloured cattle were left together. But the abnormal cattle could hardly be called Laban's even in that case, and it seems scarcely possible that Laban, who apparently was anxious to prevent any duplicity on Jacob's part (cf. ver. 35, where *he*, not Jacob, separates the normal and abnormal coloured cattle), would passively submit to this second stratagem by leaving his own cattle (i. e. those that were sent away under his sons' care, cf. ver. 32) under Jacob's charge.

41, 42. The old translators explain these verses by the fact that the strong cattle bring forth their young in winter, and the weak cattle theirs in the spring: thus המקשרות would be the winter cattle, and העטפים the spring cattle.

41. וַהַיָה . . . וְשָׂם, perfs. with waw conv. in a frequentative sense; see Driver, § 120. לְיַחֲמֶנָּה is inf. Pi'el of יחם, with the third pl. fem. suffix הּ‍ָ‍נָ‍ for ן‍ָ; cf. 41, 21 קִרְבֶּנָה, and see Ges., § 91. 1. Rem. 2; Stade, § 352 b. 2, who remarks that the dagesh should be struck out.

43. צֹאן רֲבוֹת, the collective being construed with a plural adjective; cf. 1 Sam. 13, 15 את העם הנמצאים עמו, 1 Sam. 17, 28 מעט הצאן ההנה; cf. Ges., § 112. 1. Rem. 3; M. R., § 85. Rem. b.

31.

1. הַכָּבֹד הַזֶּה = '*this wealth;*' cf. Is. 10, 3. Ps. 49, 17.

4. הַשָּׂדֶה is acc. of place; see M. R., § 41 a; Ges., § 118. 1.

5. אֵינֶנּוּ, referring to פְּנֵי; cf. Lam. 4, 16, where פְּנֵי is followed by a singular verb.

6. וְאַתֵּנָה for אַתֵּן, also pointed אַתֵּנָה (cf. the Arabic اَنْتُنَّ), is only found again in Ez. 13, 11. 20. 34, 17; see Ges., § 32. Rem. 5; Stade, § 178 c.

7. הֵתֶל for הִתֵּל, with retrogression of the tone by Ges., § 29. 3 b; Stade, § 88. 2 b. התל is Hif. of תלל; cf. the Lexic. and Ewald, § 127 d. The ה of the Hif. is retained, as though it were a radical letter, in the forms יְהָתֵלּוּ (notice the dag. in ל), Job. 13, 9; יְהָתֵלִי, Jer. 9, 4; וַיְהָתֵל, 1 Kings 18, 27: see Stade, § 145 e, and Wright, *Gram. Arab.*, i. p. 37.

התל ... והחלף. I. Either like Num. 11, 8 שטו ... ולקטו, 'the fact being stated summarily by the perfect, and this tense being followed by the perfect with waw conv.;' see Driver, § 114 a.　II. Or like Num. 21, 15 נטה ... ונשען: והחליף not being *subordinate* to התל (the imperf. with waw conv. would be required then) but *co-ordinate;* see Driver, § 132.

עֲשֶׂרֶת מֹנִים. '*Ten times;*' LXX, δέκα ἀμνῶν, possibly corrupted out of a reading μνῶν. The translators, not understanding מֹנִים, wrote the Hebrew word in Greek, and this passed over into ἀμνῶν; cf. Frankel, *Einf.*, p. 18, and ver. 41.　The word מֹנִים is peculiar to this chapter, elsewhere פְעָמִים is used, e. g. Num. 14, 22. Aq. has δέκα ἀριθμούς, Symm. δεκάκις ἀριθμῷ.

8. The account of the agreement made between Jacob

and Laban in this chapter differs from that in chap. 30, and appears to be derived from a different source.

נקדים יהיה. יהיה, the singular is perhaps due to the following שכרך; see Ges., § 147 d.

'*If he were to say thus, The spotted shall be thy hire; then all the flock used to bring forth spotted: and if he were to say thus, The striped shall be thy hire; then all the flock used to bring forth striped.*' Cf. Num. 9, 19–21. Ex. 40, 37 ואם לא יעלה הענן ולא יסעו (the apod. being in the imperf., as the waw is separated from the verb by לא); see Driver, § 136 δ. Obs., cf. § 123 β.

9. אביכם for אביכן; cf. on 26, 18.

10. ברדים = טלוא, in 30, 32; it is found twice again in Zech. 6, 3. 6 (of horses), and = '*speckled.*' ברדים probably = '*covered as it were with hailstones*' (בָּרָד), so '*white spots on a dark ground*' (Tuch).

13. האל ביתאל. '*I am the God of Bethel.*' ביתאל being loosely connected with האל, instead of being subordinated in the genitive; cf. 2 Kings 23, 17 המזבח ביתאל (but cf. Driver, § 191. Obs.). Or הָאֵל may be regarded as construct state with the article, see Ewald, 290 d (3), who cites other instances, e. g. Jer. 48, 32, etc.; see also Is. 36, 8. 16; and cf. M. R., § 76 b; Ges., § 110. 2 b.

14. ותען . . . , ותאמרנה. On the first verb with a compound subject in the singular and the second in the plural, see Ges., § 148. 2; cf. also M. R., § 138.

15. ויאכל גם אכול. '*And goes on to eat up;*' cf. on 19, 9. גם, emphasizing the verb as in 46, 4. Num. 16, 13; cf. the note on 29, 30.

16. כי. '*So that;*' so Del. and Kn., comparing Job 10, 6.

Deut. 14, 24. Di. prefers the rendering '*rather*,' or '*nay, rather*;' cf. Ps. 37, 20. 49, 11.

19. הלך לגזז. In 38, 13 we find לגז, the shorter form; cf. לסבב, Num. 21, 4, and the short form סב, Deut. 2, 3; see Stade, § 619 e; Ges., § 67. Rem. 10. הלך is pluperfect, '*had gone*.'

התרפים = '*The Teraphim*,' Laban's household gods. LXX here τὰ εἴδωλα, but the word is variously rendered by them in the other passages where it occurs. The Teraphim were of human form (1 Sam. 19, 13), and were worshipped as gods (ver. 30. Judg. 18, 24). Their worship was not re-cognised as legitimate (see 2 Kings 23, 24; cf. Gen. 35, 4 and Hos. 3, 4), yet they were at all times regarded as house-hold oracles (Judg. 18, 5. Zech. 10, 2. Ez. 21, 26), and (pos-sibly) as bringing prosperity; therefore Rachel takes them with her, to avoid bringing misfortune or ill luck on her household; cf. Judg. 18, 17, where the Danites take Micha's household gods. The pl. form may here only denote a single image, as in 1 Sam. 19, 13 (see Ges., § 108. 2 b); cf. אדונים and בעלים, both used as intensive plurals; the pl. suf. in ver. 34, and אלהי in ver. 30, not being decisive in favour of taking תרפים as a real plural; cf. Ewald, § 318 a. No certain etymology has yet been found. The one most commonly given is from the Arabic تَرِفَ '*commode vivere*,' which would agree with the idea that the תרפים were the gods who were supposed to bring good fortune to those who worshipped them; but it is not certain that تَرِفَ does not rather mean '*to be soft*;' cf. Tuch, p. 395; Del., p. 555, who also suggests a comparison with the Sanskrit *tarp*, '*to be full*.' The תרפים stood in no connection with the שׂרפים.

20. ויגנב . . . את לב = '*deceived*;' cf. 2 Sam. 15, 6

וַיְגַנֵּב אבשלום את לב, but in the sense '*to win over secretly;*' cf. κλέπτειν νόον and κλέπτειν τινά (Del.).

על בלי is only found here. בלי = לא with the finite verb, occurs in Job 41, 18. Hos. 8, 7. 9, 16 (Ktb.). Is. 14, 6; see Ewald, § 322 a. Render, '*In that he did not tell.*' On על, cf. Ges., § 104. 1 c.

21. הַנָּהָר. '*The river*' *par excellence*, i. e. the Euphrates; see Ges., § 109. 2. So often, e. g. Is. 27, 12. Ps. 72, 8.

23. את אחיו. '*His friends and fellow-tribesmen;*' cf. Lev. 10, 4. 2 Sam. 19, 13.

25. בְּהָר ... בהר הגלעד. From a comparison of vers. 21 and 23 with this verse, Jacob and Laban apparently encamped in the same place (so Vulg.); yet the narrative evidently implies that Laban encamped in one place and Jacob in another. Possibly in vers. 21, 23, and here, הר גלעד may mean the hill country of Gilead in general, הר ג״ (like ארץ ג״) in the O. T. being the name of the mountain range and country of Gilead, south of Jarmuk, up to the plain of Heshbon (Deut. 3, 12 f. Josh. 17, 1. 5. 2 Kings 10, 33, and often). In ver. 25, Jacob encamped בָּהָר, which seems to point to some special hill, possibly the hill called at the present time Ǵebel Ǵil'âd, on the south bank of the Wâdy Jabbok (cf. ver. 54). Jacob's camping ground would then be described as בהר (a special hill, with which the reader would be familiar), while Laban's is described as in the neighbourhood (cf. ver. 25, וישׂג), the actual spot not being indicated.

26. עשׂית ותגנב. The imperf. with waw conv. used to define עשׂה; so in 1 Sam. 8, 8. 1 Kings 2, 15; see Driver, § 76 a.

27. למה נחבאת לברח. ‘*Why didst thou fly in secret?*’ see 27, 20; and cf. Ges., § 142. 4. Rem. 1.

ואשלחך. ‘*And so I could have sent thee away;*’ see Driver, § 74 a. On the ⸺ in ואשׁלחֶך, see Ges., § 65. 2. note; also Stade, § 633 a.

28. הסכלת עשׂו = ‘*thou hast acted foolishly.*’ עָשׂוֹ for עֲשׂוֹת; cf. רְאֹה, 48, 11; עֲשֹׂה, 50, 20; עֲשֹׂהוּ, Ex. 18, 18; and see Ges., § 75. Rem. 2; Stade, § 619 k. In הסכלת עשׂו the construction is the same as in 8, 10 ויסף שלח.

29. יש לאל ידי. Cf. Mic. 2, 1. Prov. 3, 27; the neg. is אין לאל ידך, Deut. 28, 32. Neh. 5, 5. Hitzig explains the phrase as meaning ‘*My hand is for God,*’ which would be suitable if the meaning intended were, ‘*I am capable* or *able to do everything,*’ but scarcely suitable when the meaning is, as here, ‘*I have the power.*’ Schumann, quoted by Wright, p. 87, renders, ‘*My hand belongs to strength,*’ i. e. is strong, on which Maurer remarks that in prose this would require יש אל לידי. Del., Tuch, Ges., Di. render, ‘*It is in the power of my hand;*’ see Ges., § 152. 1.

אביכם. The plural suffix refers to Jacob and those who were with him.

30. ‘*And now (when) thou art going right away, for thou longest sore for thy father's house, why hast thou stolen my gods?*’ הלך and נכסף are infs. abs., prefixed to the finite verb for emphasis; see Ges., § 131. 3 a; Dav., § 27. Rule; M. R., § 37 a. נכסף, on the form, cf. Ges., § 51. Rem. 1.

31. כי יראתי. Cf. the note on 20, 11.

32. עם אשר ‘*with whomsoever,*’ for אשר . . . עמו; the phrase is unusual, yet imitated here by the Syriac, ܥܰܡ ܡܰܢ;

see Ewald, § 333 a; Ges., § 123. 2. foot-note; M. R., § 158. Rem. a. In 44, 9. 10 we have the regular construction אֹשֶׁר ... אתו.

33. הָאֲמָהֹת is pl. of אמה, with the insertion of a ה; see Stade, § 188; Ges., § 96; and cf. the Arabic أَمَة, pl. أَمَوَات, with و instead of the Heb. ה. The Aram. ܐܡܳܐ, pl. ܐܡܗܳܬܐ, and אָמָא, pl. אַמְהָתָא, have ה as in Hebrew.

34. כַּר. LXX, εἰς τὰ σάγματα = 'saddle.' כַּר, so called from its round basket-shaped form (root כרר), was protected by a cover or tent, in which the women sat, something like a modern palanquin; see Di., p. 334.

35. לָקוּם מִפָּנֶיךָ. Cf. Lev. 19, 32. Rachel's plan was ingenious, as any attempt to examine the camel's saddle would involve contact with an unclean thing.

36. דלקת אחרי. דלק אחרי = 'to burn after one,' i. e. to hotly pursue one; so 1 Sam. 17, 53 מדלק אחרי פלשתים.

39. טרפה לא הבאתי. Cf. Ex. 22, 12.

אֲחַטֶּנָּה, for אֲחַטְּאֶנָּה, as though from a verb ל״ה; see Ges., § 74. Rem. 4; cf. § 75. Rem. 21 c; Stade, § 111. חָטָא here is synonymous with שִׁלֵּם, Ex. 22, 12.

גְּנֻבְתִי יוֹם with the old binding vowel ־ִי; cf. on 1, 24. It always has the tone with the exception of two places, Lam. 1, 1 and Hos. 10, 11, in the former of which the accent is on the penult., on account of a word of one syllable following; cf. Ges., § 90. 3 a; Stade, § 343 d. The two imperfs. תבקשנה, אחמנה are frequentative.

40. Cf. Jer. 36, 30. In the East the cold at night is quite as intense as the heat by day.

41. עֲשֶׂרֶת מֹנִים. Cf. ver. 7. Ten here, and ver. 7, is a round number = 'often.'

42. פחד. So ver. 53; cf. מורא, Is. 8, 12. פחד is abstract for concrete; cf. σέβας = σέβασμα. The Pesh. uses ‏ܕܶܚܠܬܳܐ‎ here and Is. 8, 12 in a similar way. In the Jer.-Targ. on Deut. 32, 15, and the Targ. on Hos. 8, 6, and often else-where, we find דַחְלָא used, as פחד here, and מורא in Is., l. c.; compare also a similar use of יראה in the Talmud, *Sanh.*, 64 a הוציא יראתו מחיקו וגו׳ ‘*he takes his god* (i. e. *idol*) *out of his bosom.*’ Render, ‘*If the God of my father ... had been with me ...for then ;*’ an aposiopesis: or כי עתה may be regarded as an apodosis and rendered, ‘*indeed then thou hadst,*’ etc.; cf. 43, 10 לו יֵשׁ ; Num. 22, 29 כי לולא התמהמהנו כי עתה שבנו ; חרב ... כי עתה; 2 Sam. 2, 27 (כי אז); and see Driver, § 141. Cf. Ewald, § 358 a.

43. מה אעשה לאלה. ‘*What am I going to do to these ?*’ i. e. how am I going to harm them? For עָשָׂה ל in a bad sense, see 22, 12. 27, 45. Ex. 14, 11.

44. נכרתה ... והיה. Cf. on 1, 14. The subj. to היה cannot be ברית, as this is fem., and the action itself (the making a covenant) cannot be regarded as a witness, and so cannot be subject; Di. therefore deletes the ל before עֵד, which then becomes the subject, = ‘*and let there be a witness ;*’ otherwise we must suppose with Olshausen that something has fallen out of the text.

45. ויֲרִימֶהָ מצבה, lit. ‘*and he set it up* (*so that it became*) *a pillar ;*’ cf. 1 Kings 18, 32 בנה את האבנים מזבח ; Gen. 28, 18 וישם אתה מצבה ; see Ewald, § 284 a. 1; Ges., § 139. 2; M.R., § 45. 5.

47. יגר שהדותא = Heb. גלעד, the first occurrence of Aramaic words in the O. T. שָׁהֲדוּתָא, cf. Job 16, 19 וְשָׂהֲדִי = ‘*my witness,*’ after the form of the Aramaic participle. Del. remarks on this: ‘ We have here a historical proof which

cannot be objected to, that the language which was spoken in the ancestral home of the Patriarchs was different from that spoken in Canaan,' i. e. Abraham spoke Aramaic, but when he came to Canaan adopted the language of that country, viz. Hebrew. The naming of the place with an Aramaic and Hebrew name was perhaps occasioned by its position on the frontier, between Aramaic and Hebrew-speaking people; see Di., p. 336.

49. As the text stands, ver. 49 must be closely connected with 48, '*and Mizpah* (*he called the place*) *because he said*,' etc.; so Kn., Del.; but והמצפה is strange, as nothing has been said about a מצפה '*a look-out*,' '*watch-tower*.' Ewald emends, והמצבה המצפה '*and the pillar* (*he called*) *Hammizpah*' (*Komp. der Gen.*, p. 64), which is supported by Saadiah. The Vss. vary, and do not give any clue to solve the difficulty. Di. suggests that ver. 49 was first added by the redactor of the book, as at his time a Mizpah in Gilead was better known than a Masseba, but expresses some doubt as to whether all ver. 49 was added by the later editor, or only a portion. Del. remarks that ' The addition, vers. 49–50, says nothing more than that there was a tradition which referred back the name of Mizpah of Gilead to the scene between Laban and Jacob.'

50. אם in an oath, as in 14, 23, which compare.

52. אם with a following ואם = *sive … sive;* so Del., who compares Ex. 19, 13 אם בהמה אם איש לא יהיה '*whether beast or man, he shall not live*.' Di. prefers to take them as the אם in ver. 50, and renders, '*surely not I, I will not pass;*' the אם and then לא expressing a strong negative; but this seems unnecessary.

53. ישפטו. Perhaps the plural is used as the gods of

Naḥor are mentioned, the narrator supposing that Naḥor worshipped idols, as Laban did (cf. the תרפים); cf. Josh. 24, 2. LXX, Pesh., Sam., Vulg. give the sing. יִשְׁפֹּט.

54. Cf. 26, 30. 2 Sam. 3, 20.

32.

1. אֶתְהֶם is rare (cf. Ex. 18, 20. Num. 21, 3, and אוֹתְהֶם, Ez. 23, 45). The usual form is אֹתָם. In the fem., on the contrary, the usual form is אֶתְהֶן (אֹתָן only in Ez. 16, 54).

3. מחנים = '*two camps*.' LXX have παρεμβολαί, as though מ״ were a plural from מַחֲנַי. The dual, however, suits vers. 8–11 better than a plural. The two camps were his own, and the angel host he had just met. מחנים, belonging to the tribe of Gad, was situated north of the Jabbok, and was one of the most important towns in Gilead. Some identify it with the ruins, still extant, called مَحْنَه *Maḥneh*, but Di. considers مَحْنَه too far east and north for the מחנים of this verse.

5. תאמרון. Cf. Ges., § 47. Rem. 4; Stade, § 520 a; see on 3, 4.

וָאֵחַר is imperf. Qal, by syncope, for וָאֶאֱחַר; so אֵהַב for אֶאֱהַב, Prov. 8, 17: see Ges., § 68. 1. note; Stade, § 112 c.

6. ואשלחה. Cf. on 41, 11.

7. וגם הלך לקראתך. The participle without any subject expressed; so אַף חֹבֵב, Deut. 33, 3; אם מְשֻׁלְּחִים, 1 Sam. 6, 3; cf. Gen. 24, 30 (with הנה); 37, 15 (also with הנה): see Driver, § 135. 6. 2; Ewald, § 303 b.

8. וַיֵּצֶר is imperf. Qal from צרר, Ewald, § 232 c; Stade, § 510 g. The — in the last syllable is due to the tone being drawn back to the penult., as in Job 20, 22 יֵצֶר לֹ.

9. אל המחנה האחת. מחנה, usually masc., is here

fem., as in Ps. 27, 3; as the masc. immediately follows, the fem. is strange; the Heb.-Sam. reads הָאֶחָד.

אִם יבוא ... והכהו. Cf. 18, 26. 24, 8, and ver. 18 of this chapter, where כי takes the place of אם; see Driver, § 136 a, and cf. § 115; M. R., § 24. 2 a.

פליטה is abstract, '*escape*,' and then concrete, '*escaped ones*.'

11. קטנתי מכל, render as a present, קטן being a *stative* verb, '*I am unworthy*,' lit. '*too small*;' see Driver, § 11; M. R., § 2. 1; Ges., § 126. 3.

מכל. On the (comparative) מן here = the positive with '*too*,' see M. R., § 49. 2. Rem. a; cf. 18, 14 היפלא מיהוה דבר; 4, 13 גדול עוני מנשׂוא.

כִי במקלי. ב is pointed with dag. lene, although the previous word ends in a vowel, and has a conjunctive accent, because the aspirate in the connected sounds במ is hardened (i. e. removed), just as in כָף, כְּב, בְּפ, כְּכ, בָּב; see Ges., § 21. 1. Rem. 2, and Del., p. 416.

הייתי לשׁני מהנות. '*I have become (and still am) two camps*;' see Driver, § 8.

12. ירא ... אתו. Cf. on 22, 12 and 4, 14.

אם על בנים. The phrase occurs again in Hos. 10, 14 (cf. Deut. 22, 6), and is a proverbial expression. על depicts the mother hovering over her children, and vainly trying to defend them: or על may be taken as in Job 38, 32. Ex. 35, 22 האנשׁים על הנשׁים '*the men together with the women*.' The first explanation is perhaps preferable.

14. מן הבא בידו = '*of what he had*,' lit. '*of that which had come into his hand*;' cf. 35, 4 אשׁר בידם. A.V. '*of that which came to his hand*;' better rendered in the A.V.R. '*of that which he had with him*.'

16. בניהם. The masc. suf. for the fem., as in 31, 9; cf. 26, 18 and the note there.

פרים = '*young bullocks*,' standing in the same relation to פרות as עירים '*foals*' (here '*asses' foals*') to the אתונות.

17. עדר עדר לבדו, lit. '*flock, flock alone*,' i. e. 'by herds or flocks,' so that each flock had one servant; cf. Ges., § 108. 4; M. R., § 72. 2.

18. יִפְגָּשְׁךָ. So pointed in Baer and Del.'s edition, following Ben Asher's reading. Ben Naftali reads, however, יִפְגָּשְׁךָ. Ben Asher's reading was pronounced *yif-ghā-shăcha*, Ben Naftali's *yif-gosh-cha;* cf. Baer and Del., *Gen.*, p. 85. The imperf. יִפְגַּשׁ would be a by-form of יִפֹּשׁ; cf. 1 Sam. 25, 20. On the Ḥatef-pathach under שׁ, cf. on 2, 12 וְזָהָב.

20. תדברון. Cf. on ver. 5 תאמרון.

בְּמֹצַאֲכֶם, for בִּמְצָאֲכֶם; see Ewald, § 63. 1, and cf. הֶעֱלָה, for הֶעֱלָה. במצאכם = '*when you find*,' lit. '*in your finding*.'

23. בלילה הוא. Cf. 19, 33 and the note there.

יבק is the present Wady Zerqâ, which divides the districts of 'Aglûn and Belqâ, and falls into the Jordan about midway between the Dead Sea and lake Tiberias. The modern name Zerka, = '*blue flood*,' is derived from the clear blue colour of the water. The name יבק is probably to be derived from בקק '*to pour out;*' here it is brought into connection with the root אבק, as though יַבֹּק = יֵאָבֵק = '*striver*,' '*wrestler;*' cf. Ges., *Thes.*, p. 233 a.

25. ויאבק = '*he wrestled*,' is found only here and ver. 26. אבק is connected with חבק, or perhaps is only a dialectic variation of the same; the word is perhaps chosen on account of the pr. n. יבק. In Hos. 12, 11 ויאבק is explained by שָׂרָה. Tuch and *H. W. B.*, 9th ed., propose a derivation from

אָבָק ' *dust*,' i. e. ' *to scatter oneself with dust;*' as κονίεσθαι, from κόνις, the powder with which wrestlers were sprinkled after being oiled.

26. וַתְקַע, imperf. Qal from יקע.

29. יִשְׂרָאֵל = ' *God's striver*,' ' *he who strives with God*,' in this passage and Hos. 12, 4 (hence the choice of the rare verb שׂרה in both places), as though יִשְׂרָאֵל = אֵל עִם יִשׂרה אֲשֶׁר (Wright). The name perhaps really means—as distinct from the meaning given in the text—' *God strives*,' יִשְׂרֶה אֵל; cf. יִשְׁמָעֵאל. Ges. in *Thes.*, p. 1338 b, Tuch, Reuss, and others explain it as meaning ' *Soldier of God*,' i. e. he who fights for and with God's help. In 35, 10 we have another account of the alteration of Jacob's name.

וַתּוּכַל, (I) an imperf. Hof'. of יכל, used as the imperf. of יָכֹל (Qal); so Ewald, § 127 b: (II) Stade, § 486, and Ges., § 69. 2. Rem. 3, regard it as an imperf. Qal יֻוכַל = יוּכַל = יוּכַל = יוּכַל; cf. the Arabic imperf. يَوْجَلَ from وَجِلَ, and Wright, *Arab. Gram.*, i. pp. 89–90.

30. Cf. Judg. 13, 17.

לִשְׁמִי. ' *About my name;*' cf. 20, 2 and the note there.

31. וַתִּנָּצֵל נַפְשִׁי. Cf. Ex. 33, 20; also Judg. 13, 22. Deut. 4, 33; and the note on 16, 14. וֹ = *and yet.*

פְּנִיאֵל, or פְּנוּאֵל in ver. 32, = ' *face of God;*' cf. on 4, 18 מְתוּשָׁאֵל. In פְּנִיאֵל the י is the old binding vowel; see on נְנַבְתִּי, 31, 39. The position of פְּנִיאֵל cannot be ascertained.

33. אֵת גִּיד הַנָּשֶׁה וגו״ = ' *the hip-sinew, which is on the hollow of the thigh.*' גִּיד הַנָּשֶׁה = the Arabic نَسًا, the nerve or tendon which goes through the thigh and leg to the ancle, the *nervus ischiadicus;* see Ges., *Thes.*, p. 921 a. The law forbidding the children of Israel to eat the גִּיד הַנָּשֶׁה is not

mentioned in the O. T.   It is to be found in the Talmud, *Tract. Chullin*, chap. 7.

33.

3. **והוא** is emphatic, *he*, Jacob, as opposed to the persons mentioned in ver. 2 ; see Driver, § 160. Obs.

4. **וֹיִּשָׁקֵהוֹּ**.   Mas. note, וישקהו כלו נקור = '*with points on every letter.*' The Mid. Bem., cited by Strack, *Prol. Crit.*, p. 89, has וישקהו נקוד עליו על שלא נשקו מכל לבו, i. e. 'וישקהו *with points over it, because he did not kiss him with all his heart;*' cf. the Ber. Rab. in Strack, l. c., where Rabbi Yanai, answering Rabbi Simeon ben Eleazar, explains the points on וישקהו thus : שלא בא לנשקו אלא לנשכו '*because he did not come to kiss him* (*Jacob*), *but to bite him,*' and goes on to say that Jacob's neck was turned into marble ; an account hardly in keeping with what we are told of Esau, who is never depicted in the O. T. as an inhuman person.   The points probably here, as in the other cases where they occur, mark the word as suspicious ; cf. Ewald, § 19 d.   The translation of וישקהו is wanting in several MSS. of the LXX ; cf. Lagarde, *Gen. Graece*, p. 134.   The Targ. Ps.-Jon. explains that Jacob wept because his neck was painful, and Esau because the effort gave him the toothache ! !

5. **מִי אֵלֶה לָךְ**. '*Who are these to thee ?*' לך is an ethic. dat. ; cf. Ewald, § 315 a ; M. R., § 51. 3 ; and see Ex. 12, 26. Josh. 4, 6. 2 Sam. 16, 2.

חנן with double acc.; see Ges., § 139. 2 ; M. R., § 45. 3.

6, 7. **ותגשן**, agreeing with the subj. immediately following ; so ותגש, ver. 7.   On the gender and construction of the verbs in these verses, see M. R., § 138. Rem.; Ges., § 148. 2 ; Ewald, § 340 c.

8. מִי לְךָ כָל הַמַּחֲנֶה. ' *What to thee is all this camp?'*
i. e. the cattle (32, 14–22) which Esau had already met; cf.
מִי by attraction = מה, so Judg. 13, 17 מִי שְׁמֶךָ אֲשֶׁר פָּנִשְׁתִּי;
cf. 32, 28 מה שְׁמֶךָ. Ewald, § 325 a, and Di. prefer the rendering, ' *Who to thee is the camp?'* i. e. ' *what dost thou wish to
do with them?'* ' because he brings the people into the fore-
ground.'

10. וְלָקַחְתָּ = ' *pray take;'* cf. 40, 14 וְעָשִׂיתָ ' *pray shew
mercy;'* Judg. 6, 17 וְעָשִׂיתָ לִּי אוֹת ' *pray give me a sign;'* see
Driver, § 119 δ; Ges., § 126. 6. Rem. 1.

כִּרְאֹת פְּנֵי אֱלֹהִים. '*As one sees the face of God,'* i. e.
Jacob sees that Esau's face wears a friendly (lit. divine) aspect.
' It is a divine friendliness with which he came to meet him,'
Di. רְאֹת, the subject to the infinitive, is here indefinite, as
Ex. 30, 12.

11. הֻבָאת is third pers. fem. sing. Hof'. from בוא, with the
old feminine ending ת (instead of ה), which is preserved as
the usual ending of the third fem. perf. in Arabic, Aramaic,
and Ethiopic, and appears in Hebrew before the suffixes,
and sporadically elsewhere; cf. Wright, *Arab. Gram.,* i. p. 60;
Ges., § 74. Rem. 1; Stade, § 407 b. Other instances of the
fem. ending are אָזְלַת, שָׁבַת, נִפְלְאָת, קָרְאת (the only case with
the strong verb). LXX have here ὡς ἤνεγκά σοι, = הֵבֵאתָ, possibly not understanding the anomalous form.

בְּרַכְתִּי = ' *present;'* so 1 Sam. 25, 27 בְּרָכָה = ' *a present,'*
i. e. as a proof of favour, and often accompanied with a
blessing. Knobel compares the presents paid the clergy in
the middle ages, called *Benedictiones.*

וְכִי יֶשׁ לִי כֹל. '*And because I have everything.'* וְכִי as
in Judg. 6, 30. 1 Sam. 19, 4. Is. 65, 16; see Ewald, § 353 a.

Esau has רב '*an abundance;*' Jacob, being under especial divine protection, can say he has כל '*everything.*'

13. עֹלוֹת עָלַי = '*lactantes,*' i.e. '*with young;*' so Is. 40, 11. עָלַי = '*upon me;*' cf. 48, 7. 1 Sam. 21, 16; i.e. the cattle who were with young were a burden and responsibility to Jacob. The A.V. '*with me*' does not sufficiently express the עַל.

וּמֵתוּ ... וּדְפָקוּם, lit. = '*and they over-drive them ... and they die,*' i.e. '*if they over-drive them ... they will die,*' the death of the cattle being conditional on their being over-driven; cf. 42, 38 וְהוֹרַדְתֶּם ... וּקְרָאָהוּ אָסוֹן = '*and if trouble befall him ...ye will bring down;*' 44, 22 וְעָזַב אֶת אָבִיו וָמֵת; cf. 29. See, on two perfs. with waw conv. forming a conditional sentence, Driver, § 149; also Ges., § 155. 4 a; Ewald, § 357 a; M. R., § 28.

וּדְפָקוּם, the masc. suffix for the fem.; cf. on 26, 15; and on the third pers. pl. used impersonally, see Ges., § 137. 3; M. R., § 123. 1.

14. לְרֶגֶל הַמְּלָאכָה = '*according to the pace of the cattle.*' מְלָאכָה = '*property*' (cf. מִקְנֶה), here, from the context, including cattle; cf. Ex. 22, 7 with vers. 9 and 10; 1 Sam. 15, 9.

17. בַּיִת = perhaps, as Del. suggests, '*a house,*' i.e. not a tent, אֹהֶל 27, 15, but '*a building;*' here opposed to סֻכֹּת '*booths,*' '*tents.*' Hence the name of the place, סֻכֹּת.

סֻכּוֹת was probably on the *eastern* side of Jordan, in a valley, a little further west than Peniel; cf. Judg. 8, 5. 8. Ps. 60, 8. Its exact position is uncertain. At the present day a Sâkût (ساكوت) exists, south of Bethshan, on the *western* side of Jordan, which is apparently distinct from the סֻכֹּת here mentioned; see Di., p. 348; Del., p. 421.

18. שָׁלֵם = בְּשָׁלוֹם, 28, 21, '*safe and sound,*' after his late meeting with Esau, and the danger there might possibly have been in encountering him. The LXX, Syr., Hier. take שלם as a proper name. The Heb.-Sam. reads שלום here; cf. 43, 27.

שְׁכֶם, afterwards one of the cities of refuge (Josh. 20, 7), in the hill country of Ephraim, called in the time of the Romans *Flavia Neapolis*, and at the present day by the Arabs *Nablous* (نابلس).

אֶת פְּנֵי = '*before ;*' cf. on 19, 13.

19. מִיַּד בְּנֵי חֲמוֹר אֲבִי שְׁכֶם. '*From the sons of Ḥamor, the father of S.,*' i. e. the father of Shechem (34, 2), after whom the city was called Shechem; cf. 4, 17. The LXX omit בני, ' in order to agree with 34, 1 ff.,' Di.

קְשִׂיטָה. LXX, Onq., Hier. render, '*lambs ;*' cf. Ber. Rabba, c. 79; Targg. Ps.-Jon. and Jer. '*pearls.*' Rabbi Akiba, in the Talmud, *Tract. Rosh ha-shana*, 26 b, relates that in Africa he heard a coin (מָעָה) called קשיטה. Probably the word = '*that which is weighed,*' from קשט = Arab. قَسَطَ = '*to divide,*' '*fix ;*' cf. قِسْطٌ '*a weight,*' '*pair of scales,*' then '*a fixed weight,*' equally used with the shekel by the patriarchs. From a comparison with 23, 15. 16 some have supposed the ק" to be equivalent to four shekels, but this is quite uncertain. קשיטה occurs twice again, Josh. 24, 32. Job 42, 11, but neither passage throws any additional light on the word.

34.

1. בַּת לֵאָה אֲשֶׁר יָלְדָה לְיַעֲקֹב (cf. 16, 15 f. 25, 12), an instance of P's circumstantial style.

2. וַיִּשְׁכַּב אֹתָהּ. שכב with the acc., as in Lev. 15, 18.

24. Num. 5, 13. 19. 2 Sam. 13, 14. Deut. 28, 30. Kri; cf. שׁגל, which is construed with an acc. and always has a Kri שׁכב. There is no need to emend the pointing to אֹתָהּ (cf. 26, 10), as some desire.

3. הַנַּעֲרָ.   Cf. the note on 24, 14.

וידבר על לב הנער = 'and he spake kindly to the damsel;' cf. 50, 21 וידבר על לבם; Is. 40, 2. Hos. 2, 16.

5. '*Now Jacob had heard that he (Shechem) had defiled Dinah his daughter, while his sons were with his cattle in the field, and Jacob was silent until they came.*' והחרשׁ probably, as in 37, 3 ועשׂה לו כתנת, frequentative; cf. Driver, p. 190. foot-note 1.

7. ויחר להם.   Cf. on 4, 5.

כי נבלה עשׂה בישׂראל = '*for he had wrought folly in Israel.*' עשׂה נבלה is the constant expression for any carnal offence; cf. Deut. 22, 21. Judg. 20, 6. 10.

לִשְׁכַּב.   See Ges., § 45 a; Stade, § 619 a. Notice that with the prefix ל (but not כ and ב) the inf. cstr., if the second radical is one of the letters ת, פ, כ, ד, ג, ב, takes usually a *dag. lene*, e. g. שָׁכַב with ל = (by Ges., § 28. 1; Dav., § 6. 2 d) לִשְׁכַּב, and with the *dag. lene* לִשְׁכַּב; cf. Dav., p. 16. foot-note (where a list of the so-called half-open syllables is given which is useful for reference), and Ges., § 45. 2. note.

וכן לא יעשׂה.   Cf. on 20, 9. 29, 26; and see Driver, § 39 a.

8. שְׁכֶם בני חשׁקה נפשׁו.   '*Shechem my son, his soul cleaves*' etc.   שׁכם בני, a *casus pendens;* cf. Deut. 32, 4 הצור תמים פעלו, Is. 11, 10 שׁרשׁ ישׁי ... אליו נוים ידרשׁו; see Driver, § 197. 2; Ges., § 145. 2; M. R., § 132.

בבתכם. The pl. suffix includes the brothers with the father; cf. 17 בתנו; 24, 59 f.

9. התחתנו אתנו. So Deut. 7, 3 = '*intermarry*.' אֹתָנוּ (cf. ver. 2) might possibly be pointed אַתָּנוּ; cf. the construction הַתחתן בְּ; but the acc. is found again in 1 Kings 3, 1; cf. Ewald, § 124 b.

10. וסחרוה. סחר is construed with an acc. like a verb = *going*; cf. 42, 34 ואת הארץ תסחרו = '*traffic in the land*,' i. e. go to and fro in the land for the purpose of trading.

האחזו בה = '*settle down therein*,' lit. '*hold yourselves fast therein*.' The word is peculiar to P; so again 47, 27.

12. מהר ומתן. מהר = the price paid the parents for their daughter; cf. Ex. 22, 15. 1 Sam. 18, 25 : מתן = the gifts given to the bride; cf. 24, 53, where a like distinction is made.

13. וידברו אשר טמא. LXX, καὶ ἐλάλησαν αὐτοῖς, ὅτι ἐμίαναν, which would mean, '*and spoke, because they had defiled*,' or, (?) '*and said, that they had defiled*,' which would be better expressed by ויאמרו כי טמא. The first meaning being very lame and the second doubtful, it has been conjectured that דבר here must = the Arabic دَبَرَ, and mean, '*to act craftily behind one's back*,' '*lay snares for*;' cf. 2 Chron. 22, 10 (but see Bertheau); so Ges. in *Thes.*, p. 315 a, Kn., Del. This, however, is not certain (see Di., p. 353); so perhaps it is simpler to read וידברו במרמה instead of במרמה וידברו; so Pesh. ܘܐܡܪܘ ܠܗ ܒܢܟܠܐ. Kuenen emends, אחותנו for אחותם, but then וידברו would have to mean ויאמרו איש אל אחיו.

15. בזאת = '*on this condition*,' ב being the ב of price; cf. ver. 22. 1 Sam. 11, 2.

נאות, imperf. Nif'. of אות; it occurs again in vers. 22, 23, and 2 Kings 12, 9, but nowhere else. In Rabb. the part. Nif'. נאות is found, = '*suitable*.' Hitzig and Stade, § 585 a, prefer to take it as imperf. Qal, like יָבוֹשׁ; cf. on 23, 13, where Hitzig reads אם אתה as perf. Qal from אות.

לְהִמֹּל. Cf. 17, 10 and the note there. המול לכם כל זכר is a phrase characteristic of P; so 17, 10. Ex. 12, 48.

16. וְנָתַנּוּ. *'Then we will give.'* The perf. with waw conv.; the apodosis to אם תהיו כמנו in ver. 15; cf. vers. 17, 18, 26, and often.

19. אַחַר = אֵחַר, cf. מֵאֵן, the vowel being lengthened by way of compensation for the non-doubling of ח; see Stade, § 386 d. 2; Ges., § 64. 3.

20. אֶל שַׁעַר עירם. Cf. 23, 4. 10. Is. 29, 21. Am. 5, 10. שער העיר was the oriental Forum (Del.).

21. *'These men, they are peaceably disposed towards us.'* *Casus pendens;* cf. on ver. 8; see Driver, § 198. Cf. also 41, 25. 45, 20. 47, 6. 48, 5 (לִי הם).

שְׁלֵמִים *'peaceable.'* Geiger, *Urschrift,* p. 76, renders '*Salemites,'* also taking שָׁלֵם, 33, 18, as the name of a city belonging to Shechem, which Di. describes as '*sonderbar*' (strange).

רַחֲבַת ידים. *'Wide on both sides;'* so Judg. 18, 10. Is. 22, 18; also Ps. 104, 25 (הים ... רחב ידים).

וַיֵּשְׁבוּ. LXX, Sam., Pesh., Vulg. omit the ו and connect ישבו with אתנו.

24. כל יצאי שער. Cf. 23, 10. 18, and the note on ver. 10. On the verbs יצא and בא with the accusative, and so capable of the genitive construction with the participle, see Ges., § 135. 1. note.

25. בהיותם כאבים, i. e. when they were attacked with the fever that appears on the third day after circumcision in the case of adults. The third day was the most critical time for the circumcised person; cf. Tuch, p. 409.

שִׁמְעוֹן וְלֵוִי, i. e. Simeon and Levi with their fellow-tribesmen.

אִישׁ חַרְבּוֹ. '*Each one his sword;*' see Ges., § 124. Rem. 1; M.R., § 72. 3. Rem. a; and cf. 42, 25 אִישׁ אֶל שִׂקּוֹ.

בֶּטַח, elsewhere usually לָבֶטַח, = '*in security,*' a circumstantial accusative, as in Ez. 30, 9 לְהַחֲרִיד אֶת כּוּשׁ בֶּטַח; cf. Ewald, § 287 c.

26. לְפִי חֶרֶב, not '*with the edge,*' but '*according to the mouth of*' etc., i. e. according to its ability to devour; cf. 2 Sam. 2, 26. 11, 25 כִּי כֹזֶה וְכָזֶה תֹּאכַל הֶחָרֶב. Usually לְפִי חֶרֶב is connected with הִכָּה '*to smite,*' but it is also found with other verbs, though only here with הרג (Di.).

27. בְּנֵי יַעֲקֹב. LXX, Syr., Saadiah, Sam., and two MSS. (Wright) read וּבְנֵי, which is not so abrupt; possibly waw originally stood before בני, and dropped out on account of the final ו of וַיֵּצְאוּ, ver. 26; or the Vss. might have added it, to remove the abrupt commencement of the verse. The בני are probably only Simeon and Levi, not the other sons of Jacob; cf. ver. 30, where only Simeon and Levi are blamed.

30. לְהַבְאִישֵׁנִי, lit. '*by making me stink,*' i. e. bringing me into evil repute; so Ex. 5, 21. 1 Sam. 13, 4. 2 Sam. 10, 6. Cf. the English phrase, '*To be in bad odour with any one.*'

מְתֵי מִסְפָּר, lit. '*men of number,*' i. e. so few that they might easily be counted; cf. Ges., § 106. 1; M.R., § 79. 4. Rem. a: so Deut. 4, 27. Ps. 105, 12; cf. Is. 10, 19. For מְתֵי, see on 4, 18. It is only found in the plural; see Ewald, § 178 d; Stade, § 183.

וְנֶאֱסְפוּ ... וְהִכּוּנִי. Cf. on 33, 13 וּמֵתוּ ... וּרְפָקוּם.

31. הַכְזוֹנָה, so Baer and Del., with כ aspirated; cf. 27, 38. Job 15, 8. 22, 13; and the metheg (Ga'ya) before the

pathach, to distinguish the ה interrog. from the ה of the article (Del.).   The ordinary text has ו *majusculum*.

יַעֲשֶׂה.   Cf. Lev. 16, 15 וְעָשָׂה אֶת דָּמוֹ.

35.

1. עֲלֵה בֵיתאֵל.   Bethel was situated on a hill; cf. ver. 8 מִתַּחַת לְבֵיתאֵל; 1 Sam. 10, 3.

2. אֶת אֱלֹהֵי הַנֵּכָר, especially the Teraphim (31, 19) which Rachel had taken with her.   אֱלֹהֵי נֵכָר = '*strange gods*,' lit. '*gods of strangeness;*' cf. Josh. 24, 23. Judg. 10, 16.   So בֶּן נֵכָר '*son of strangeness*'='*stranger*' (17, 10. Ex. 12, 43).

הִטַּהֲרוּ for הִתְטַהֲרוּ, by Ges., § 54. 2 b; Dav., § 26. 3.

3. הָעֹנֶה אֹתִי . . . וַיְהִי.   The participle continued by an imperf. with waw conv., a fact being stated; so 49, 17. Num. 22, 11 הַיֹּצֵא מִמִּצְרַיִם וַיְכַס אֶת עֵין; cf. on 27, 33.

4. הַנְּזָמִים, i. e. the earrings that were worn as talismans and amulets, and so belonging to the heathen practices, which Jacob required them to give up.

תַּחַת הָאֵלָה.   '*Under the terebinth*,' i. e. the well-known terebinth, which would be familiar to the reader; hence the article; cf. 12, 6.   Possibly, as Tuch suggests, the tree mentioned here is the same as the one in Judg. 9, 6, where Abimelech was made king.

The LXX have here the addition, καὶ ἀπώλεσεν αὐτὰ ἕως τῆς σήμερον ἡμέρας; which Frankel, *Einf.*, p. 56, explains as a marginal gloss, added by a pious reader who objected to וַיִּטְמֹן.

5. חִתַּת אֱלֹהִים, not '*a mighty terror*,' but '*a terror of God*,' i. e. one caused or sent by Him; cf. פַּחַד אֱלֹהִים, 2 Chron.

20, 29; פַּחַד יהוה, 2 Chron. 14, 13. חִתַּת is a ἅπαξ λεγόμ. The genitive is an objective genitive; cf. on 9, 2.

7. נגלו אליו האלהים plural, perhaps because האלהים here includes the angels; cf. 28, 12; see also 20, 13. Josh. 24, 19. Onq. here has מַלְאֲכַיָּא דַיָי 'angels of Y.;' but Berliner in his edition gives אִיתְגְּלִי לֵיה יְיָ, i.e. 'Y. appeared to him;' cf. M. R., § 135. 2. Rem. a; Ges., § 146. 2. foot-note 2.

8. אלון בכות, probably identical with the palm tree of Deborah, Judg. 4, 5, and perhaps with the Terebinth of Tabor, mentioned in 1 Sam. 10, 3.

10. Cf. 32, 29.

11. מחלציך. In 46, 26 we have יצאי ירכו; מתנים is never used in this connexion.

14. מצבה ... מצבת אבן. מצבת אבן is epexegetical; cf. 15, 18. 25, 30; and see M. R., § 72. 3.

ויסך עליה נסך. Cf. 28, 18 ויצק שמן. נסך was probably a libation of wine (Targ. Ps.-Jon., wine and water). Some (Kn., Wel.) take ויצק ... שמן as epexegetical to ויסך.

15. אשר דבר אתו שם. Contrast ver. 13 and ver. 14, where שם is omitted, as no confusion can arise in the sentence through its absence; see M. R., § 157 c; Ewald, § 331 c. 3.

16. כברת הארץ occurs again 48, 7 and 2 Kings 5, 19; but neither of these passages throws any light on the word כברת; however, from 2 Kings, l. c., it could not have been a very great distance. LXX have here Χαβραθά, but in 48, 7 τὸν ἱππόδρομον Χαβραθά (a double translation), i. e. either a stadium, or like the Arabic شوط فرس (i. c. as far as a horse can run), a measure common among the Arabs; see H. W. B., 9th ed., p. 368. Syr. ܦܪܣܚܐ, a 'parasang,' =

eighteen thousand paces or three German miles; cf. Bernst., *Syr. Lex.*, p. 408 b. Onq. has כְּרוֹב אַרְעָא = '*about an acre*,' etc.; cf. Levy, *Chald. W. B.*, i. 384 a. Del. and Tuch take it as = '*about an hour's journey.*' Cf. Ges., *Thes.*, p. 658 b.

17. כי גם זה לך בן. Cf. 30, 24, where Rachel wishes that she may have another son.

18. בן אוני = '*son of my sorrow;*' inasmuch as giving birth to him cost her her life. His father, however, instead of this ill-omened name, called him בנימין '*son of the right hand,*' i. e. son of good luck, the right side being considered by the ancients as the lucky side; cf. Ges. in *Thes.*, p. 599, and δέξιος and ἀρίστερος in Greek. בְּ is pointed with ḥireq like the pr. n. בְּן יקה in Prov. 30, 1; בְּן נן, Num. 11, 28, etc.; cf. בְּן לילה, Jon. 4, 10. Del. gives two other explanations of the name '*son of good fortune.*' I. He might have been so named because he was born when Jacob was free, his other children having been born when he was in Laban's service. II. Because he completed the lucky number (twelve) of his sons. In Ps. 89, 13 ימין = '*the south,*' so Rashi explains the name as meaning the '*south son,*' as opposed to the others, who were '*north sons,*' being born in Aramea; but Canaan is nowhere called '*the south land.*'

19. אפרתה הוא בית לחם. So 48, 7, i. e. Bethlehem, two hours south of Jerusalem; cf. Mic. 5, 1 בית לחם אפרתה; 1 Chron. 4, 4. Matt. 2, 16–18. Di., Thenius, and others, from 1 Sam. 10, 2 ff. (cf. Jer. 31, 15), consider that Rachel's grave must be sought for much further north, in the territory of Benjamin, or on the boundary between Benjamin and Ephraim, on the way between Ramah of Samuel and Gibeah of Saul, not far from Bethel. Di. points out that this would be more natural, as Rachel was the mother of Joseph and

Benjamin; הוא בית לחם here and 48, 7, therefore, is considered by them as a gloss, which was caused by the fact that Ephrath Bethlehem was better known than Ephrath near Bethel.

21. מהלאה למגדל עדר. '*On the other side of Migdal 'Eder;*' so Amos 5, 27 מהלאה לדמשׂק '*on the other side of Damascus,*' beyond Damascus.

מִגדל עדר = '*Herd's tower;*' cf. 2 Kings 17, 9. 18, 8. 2 Chron. 26, 10. It is placed by Di., who holds that there were two Ephraths, near Hebron. Knobel places it at Jerusalem (cf. Mic. 4, 8); so the LXX, who place ver. 21 after מביתאל in ver. 16. Del. considers that it was near Bethlehem.

22. בִּשְׁכֹן with כ with dag., an exception to the rule given in the note on 34, 7.

וישׁכב וגו״. Cf. 2 Sam. 16, 22. 1 Kings 2, 22.

The Massoretes here have a note, פִּסְקָא בְּאֶמְצַע פָּסוּק, i. e. '*a gap in the middle of the verse.*' There are three of these פִּסְקָאוֹת in the Pent., and twenty-eight in the books from Joshua to Ezekiel. They are not mentioned in the Talmud or Midrash (Del.). Verse 22 down to ישׂראל has a double accentuation, according as it is read as a complete verse or as a half-verse. Geiger, *Urschrift*, p. 373, points out that in the public reading of the text the two verses 22 and 23 were read as one, so that the passage might be passed over in reading as quickly as possible, and the attention of the audience diverted from the evil deed of Reuben. The correct accentuation makes ver. 22 end at ישׂראל, and ver. 23 begin at ויהיו, one section ending at ver. 22, and a fresh one beginning with ver. 23. The first way of accenting the verses here (viz. making 22 end at ישׂראל, and 23 begin with ויהיו)

is called טעם תחתון ('*lower accentuation*'); the second way
(viz. making the two verses one), טעם עליון ('*upper accentuation*'). Cf. the double set of accents in the Decalogue in
Exodus and Deut., and cf. Num. 25, 19 and Deut. 2, 8, where
there is a gap in the middle of the verse. The LXX have
the addition, καὶ πονηρὸν ἐφάνη ἐναντίον αὐτοῦ = וירע בעיניו, possibly added to avoid the abrupt ending, which is regarded by
Di. as intentional, to draw attention to 49, 3 f.

26. יָלַד. Sam. and Heb. MSS. (Di.) יָלְדוּ, as in 36, 5.

אשר is acc. case by Ges., § 143. 1 b; M. R., § 47. 2; cf.
4, 18.

36.

The Toledoth Esau follow in this chapter, preceding those
of Jacob, just as Ishmael's preceded Isaac's; the object of
the chapter, and its position before the account of Jacob's
family, being to dispose of Esau, and leave the course of the
narrative entirely free for Jacob's history. The Edomites,
Esau's descendants, first appear again in Num. 20, 14 ff.
Such a detailed account of the history of Edom can be explained sufficiently from the fact that Edom always passed as
Israel's brother (cf. Num., l. c.), and occupied an important
position in the history of Israel. A partial list of the
descendants of Esau is given in 1 Chron. 1, 35–54.

2. In 26, 34 Esau married Yehudith the daughter of Beeri
the Hittite, and Basemath the daughter of Elon the Hittite.
In 28, 9 he takes, in addition to his other wives (על נשיו)—
i. e. those of 26, 34—Mahalath, Ishmael's daughter. Thus,
according to 26, 34. 28, 9, Esau's three wives were, 1. Yehudith, Beeri the Hittite's daughter; 2. Basemath, Elon the
Hittite's daughter; and 3. Mahalath, Ishmael's daughter.

Here Esau's wives are given, 1. Adah the daughter of Elon
the Hittite; 2. Oholibamah the daughter of Anah, the daughter
of Tsibeon the Hivite; 3. Basemath the daughter of Ishmael,
the sister of Nebayoth. There are three serious discrepancies
in the two accounts. 1. The Basemath of 26, 34 is here
called Adah; 2. the Oholibamah the daughter of Anah, the
daughter of Tsibeon the Hivite (cf. below) = (apparently)
Yehudith the daughter of Beeri the Hittite of 26, 34; and
3. Ishmael's daughter Maḥalath, 28, 9, is here called Basemath. With regard to 2. בת צבעין החוי we must read (i) for
חוי, הֹרִי, as ver. 25 (cf. ver. 20) shews; and (ii) either render
בת 'granddaughter,' cf. ver. 39 (?) and 29, 5 (where בן must=
'grandson'); or emend and read בן, so Sam., LXX, Pesh.;
cf. ver. 24. note, where Anah is Tsibeon's son, and ver. 25,
where Oholibamah is Anah's daughter. Various hypotheses
have been adopted to reconcile the different accounts of
Esau's wives. Some have held that Esau had five wives;
others (Hengst., Ros.) that the wives had two names, or had
their names changed. Kn. and Ewald suppose that the
names have been corrupted by copyists. If this is the case,
the corruption must have been, as Di. points out, very great.
Others (Del., Tuch, Nöld.) explain the difference in the two
accounts as arising from two different traditions. This
seems the most natural solution, this chapter (36) embodying
one account, and 26, 34 f. 28, 9 another; see further, Del.
and Di.

6. Esau takes his wives and children, and all his property,
and leaves Canaan for the land of Seir, out of the way of his
brother Jacob.

אל ארץ as it stands yields no suitable sense. The
Targums and Vulg. read אל ארץ אחרת. Ges. renders the

text, '*to a land east of* (lit. *before*) *Jacob;*' but מפני can hardly mean this. LXX and Sam. read מארץ כנען, possibly a correction. The Syriac has ܠܐܪܥܐ ܘܡܚܟܝ, cf. vers. 8, 9, which is probably the correct reading of the text; so Di., Tuch.

7. מֹשָׁבֹת. Cf. 4, 13 מנשוא.

8. שֵׂעִיר, embracing the hill country of Edom east of the Arabah, reached from the Dead Sea to the Elanitic Gulf. The northern half is at the present day called Gebâl, and the southern eṣ-Ṣerâh.

11. The Canaanitish line.

תֵּימָן is the name of a district of Edom (Jer. 49, 20. Amos 1, 12. Hab. 3, 3) celebrated for its wise men (Jer. 49, 7. Bar. 3, 22 f.); the home of Eliphaz, Job 2, 11.

אוֹמָר, צְפוֹ, and גַעְתָּם are quite unknown.

קְנַז. Cf. 15, 19, where the Kenizites are mentioned among other tribes dwelling in the south of Canaan.

12. עֲמָלֵק, 'not identical with the Amalekites of 14, 7, who dwelt in the south of Canaan; but probably only a portion of those, who attached themselves to the families of Eliphaz, or were subject to them' (Di.); cf. ver. 22.

13. The Ishmaelitish line.

The names are not further known.

14. The Horite line.

Nothing further is known about the names here given.

15–19. The tribal princes of Edom.

15. אַלּוּף, a denom. from אֶלֶף '*a thousand*' = *chiliarch* or *phylarch*, mostly used of the tribal princes of Edom, more rarely of those of Judah, Zech. 9, 7. 12, 5. 6; see Prof. Driver, *The Expositor*, July, 1885.

16. אַלּוּף קֹרַח, mentioned in ver. 18 as the son of Esau by Oholibamah, is wanting in the Sam. Codex and Vs.,

and one Heb. MS. (Wright), and is rejected as spurious by
Tuch, Knobel, Del. Di. considers that it either crept in
here by the oversight of a copyist from ver. 18, or is a gloss
assigning Korah, according to another theory, to the family
of Eliphaz.

20–30. The tribes of the Horites.

The inhabitants of the land, as opposed to the descendants
of Esau, who took possession of it (Deut. 2, 12).

20. החרי from חור 'a hole,' so 'a dweller in a hole or cave.'
'The land of Edom abounds in holes or caves' (Di.). The
identification of the names in the following verses is uncertain; cf. Di., p. 366 f.

24. ואיה. Most commentators read איה with 1 Chron.
1, 40, LXX, Syr., and Vulg.; the text as it stands yields no
suitable sense.

הימם. Targ. Jer., Saad., Kimchi, Luther, 'mules;' so
the A.V.; more probably 'hot water springs' (A.V.R. 'the
hot springs'), which Del. identifies with the hot springs of
Kalirrhoë, beneath Zerka Maein, on the east side of the Dead
Sea, about two hours distant from it; cf. Hieron., Quaest. ed.
Lag., p. 56. Onq. and Ps.-Jon. seem either to have read
האימים, 'the giant race' mentioned in Deut. 2, 10, or to have
taken הימם as meaning this. Pesh. gives מים, and one Heb.
MS. (Wright).

26. דִּישָׁן. LXX, Pesh., Vulg., 1 Chron. 1, 41, and most
commentators read דִּישׁן.

30. לאלפיהם. 'According to their tribal princes.' LXX,
ἐν ταῖς ἡγεμονίαις, reading לְאַלְפֵיהֶם, possibly the correct reading, as this is the only place in this chapter where אלוף is
written without the ו. It is worthy of notice that many of
the names in this list, vers. 20–30, are names of animals, e. g.

שׁוֹבָל = in Arabic '*young lion*;' עֲנָה '*wild ass*;' דִּישׁוֹן, a name of an animal in Deut. 14, 5; צִבְעוֹן = in Arabic '*hyena*,' etc. Di. remarks, 'that it is a natural thing for peoples amongst whom the arts and trades were not developed to be fond of choosing their family names from the names of animals.' Cf. Rob. Smith, *Journ. Phil.*, ix. 75 ff.

31–39. The names of the kings who ruled in the land of Edom. The names in this list are also doubtful; cf. Di., p. 368 ff.

33. מִבְצָרָה, now a little village in Gebâl, El-Butseirah, four miles south of the south end of the Dead Sea.

37. מְרְחֹבוֹת הַנָּהָר. Several places in the O. T. are called Reḥoboth. The one mentioned here has been identified with رَحْبَة, Raḥba, on the Euphrates (הַנָּהָר elsewhere being the river *par excellence*, i. e. the Euphrates), south of Circesium. But this identification is not certain.

40–43. A brief review of the tribal princes of Esau. The list contains partly names of individuals, e. g. קְנַז, אָהֳלִיבָמָה, and partly names of districts, e. g. פִּינֹן, אֵלָה. Most of the names of places in this list are uncertain.

אֵלָה, perhaps the seaport אֵילַת; cf. on 14, 6.

פִּינֹן, also called in Num. 33, 42 פּוּנֹן, in Idumea, between Petra and Zoar, well known through its mines.

37.

2. '*Joseph, being seventeen years old, was tending the flock with his brethren, while yet a lad, with the sons of Bilhah, and with the sons of Zilpah, his father's wives, and Joseph brought an evil report about them to their father.*'

הָיָה רֹעֶה. Cf. the note on 4, 17.

וְהוּא נַעַר‎. LXX, ὧν νέος. A.V. renders incorrectly, '*and the lad was with the sons of Bilhah,*' for the clause is a circumstantial one; cf. Driver, § 160; M. R., § 152. Pesh. and Onq. seem to have misunderstood the words; the Syr. has ܣܘܐ ܗܘܐ ܝܬܒ ܥܡ ܒܢܝ '*and he was growing up with;*' and Onq. וְהוּא רָבֵי עִם בְּנֵי '*and he was growing up with the sons of*' etc. אֶת בני‎ has been rendered variously. Knobel gives the following meaning to the words. Joseph was feeding the flock with his brethren, as servant to the sons of Bilhah, etc.; i. e. he was handed over to their charge to learn, or to help them in their business; comparing, for this use of נַעַר‎, Judg. 7, 11. 9, 54. 19, 13, but this is giving the words of the text a very forced meaning. Del. has also a far-fetched translation, '*While yet a young man in comparison with the sons*' etc. The rendering of the LXX, '*being yet a lad, with the sons*'—אֶת‎ in the same sense as the אֶת‎ in אֶת אחיו בצאן‎, just before—is unobjectionable. וְהוּא נער‎ is perhaps a duplette of בן שבע עשׂרה שנה‎ (Di.).

דבתם רעה‎. '*An evil report about them;*' רעה‎ is intentionally indefinite, דבתם הרעה‎ would mean, '*their evil report;*' see Ges., § 111. 2 b. Possibly the words should be rendered, '*the report of them (as) an evil one,*' a sort of tertiary predicate; cf. Num. 14, 37 דבת הארץ רעה‎; 1 Sam. 2, 23 אֶת דבריכם רעים‎.

3. כי בן זקנים הוא לו‎. Cf. 21, 2. 44, 20.

וְעֶשׂה לו‎. Either a case of the perf. with simple waw; or, possibly, with waw conv. in a freq. sense (29, 3); cf. 1 Sam. 2, 19.

כתנת פסים‎ only in this chapter and 2 Sam. 13, 18 (of Tamar's garment as the clothing of a king's daughter). פס = '*an end,*' '*extremity,*' used of the hands and feet; so

כתנת פסים = '*a coat of extremities,*' i. e. one reaching to the wrists and ancles; and, as is apparent from 2 Sam. l. c., worn by the upper classes. The ordinary כתנת only reached to the knees, and had no arm-holes. Cf. פס in Aramaic (e. g. Dan. 5, 5. 24), of the extremities of the hand and foot, and ܦܣܬܐ used in a similar way. This meaning is supported by the Pesh. here, and the Vulg., LXX, and Aquila in 2 Sam. l. c. The LXX and Vulg. here, and the Pesh. in 2 Sam., and A.V. here and 2 Sam., '*a coat of (many) colours,*' margin ('*pieces*'), but this meaning of פס = '*a piece*' or '*patch,*' and so פ״ כ״ '*a variegated garment,*' is very doubtful. The A.V.R. retains the rendering, '*a coat of many colours,*' but gives in the margin, '*a long garment with sleeves.*'

4. דברו לשלם. '*To speak peaceably to him,*' or '*to address him in greeting,*' i. e. to greet him and answer his inquiries after their health (Del.). There is only one other instance of דבר with the acc., viz. Num. 26, 3.

5. ויוספו עוד שנא. Cf. on 8, 10.

7. '*And behold we were binding sheaves* (partic.) *in the midst of the field, and behold my sheaf rose, and also stood up ; and behold your sheaves were moving round* (imperf.), *and bowed down* (imperf. with waw conv., denoting a single action) *to my sheaf.*' מאלמים '*were binding,*' participle, as in 9, 18; cf. the note there. תסבינה = '*began to move round.*' 'Joseph represents the sheaves as being in motion' (Driver, § 27 γ).

ותשתחוין, ־ן *scriptio defectiva* for נָה, '*and they did bow down,*' i. e. once, and not more ; the imperf. with waw conv. describing a fact that happened once only in the past ; contrast תסבינה, where the action has begun, and is still going on to completion.

10. הבוא נבוא. See Ges., § 131. 3 a; M.R., § 37 a.

T

11. ‏וְאָבִיו שָׁמַר אֶת הַדָּבָר‎.   Cf. Luke 2, 19. 51.

12. ‏אֵת צֹאן‎.   ‏אֵת‎ with two dots over it, probably because it was regarded as **a** doubtful reading. The Bereshith Rabba, cited by Strack, p. 89, explains the points as follows, ‏וְנָקוּד‎ ‏עַל אֵת לוֹמַר שֶׁלֹּא הָלְכוּ אֶלָּא לִרְעוֹת אֶת עַצְמָן‎, i. e. ‘ *With points on the* ‏אֵת‎, *meaning that they only went to feed themselves* (*not the flocks*)!’   So the Midr. Bem., cited by Strack at the same place.

14. ‏שָׁלוֹם‎ = ‘*well-being*,’ applied to the flocks and to Joseph's brethren.

15. ‏וְהִנֵּה תֹעֶה‎ for ‏הִנְנוּ תֹעֶה = וְהִנֵּה הוּא תֹעֶה‎; cf. on 32, 7.

17. ‏שָׁמַעְתִּי אֹמְרִים‎.   Cf. 27, 6 ‏שָׁמַעְתִּי אֶת אָבִיךָ מְדַבֵּר‎; here the object is omitted; cf. M. R., § 46. 2; see also Ewald, § 284 b.

‏דֹּתָיְנָה‎ ‘*towards Dothan*.’ Dothan or Dothain, = ‘*two fountains* (?),’ or perhaps ‘*cisterns*,’ was about five hours north of Samaria. In Judith 3, 9 f. 4, 6. 7, 3. 8, 3, it is called Δωταία or Δωθαίμ, and is described as on the south side of the plain of Jezreel, between Scythopolis and Gabae, near the ancient Ginnaea (Génin). Through the plain of Tell Dothan, south of Génin, the road from Bethshan and Jezreel to Ramleh and Egypt passes (Di.); cf. ver. 25 and Ebers, *Egypten und die B. Mose's*, p. 288. The form ‏דֹּתָיִן‎ is the Aramaic dual, of which ‏דֹּתָן‎ is a contraction; cf. ‏קַרְתָּן‎ and ‏קִרְיָתַיִם‎, ‏עֵינָם‎ and ‏עֵינַיִם‎, and see Ges., § 88. 1. Rem. 1, and the forms found on the Moabite stone, e. g. ‏קריתים = קריתן‎, line 10; ‏מאתים = מאתן‎ (‘ *two hundred*’), line 20; ‏דבלתים = דבלתן‎, line 30; ‏חורונים = חורנן‎, line 31.

18. ‏וּבְטֶרֶם יִקְרַב … וַיִּתְנַכְּלוּ‎.   Cf. the note on 2, 5; also Driver, § 127 β.

‏וַיִּתְנַכְּלוּ אֹתוֹ‎.   ‘ *They plotted against him*.’ Hithpa‘el with the acc. as in 1 Chron. 29, 17 ‏הִתְנַדַּבְתִּי כָל אֵלֶּה‎; see Ewald,

§ 124 b; Ges., § 54. 3 c; cf. Ps. 105, 25, where התנכל takes the prep. ב, not the acc. as here.

19. בעל החלמות. Cf. on 14, 13. הלזה as in 24, 65; cf. the note there.

21. לא נכנו נפש = '*let us not smite him as to life*,' i. e. mortally; so Deut. 22, 26 ורצחו נפש; see Ges., § 139. note, and cf. the note on 3, 15.

24. הברה. Cf. Jer. 38, 6 (where Jeremiah is cast into a pit with no water in it, but mud); Lam. 3, 53.

25. לאכל לחם = '*to take their meal*,' lit. '*to eat bread*,' the meal being so called from the chief article of food; cf. 31, 54. 43, 25. Matt. 15, 2.

ארחת ישמעאלים. So Is. 21, 13 ארחות דדנים; Job 6, 19 ארחות תמא. ארחת is the part. Qal fem. of ארח, used in a collective sense. אֹרַח = '*a single traveller*,' אָרְחָה '*a company of travellers*,' '*a caravan*.' Other feminines used collectively are אַחֲוָה '*brotherhood*,' from אָח '*brother*;' עֲנָנָה '*a mass of clouds*,' from עָנָן '*a cloud*;' גּוֹלָה '*a band of exiles*;' see Ges., § 107. 3 d; Stade, § 312 b.

נכאת = '*tragacanth gum*;' צרי = '*balsam*' (צְרִי for צֳרִי, like רְאִי for רֳאִי, Job 37, 18; דְּמִי for דֳּמִי, Is. 38, 10): לט = '*ladanum*;' three articles which even at the present day form the chief trade of the Arab-Egyptian caravans. Ebers, *Ægypten* etc., p. 292, has found נכאת and צרי on the Egyptian inscriptions, but not לט; he also (p. 293) mentions that gum, balsam, and incense are the chief imports from the East to Egypt at the present day, and—with the exception of a short distance by rail—are brought by the same method, i. e. caravans, as in the days of the patriarchs. The caravan road from Damascus to Egypt is the same now as in the time of Joseph.

26. מַה בֶּצַע = '*what gain, that we kill?*' on the construction, cf. M. R., § 93. Rem. b; see also Ewald, § 326 a.

28. מְדָנִים. Cf. on 25, 2. The name of Ishmaelites was probably of more modern origin than that of Midianites, and applied generally to all Arabs (Di.).

בְּעֶשְׂרִים כֶּסֶף. שֶׁקֶל being omitted by Ges., § 120. 4. Rem. 2. The LXX have εἴκοσι χρυσῶν, so in 45, 22. The price of a slave between five and twenty years was twenty shekels; see Lev. 27, 5. On slavery in Egypt, see Ebers' note, *Egypten und die Bücher Mose's*, p. 293 ff., where he shews that the narrative in this chapter is quite in accordance with what used to take place at the time of the Pharaoh, whose favourite Joseph became.

33. טָרֹף טֹרַף. Cf. Ges., § 131. 3. Rem. 2, and see Job 6, 2 שָׁקוֹל יִשָּׁקֵל, the inf. abs. Qal and imperf. Nif., Gen. 46, 4 אַעַלְךָ גַם עָלֹה, inf. Qal and imperf. Hif.

35. כִּי, either (1) introducing the words of the speaker, or (2) the Latin *imo*, '*no*.'

שְׁאֹלָה = '*to Sheol*,' '*the underworld;*' always without the article. The word probably = '*the hollow place*,' from שָׁאַל = שָׁעַל. Another derivation, now almost obsolete, is from שָׁאַל '*to ask*,' with reference to the inexorable demand made by death on all mortals, and then transferred to the place of death, to which all mortals must come, '*the house of meeting for all living*,' Job 30, 23; cf. Is. 5, 14. Hab. 2, 5.

36. הַמְדָנִים either abbreviated or corrupted from מְדָנִים, which is the reading of all the versions here.

לְפוֹטִיפַר. פּוֹטִיפַר is the same as פּוֹטִי פֶרַע, 41, 45. 46, 20, the former name being abbreviated from the latter. LXX have both Πετεφρῆς and Πεντεφρῆς, see Lagarde, *Gen. Graece*, pref., p. 20. The name is the Egyptian *Peti-pa(pha)-ra*,

meaning, '*one devoted to Ra*,' the sun god, see Ebers, p. 296.
Ra is the Egyptian sun god, the chief place of his worship
being Heliopolis.   Brugsch, *Gesch.*, p. 248, explains the
name as=*puti-par*, '*Gift of him that has appeared*.'

סריס, either to be taken in its literal sense, cf. Ebers,
p. 299, or merely equivalent to '*officer*,' '*official*;' see further,
Ebers, pp. 297, 300, who renders סרים '*courtier*;' remarking
that סרים, among the Orientals, had much the same meaning
as '*Schranz*' in German ('*parasite*,' '*courtier*').

שׂר הטבחים='*captain of the executioners*.'   The captain
of the executioners was also chief of the body-guard and
superintendent of the state prison (40, 3 f.), see Ebers, p. 301,
who describes Potiphar's office as that of chief minister
of police.   A similar office existed among the Babylonians,
2 Kings 25, 8 ff. Jer. 39, 9. 52, 12. Dan. 2, 15.   See further,
Ebers, p. 300 ff.   The LXX have ἀρχιμάγειρος, which rendering is perhaps due to 39, 6.

38.

1. ויט '*turned aside*,' Del. renders, '*removed his dwelling*,'
sc. אהלו; but ויט without אהלו is not found in this sense,
and further, no pr. name of a place follows עד.

עדלמי.   Adullam was in the plain (שׁפלה) of Judah,
presumably north-west of Hebron (Di.), identical, perhaps,
with the modern Deir Dubbân, north of Eleutheropolis.

2. איש כנעני.   Onq. renders גְּבַר תַּגָּרָא (cf. Prov. 31, 24.
Is. 23, 8) '*a merchant*,' possibly finding Judah's marriage
with a daughter of Canaan objectionable.   Berliner, however,
in his edition has גְּבַר כְּנַעֲנַי, but mentions the other reading
in his notes, p. 14 of part ii.   Cf. Levy, *Chald. W. B.*, ii.
p. 528.

3. ויקרא. Sam., Targ. Ps.-Jon., Heb. Codd. (Di.) read ותקרא, see 29, 34 and vers. 3, 4.

5. והיה, see Driver, § 133. LXX has αὔτη δὲ ἦν, which points to a reading והיא (hardly והיתה, Di.), which gives a suitable sense; cf. 1 Sam. 23, 15. 24. 2 Chron. 10, 2; see also Geiger, *Urschrift*, p. 462. As the text stands it must be rendered, '*he (Judah) was*,' but the perf. with waw is very harsh, and a reference to Judah is not what we should expect.

בכזיב=the אכזיב of Mic. 1, 14. Josh. 15, 44; it was also in the low country (שפלה) of Judah.

8. ויבם=to perform the duty of marrying the deceased brother's widow when he left no son; see Deut. 25, 5. The brother-in-law in this case was called יָבָם.

9. והיה . . . . ושחת. The perfect with waw conv. in a frequentative sense, see Driver, § 121; also Ewald, §§ 342 b, 345 b. Other examples are Num. 21, 9 . . . והיה אם נשך הנחש; Ex. 33, 9 והיה אם זרע . . . ועלה; Judg. 6, 3 והביט . . . וחי; והיה . . . ירד, with a simple impf. following. Other instances of אם in a temporal sense with the perf. are Ps. 41, 7. Amos 7, 2. Is. 4, 4; compare Ewald, § 355 b.

ושחת ארצה; a pregnant construction, see Ges., § 141. זֶרַע must be understood after ושחת.

נתן. Cf. the note on נשא, 4, 13.

11. בית אביך is acc. of place, see Ges., § 118. 1.

12. ויעל על גזזי וגו״, lit. '*he went up about the shearers of his flock*,' i.e. to see after them; cf. the use of על in 30, 33 על שכרי.

רֵעֵהוּ. '*His companion*.' LXX and Vulg. read the consonants as רֹעֵהוּ '*his shepherd*;' so Luther.

תמנתה is probably the Timnah near Gibea, in the hill country of Judah (Josh. 15, 57), and not identical with the Timnah belonging to the Danites (Josh. 19, 43), on account of עלה; Di. after Kn. Tuch (cf. Merx's note however) and Del. consider that there was only one Timnah. The name is found on the inscriptions in the form *Tamnaa*, Schrader, *K. A. T.*², 170. Rob., *Pales.*, ii. 343, mentions three Timnahs, and considers the one occurring here to be in the hill country of Judah.

14. ותסר בגדי אלמנותה. Cf. Judith 10, 3.

ותכס, i. e. the face; cf. Deut. 22, 12. Jon. 3, 6, where the object of כסה is omitted.

ותתעלף. '*And veiled herself;*' cf. Prov. 7, 10. LXX, Pesh., Onq. render, '*adorned herself.*'

בפתח עינים='*at the gate of Ainaim.*' עֵינָיִם being the same as עֵינָם (cf. on 37, 17 דתינה), Josh. 15, 34 (with the article), and עֵינַיִם in ver. 21. So most modern commentators; cf. ver. 21. The Vss. took the word as a *nom. appell.*, contrary to ver. 21, excepting the LXX who give Αἰνάν. The Pesh. has ܦܳܠܓܽܘܬ ܐܽܘܪ̈ܚܳܬܳܐ '*dividing of roads,*' Onq. פָּרָשׁוּת עֵינַיִם, lit. '*division of eyes,*' i. e. cross-way; cf. Levy, *Chald. W. B.*, ii. p. 212 and p. 304. Targ. Ps.-Jon. פָּרֵשַׁת אָרְחִין דְּכָל־עַיְינִין מִסְתַּכְּלִין, i. e. '*the cross-ways whither every one's eyes look!*' Vulg. '*in bivio itineris.*' Saad. مَنْظَر '*a watch tower.*' The A. V. has, '*in an open place,*' margin, '*The door of eyes.*' A. V. R. '*in the gate of Enaim.*'

והוא לא נתנה לו לאשׁה='*without her being given him to wife;*' circ. cl.

15. ויחשׁבה לזונה. Cf. 1 Sam. 1, 13 ויחשׁבה עלי לשׁכרה.

כי כסתה פניה. LXX and Vulg. add ולא ידעה '*and*

he did not know her,' to explain פ״ כי ב״, which gives the reason why Judah did not recognise her, and not why he took her for a harlot.

18. חתמך. ' *The signet ring,'* which was worn round the neck on a chain (פתיל). As these were always worn by their owners, they would be easily identified again by them; cf. Song of Songs 8, 6. On חותם, cf. a note in Del., *Gen.*[4], p. 557, where he regards the word as the only possible trace of the use of writing in Genesis (die einzige mögliche Spur des Schriftgebrauches in der Genesis).

ומטך. ' *And thy staff.'* מטה was a carved or ornamented staff, and so different from מקל, a stick in its natural condition. Among the Babylonians every man carried a stick with an ornamented top, and wore a signet ring; see Herod. i. 195. The Versions render פתיל differently. LXX have ὁρμίσκον, ' *a necklet.'* Hieron. ' *armillam.'* Onq. שׁוֹשׁיפָך ' *thy cloak.'* Syr. عَـمْـقـي ' *thy cloak.'*

21. הקדשה הוא. Cf. the note on 19, 33. קדשה=' *a religious prostitute,'* lit. ' *one dedicated'* (קָדֵשׁ ' *to set apart,'* ' *dedicate'*) to the goddess Ashtoreth (עשׁתרת). Cf. Deut. 23, 18 for the law forbidding this dedication to Ashtoreth in Israel.

24. ויהי כמשׁלשׁ חדשׁים. ' *And it happened after about three months;'* the double preposition is exceedingly rare, but cf. 1 Sam. 10, 27 LXX כמחדשׁ; 1 Sam. 14, 14 כבחצי; Lev. 26, 37 כמפני חרב, also כבראשׁנה. חדשׁ is here fem., but nowhere else; the Heb.-Sam. reads the more correct שׁלשׁת.

ותשׂרף. This punishment in the Levitical law was applicable only to the daughters of a priest; see Lev. 21, 9. In other cases the offender was stoned, Lev. 20, 10. Deut. 22, 23 ff. John 8, 5.

25. '*She was being brought out, and she sent to her father-in-law, saying, By a man to whom these belong am I with child;*' a more expressive way of saying, '*As she was being brought forth, she sent*' etc.; so Judg. 18, 3 הֵמָּה עִם בֵּית ... וְהֵמָּה; 1 Sam. 20, 36 הַנַּעַר רָץ וְהוּא יָרָה, also Gen. 29, 9. 44, 3. 4; see Driver, § 169; Ewald, § 341 c.

מוּצֵאת is fem. partic. Hof. of יצא for מוּצֶאֶת; cf. לֵאמֹר for לֵאֱלֹהִים for לֵאלֹהִים; see Stade, § 112 c; Ges., § 23. 2 b.

28. וַיִּתֶּן יָד. '*And one stretched out a hand,*' i. e. a hand appeared; cf. יתן in Job 37, 10 מִנִּשְׁמַת אֵל יִתֶּן קֶרַח; Prov. 13, 10 רַק בְּזָדוֹן יִתֵּן מַצָּה; so Del. Di. prefers to render, '*then he* (sc. הַבֹּהֵן) *stretched out*' etc., i. e. there was stretched out; see Ges., § 137. 3. Rem. 1; M. R., § 123. 3; and cf. Cheyne's crit. note on Is. 14, 30.

שָׁנִי, i. e. '*a thread coloured with crimson.*' שָׁנִי is the crimson colour derived from the cochineal; called in Heb. either שָׁנִי, or more fully תּוֹלַעַת שָׁנִי.

29. וַיְהִי כְמֵשִׁיב, hardly, '*and he was as one drawing back his hand,*' i. e. made an attempt to draw back (Del.); but rather equivalent to כְּהֱיוֹתוֹ מֵשִׁיב, or כַּהֲשִׁיבוֹ, '*and it came to pass when he drew back;*' so Di., who compares 40, 10. Jer. 2, 17; Ewald, § 337 c; but see Driver, § 135. 6. Obs. 2, who suggests the emendation כְּהָשִׁיב as more in accordance with Biblical analogy.

מַה פָּרַצְתָּ עָלֶיךָ פָּרֶץ=' *Why hast thou made a rent for thyself?*' (20, 3) עָלֶיךָ '*for thyself,*' '*on thy account*'); so LXX, Aquila, Luther, Di., Del. Others (Ges., Kn.) render, '*Why hast thou made a breach?*' '*Upon thee a breach!*' cf. 16, 5 חֲמָסִי עָלֶיךָ: i. e. either (Ges.) '*thou must bear the guilt of this breach;*' or Knobel, '*may a breach come upon thee;*' but this is not so natural, and would rather require הַפֶּרֶץ.

39.

1. הישמעאלים. '*Ishmaelites*,' i.e. Arabs; cf. 37, 28, the name being given to Arabs in general.

2. איש מצליח. '*A prosperous man*;' מצליח in the next verse is slightly different=' *to cause to prosper*.'

3. וכל אשר הוא עשה. '*All that he was doing*,' almost equivalent to וכל אשר הוא יעשה; so ver. 6 אכל, ver. 22 עשים; 1 Kings 3, 2 מזבחים; see Driver, § 135. 2. Obs., 'the participle denoting not a *continuous state*, but a fact liable to recur.'

The position Joseph held in Potiphar's household was that of steward, somewhat similar to the post Eliezer occupied in Abraham's family (15, 2 f.); cf. Ebers, p. 303, who speaks of the position of steward as 'a dignity which we meet with at the earliest times in every great Egyptian household.'

4. וכל יש לו for וכל אשר יש לו; cf. ver. 5. Ex. 9, 4. 18, 20. On the omission of the relative, see Ges., § 123. 3 a; M. R., § 160; Ewald, § 333 b, who remarks that 'the omission of the relative in *prose* is almost entirely confined to the books of Chronicles.'

5. מאז הפקיד. מאז with the perfect, as in Ex. 5, 23 ומאז באתי אל פרעה; 9, 24 מאז היתה לגוי. In Ex. 4, 10 the inf. follows מאז.

6 ff. On the history of Joseph and Potiphar's wife, cf. the Egyptian tale, contained in the Papyrus d'Orbiney, translated by Ebers, p. 311 ff.

ולא ידע אתו. אִתּוֹ referring to Joseph; cf. ver. 8 אִתִּי; '*and he did not know anything with him (Joseph)*'=he did not trouble himself about anything that was with him, i. e. he left everything to Joseph's care, except his food, which

could not be entrusted to him on account of the strictness
of the Egyptian laws as to cleanness and uncleanness; see
43, 32. 46, 34; so Kn., Ebers. Del., however, explains
differently. Potiphar left everything he could to Joseph's care,
except eating his food, which naturally could not be done by
deputy. אתו may also be taken reflexively, and referred to
Potiphar = 'with himself,' i.e. in his own mind; cf. Ges., § 124.
1; M. R., § 89 a. The A. V. offers a third rendering, also
regarding אתו as reflexive, '*And he knew not aught he had.*'

8. מה בבית. '*What is in the house;*' or מה = '*anything,*'
as in Prov. 9, 13. Job 13, 13. The Heb.-Sam. has מאומה.

9. איננו גדול בבית הזה ממני = '*he is not greater
in this house than I am,*' i.e. I hold the same position in this
house that he does. These words are taken differently by
Maurer, '*There is nothing in this house too great for me;*'
and by the A.V., '*There is none greater in this house than I.*'
But איננו cannot be translated indefinitely, as it would be in
these two renderings.

10. יום יום = '*day by day,*' '*daily;*' so Ex. 16, 5. Prov.
8, 30; see Ges., § 108. 4; Ewald, § 313 a; M. R., § 72. 2.

11. ויהי כהיום הזה. '*And it came to pass, just about
that time;*' cf. Deut. 6, 24 לחיתנו כהיום הזה; Neh. 5, 11
השיבו נא להם כהיום. In 50, 20 we find the more usual form
כיום הזה.

12. בבגדו. In the singular we should—from the analogy
of other words of the same kind, e. g. מַלְכִּי from מֶלֶךְ, דַּרְכִּי
from דֶּרֶךְ—expect בִּבְגְּדוֹ; cf. יְקָבְּךָ from יֶקֶב, in Deut. 15, 14;
בִּגְדִי, Ez. 9, 3; עָמְדִי, Dan. 8, 17; and see Ges., § 93. Rem. 1;
Stade, § 345 b. In the plural the aspirate has no dagesh.

14. הביא לנו איש עברי = '*he (Potiphar) hath brought
us a Hebrew man;*' or impersonally, '*one has brought,*' i.e.

'*there has been brought.*' אִישׁ עִבְרִי, i. e. one whom the Egyptians would regard with little favour; cf. 43, 32. 46, 34. On עברי, cf. on 14, 13; the name has been supposed to be found in the Egyptian inscriptions, in the form '*apuriu;*' see Ebers, p. 316, but the *p* for *b* is a difficulty, and this opinion is now generally given up.

לְצַחֶק בָּנוּ. Retrogression of the tone, by Ges., § 29. 3 b; cf. on 4, 17. See also Ges., § 64. Rem. 2; Stade, § 88. 2 b; so in ver. 17. לצחק בנו, as in Prov. 1, 26 = '*to wanton with us,*' different from צחק את, 26, 8. The LXX have ἐμπαίζειν; cf. Ewald, § 217. f. 2 δ.

בנו. Potiphar's wife wishes to imply that the other females of the household had been similarly treated by Joseph.

15. אצלי. Sam. has בידי, but Del. points out that with this reading she would betray herself.

18. ואקרא ... כהרימי. So Lev. 16, 1 בקרבתם ... וימתו; Josh. 8, 24 כבלות ... ויפלו; 1 Kings 18, 18 בעזבכם ... ותלך; see Driver, § 118; Ges., § 132. 3. Rem. 2, and cf. the note on 18, 25. Render, '*When I lifted up my voice and cried.*'

20. אדני יוסף. So 42, 30. 33. *Pluralis excellentiae,* see Ges., § 108. 2 b; M. R., § 135. 2.

בית הסהר = perhaps '*the house of surrounding,*' or '*shutting in,*' i. e. a prison surrounded by a wall, if סהר be related to סחר, סגר; cf. the Syriac ܣܝܳܐܪܐ. Ebers, p. 317 f., compares the fortress at Memphis called '*White wall*' (a name found on many inscriptions), with which he identifies the בית הסהר of this chapter, and 40, 3. 5. The LXX have ὀχύρωμα. The name for prison better known to the Hebrews was either בית הבור, Ex. 12, 29; בית כלא, Is. 42, 7; or מסגר, Is. 42, 7.

מקום אשר. The sentence commencing with אשר is a

genitive after the construct state מקום; see Ges., § 116. 2;
M. R., § 82 c; so 40, 3 מקום אשר יוסף אסור; 2 Sam. 15, 21
במקום אשר יהיה שם.

אסורי, Kri אֲסִירֵי, the Ktb. being the part. pass. Qal, the
Kri the adj. of the form קָטִיל; cf. Ges., § 84. 5.

אסורים. שם is omitted after אסורים, as in 35, 13; contrast 40, 3, and see Ewald, § 331 c. 3; cf. ver. 22, where the
ordinary editions have Ktb. האסורים, with the Kri האסירם,
as here, while Baer and Del. have האסירים in their text.

21. ויתן חנו, lit. 'gave his (*Joseph's*) *favour in the eyes
of*,' i.e. and gave him favour in the eyes of, etc.; cf. Ex. 3,
21. 11, 3. 12, 36 (all).

שר בית הסהר. Cf. 40, 3, where the captain of the
prison is Potiphar. Del. and Ebers, however, regard the person
mentioned in this verse as the special governor of the prison
for state prisoners. Potiphar was, as police minister, in
control over all the prisons; but not an actual prison
governor. Otherwise we must suppose that these conflicting
statements emanate from different sources.

22. היה עשה. Cf. the note on 4, 17.

23. Render, '*There was no governor of the prison overlooking* (lit. *seeing*) *anything that he did* (lit. *anything in his
hand*), *in that Yahweh was with him, and that which he was
doing Yahweh made to prosper*.'

40.

1. ויהי . . . החטאו. So 14, 1. 2 עשׂו . . . ויהי בימי; Ex.
12, 41 b ויהי בעצם היום הזה יצאו; where instead of the *perfect*
in the second half of the clause, the *imperfect* with *waw
conversive* might stand, and most frequently does stand; see
Driver, § 78.

משקה מלך מצרים והאפה = '*the cupbearer and baker of the king of Egypt.*' Notice the difference in the idiom in English and Hebrew. English says, '*the cupbearer and baker of the king ;*' Hebrew, '*the cupbearer of the king and the baker,*' or more commonly with the third pers. suffix, '*his baker ;*' see Ewald, § 339 b; M. R., § 75. 2. Rem. a; Ges., § 114, footnote. The אפה has been discovered on the Egyptian inscriptions, but not the משקה; see Ebers, p. 321.

2. סָרִיסָיו with firm qameç, as in בְּרִית, though the more usual form with simple shewa under the ס is also found. The form with qameç is explained by Stade, § 209, either from a by-form kaṭṭil, i. e. for סַרְּים, and as ר cannot be doubled, סָרִים, so בְּרִית; or through the influence of the counter-tone on the first syllable; for this he compares שְׁלָישִׁים for שְׁלִישִׁים, from שָׁלִישׁ. Cf. also פָּרִיצֵי and פְּרִיצֵי, and Ges. in the *Thes.* s. v.

3. מְקוֹם אֲשֶׁר. Cf. the note on 39, 20.

4. וַיִּהְיוּ יָמִים בְּמִשְׁמָר, lit. '*and they were days*' etc., i. e. some time; cf. 4, 3 מִקֵּץ יָמִים = '*after some time;*' so we find יָמִים used indefinitely in 1 Sam. 29, 3. Dan. 8, 27. Neh. 1, 4.

5. אִישׁ כְּפִתְרוֹן חֲלֹמוֹ. '*Each according to the interpretation of his dream,*' i. e. each one dreamt a dream that had its special reference to himself, and its own interpretation.

הַמַּשְׁקֶה וְהָאֹפֶה אֲשֶׁר לְמֶלֶךְ מִצְרַיִם. Cf. the note on 29, 9. This construction is closer to the English idiom than the one noticed in ver. 1, and must be used if the two words that should be in the construct state are to stand together; the construction מַשְׁקֵה וְאֹפֶה מֶלֶךְ מ״ hardly occurs (two construct states and one genitive), so we must, if we wish to keep אפה and משקה together, use אֲשֶׁר לְ or לְ, as in 7, 11; otherwise the alternative construction followed in ver. 1 must be adopted.

6. זֹעֲפִים = '*of a sad countenance*,' '*cast down*;' so Dan. 1, 10; cf. פנים נזעמים in Prov. 25, 23. Symm. has σκυθρωποί here. On the importance attached to dreams among the Egyptians, see Ebers, p. 321.

7. מדוע פניכם רעים. Cf. Neh. 2, 2 מדוע פניך רעים = '*why dost thou look so troubled?*'

8. ופתר אין אתו = '*and there is no one to interpret it*;' cf. 41, 8 ואין פותר אותם; on אין, see Ges., § 152. 1; M. R., § 128. 2 b.

9. בחלומי והנה וגו׳. '*In my dream, behold a vine was before me*;' the apodosis without a verb being introduced by waw; so ver. 16 (cf. 41, 17, where waw is omitted); 2 Sam. 15, 34. Prov. 10, 25 a; see Driver, § 125. Obs.; M. R., § 132 b. הנה is inserted to attract the attention of the reader to the nature of the dream; contrast 41, 22 וארא בחלמי, where no especial stress is laid.

10. והוא כפרחת עלתה וגו׳. I. The A.V., Knobel, Tuch, Driver render, '*And it was as though it budded, and its blossoms shot forth*;' cf. the analogous use of היה כ in 19, 14, in the sense '*to appear*,' '*to seem*.' II. Di. and apparently Del. prefer taking כ in a temporal sense, and render, '*And it, as it budded, its blossoms shot forth*,' comparing 38, 29 כמשיב; cf. the note there, and Driver, § 135. 6. Obs., who points out that this usage of the participle, though common in the Mishna (see Geiger, *Lehr- und Lesebuch zur Sp. der Mishna*, p. 52), is without analogy in Biblical Hebrew.

נִצָּהּ '*its blossom*.' נִץ occurs nowhere else in the Bible in the sense '*blossom*,' but is common in the Mishna; the feminine נצה being used in Biblical Hebrew (as a *nomen unitatis* according to Ges., § 107. 3 e). The masc. here may be explained as a collective, and so construed with the fem. עלתה (Wright). Others take נצה as abbreviated from נִצָּתָה; see Ewald, § 257 d; Stade, § 347 c. 2 (and Del. on Ps. 27, 5), who gives as other examples, מִדָּה, פִּנָּה, צֵידָה, נֻלָּה. נצה may be taken, by Ewald, § 281 d, as accus. to עלתה='*and it (the vine) went up into blossoms;*' cf. עלה in Is. 5, 6. 34, 13. Prov. 24, 31; so הבשילו in the second half of this verse. Possibly the text ought to be pointed נִצָּה, the fem. ending ה— being altered into ה— (the suffix), to conform with אשכלתיה in the second half of the verse. Prov. 7, 8 (פנה); Job 11, 9 (מדה); Zech. 4, 2 (נלה), cited by Stade above, are similar to נצה in this verse, and may possibly be mistakes for the fem. forms.

אשכלתיה = '*its clusters.*' ענב = '*the ripe grape.*' On the use of wine in Egypt, see Ebers, p. 322 f.

12. שלשת השרגים, *casus pendens.* ' *The three branches, they are three days;*' cf. ver. 18.

13. ישׂא . . . את ראשך. '*Shall lift up thy head,*' i. e. shall take thee from prison; cf. 2 Kings 25, 27.

כמשפט הראישון, lit. '*according to the former custom,*' i. e. as thou wert accustomed to do.

14. כי אם זכרתני. Di., following Ewald, § 356 b, cf. § 342 b. 2, renders, '*only that thou rememberest me, with thee* (i. e. *thyself*), *when it is well with thee, and wilt shew me kindness,*' comparing 2 Sam. 5, 6. 2 Kings 23, 9, which are different from this passage, as the כי אם in both is dependent on a previous verb. Wellhausen emends to אך; cf. Driver, § 119 δ. foot-note 2; and 23, 13; which would remove any difficulty, אם זכרתני . . . ועשית being a conditional sentence, exactly like 43, 9. 47, 6; see Driver, § 138. 1 a; M. R., § 26.

אתך. Cf. Job 12, 3. 14, 5.

15. כי שׂמו אתי בבור. ' *That they should have put me in prison;*' cf. Ruth 1, 12 כי אמרתי ' *that I should have said;*' 1 Sam. 17, 26 b כי חרף ' *that he should have reproached;*' see Driver, § 39. 8. Obs.

16. סלי חרי. ' *Baskets of white bread.*' חרי from חור ' *to be white,*' properly an adj. = ' *what is white,*' and then applied to what is baked; so the Arab. خُوَارِى (Del.). Vulg. ' *canistra farinae,*' LXX κανᾶ χονδριτῶν; cf. ver. 17 מאכל פרעה. The baker carried his wares on his head, an exceptional mode of carrying things among the Egyptians; see Ebers, p. 331 f.

17. מכל מאכל פרעה. ' *Of all kinds of food for Pharaoh,*' cf. Dan. 1, 5 פת בג המלך; Gen. 49, 20 מעדני מלך. מכל, מן partitive; cf. on 4, 3.

19. ישׂא . . . מעליך. ' *Shall lift up thy head from off thee,*' i.e. shall behead thee. There is a play on the words here, the phrase being the same as in ver. 13. Wright compares John 12, 32. The punishment of the chief baker was one of the heaviest that could befall an Egyptian. The exposure of the body was intended to make the sentence more severe, and was especially repugnant to the superstitious Egyptians, who regarded the life after death as dependent on the body remaining unmutilated; see Ebers, p. 334.

20. יום הלדת את פרעה. The construction is the same as in 4, 18; see the note there. הֻלֶּדֶת is inf. Hof. of ילד, for the ordinary form הוּלֶדֶת; cf. Ez. 16, 4 הֻלֶּדֶת, and מוּסָד, Is. 28, 16 (see Dav., § 3. 2; Stade, § 29), the ל being doubled to compensate for the shortened vowel.

21. על משקהו = ' *to his butlership*' or ' *cupbearership.*'

41.

1. יָמִים. Cf. on 29, 14.

הַיְאֹר. Always with י without the dagesh. הַיְאֹר '*the river*' *par excellence*, the Nile, is the Hebrew form of the Egyptian *aur-áa*, i. e. '*the great stream*,' Ebers, p. 338, which became in the mouth of the people *iar-á*, *iaro*.

On the participle in this and the two following verses, cf. on 9, 18.

2. בָּאָחוּ. אחו, LXX ἄχει, '*Nile-grass*,' is the Hebrew form of the Egyptian *axu* or *axuu*, '*reeds*' or '*grass*' growing in marshy ground; see Ebers, p. 338; also notice Hieron. ad Jes. 19, 7, who describes it as 'omne quod in palude virens nascitur.'

2–4. The number of the cows, seven (cf. the same number in the next dream), was a sacred number among the Egyptians, as among other Oriental nations (Ebers, p. 337); cf. 21, 28. 30. On the first dream Di. remarks, 'The Nile floods are what the fruitfulness of Egypt chiefly depends on. The ox was the symbol of the Nile (Diod. i. 51), and especially sacred to Osiris, the discoverer of agriculture (Diod. i. 21). The cow was, in the Egyptian hieroglyphic writing, the sign for the earth (Macrob., *Sat.*, i. 19), agriculture, and food (Clem. Alex., *Strom.*, v. p. 567). At the same time Isis was the goddess of the earth, that nourishes everything (Macrob., *Sat.*, i. 20), and is rendered fruitful by the Nile (Plut., *de Is.*, 38); the cow was especially sacred to her (Her. ii. 41; Aelian., *h. an.*, x. 27). She was also goddess of the moon (Diod. i. 11), and her picture serves in the hieroglyphics as a sign for the year (Horapollo, i. 3); therefore the seven fat cows mean seven fruitful, and the seven lean cows seven unfruitful years; the seven lean cows coming closely upon the seven fat ones, points to the close succession of the unfruitful years to the fruitful years.'

6. שְׁדוּפֹת קָדִים. '*Blasted by the east wind.*' The narrator here mentions the wind that was most destructive in Palestine; cf. Hos. 13, 15. Jon. 4, 8. Ez. 17, 10. The winds in Egypt that were most hurtful came usually from the N.W. or S.E.; see Ebers, p. 340. Del. understands קדים here as the destructive Chamsin, which blew, in the spring months, from the S. E. quarter; see Ebers, l. c.

7. Knobel remarks on the dreams, 'The order in which they come is well chosen. First the Nile, which causes the fruitfulness, then the cows representing fruitfulness, and lastly the ears, as an evidence of fruitfulness.'

8. חרטמי מצרים. LXX ἐξηγητάς. '*The lettered men of Egypt.*' The חרטמים are the Egyptian ἱερογραμματεῖς, represented on the inscriptions with writing materials in their hands, and a pen on their temples (Ebers, p. 345). They belonged to the Egyptian priesthood, and employed themselves in the study of the hieroglyphic writing and astronomy, and were also noted as seers or foretellers of future events; see Ebers, p. 344 f.; Di., p. 392. They also had a great reputation as magicians, as is clear from Ex. 7, 11. 22. 8, 3, etc. The word חרטם is taken by Harkavy (*Journ. Asiatique,* 1870, p. 168 f.) as equivalent to the Egyptian '*Cher-tum,*' '*Revealer of secrets.*' It may, however, be equally well derived from חָרַט '*to grave,*' or חֶרֶט '*a stylus,*' with the formative ending ōi, like דָּרוֹם from דַּר, עֵירוֹם, פִּדְיוֹם; see Ewald, § 163 g; Stade, § 295. Tuch gives another derivation (*Comm.,* p. 443 f.), according to which חרטם is a quadriliteral form from חרט '*to write with a stylus,*' and חרם '*to be sacred;*' cf.

חרגל from חגל, and רגל; this, however, is doubtful; see Stade, §§ 149, 150, on the formation of quadriliterals.

חכמים = '*the wise men*,' identified by Ebers, p. 345, with the *reχχal-u* of the inscriptions, '*those who know things*' (die wissenden der Dinge), probably a wide term, embracing all the higher classes of priests, especially the ὡροσκόποι of Clement, who were astrologers, calendar makers, and interpreters of signs or omens.

חלמו ... אותם. אותם, the plural suffix, may be used with reference to the double nature of the dream, or the reading may be a *scriptio defectiva*, חֲלוֹמוֹ for חֲלֹמָיו, which the Sam. gives; so Syr. and Saadiah.

9. אני מזכיר, not '*I remember*,' A.V.—for הזכיר means '*to cause another to remember*'—but '*I make mention of.*'

10. אתי. LXX and Sam. read, more correctly, אתם.

11. ונחלמה. The first person imperf. with waw conv. and the ה cohortative is rare; there are two other instances in Gen., viz. 32, 6 ואשלחה, and 43, 21 ונפתחה; see other instances in Driver, § 69. Obs.; Ewald, § 232 g.

12. איש כחלמו. See on 9, 5.

14. ויריצהו. '*And they brought him quickly*,' lit. '*made him run;*' cf. 1 Sam. 17, 17 והרץ המחנה לאחיך; 2 Chron. 35, 13 ויריצו לכל בני העם.

ויגלח ויחלף שמלתיו. No one was allowed to appear before the king of Egypt unless he was quite clean; see Ebers, p. 350. Del. and Tuch explain the verse from the Egyptian custom of regarding a prisoner as a mourner. He would then wear his beard and hair; see Ebers, p. 350. footnote, against this view.

15. ואני שמעתי. '*And I have heard about thee, saying*

thou canst understand a dream,' or '*thou hearest a dream,'* i. e.
hast only to hear it, and can interpret it.

עָלֶיךָ, as in 1 Kings 10, 6 עַל דבריך ועל חכמתך.

On the construction—*oratio indirecta* without כִּי to introduce it—cf. 12, 13. 23. 21, 4; Ges., § 155. 4 c; Ewald,
§ 338 a; see also M. R., § 162.

16. בִּלְעָדַי. '*Not I,'* as in 14, 24. The LXX have ἄνευ
τοῦ Θεοῦ οὐκ ἀποκριθήσεται, which means really the same as
the Mass. text, and does not of necessity suppose a reading
בִּלְעָדַי אלהים, and the addition of לֹא. The Sam. Ver. has a
similar rendering to the LXX.

יַעֲנֶה אֶת־שְׁלוֹם, lit. '*answer the welfare,'* i. e. give such
an answer as will be most conducive to Pharaoh's welfare.

19. רַקּוֹת, so vers. 20, 27, possibly a mistake for דַקּוֹת,
which occurs in ver. 3.

לֹא רָאִיתִי כָהֵנָּה וגו״ = '*such as I have not seen in all
the land of Egypt for badness,'* lit. '*I have not seen like these'*
etc.; see ver. 38, and cf. M. R., § 56.

21. קִרְבֶּנָה. Cf. the fuller forms in 21, 29 לבדנה; 31, 6
אתנה; the ‒ָ, defective for י‒ָ, has arisen out of the diph-
thong י‒ָ; see Stade, § 352 b; cf. § 99. 2; Ges., § 91. 1.
Rem. 2.

וּמַרְאֵיהֶן. The form is singular, not plural, the י‒ָ
being the ending י‒ָ, מַרְאֶה = מַרְאַי; see Stade, § 353 a. 1 β;
cf. § 99. 2; Ges., § 93. 3. Rem. 3.

23. אַחֲרֵיהֶם. Masc. suffix for fem.; cf. on 26, 15; in
ver. 27 we find the fem. suffix used.

25. חֲלוֹם פַּרְעֹה אֶחָד הוּא. Cf. on 34, 21.

26. שֶׁבַע פָּרֹת הַטֹּבֹת. See the note on 1, 21 כל נפש
החיה. שֶׁבַע פרת וגו״ is a *casus pendens*, as in ver. 25 (see
40, 12).

32. '*And with respect to the repetition of the dream unto Pharaoh twice, (it is) because the matter is resolved on by God, and God hastens to do it.*' ועל השׁנות ; cf. Ruth 4, 7 על הגאלה ועל התמורה '*with respect to ransoming, and with respect to exchanging.*' השׁנות is the Nif. inf. cstr. of שׁנה. The Nif‘al of this verb is not found elsewhere.

33. יֵרֶא. So the ordinary editions; but Baer and Del. in the text have יֵרֶא, and in the notes to their edition, p. 78, they refer to Ibn Ezra in favour of the reading with ־ֶ. On יֵרֶא for יֵרָא, cf. Zech. 9, 5 תֵּרֶא (Baer and Del. תֵּרֶא in text and notes, p. 83), and see Ewald, § 63 d; cf. Stade, § 489 b. 1. On יֵרָא, also an abnormal form, see Stade, l. c., and Ges., § 75. note 3 b. The jussive is used in making a suggestion, see Driver, § 50 b (cf. Ex. 8, 25. 1 Kings 1, 2), and M. R., § 8. 2.

34. יעשׂה פרעה ויפקד = '*let P. set up and appoint*' etc.; cf. the use of עשׂה in 1 Sam. 8, 16. 1 Kings 12, 31. Ges. in *Thes.*, p. 1077, renders, '*faciat* (hoc) *P.* (sequatur consilium meum) *et praeficiat;*' cf. Ges., § 121. 6. Rem. 2.

חמשׁ, a ἅπαξ λεγόμ.='*let him exact the fifth part;*' cf. עָשֵׂר = '*to take the tenth part of anything.*'

35. תחת יד פרעה = '*under Pharaoh's control.*' יד used as in 2 Kings 13, 5. Is. 3, 6.

39. אחרי הודיע אלהים אותך את כל וגו״. On the construction, see Ges., § 133. 3; M. R., § 116.

40. על פיך ישק כל עמי. I. Gesenius and Knobel render, '*And all my people shall kiss thy mouth;*' cf. 1 Sam. 10, 1. 1 Kings 19, 18. Hos. 13, 2. But the kiss of homage was not given on the mouth; and that Joseph had to receive the kiss from all the people would be a very unnatural thought; further, נשׁק על is not used in the sense '*to kiss,*'

for which we find the acc. or לְ. II. The LXX, Sam. Ver., Vulg., and most 'moderns, e. g. Del., Tuch, Di., prefer taking עַל פִּי, as in 45, 21. Ex. 17, 1. Num. 3, 16, etc. = '*according to thy mouth*,' i. e. '*command*' etc., and render נשק '*dispose themselves*,' taking it intransitively. Cf. the Arabic نسق '*ordinare et disponere rem*.'

רק הכסא אגדל ממך. '*Only with respect to the throne will I be greater than thou*.' הכסא, accus. of respect; see Ges., § 118. 3; M. R., § 44; Ewald, § 281 c.

41. נתתי. See on 1, 29.

42. טבעתו. Cf. Esther 3, 10. 8, 2, where the Persian monarch gives his signet first to Haman, and then to Mordecai.

שֵׁשׁ = '*byssus*,' '*fine white cotton*;' here בגדי שש = '*clothing made of byssus*;' cf. Del., *Comm.*, p. 557. The priests' clothing was of byssus; cf. Her. ii. 37. For שׁשׁ, at a later period of the language, בוץ was used, e. g. in the books of Chronicles and Esther.

43. מרכבת המשנה = '*a carriage of the second rank*;' cf. כהן המשנה '*a priest of the second rank*.'

אשר לו. Cf. on 40, 5.

אַבְרֵךְ. Most probably the Hebrew form of an Egyptian word. De Rossi explains it as = *ape-rek*, '*bow the head*.' Harkavy (in the *Berlin Aegyptological Journal*, 1869, p. 132) as the Egyptian *ap-reχ-u*, '*head of the wise*.' Benfey (*Ver-hältniss der Ägypt. Sprache*, p. 302 f.) takes it as equivalent to *a*, the sign of the imper., *bor* = '*projicere*,' and *k* the sign of the second person; so '*cast thyself down*.' Jablonski (*Opusc.*, i. p. 6) explains it as meaning *ouberek*, '*bow towards*' (Joseph); and Cook (*Speaker's Comm.*, p. 482) renders it '*welcome*,' or '*rejoice*,' addressed to Joseph. The Versions

give various renderings. The LXX have καὶ ἐκήρυξεν ἔμπροσθεν αὐτοῦ κῆρυξ, apparently taking אברך as 'a herald;' so
Sam. Ver., which has ﭏﻃﯖﻻ. The Targums of Onq. and
Jer. give אַבָּא לְמַלְכָּא, as though אברך were compounded of
אב 'father,' and רֵךְ = the Latin *rex* ! (cf. 45, 8). The Syr.
paraphrases ܐܒܐ ܘܫܠܝܛܐ ܟܠܗ ܩܕܡ "ܐܒܐ ܘܡܫܠܛ ' *Father
and ruler over all the land of Egypt;*' also the Vulgate, which
has ' *Ut omnes coram eo genu flecterent.*' A possible explanation from the Hebrew is to take אברך as inf. abs. Af'el for
Hif'il, instead of the imperative; cf. ver. 51 נשני, Pa'el for
Pi'el, and accordingly Jose b. Dormaskith, quoted by Del.,
Comm., 4th ed., p. 470, explains it by לְבִרְכַּיִם; cf. the Vulg.
rendering, and Aquila's rendering cited by Hieron. (*Quaest.*,
ed. Lag., p. 60), 'et clamavit in conspectu ejus ad geniculationem.' Hieron. himself follows the Targ. Ps.-Jon., and
renders, ' *tender father ;*' cf. רך, 18, 7.

וְנָתוֹן. The inf. abs. continuing the narrative instead of וַיִּתֵּן ;
cf. the inf. abs. again in Ex. 8, 11 והכבד את לבו ; Judg. 7, 19
ונפוץ הכדים ; and see Ges., § 131. 4; M. R., § 106. 2; Ewald,
§ 351 c. Probably the inf. abs. is used instead of the ordinary
construction of the imperf. with waw conv., to shew that the
appointment of Joseph over the land of Egypt was contemporaneous with the announcement of the herald, and the
setting him in the second chariot; not subsequent (as it
would be with waw conv. and the impf.); we might therefore
render ונתון ' *thus setting him.*' To connect ונתון with אברך
is against the accents, besides giving an improbable sense, as
the people would not have the appointment of vizier in their
hands; cf. the next verse.

45. צפנת פענח. LXX, Ψονθομφανήχ—probably = *p-sotom-ph-ench*—comes nearer the original name than the Hebrew

form of the word preserved in the Mass. text. The name is explained by Hieron. as '*Salvator mundi*,' i. e. *p*, the article, masculine, *sot* or *sole*=*salus*, *ph m* the sign of the gen., and *eneh*=*aetas* (Di.). Ges. in the *Thes.*, p. 1181, considers the *sont* of the LXX for *sot* difficult, and renders it *p-sont-m-ph-eneh* = '*the preserver* or *supporter of the age.*' Di. renders slightly differently, '*the support,*' or concrete, '*the supporter of life;*' so Bunsen and Lepsius, taking פענח as equal to the Egypto-Kopt. *ph-aneh*, '*life.*' The word צפנת is apparently, in the Hebrew form, transposed for פצנת; see Ewald, § 78 b. Brugsch, *Gesch.*, p. 248, explains the word as equivalent to *za-p-u-nt-p-àa-ānkh*, i. e. '*guardian* (*Landpfleger*) *of the district of place of life.*' Cook, *Speaker's Comm.*, p. 481, renders it '*food of the living.*' The Jewish interpreters, Onq., Pesh., Saad., make it mean '*revealer of secrets,*' taking פען as equivalent to φαίνω !

אסנת = '*she who belongs to Neith*' (Pallas). LXX, 'Ασενέθ. Brugsch, *Ges.*, p. 248, makes it = *Snat* or *Sant*, the name of a woman.

אן. LXX, 'Ηλιούπολις, situated on the north-east of Memphis, on the eastern bank of the Nile. In Coptic the name of אן is *Un* or *On*, meaning '*light*' or '*sun*(?);' cf. the Hebrew בית שמש '*house of the sun.*' Hieroglyphically it was *Anu* or *An*, more closely *Anu-mhit* (Brugsch and Ebers, cited by Di., p. 395). Heliopolis was the chief seat of the worship of the sun-god *Ra;* cf. its name in Is. 19, 18 עיר ההרס ('*city of destruction*'), a play on the words for עיר החרס; cf. Jer. 43, 13, where it is called 'בית שמש *in the land of Egypt.*'

48. שבע שנים, as the text stands, quite indefinite, seems hardly correct. Del. reads שבע השנים. Ols. proposes to read

(cf. ver. 53) for שנים, שְׁנֵי הַשָּׂבָע. The LXX and Sam. read
for שנים, הַשָּׁנִים אֲשֶׁר הָיָה הַשָּׂבָע—היו for.

51. מנשה כי נשני = '*Manasseh, for he hath made me
forget.*' The form נַשַּׁנִי, for נִשַּׁנִי, is used on account of its
similarity in sound with the name מנשה; cf. Ges., § 52.
note 1; Stade, § 387 a. In Arabic and Aramaic the *a*
sound is regular, e. g. Heb. קִטֵּל, Arab. قَتَّلَ, Aramaic مَقْطֵל,
and קַטֵּל; and that *a* was once the original sound in
Hebrew is proved from the imperf. and partic. of the Pi'el;
cf. Wright, *Arab. Gram.*, i. pp. 32, 33. The Pi'el with a
double acc. may possibly, as Tuch and Di. suggest, have
been chosen instead of the commoner Hif'il on account of
the name מנשה.

52. אפרים, meaning perhaps '*double fruitfulness;*' cf.
Hos. 13, 15. Other dual names are דִּבְלַיִם, Hos. 1, 3; דִּבְלָתַיִם
(in בית דבלתים, Jer. 48, 22; called on the Moabite stone,
l. 30, בית דבלתן; cf. Gen. 37, 17 (בְּדֹתָן); also קִרְיָתַיִם and חֹרֹנַיִם
(*ibid.*, lines 10, 31 קריתן and חורנן); see Schlottmann's mono-
graph, p. 48, and the proper names of places, as עֵינַיִם,
מַחֲנַיִם; etc.

53. היה is neuter, '*which there was*' (Germ. *die es gab*);
contrast ver. 48; or היה may be referred to השבע.

56. את כל אשר בהם. LXX, πάντας τοὺς σιτοβολῶνας,
Syr. ܐ̈ܘܨܪ̈ܐ, Vulg. '*universa horrea,*' Onq. יַת כָּל אוֹצְרַיָּא דִּבְהוֹן
עִיבוּרָא = '*all the storehouses wherein was grain,*' which point
to a reading אוצרות בר. The true reading here seems to
have been lost.

וישבר is probably to be emended to וַיַּשְׁבֵּר, cf. 42, 6, as
שבר, Qal, always means, when a denom. from שֶׁבֶר, '*to buy,*'
not '*to sell.*'

57. ‏וכל הארץ באו‏. The plural verb as ‏הארץ‏ = ' *the inhabitants of the land;*' see Ges., § 146. 1 ; M. R., § 135. 2 ; so 1 Sam. 14, 25. 2 Sam. 15, 23.

42.

1. ‏שבר‏. In all the passages where ‏שבר‏ occurs it means '*grain,*' as an article of merchandise, hence its frequent use from this chapter onwards. It is usually derived from ‏שָׁבַר‏ '*to break,*' from the corn being crushed in the mill; see the Lexica.

‏תתראו‏. ' *Look at one another,*' i. e. look helplessly, one to the other, expecting aid and advice. It is not found elsewhere in this sense.

4. ‏פן יקראנו אסון‏. ' *Lest harm befall him.*' ‏קרא‏ is here equivalent to ‏קרה‏, as in ver. 38. 49, 1. Ex. 1, 10.

‏אסון‏ is only found again in ver. 38. 44, 29. Ex. 21, 22. 23.

6. ‏ויוסף הוא השליט‏. ‏ויוסף‏ is a *casus pendens;* so 9, 18 ‏והם הוא אבי‏; 15, 2 ‏ובן משק ביתי הוא דמשק‏; see Driver, § 199.

‏השליט‏ = ‏המשל‏ in 45, 8. ‏שליט‏ is a word common in Aramaic, and occasionally found in late Hebrew, e. g. Eccl. 8, 8. 7, 19 (pl.). 10, 5 ; and in the fem. sing. ‏שלטת‏, Ez. 16, 30 (all). Di. suggests that it is a technical word here, that has come over with tradition, as it agrees remarkably with *Salatis,* or *Silitis,* the name of the first ruler of the Hyksos in Egypt, Jos., *Contra Ap.,* i. 14; so Tuch and Del. in their commentaries; cf. the Assyrian *salat,* '*viceroy.*'

7. ‏וידבר אתם קשות‏. ‏קשות‏, the fem. pl., is here used as neuter; so ‏קשה‏, fem. sing. in Ps. 60, 5 ‏הראית עמך קשה‏,

and 1 Kings 12, 13 וַיַּעַן הַמֶּלֶךְ אֶת הָעָם קָשָׁה; other instances of the pl. fem. as neuter are Ps. 12, 4 גְּדֹלוֹת; Ps. 16, 11 נְעִימוֹת; Zech. 4, 10 קְטַנּוֹת; see Ewald, § 172 b; M. R., § 63; Ges., § 80. 1.

8. וְהֵם is emphatic, *they*, as opposed to Joseph; see on 33, 3.

9. לָהֶם. '*About them;*' see on 17, 20.

אֵת עֶרְוַת הָאָרֶץ. '*The bareness of the land;*' cf. a similar use of the Arabic عَوْرَة, Qor. 33, 13. Knobel further compares γυμνοῦσθαι (Homer, *Iliad*, 12. 339) and *nudari* (Caesar, *Gallic War*, vii. 70), and points out that the Hyksos were in constant dread of attacks from the Assyrians, who were at that time very powerful, and therefore fortified the eastern portion of the land of Egypt (Jos., *Contra Ap.*, i. 14).

10. וַעֲבָדֶיךָ. ו is here used after the negative, after which כִּי usually stands; so 17, 5 וְהָיָה, for the more usual כִּי יִהְיֶה; see Ewald, § 354 a; Ges., § 155. 1 b; cf. Deut. 11, 10 f.; 2 Sam. 23, 7.

11. נַחְנוּ for the longer form אֲנַחְנוּ is only found here, Ex. 16, 7. 8. Num. 32, 32. Lam. 3, 42; see Ges., § 32. Rem. 2; Stade, § 179 b; Dav., § 12. Rem. a. נָחְנוּ is the pausal form.

כֵּנִים in the sense of '*upright,*' '*honest*' (masc.), is only found in this chapter; כֵּן occurs, Num. 27, 7. Is. 16, 6. Prov. 11, 19, and elsewhere, in the *neuter* sense of '*right.*'

הָיוּ is here a stative verb = '*thy servants have not been, nor are they now, spies;*' so Is. 15, 6; see Driver, § 11.

מְרַגְּלִים. '*Spies.*' Del. remarks that the term מְרַגְּלִים ('*those who go about with the object of spying*') was a more insulting term than תָּרִים ('*those who go about with the object of exploring*').

12. כי ערות הארץ באתם לראות. The obj. is intentionally emphasized by being placed first.

13. אנחנו seems superfluous; possibly, as Olshausen suggests, it is a gloss from ver. 32, and should be rejected. Del. renders, against the accents, ' *Twelve are thy servants, brothers are we, the sons of* ' etc.

הקטן = ' *the youngest;* ' see on 9, 24, and cf. M. R., § 86; Dav., § 47. 2; Ges., § 119. 2.

איננו, as in 5, 24.

14. הוא is here neuter, as in 20, 16. Job 13, 16.

15. חי פרעה. The Mass. pointed חֵי with a created object, but חַי with God; so Lev. 25, 36 וְחֵי אָחִיךָ עִמָּךְ. Cf. 1 Sam. 17, 55 (Saul). 2 Sam. 11, 11 (David). Di. remarks ' that this oath is very suitable here, as the Egyptians honoured their kings, ὡς πρὸς ἀλήθειαν ὄντας θεούς (Diod. i. 90).'

אם. On this use of אם, cf. on 14, 23.

Render, ' *As sure as P. lives ! ye shall not go hence, except your youngest brother come hither.* '

16. כי (introducing the oath) = ' *surely;* ' see Ewald, § 330 b, and cf. 1 Sam. 14, 44. 1 Sam. 20, 3. 2 Kings 3, 14.

17. ויאסף. Cf. Josh. 2, 18. Is. 24, 22.

18. זאת עשׂו וחיו, lit. ' *Do this and live,* ' i. e. ' if ye do this ye shall live ;' see Ges., § 130. 2; M. R., § 10; Driver, § 152 i, and cf. Amos 5, 4 דרשׁוני וחיו ; Prov. 3, 3 f. . . . כתבם ומצא.

19. אחיכם אחד. Cf. ver. 33 אחיכם האחד. On the absence of the art. here, see Ges., § 111. 2 b; M. R., § 76. Rem. c ; Ewald, § 290 f. ; so in 43, 14 אחיכם אחר.

שׁבר רעבון בתיכם. Cf. Is. 30, 23 מטר זרעך.

23. שׁמע. Cf. on 9, 18.

כִּי הַמֵּלִיץ, i. e. the interpreter that was usually present in such cases; hence the article.

בִּינָתָם. Cf. בִּינוֹתֵינוּ in 26, 28.

25. כַּסְפֵּיהֶם here, and ver. 35, the plural is used, because the silver of more than one is intended, Ewald, § 176 c; Ges., § 108. 4. Rem. 1, explains the plural differently. The dag. in the פ is unusual, though it is found in the sing. and dual, the aspiration is generally preserved in the pl.; so רִשְׁפֵּי, צִמְדֵּי, טַרְפֵּי, etc.; see Ges., § 93. Rem. 1 ; Stade, § 71. 2.

אִישׁ אֶל שַׂקּוֹ, so ver. 35. Cf. the note on 9, 5.

וַיַּעַשׂ. The sing. is harsh; after וַיְמַלְאוּ a plural would be natural. The Syr. and Vulg. read the pl., while the Sam. and Onq. have the sing.; the LXX have ἐγενήθη αὐτοῖς οὕτως. If וַיַּעַשׂ (sing.) is read it must be rendered impersonally, '*one did,*' i. e. '*it was done;*' the implied subj. being הָעֹשֶׂה.

27. הָאֶחָד, i. e. the one who, as it were, made a beginning, and opened his bag (the others naturally opening theirs afterwards), so = '*the first;*' cf. 2, 11. 4, 19.

אַמְתַּחְתּוֹ, '*distinguished from שַׂק as being more specially the sack which the ass carried,*' Tuch. The word is only found in Gen., chaps. 42–44 (in J, see App. I).

28. וַיֶּחֶרְדוּ וגו׳. A pregnant construction; see Ges., § 141; Ewald, § 282 c; cf. 43, 33 וַיִּתְמְהוּ הָאֲנָשִׁים וגו׳.

30. אֲדֹנֵי הָאָרֶץ. See on 39, 20.

כִּמְרַגְּלִים is Ben Asher's reading. Ben Naftali reads כַּמְרַגְּלִים (with the article), see Baer and Del., *Gen.*, p. 86 [where, in note 3, Judg. 21, 29 should be Judg. 21, 19].

35. וַיְהִי הֵם מְרִיקִים. '*And it came to pass, as they were emptying their sacks, that they found*' etc. A circumstantial clause; so 2 Kings 2, 11 וַיְהִי הֵמָּה הֹלְכִים . . . וְהִנֵּה, see Driver, § 165; M. R., § 154.

36. בלנה. See on 21, 29. בלנה occurs again, Prov. 31, 29.

37. תמית='*thou mayest kill.*'

38. וקראהו . . . והורדתם. Cf. the note on 33, 13.

43.

3. העד העד '*protested strongly;*' the inf. abs., by Ges., § 131. 3 a; M. R., § 37 a.

בלתי אחיכם. Cf. Ex. 22, 19 בלתי ליהוה לבדו (Del.), see Ewald, § 322 a; cf. also M. R., § 153.

4. אם ישך משלח. Cf. the neg. in ver. 5 ואם אינך משלח, and the note on 24, 42; here an imperf. (voluntative) alone follows the participle with יש אם, in 24, 42 a perf. with waw conv.

6. למה, here pointed with two qameçs and no dag., and the tone on the last syllable, as the next word begins with a guttural; see Ges., § 102. 2 d.

7. '*The man asked particularly about us, and our kindred, etc.,* . . . . . *so we told him according to these words; how were we to know that he would say?*' etc.   על פי, as in Ex. 34, 27. Lev. 27, 8, and often.

הידוע נדע. On the inf. abs. see above on ver. 1, and for this (potential) use of the imperf., cf. Driver, § 39 β; Ewald, § 136 d; M. R., § 7. 2. Rem. c; Ges., § 127. 3 d; so ver. 25 הכמות נבל ימות אבנר 2 Sam. 3, 33 כי שם יאכלו, etc.

9. אם לא הביאתיו . . . וחטאתי. Cf. 47, 6 ואם ידעת . . . והית 2 Sam. 15, 33 אם עברת . . . ושמחתם; and see Driver, § 138 i. (a); M. R., § 3. 1 c. וחטאתי לך. Cf. 1 Kings 1, 21 אני ובני שלמה חטאים.

10. *'For had we not tarried, surely now we had returned'* etc. כִּי עַתָּה, as in 31, 42; cf. the note on that passage.

11. מִזִּמְרַת הָאָרֶץ is usually rendered, *'from the song of the land,'* i. e. of the products of the land of Canaan that are celebrated and praised in song; cf. Jer. 51, 41. But Kn. and Del. point out that such a highly poetical expression would be very strange in this passage, and further that זמר and its derivatives are only used of songs in divine service. Del. derives זמרה here from זמר (cf. מזמרה) in the sense *'to cut off,'* so זמרה would mean *'produce'* or *'portion.'* But, as Di. remarks, *'*זמר* is only used of cutting off what is useless, or in the way.'* Norris, *Assyrian Dict.*, ii. 354, gives an Assyrian word *zumri* = *'fruit, produce,'* Di. Di. renders *'fruits.'* LXX, καρποί.

צְרִי, נְכֹאת, לֹט, see on 37, 25.

דְבַשׁ, here probably not the honey of bees, but a syrup prepared by boiling from the juice of the grape, Arab. *dibs*, which is at the present day brought to Egypt from the neighbourhood of Hebron.

בָּטְנִים. *'Pistacia nuts'* (see Ges. in the *Thes.*, s. v.), the fruit of the *Pistacia vera*.

וּשְׁקֵדִים. *'And almonds,'* the fruit of the *Amygdalus communis*. Almonds are found in Egypt, but only very rarely.

12. וְכֶסֶף מִשְׁנֶה. מִשְׁנֶה is here an adverbial acc.; cf. לֶחֶם מִשְׁנֶה, Ex. 16, 22. In verse 15, in מִשְׁנֶה כֶסֶף, כֶסֶף is the acc., *'double in silver;'* cf. Deut. 15, 18 כִּי מִשְׁנֶה שְׂכַר שָׂכִיר; Jer. 17, 18 וּמִשְׁנֶה שִׁבָּרוֹן. See Ges., § 118. 3; Ewald, § 286 d.

14. אֶת אֲחִיכֶם אַחֵר. See the note on 42, 19. LXX and Heb.-Sam. read הָאַחֵר here.

וַאֲנִי כַּאֲשֶׁר שָׁכֹלְתִּי שָׁכָלְתִּי. *'And I, if I am bereaved,*

I am bereaved;' cf. Esther 4, 16 וכאשר אבדתי אבדתי; 2 Kings 7, 4 ואם ימיתנו ומתנו. In שְׁבָלְתִּי notice the — in pause for —, and cf. 49, 3 עָז for עֹז; 49, 27 יִטְרָף for יִטְרֹף; see Ewald, § 93. 3; Stade, § 459 c. 1 (who accounts for the use of the pausal form with — here, ‘der Euphonie wegen,’ for euphony).

16. טְבֹחַ is imperative for the usual form טְבַח, but only in this passage, possibly, as Böttcher suggests, on account of the following טְבֹחַ, to produce a change in the sound of the final syllable of the first word (טְבֹחַ).

18. הֻשַׁב, ‘because how it came there was unknown to them and inconceivable,’ Del.

לְהִתְגַּלֵל, lit. ‘*to roll oneself upon any one;*’ cf. Job 30, 14 תחת שאה התגלגלו. לְהִתְגַּלֵל is inf. cstr. Hithpo’al from גלל.

20. בִּי is a precative particle, always followed by אדוני, = ‘*pray!*’ בִּי has probably arisen out of בְּעִי, as בֵּל out of בְּעֵל; cf. in Aramaic the precative particles בְּבָעוּ and ܒܳܥܶܐ. See Prof. William Wright's *Book of Jonah in Four Semitic Versions*, p. 11.

23. שָׁלוֹם לכם. Cf. Judg. 6, 23. 1 Sam. 20, 21. ‘שלום לכם in the O. T. is always a formula of encouragement or congratulation, never of greeting,’ Del.

25. כי שם יאכלו לחם. ‘*That they were to eat bread there.*’ Imperf., as in ver. 7.

26. וַיְבִיאוּ. א with mappiq, perhaps to mark that it is a consonant; cf. Lev. 23, 17 תָּבִיאוּ; Job 33, 21 רֻאוּ (‘cum א dagessato teste Masora, vide Michlol, 63 b;’ note in Baer and Del.’s ed. of *Job*, p. 52); Ezra 8, 18 וַיָּבִיאוּ (‘א dagessatum auctore Masora;’ note in Baer and Del.’s ed. of *Daniel, Ezra, and Neh.*, p. 108). Di. points out that we now know

(Ginsburg, *Verhandl. des 5 intern. Orient. Congr.*, ii. 1. 136 ff.)
that the four examples of a mappiq in א *mobile* are only
remains of a much wider system of pointing the א *mobile*
with mappiq, which was once more consistently carried out
in MSS. See further, Ewald, § 21 e; Ges., § 14; Stade,
§ 42 b; Strack, *Proleg. Critica*, p. 19.

27. השלום אביכם. שלום is here used as an adj.; cf.
1 Sam. 25, 6. 2 Sam. 20, 9.

28. ויקדו, impf. Qal of קדד; see Ges., § 67. N.B.; Dav.,
§ 42. 6. foot-note 2. קדד and השתחוה occur together again
in 24, 26. 48.

29. יָחְנְךָ. So again Is. 30, 19 for יְחָנְךָ; cf. Ges., § 67.
Rem. 2; Ewald, § 251. 2 d.

30. כי נכמרו רחמיו. Cf. 1 Kings 3, 26. Hos. 11, 8
(with רחמים for נחמים).

32. כי לא יוכלון. Cf. Num. 9, 6. Deut. 22, 19. 12, 17,
of legal and moral incapability. Kn. remarks on this verse:
'The predilection of the Egyptians for their own people and
land, and their exclusiveness towards strangers (Diod. i. 67;
Strabo, xvii. 1. 6), is well known. The priests neither ate
nor drank anything that came from a foreign land (Porph.
iv. 7); the Egyptian would use no eating utensils belonging
to a Greek (Her. ii. 41). In a similar way they conducted
themselves towards the Hebrews, especially as they were a
nomad people, "tenders of flocks and herds" (see 46, 34;
and cf. also 39, 6).'

33. ויתמהו. Cf. on 42, 28.

34. וישא is impersonal, the implied subject being הַנֹּשֵׂא;
cf. 42, 25; Deut. 22, 8 כי יפל הנפל; 2 Sam. 17, 9 וּשְׁמֹעַ הַשֹּׁמֵעַ.
The LXX and Syr. have the plural here.

חמש ידות. Knobel calls attention to the frequency of

the number five in matters relating to Egypt, e. g. 41, 34.
45, 22. 47, 2. 24. Is. 19, 18.   For יד in the sense of '*portion*,'
cf. 47, 24. 2 Sam. 19, 44. 2 Kings 11, 7.

וישכרו ' to be understood according to Hagg. 1, 6,' Del.

44.

1. כסף איש.   See Ges., § 124. Rem. 1 ; M. R., § 94 b.

3. "הבקר אור והאנשים וגו.   ' *The morning dawned,
and the men were sent away.*'   The construction is the same
as in 38, 25 הוא מוצאת והיא שלחה, see the note there ; so in
the next verse, הם יצאו . . . ויוסף אמר.   Cf. also M. R., § 154.

אור, intrans. perf. like בוש, טוב (all);   see Ges., § 72.
Rem. 1 ; Stade, § 385 f.

4. לא הרחיקו.   ' *Without having gone far;*' so Ex. 34,
28 לחם לא אבל ומים לא שתה ' *without eating bread, or drinking
water;*' Lev. 13, 23 לא פשתה ' *without having spread.*'   The
perfect is here equivalent to our past part. act.; see Driver,
§ 162.

5. The LXX (cf. the Syr. and Vulg.) insert at the end of
ver. 4, ἵνα τί ἐκλέψατέ μου τὸ κόνδυ τὸ ἀργυροῦν; perhaps an explanatory gloss.

' *Is not this that wherein my lord is wont to drink, and he*
(emphatic) *would surely practise divination therewith*' etc. ?
On בו, cf. Ges., § 154. 3 a; and M. R., § 52. 1. Rem. a, who
compares πίνειν ἐν χρυσῷ, *bibere in ossibus*, and *boire dans un
verre*, with the plural used here.   שתה ב occurs again in
Amos 6, 6 השתים במזרקי יין.   Tuch takes the sentence
slightly differently, supplying בידכם after הלא.   But this
seems unnecessary.

נחש ינחש בו.   Cf. 30, 27.   This species of divination

X 2

with cups, called κυλικομαντεία or ὑδρομαντεία, was much practised in Egypt; cf. Jamblich., *Myst.*, 3. 14, and Varro in
Augustine's *Civ. dei*, 7. 35, cited by Di., p. 407. Di., l. c.,
says: 'Water was poured into a glass or some other vessel,
or pieces of gold, silver, or precious stones were thrown into
the water, and the figures or rings that appeared were supposed to give information about the future, or what was
obscure to the inquirer.' The LXX have here αὐτὸς δὲ
οἰωνισμῷ οἰωνίζεται ἐν αὐτῷ. So the Syr. and Vulg. Onq. has
וְהוּא בַּדְקָא מְבַדֵּיק בֵּיהּ 'and he makes discoveries through it,'
sc. the cup. Saadiah, quoted by Wright (*Genesis*, p. 109),
has وَهُوَ إِنَّمَا ٱمْتَحَنَكُم بِـ 'and he only proved you by it.'
'Wishing to screen Joseph from such practices.'

נָחֵשׁ = properly '*to whisper*,' viz. magic formulae or oracles.

7. לָמָה יְדַבֵּר. 'After למה the imperfect, as more courteous and adapted to a tone of entreaty, is often preferred to
the perfect,' Driver, § 39 γ; so Ex. 2, 13 למה תכה; 1 Sam.
21, 15 למה תביאו אתו.

חלילה ... מעשות. Cf. on 18, 25.

9. אשר ימצא ... ומת. The perf. with waw conv. to
introduce the apodosis; contrast ver. 10, where the simple
imperf. follows; cf. ver. 17 (where 'the subject is reinforced
by the personal pronoun' הוא); Judg. 8, 7. 9; and see
Driver, § 123 γ. Obs.; M. R., § 26.

12. בגדול החל ובקטן כלה, circ. clause; see on 21,
14. LXX, ἀρξάμενος; so 48, 14 שׂכל את ידיו. See also
M. R., § 153. Render, '*Beginning with the eldest, and finish-
ing with the youngest.*'

הגביע is a cup shaped like the bell or calix of a flower;
cf. Ex. 25, 31, where the word is used of the cup of a flower
used in the workmanship of the golden candlestick.

15. הלוא ידעתם וגו׳ . ‘ *Did ye not know that a man like me would be certain to practise divination,*’ and so at once discover the thief? איש אשר כמני, i. e. one of the wise men of Egypt; cf. Is. 19, 11; Kn.

16. ומה = ובמה, as in Ps. 116, 12.

18. כמוך כפרעה, lit. ‘ *like thee, like Pharaoh,*’ i. e. ‘*for thou art as P.;*’ cf. 18, 25. Is. 24, 2. Hos. 4, 9. Ps. 139, 12; and see M. R., § 56. 1. Rem. a; Ges., § 154. 3 f.

21. ואשימה עיני עליו, i. e. take him under my protection; cf. Jer. 39, 12. 40, 4. Ps. 33, 18. 34, 16.   LXX, καὶ ἐπιμελοῦμαι αὐτοῦ.

22. ועזב . . . ומת.   See the note on 33, 13. וָמֵת; cf. the note on 3, 22.

29. וקרהו . . . והורדתם.   Cf. on ver. 22.

31. והיה introduces the apodosis to ועתה כבאי in ver. 30; and ומת is apodosis to כראותו.

33. ישב . . . יעל.   The jussive is here used in making a request, as in 9, 27. 31, 49, and often; see Driver, § 50 γ; M. R., § 8; Ges., § 127. 3 b.

45.

1. לכל הנצבים עליו.   ‘ *Before all those that stood by him,*’ lit. ‘ *with regard to all those*’ etc.   ל as in 17, 20 לישמעאל; cf. the note on that passage.

בהתודע.   ‘ *When he made himself known.*’ התודע, cf. Num. 12, 6 (all), is the inf. Hithp׳. of ידע, a verb פ״י, really פ״ו; in the Nif׳., Hif׳., and Hof׳. the waw reappears, הִוָּדַע = הוּדַע, הוֹדִיעַ = הוֹדִיעַ, נוֹדַע = נַוְדַע; but in Hithpa‘el the י usually remains, as התילד, התיעין, יעין, התיצב, יצב (den.

from יָלַד), התיחש (den. from יַחַשׂ), etc. With התודע, cf.
התודה.

4. אֲשֶׁר מכרתם אתי. See Ges., § 123. 1; M. R.,
§ 156. Rem. c.

5. כי למחיה. '*For for the preservation of life*,' i. e. for
the preservation of your life and that of other people; cf.
Ezra 9, 8. 9.

6. זה שנתים. On this use of זה, cf. 27, 36. 31, 38. 43,
10, and see Ges., § 122. 2. Rem. Render, '*Now two years
has the famine*' etc.

7. וישלחני is connected only in *thought*, and not *chrono-
logically*, with ver. 6; so ותלד, 36, 14. 46, 18. 25. See
Driver, § 76 a.

לשׂום לכם שׁארית. '*To give you a remnant*' etc., i. e.
that your descendants may live and your family not be
destroyed from off the earth; cf. 2 Sam. 14, 7. Jer. 44, 7.
To take שׁארית as the residue of the corn which the earth has
brought forth is unsuitable, as שׁארית is never used of things.

ולהחיות לכם לפליטה גדלה. Del. renders '*to pro-
long for you life* (להחיות=מחיה לתת, Ezra 9, 8 f.), *to a great
(numerous) deliverance*,' i. e. that you may be preserved, and
become a numerous body of people, the second ל being
the dat. of the product. החיה everywhere else is construed with the acc., but, as Del. on Is. 53, 11 shews, verbs
in Hif'. are sometimes construed with a dative. Others
(Schumann, Wright) take לפ״ ונ״ as in apposition to לכם,
and render, '*to keep you alive, a great body of fugitives.*' LXX
and Heb.-Sam. strike out the ל before לפליטה.

8. לאב לפרעה. Cf. 1 Macc. 11, 32. A title bestowed
on the first minister in the kingdom; see Ges., *Thes.*, p. 7.
Di., referring to Brugsch, *Gesch.*, 248, 252, 592, says *ab en*

pirāo was, in documents of the nineteenth dynasty, the official title of the first (domestic) minister, and that '*adon* of the whole land' occurs in a similar sense in a document of the eighteenth dynasty.

10. בְּאֶרֶץ גֹּשֶׁן, called in P אֶרֶץ רַעְמְסֵס, 47, 11 (cf. Ex. 12, 37. Num. 33, 5); the LXX also, in 46, 28, render גֹּשֶׁן by εἰς γῆν Ῥαμεσσῆ. גֹּשֶׁן must, probably, be sought for on the eastern side of the Nile. From Ex. 2, 3 f. Num. 11, 5 the Israelites seem to have dwelt near the Nile, and there is no reason to suppose that they ever crossed that river, as neither when they enter, nor when they leave Egypt is any mention made of their crossing the Nile. The LXX render גֹּשֶׁן here, and 46, 34 Γεσὲμ 'Αραβίας, hence we may infer that גֹּשֶׁן must have been a portion of lower Egypt, on the right bank of the Nile. This portion of Egypt was regarded by the ancients as Arabia, so that to them Heliopolis and Heroopolis, for example, were situated in Arabia (Her. ii. 15; Strabo, xvii. 1. 21. 30), or ἐν μεθορίοις 'Αραβίας (Ptol. iv. 5. 54); cf. also Ps. 78, 12. 43 ('*his* [Moses'] *wonders in the field of Zoan*' [Tanis]). Di., p. 411, after citing authorities, says, ' Goshen is the district on the east side of the Pelusian, or rather Tanitic arm of the Nile, north-east of Cairo.' This part of Egypt was considered one of the best portions of the country (47, 6. 11), and was a land well adapted for shepherds (46, 34); see further, Di., p. 411; Del., p. 493. The name גֹּשֶׁן was probably Semitic, as it is also found in Josh. 10, 41. 15, 51 as the name of a district and town in southern Canaan.

11. וְכִלְכַּלְתִּי. The Pilpel of כּוּל; see Ges., § 55. 4; Dav., § 26. 3. Rem. c. The pass. וְכָלְכְּלוּ occurs in 1 Kings 20, 27.

פֶּן תִּוָּרֵשׁ. '*Lest thou be brought to poverty*,' Nif'. of יָרֵשׁ=
רוּשׁ; so most of the Vss. Another rendering, which is less
natural, is '*lest thou be taken possession of*,' from יָרֵשׁ *possidēre*,
i. e. through poverty became the property of some one else ;
cf. 47, 19 f.

12. כִּי פִי הַמְדַבֵּר, lit. '*that my mouth is the one speaking*'
etc., i. e. '*that it is I myself that speaketh*.'

17. טַעֲנוּ '*load*,' a ἄπαξ λεγόμ.; cf. 44, 13, where עָמַס occurs.

18. טוּב וגו״. '*The best of the land of Egypt*,' i. e. its best
products ; cf. vers. 20. 23, also 24, 10. 2 Kings 8, 9, etc.; so
LXX, Vulg., Tuch, Del., Di., Rashi, and others take טוּב as=
'*the best portion*,' i. e. Goshen ; but this is מֵיטַב, 47, 6. 11.

19. וְאַתָּה צֻוֵּיתָה וגו״ must mean, '*And thou* (Joseph)
art charged, do ye (the brethren) *this*,' which is very harsh.
Possibly the text is corrupt. The Syr. inserts after צֻוֵּית,
אֱמֹר אֶל־אַחֶיךָ; while the LXX, σὺ δὲ ἔντειλαι, and the Vulg.,
'*praecipe etiam*' etc., read the text צַוֵּה אֹתָם.

20. Compare the note in 34, 21 for the *casus pendens*,
כִּי טוֹב וגו״, taken up by the pronoun הוּא.

22. חֲלִפוֹת שְׂמָלֹת, i. e. '*changes of raiment*,' costly robes,
which would be worn on special occasions, cf. 27, 15 ; see
Judg. 14, 12 f. 19. 2 Kings 5, 5. 22 f. The brothers received
a complete outfit, while Benjamin has five times as much,
and three hundred shekels besides.

23. כָּזֹאת '*as follows*.' Usually pointed כָּזֹאת, and only
here with no pretonic ־ָ.

מָזוֹן occurs only once again in the O.T., 2 Chron. 11, 23.
The word is frequent in Aramaic.

24. אַל תִּרְגְּזוּ, scarcely '*do not fear*,' for such a warning
would be superfluous in the case of persons who had already

made the journey more than once, but rather '*do not quarrel,*'
i. e. do not dispute about your conduct to me; cf. 42, 22, also
Prov. 29, 9. Is. 28, 21.

26. וכי = '*and that,*' introducing the *oratio obliqua.*

ויפג לבו. '*And his heart grew cold.*'

27. ותחי רוח יעקב ... וירא, lit. '*and he saw ... and
the spirit of J. revived;*' almost='*when he saw ...*' etc. (46,
29); cf. Driver, p. 216. ותחי רוח; cf. Ps. 22, 27 יחי לבבכם
ויחי לבבכם ;69, 33; לעד.

28. רב. '*It is enough;*' so 2 Sam. 24, 16. Num. 16, 3. 7.

46.

3. מרדה. רְדָה for רֶדֶת, like דֵעָה for דַּעַת, Ex. 2, 4; לֵדָה
for לֶדֶת, Is. 37, 3; see Ges., § 69. Rem. 1; Stade, § 619 h.

4. ואנכי אעלך גם עלה. On the inf. Qal and imperf.
Hif., see the note on 37, 33. The emphatic inf. abs. usually
precedes the finite verb; see Ges., § 131. 3. Rem. 1; M. R.,
§ 37 a; Ewald, § 312 b, who remarks that Qal after Hif. is
very rare; cf. Is. 31, 5. The inf. abs. is here further emphasized by גם, as in 31, 15 ויאכל גם אכול.

6. ומקניהם, sing. not plural; see the note on 41, 21.

8–27. A list of the family of Jacob who went down into
Egypt with him. The names in this list are found again,
with several variations, in Num. 26. 1 Chron. 2–8 (cf. also
Ex. 6, 14–16), the variations being most numerous in the
case of the sons of Benjamin.

Jacob's sons are classified according to his wives, the list
falling under four heads: Leah, Zilpah, Rachel, Bilhah. Under

the first head, Leah, come Reuben, with four sons; Simeon, with six; Levi, with three; Judah, with five; Perez and Zerah being regarded as his sons, though they really were his grandsons; Perez has two sons, and as Er and Onan died in Canaan, Judah's sons and grandsons amount to five; Issachar has four sons; Zebulun, three; Leah's daughter Dinah is also mentioned: thus Leah's children and grandchildren amount to 26; and these 26 + Reuben, Simeon, Levi, Judah, Issachar, and Zebulun = 32, and with Jacob himself, 33. Under the second head, Zilpah, come Gad, with seven sons; Asher, with four sons, a daughter (Serah), and two grandsons (7): thus 7 + 7 + 2 (Gad and Asher) = 16. Under the third head, Rachel, come Joseph and Benjamin; Joseph has two sons, Ephraim and Manasseh; and Benjamin, ten: thus 2 + 2 + 10 = 14. Under the fourth head, Bilhah, come Dan, with one son; and Naphtali, with four sons: in all, 1 + 4 + 2 (Dan and Naphtali) = 7. Thus all the family of Jacob, including himself, was (33 + 16 + 14 + 7) 70. The LXX here (ver. 27), cf. Acts 7, 14, make the total number 75, counting (ver. 20) three grandchildren and two great-grandchildren among Joseph's descendants; from 50, 23. Num. 26, 28 ff. 1 Chron. 7, 14 f. The number 70 is mentioned again in Ex. 1, 5. Deut. 10, 22 (LXX in Ex. 75, but in Deut. 70). On the variations in the lists given in this chapter, Num., l. c., and 1 Chron., l. c., cf. the larger commentaries, i. e. Del., p. 487; Di., p. 417 f.; also on the difficulty that arises in the case of Perez, who, being born after the sale of Joseph into Egypt, and before Jacob came to Egypt, had, according to our list, two sons. Thus, as the time between Joseph's sale into Egypt and the coming of Jacob is only twenty-two years, the birth of Perez and his sons must have occurred within twenty-two years, which, of course, ` is not impossible, but not very probable. Another difficulty is also discussed by Di. and Del., viz. that Benjamin, the youth (43, 8. 44, 20, etc.), is represented here as the father of ten sons.

15. ואת דינה. If the את is not corrupt, we must render, '*and also Dinah*' (governed by ילדה).

20. אשר refers to the object that is implied in ויולד ליוסף, viz. בנים.

27. הבאה. See the note on 18, 21.

28. להורת. '*That he (Joseph) might give him instruc-tions*,' or '*direct him*,' i. e. that Joseph might instruct Judah, and give Jacob, with his flocks and herds, every facility to enter the land; so Ges., Kn. Del. makes Judah the subj. to להורת, i. e. Judah went before Jacob to shew him the way, which he (Jacob) could find as easily as Judah. The Sam. Ver., LXX, Pesh. apparently read להורת, as inf. Nif.=לְהֵרָאוֹת (which is found in the Heb.-Sam.), or had this word in their text, which reading is accepted by Di., who considers it con-firmed by וירא אליו in ver. 29, and renders, '*That he (Joseph) should appear before him* (i. e. *come to meet him*) *to Goshen*.'

לפניו, i. e. '*before his (Jacob's) arrival*.'

29. ויעל, i. e. from the Nile land to Goshen, which lay on higher ground, Di.

עוד = '*again and again*;' cf. Ruth 1, 14.

30. הפעם, as in 2, 23. 18, 32. 29, 34.

31. אעלה, possibly used with reference to the ideal, or real high position of Pharaoh's royal residence, Di.; cf. Ges., *Thes.*, 1022.

33. מעשיכם, singular; cf. on 41, 21.

34. כל רעה. Cf. on 4, 2. The Sam. has the pl. רעי.

47.

2. ‏ומקצה אחיו‎. ‘*Out of the whole number of his brethren;*’ so 1 Kings 12, 31 ‏מקצות העם‎ (not as A.V., ‘*of the lowest of the people*’); Ez. 33, 2 ‏איש אחד מקציהם‎; 19, 4 is different, cf. the note on that passage.

3. ‏רעה צאן‎. On the predicate in the sing., see Ges., § 147 c; M. R., § 133. Di., however, considers that ‏רעה‎ is miswritten for ‏רעי‎, comparing 46, 32; Ewald, § 16 b. The Sam. and several codices (Wright) read the plural.

5 and 6. In the LXX text 6 b is continued with ἦλθον δὲ εἰς Αἴγυπτον πρὸς Ἰωσὴφ Ἰακὼβ καὶ οἱ υἱοὶ αὐτοῦ· καὶ ἤκουσε Φαραὼ βασιλεὺς Αἰγύπτου, καὶ εἶπε Φαραὼ πρὸς Ἰωσὴφ λέγων, then 5 b and 6 a follow.

6. ‏ארץ מצרים לפניך הוא‎. *Casus pendens;* see on 34, 21.

‏ואם ידעת ויש בם אנשי חיל‎. ‘*And if thou knowest that there are capable men among them,*’ lit. ‘*and if thou knowest, and there are*’ etc. On this union of the subordinate clause by waw, see Driver, p. 235, and cf. Job 23, 3 (‘*knew so that I might find him*’).

‏אנשי חיל‎. ‘*Able* or *worthy men;*’ cf. Ex. 18, 21. 25, and 1 Kings 1, 52 (‏בן חיל‎).

‏ושמתם‎, the perf. with waw conv. used in making a suggestion; see on 24, 14.

‏שרי מקנה‎. Cf. 1 Sam. 21, 8, where Doeg the Edomite is called ‏אביר הרעים אשר לשאול‎.

7. ‏ויעמדהו‎. Cf. ‏העמיד‎ in P with ‏הציג‎ in ver. 2.

‏ויברך‎, as in 2 Kings 4, 29, used of greeting any one; cf. 2 Sam. 16, 16.

11. רעמסם. Cf. on 45, 10. רעמסם is here the name of
the district, so called from the town of the same name mentioned in Ex. 1, 11. 'The designation "land of Ramses" is
only found in this passage,' Kn.

12. ויכלכל ... את אביו ... לחם. On כלכל with a
double acc., see Ewald, § 283 b.

לפי הטף, lit. 'according to the little children,' i. e. 'according to their number and wants,' 'little children being mentioned
because they would require much food, and also because
people would be less willing to see them in want,' Del. לפי
as in Lev. 25, 16. 27, 16.

13. ותלה, ἅπαξ λεγόμ. Imperf. apoc. Qal of להה for לאה;
on the form of the imperf. apoc., see Ges., § 75. Rem. 3 b.

14. הנמצא. Cf. הנמצאת, 19, 15.

15. אפס occurs only in this and the next verse in the
Pent.; it is also found in Ps. 77, 9. Is. 16, 4. 29, 20 (all).

17. וינהלם. 'And he sustained them.' נֵהֵל is only used
in this passage in the sense, 'sustain,' 'nourish.' Elsewhere
it means 'to lead' or 'guide;' so Is. 40, 11. Ps. 23, 2.

18. לא נכחד מאדני וגו'. 'We will not hide it from
my lord, that if the money is spent, and the cattle we own be my
lord's, there is nothing left' etc.; כי אם being taken separately,
according to the accentuation. Del. prefers to render them
together, 'but,' comparing 2 Sam. 15, 21. 1 Kings 20, 6.
2 Kings 5, 20 (where כי אם is preceded by a protestation),
which are not quite parallel to this passage. Others (Kn.,
Ges.) render כי אם 'but, since,' or 'but, because,' which renderings assign to אם a meaning it can hardly bear. Di., following
Kn., renders the words from כי אם down to אדני slightly
differently, 'that if our money, and the cattle we own, are

entirely at an end, (and come) to my lord,' comparing for the pregnant construction 14, 15. 42, 28. 43, 33, a rendering that seems somewhat harsh and unnatural. אדני is used here, as in Num. 32, 25. 27. 36, 2, where more than one person is speaking. Del. compares the French '*Monsieur.*'

גויתנו = '*our bodies,*' i.e. '*ourselves,*' גויה being used of living beings, as in Dan. 10, 6. Ez. 1, 11. 23. Neh. 9, 37; elsewhere it is only used of a corpse.

19. Notice that נמות is zeugmatically connected with ישׁב אהל ומקנה; cf. 4, 20 אדמתנו.

גם אנחנו גם אדמתנו. נם ... נם='*both ... and,*' as in ver. 3, 43, 8. 44, 16. 46, 34.

תשׁם, impf. Qal (intrans.) from שׁמם; cf. Ges., § 67. Rem. 3; Stade, § 509. 2; see on 16, 4 (וַתֵּקַל). With this use of שׁמם, cf. Ez. 12, 19 למען תשׁם ארצה; 19, 7 ותשׁם ארץ ומלאה.

21. ואת העם העביר אתו וגו״, usually rendered, '*and the people, he removed them into the towns;*' but such a removal of all the people into the towns would be scarcely possible, and it is very doubtful whether העביר can mean this. It is better, if the text is left unchanged, to render, '*and the people he caused to pass over to the towns*' (ואת העם being a *casus pendens*; cf. 13, 15. 21, 13; Driver, § 197. 6; M. R. § 132 a). The meaning being, the people were brought to the towns so that they might be fed from the stores of grain that were there; cf. 41, 48. Tuch interprets the Mass. text as meaning, '*he moved the people from one city into another, throughout the whole land;*' possibly to remove them from the districts in which the land they formerly owned lay. But this would require מעיר לעיר; cf. 2 Chron. 30, 10. The LXX, καὶ τὸν λαὸν κατεδουλώσατο αὐτῷ εἰς παῖδας, so the Sam. ⸂Samaritan script⸃, and Vulg.

'*Subjecitque eam (omnem terram) Pharaoni, et cunctos populos ejus*,' which point to a reading ואת העם העביר אתו לעבדים (cf. Jer. 17, 4) = '*the people he made serve him (the king) as slaves*.' Di. adopts this reading, following Knobel. Onq. has וְיַת עַמָּא אַעֲבַּר יָתֵיהּ מִקְּרֵי לִקְּרִי, and the Pesh. ܘܟܠܗ, both = '*and the people, he removed them from town to town*,' a meaning which (see above) the Heb. text cannot bear. Di. remarks, in favour of the rendering of the text adopted by him, that the purchase of the people, corresponding to the purchase of the land, is demanded by the emphatic position of ואת העם; cf. 19 and 23.

22. כי חק. חק as in Prov. 30, 8. 31, 15; Ez. 16, 27.

23. הא = הנה occurs only once again in Heb., Ez. 16, 43. It corresponds with the Arab. ها, Syr. ܗܐ.

וזרעתם. Cf. on 24, 14.

24. וארבע הידת יהיה לכם. '*And four portions ye shall have.*' וארבע הידת must be regarded as object after יהיה לכם, which is nearly equivalent to '*ye have.*' Cf. Ex. 12, 49 חקה אחת יהיה לכם; Num. 9, 14 תורה אחת יהיה לאזרח; see Ewald, § 295 d; Ges., § 147. Rem. 2. Di. accounts for the sing. here on the ground that the numeral is regarded in much the same way as כל.

הידת. See 43, 34.

26. לפרעה לחמש. '*For P. with regard to the fifth part.*' It would be less harsh if the text were read לפרעה חמש, with the Syriac, as an explanation of אתה. The LXX have τῷ Φαραῷ ἀποπεμπτοῦν, as though the text were לפ״ לַחֲמֵשׁ.

27. ויאחזו. See on 34, 10.

29. שים נא ידך תחת ירכי. See the note of 24, 2.

31. וישתחו ישראל על ראש המטה. '*And Israel*

bowed down towards the head of the bed;' so Di., Del. The aged patriarch sat upright while speaking with Joseph, and as he was too weak to rise, turned and inclined himself towards the upper end of the bed, and offered up thanks to God that his request was granted; cf. the Vulg., '*adoravit Israel Deum, conversus ad lectuli caput,*' and 1 Kings 1, 47. Tuch renders, '*leant back upon the head of the bed.*' The LXX, Syr., and Itala read הַמִּטָּה as הַמַּטֶּה, the LXX being quoted thus in Heb. 11, 21 (ἐπὶ τὸ ἄκρον τῆς ῥάβδου αὐτοῦ), Jacob being represented as bowing over the top of his staff, or, as others suppose, over the staff of Joseph (which he carried as a token of his authority) as a mark of homage to him; cf. 37, 7. But this reading is not so natural as הַמִּטָּה, and a suffix would be required (מַטֵּהוּ), which the Vss. express.

48

1. **ויאמר ליוסף**. '*And one told Joseph*' (sc. הָאֹמֵר). The third pers. sing. being here used like the impersonal, '*man sagte,*' '*on dit,*' Ewald, § 294 b; Ges., § 137. 3; M. R., § 123. 2. In 22, 20 we find ויֻגַּד used; but here the active is employed by the narrator, as ויאמר is not used in this sense; so in ver. 2 ויֻגַּד, and again ויאמר.

4. **הנני מפרך והרביתך**. The perf. with waw conv. after a word pointing to the future, as in 7, 4 ממטיר ... ומחיתי; Is. 7, 14 הִנֵּה הָעַלְמָה הָרָה ... וְקָרָאת; see Driver, § 113. 1; M. R., § 24. 2 a; Ges., § 126. 6 a.

מפרך. On the part. as *futurum instans*, see on 6, 17.

5. **ועתה שני בניך** . . . **לי הם**. On the *casus pendens*, see on 34, 21.

6. וּמוֹלַדְתְּךָ. '*And thy offspring;*' מוֹלֶדֶת, as in Lev. 18, 9. 11.

עַל שֵׁם אֲחֵיהֶם וגו׳. '*According to the name of their brethren shall they be called in their inheritance,*' i. e. their descendants shall dwell among the posterity of Ephraim and Manasseh, and be reckoned as belonging to them, and not as separate tribes.

7. מִפַּדָּן. Everywhere else P calls Mesopotamia פדן ארם ; cf. on 25, 20. Possibly the omission of ארם is due to a copyist's mistake. The Sam. has פדן ארם.

מֵתָה עָלַי. '*Died, to my sorrow.*' For this use of עָלַי, cf. Eccl. 2, 17 כי רע עלי המעשׂה. See also 33, 13 and the note on that passage.

כִּבְרַת אֶרֶץ. Cf. the note on 35, 16.

9. בָזֶה '*here;*' so 38, 21.

קָחֶם נָא. Ewald, § 253 a, and Stade, § 631 e, compare קָחֶם here with בְּצָעַם (Amos 9, 1), the suffix being attached to the word ending in a guttural, the tone being placed on the penult. קחם, however, here has no accent at all, as it is connected with נא by Maqqef, and so deprived of its accent; and the ⸗ of ◌ֶ⸗ is consequently shortened into ◌ֱ⸗: and in Amos l. c. the tone on בְּצָעַם is drawn back on to the penult. to avoid two tone-syllables coming together, the next word being בְּראשׁ.

וַאֲבָרְכֵם. For the pausal seghol, cf. 21, 9 מִיִּצְחָק and the note there; also the frequent לְעוֹלָם וָעֶד. In Num. 6, 27 we find אֲבָרְכֵם in pause, also in ordinary editions in this passage.

11. רְאֹה for רְאוֹת, like עֲשׂוֹ for עֲשׂוֹת in 31, 28 (see the note on that passage), and עֲשֹׂה for עֲשׂוֹת, 50, 20.

פִּלָּלְתִּי. According to Ben Asher in the *Dikduke Haṭ'a-*

mim, ed. Baer and Strack, Leipzig, 1879, § 49, the $-\!\!\!\cdot$ in the first person perf. Pi'el is always preserved in pause, except in this word; הִלַּכְתִּי, Ps. 38, 7; יִחַלְתִּי., Ps. 119, 43, etc.; יִשַּׂרְתִּי., Ps. 119, 128.

12. לְאַפָּיו, as in Num. 22, 31. In 19, 1. 42, 6 we find אפים alone used after וישתחו and וישתחוו respectively.

14. שִׂכֵּל אֶת יָדָיו. '*Crossing his hands;*' the construction is the same as in 44, 12; cf. the note on that passage. This rendering is the same as that of the LXX, Syr., Vulg., and most moderns, and is suitable to the context; cf. ver. 13. Cf. the Arab. شَكَلَ '*plexuit,*' '*ligavit.*' Onq. and Saadiah render, '*he made his hands wise,*' i. e. 'he placed them so intentionally,' which assigns a doubtful meaning to שִׂכֵּל (=הִשְׂכִּיל); moreover with this rendering בידיו would be more natural, as Di. points out. With this verse cf. Matt. 19, 13 f. Mark 10, 16, where Christ in blessing lays His hands on those whom He blessed.

15. מֵעוֹדִי עַד הַיּוֹם הַזֶּה. This phrase is only found once again in the O. T., viz. Num. 22, 30 מעודך עד היום הזה.

16. וְיִקָּרֵא בָהֶם שְׁמִי. Cf. 21, 12 and the note there. '*In them let my name be named,*' i. e. 'be made famous through their offspring.' Del. renders, '*On them let my name be called.*' בָּהֶם=עֲלֵיהֶם, i. e. 'let them be regarded as my children, and sharers of the promises made to me and mine.'

יִרְגּוּ. דגה is only found in this passage in the O. T.

17. יָשִׁית. Notice the tense, '*was placing;*' Jacob had not *actually* placed his hands on the heads of Ephraim and Manasseh, but was in the act of placing them; cf. Driver, § 39 β. The imperfects with waw conv. give details of Jacob's blessing which have been omitted, though the actual blessing

is given in the preceding verses; cf. 27, 24. 37, 6. 42, 21 ff.
45, 21–24; Driver, § 75 β.

19. מלא הגוים (cf. Is. 31, 4)=המון גוים in 17, 5.

22. ואני נתתי לך שכם אחד על אחיך. ‘*And I
give thee one mountain slope above thy brethren.*’ שכם =
‘*shoulder*,’ then applied to the slope of a mountain, like כתף,
Num. 34, 11. Josh. 15, 18. Is. 11, 14; see Ges., *Thes.*, 1407.
אֶחָד is *status absolutus* with the vocalisation of the *status con-
structus*, the shorter pronunciation being sometimes chosen
in the flow of speech; see Ewald, § 267 b; Ges., § 116. 6; and
cf. Zech. 11, 7 וּלְאַחַד קָרָאתִי ... לְאַחַד קָרָאתִי; Is. 27, 12 לְאַחַד
אֶחָד. שכם is taken by Onq. and Pesh. in the sense ‘*portion*,’
a translation that is too indefinite. לקחתי and נתתי are perhaps best taken with Tuch and Del. as prophetic perfects
(see, however, Di., p. 431). The meaning of the promise
seems to be that the descendants of Joseph should have a
mountain tract, in addition to their other territory. Possibly
the word שכם is chosen with reference to the well-known
place of that name in the territory of Ephraim; cf. the LXX
rendering, Σίκιμα ἐξαίρετον, and John 4, 5. Tuch and others
consider that שכם אחד means that two portions of territory
should be assigned to Ephraim and Manasseh (cf. ver. 5), as
contrasted with the one portion that the other tribes were to
receive. But שכם אחד can hardly mean ‘*one portion*,’ unless
the rendering of Onq. and the Pesh. be adopted, which, as
was remarked above, does not adequately represent the
Hebrew words. A portion of land would embrace more
than one ‘mountain slope.’

בחרבי ובקשתי are curiously rendered in some texts, cf.
Onq. בִּצְלוֹתִי וּבְבָעוּתִי ‘*with my prayer and entreaty*’ (Berliner's
text follows the Mass. text, see the notes in his edition,

part ii, p. 17). Another curious paraphrase is proposed by Hieron. (*Quaest.*, ed. Lagarde, p. 66), 'dabo tibi Sicimam, quam emi in fortitudine mea, hoc est in pecunia quam multo labore et sudore quaesivi.' In his translation, however, he follows the Heb. text.

49.

In this chapter is contained the so-called 'Blessing of Jacob,' a name which owes its origin to ver. 28, which however probably belongs, not to the ' Blessing,' but the following narrative, and was derived from a different document. This designation cannot be regarded as a suitable one, as in point of fact only two of the tribes are really blessed, viz. Judah and Joseph, the utterances of the patriarch in the case of Reuben, Simeon, and Levi being full of reproach, and a future predicted for them the reverse of prosperous. It would be better designated by the title Del. gives it, ' The prophetic sayings of Jacob concerning the Twelve.' The six sons of Leah are first mentioned, then Bilhah's eldest son, Zilpah's two sons (the eldest first), Bilhah's second son, and Rachel's two sons, Joseph the eldest first. The order in which they occur is partly that in which they were born, and partly that in which the territories represented by them geographically stand, starting from the south of Canaan and going northwards (Ewald, *Hist.*[3], ii. p. 435 ; Eng. trans., ii. p. 308). Thus the four elder sons come first, Reuben, Simeon, Levi, Judah ; but then the order of birth is abandoned, and Leah's other two sons, Zebulon (Jacob's tenth son) and Issachar (Jacob's ninth son), are inserted, Zebulon being placed before Issachar, as the future that Jacob predicts for him is more prosperous and honourable than that of Issachar (Di.). Cf. Deut. 33, 18.

where Zebulon and Issachar come together, but Zebulon first, as here. The four last sons are cited according to their geographical position; Benjamin, Joseph, Naphtali, Asher (from south to north), Joseph and Benjamin also being in the proper order of their birth. Dan is probably placed after Issachar, as being the first son of Jacob by his wives' hand-maidens (in order of birth he follows Judah, but as the order of birth is abandoned to enumerate Leah's six sons, Dan, the fifth, is mentioned first, after the six sons of Leah). Gad would then be placed after Dan, and before Naphtali, who was born before him, so as not to disturb the geographical arrange-ment—Benjamin, Joseph, Naphtali, Asher—and possibly to keep Zilpah's two sons together. In Deut. 33, the 'Blessing of Moses,'—which has many points of contact with this chapter, both in the figures it employs and the language used,—the order is varied; viz. Reuben, Judah, Levi (whose blessing contrasts strangely with Jacob's words in ver. 5), Benjamin, Joseph (Ephraim and Manasseh are mentioned by name), Zebulon, Issachar, Gad, Dan, Naphtali, Asher, while Simeon in the text as we now have it is not mentioned at all.

The language of this chapter should be noticed. In its elevated tone, in vigour and force, and in the numerous figurative expressions employed, it surpasses the other poeti-cal passages in Genesis (9, 25 ff. 14, 19 ff. 24, 66. 25, 23. 27, 27 ff. 39 f.). Many of the expressions employed are rare, and unusual in the later stages of the language, e. g. פַּחַז (ἅπαξ λεγ.) and הותיר, ver. 4; מברה, ver. 5 (a ἅπαξ λεγ. of uncertain meaning); מחקק, ver. 10 (occurring again (in the poetical fragment) Num. 21, 18. Deut. 33, 21. Judg. 5, 14. Ps. 60, 9); סות, ver. 11 (ἅπαξ λεγ.); חכלילי, ver. 12 (ἅπαξ λεγ.); משפתים, ver. 14 (only found once again, Judg. 5, 16); שְׁפִיפן, ver. 17 (ἅπαξ λεγ.); שְׁלוֹח, ver. 21 (only used thus in this passage);

פרת, ver. 22 (observe the archaic fem. ending), only in this passage for פֹּרָה; רבו: ver. 23 (רבב is perhaps found again in Ps. 18, 15 ברקים רב, see the note on this verse); ותשב ... קשתו, ver. 24, etc.; also the archaic ending יִ (the old binding vowel) in בני אתנו, אסרי לגפן; the suffix הֹ for וֹ, in עירה and סוּתה, and possibly in שׁילה (cf. the note on this word); the poetical עֲלֵי for עַל; כבוד, poetical for נפש, with which it is here parallel, ver. 6; אמרי, ver. 21, poetical for דברי; the poetical זרעי ידיו, ver. 24, etc. Probably this chapter is the oldest portion of the book of Genesis, being incorporated into one of the original documents, out of which the present book grew, from a still older source. On the special literature of this chapter, see Tuch, p. 479 f., and Di., p. 435 f.

1. יקרא אתכם. קרא = קרה, as in 42, 4; cf. the note on that passage.

באחרית הימים. *'In days to come,'* lit. *'in the end of days.'* אחרית is used here as in Num. 24, 14. Deut. 4, 30. Jer. 23, 20, etc., denoting the end of the period which the prophet sees, or which he has in view. The LXX have ἐπ' ἐσχάτων τῶν ἡμερῶν; cf. Heb. 1, 1 and 1 Pet. 1, 20 (ἐπ' ἐσχάτων τῶν χρόνων); Syr. ܒܝܘܡܬܐ ܐܚܪܝܐ; Onq. בְּסוֹף יוֹמַיָא; Vulg. *'in diebus novissimis.'* The formula is also common in prophecy in a somewhat different sense, e. g. Hos. 3, 5. Mic. 4, 1. Ez. 38, 16.

2. *' Gather yourselves and hear, sons of Jacob;*
   And hearken unto Israel your father.

3. *Reuben—my firstborn art thou, my strength and the*
   firstfruits of my vigour.
   Excelling in dignity and excelling in might.
   Boiling over like water, excel not thou;
   For thou didst go up to thy father's bed:
   There thou didst pollute it; he went up to my couch !'

Reuben, Jacob's firstborn, excels his brethren in dignity and power, but loses his privileges through his sin. In the post-Mosaic time the tribe of Reuben sinks into obscurity. With the exception of one successful campaign against the Hagarenes (1 Chron. 5, 8–10), nothing more is known of the doings of this tribe.

בכרי אתה might be rendered, '*my firstborn, thou,*' regarding אתה as a vocative; the rendering given above is, however, better.

כחי = '*my manly strength.*' אוני, און, as in Deut. 21, 17. Ps. 78, 51. 105, 36, of genital power. LXX, σὺ ἰσχύς μου καὶ ἀρχὴ τέκνων μου; Vulg. '*et principium doloris mei*' (as though אוֹן were אָוֶן), following (as often) Aq. κεφάλαιον λύπης μου, and Symm. ἀρχὴ ὀδύνης μου.

יתר שאת ויתר עז, lit. '*excellence of dignity and excellence of power,*' יתר both times being abstract for concrete. שאת as in Ps. 62, 5. Job 13, 11. 31, 23. Hab. 1, 7. עָז not an adj. but pausal form of עַז, see on 43, 14; so יִטְרָף in ver. 27 in pause for יִטְרֹף. The LXX render σκληρὸς φέρεσθαι, καὶ σκληρὸς αὐθάδης, while Onq. renders as follows: לָךְ הֲוָה חָזֵי לְמֵיסַב תְּלָתָה חוּלָקִין בְּכֵירוּתָא כְּהוּנָתָא וּמַלְכוּתָא '*for thee it was provided to receive three portions, the right of firstborn, priesthood, and the kingdom,*' in accordance with the Jewish tradition, which assigned these three privileges to Reuben as the firstborn.

4. פחז כמים, lit. '*a bubbling over like water.*' The root פחז in Arabic (فَخَزَ I, V) = '*to boast;*' in Aramaic the subs. فَخُوثَا occurs in the Pesh. Vers., 2 Cor. 12, 21. Eph. 4, 19 = ἀσέλγεια. The root properly = '*to exceed bounds, be inordinate;*' LXX well, ἐξύβρισας. Only the comparison gives the idea of *boiling* or *bubbling*. פַּחַז, like יֶתֶר in the preceding

verse, is abstract for concrete; cf. Ewald, § 296 b; Driver, § 189. Obs. The words may be taken as vocative, or (with Del.) as a descriptive apposition to the subject ראובן. The Heb.-Sam. has פָּחַזְתָּ, and the other Vss. render as though פָּחַזְתָּ stood instead of פַּחַז; but it is not necessary to suppose that the text they translated from actually had the second pers. of the verb, their renderings are probably chosen to express פַּחַז with greater clearness. פֹּחֲזִים, part. of פָּחַז, occurs twice in the O. T., Judg. 9, 4. Zeph. 3, 4; in the sense of 'wanton' in Judg. l. c., and 'boasting' in Zeph. l. c., of false prophets.

אל תותר, i. e. with reference to the יתר mentioned in ver. 3. Render, 'Do not thou excel' (the jussive, with a negative, expressing a desire or wish, Driver, § 50 γ), i. e. 'mayest thou lose the privileges that belong to thee as firstborn,' viz. those mentioned in ver. 3. LXX, μὴ ἐκζέσῃς (cf. Lagarde's *Genesis Graece*, p. 202, notes), which Geiger, *Urschrift*, p. 373, regards, not as indicating a different reading, but as a paraphrase on the part of the LXX, who refer תותר back to פחז, the paraphrase being due to a desire to mitigate the effects of Reuben's sin. The Syriac has ܬܬܝܬܪ, reading the text as תִּוָּתֵר.

כי עלית משכבי אביך. עלה is here construed with the acc., as in Num. 13, 17 ועליתם את ההר. משכבי, Di. explains the plural as meaning a double bed; Del. explains it by Ges., § 108. 2 (nouns denoting extension of *space* or *time*, used in the plural). With the plural here, יְצוּעֵי אָבִיו of 1 Chron. 5, 1 may be compared, Reuben also being referred to.

יצועי עלה. These words are addressed, in astonishment at Reuben's sin, by Jacob to his other sons; therefore the third pers.; cf. Is. 42, 20. 51, 18. 52, 14. The LXX, Pesh.,

Onq. render as though the text had עָלִיתָ, possibly an attempt to amend the Heb. text, which is not necessary, while the Vulg. leaves עלה untranslated, and makes יצועי the obj. of חללת. Geiger, *Urschrift*, p. 374, supposes that these words were not the real text, but that יְצוּעֵי בִלְהָה was written originally, which afterwards was changed into יצועי עלה, as being too clear. He objects to our present text because everywhere else יצוע is used in the plural, and only in this passage in the singular. Di. describes his emendation, which is very needless, as 'the purest prose.' Ewald, *History*[3], i. p. 535, Eng. trans., i. p. 373, foot-note, renders, '*my couch of highness*,' '*my lofty couch*,' pointing עָלָה as עֲלָה = '*a step*,' a rendering that can scarcely be justified. In 1 Chron. l. c. the right of firstborn, which Reuben lost, is given to Joseph, while Judah received his (Reuben's) privilege of royalty. In Deut. 33, 6 Reuben's blessing is as follows: יחי ראובן ואל ימת ויהי מתיו מספר '*Let R. live and not die, yet let his men be few.*'

> 5–7. '*Simeon and Levi are brethren;*
> *Weapons of violence are their shepherds' staves.*
> *Into their council, let not my soul come;*
> *With their assembly, let not my honour be united;*
> *For in their anger they slew men,*
> *And in their wantonness houghed oxen.*
> *Cursed be their anger, for it was fierce;*
> *And their wrath, for it was cruel:*
> *I will divide them in Jacob,*
> *And scatter them in Israel.*'

5. אחים, either predicate or in apposition to שִׁמְעוֹן ולוי. Simeon and Levi are brothers, not only as sons of the same parents, but as being alike in their dispositions.

מכרתיהם. The meaning of this word, which only

occurs in this passage, is very uncertain. (1) It is commonly
rendered '*sword*,' a meaning which was first hinted at by the
Jews, who compared מכרה fancifully with the Greek μάχαιρα;
see Bereshith Rabba, c. 99 אמר רבי יוחנן לשון יוני
מברותיהם. הוא מכירין פי" קורין לחרבות מכירין ויש אומרים מברותיהן
מגורותיהם כמה דאת אמר מכורותיך ומולדותיך: '*Rabbi Joḥanan
says the word* מברות *is a Greek word, as they* (*the Greeks*)
call swords מבירין (μάχαιραι). *Others think that* מכרות =
מגורות, *comparing Ez.* 16, 3.' Del. also assigns the meaning
'*sword*' to מכרה, deriving it from בּוּר, or rather בָּרַר=בּוּר
(after the analogy of מְקֵרָה, מְגֵרָה, מְאֵרָה), which has the
meaning '*to dig*' or '*pierce.*' Hieron. and Rashi also render
'*sword*;' see Ges., *Thes.*, p. 672. (2) Tuch assigns to the
word the meaning '*plot*' or '*contrivance*,' lit. '*windings*,' from
כרר='*to wind*,' but, as Del. points out, כרר does not mean
'*to wind*,' but '*to be round*;' while L. de Dieu and Maurer
also render '*plots*,' but get this meaning from מכר = măkără
in Ethiopic and مَكَرَ in Arabic, '*to plan*,' '*contrive.*' We
must then, however, point the form מִכְרֹתֵיהֶם, not מִכְרֹתֵיהֶם;
see Ewald, § 260 a. (3) Kn., Boettcher, § 791 (though he
adheres to the Mass. pointing), and others render, '*marriage
contracts*,' as though מכר = the Syriac ܡܟܰܪ '*desponsavit*;'
מבר, however, means '*to sell*,' and if מכר can = ܡܟܰܪ (which
in Heb. would usually be rendered by מהר), as ܡܟܰܪ is
always used of 'the wooer' or 'suitor' (Del.), (see, however,
Payne Smith, *Thesaurus Syriacus*, col. 2107), the reference
to Dinah's brethren would be hardly suitable—though the
next verse certainly refers to the incident narrated in chap.
34—and 'marriage contracts' could scarcely be called כלים.
Knobel alters the reading into מִכְרֹתֵיהֶם. (4) Di. derives the
word from כרר '*to be round*,' and says it means a '*round
curved instrument*,' perhaps a '*curved knife*' or '*sickle.*'

Ewald, *Hist.*[8], ii. p. 493, Eng. trans., ii. p. 349, and Wellhausen, *History of Israel*, Eng. trans., p. 144, render (also from כרר), '*shepherds' staves*,' or as we should say in English, '*shepherds' crooks*,' which perhaps is the most suitable rendering. The LXX have συνετέλεσαν ἀδικίαν ἐξ αἱρέσεως αὐτῶν, as though the text were כִּלּוּ חֲמַס מְכֵרוֹתֵיהֶם '*they ended the violence of their nature;*' so Geiger translates, *Urschrift*, p. 374 f., regarding this translation of the LXX as intended to tone down the violence of Simeon and Levi's conduct. The Syriac has ܟܠܘܡܣ ܡܢ ܐܘܣܝܐ ܕܝܠܗܘܢ '*instruments of violence from their nature;*' possibly they connected מְכֵרָה with כִּיכוּרָה '*birth*,' '*descent.*' Onq. renders גֻּבְרִין גִּבָּרִין בְּאֲרַע תּוֹתָבוּתְהוֹן עָבָדוּ גְּבוּרָא '*mighty men, in the land they dwelt in they did a mighty deed*,' as though מְגוּרֵיהֶם = מְכֵרֹתֵיהֶם; so Kimchi and the A.V., who supply '*in*,' which is wanting in the Heb. text. Onq.'s rendering seems an endeavour to transform Simeon and Levi's cruel deed into a noble one. The Vulg. gives '*vasa iniquitatis bellantia.*'

6. The first portion of this verse is rendered as follows in the A.V. and A.V.R.: '*O my soul, come not thou into their secret* (A.V. R. "*council,*" marg. "*secret*"); *unto their assembly, mine honour* (A.V.R. "*my glory*"), *be not thou united,*' taking תבא and תחד as second pers. sing. masc. (though נפש is more commonly fem.), and נפשי and כבדי as vocatives. The rendering given above is that adopted by Di. and Del.

תֵּחַד is imperf. Qal of יָחַד. The Heb.-Sam. reads אל יחר.

כבדי, '*my honour*' or '*glory*,' is rhythmically interchanged with נפש here. In Ps. 7, 6 כבדי is parallel to נפשי, and in Ps. 16, 9. 108, 2 to לבי; cf. also Ps. 30, 13. 57, 9, where it is used in the sense of נפש. כבד is here fem. by Ewald,

§ 174 b (names of invisible active powers are fem.; so נֶפֶשׁ is usually fem., and כבדי being parallel to it, is also regarded as fem.). The LXX render אל תחד כבדי with μὴ ἐρίσαι τὰ ἥπατά μου, as though the text were אַל־יֵחַר כְּבֵדִי; see Geiger, *Urschrift*, p. 319, who regards the rendering of the LXX as intentional, to avoid the possibility of confounding the human כבד (Doxa) with the divine, the word כבד, when equivalent to נפשׁ, having 'both the idea of divine majesty and the idea of the higher human nature.'

אִישׁ may be either collective—cf. the rendering given above—or the sing. may be used poetically for the plural.

וברצנם. '*In their wanton wrath.*' רצון, here parallel to אַף, means '*unrestrained passion;*' cf. Esther 9, 5 ויעשו בשׂנאיהם כרצונם.

עִקְּרוּ שׁוֹר. '*They houghed oxen,*' i. e. severed the sinews of the thigh and so rendered the animals useless; so LXX, ἐνευροκόπησαν ταῦρον; cf. Josh. 11, 6. 9. 2 Sam. 8, 4. Onq., Pesh., Aq., Symm., Hieron., Vulg., and A.V. (but not A.V. R.) take שׁוֹר as שׁוּר, and render, '*a wall*' (this reading, according to Wright, being found in three MSS.), pointing עָקְרוּ, עִקְּרוּ (cf. Zeph. 2, 4), and taking עָקְרוּ in the sense, '*they destroyed,*' a meaning of the root which is common in Aramaic. Kn. points out that in 34, 28 f. Jacob's sons carried off the cattle as spoil, and Di., p. 439, suggests that the rendering '*wall*' may have been adopted to avoid a discrepancy in the narrative here and in chap. 34. Schumann and others consider that שׁוֹר refers to שׁכם, the son of חמור, comparing Ps. 68, 31. Deut. 33, 17, also Ps. 22, 13. Is. 14, 9, but this reference to שׁכם is very doubtful, and seems hardly justified by the passages cited in its defence.

7. עֹז is the pausal form of עַז; so חָי pausal form of חַי, 25, 7, and דָּק pausal form of דַּק, Ex. 32, 20.

כִּי עַז ... כִּי קָשָׁתָה. Cf. a similar change in Song of Songs 8, 6 כִּי עַזָּה כַמָּוֶת אַהֲבָה קָשָׁה כִשְׁאוֹל קִנְאָה.

The Heb.-Sam. text has אַדִּיר for אָרוּר, and וְחִבַּרְתָּם for וְעִבַרְתָּם, probably an intentional change, so that Jacob should not be represented as cursing them. The Sam. Version renders in the same way as the Heb.-Sam. text; cf. Targ. Ps.-Jon.

In Deut. 33, 8 f. Levi's blessing is entirely different in its tone from the severe language used by Jacob in this chapter; while Simeon is not mentioned in Deut. 33, at least in our present text.

The Simeonites received as their portion several cities in the נגב, i. e. the southern portion of Palestine, in the midst of the territory of Judah (cf. Josh. 15, 26–32. 42 with Josh. 19, 1–9. 1 Chron. 4, 28–32); while Levi, according to Num. 35. Josh. 21, receives no special portion of territory, but has forty-eight cities assigned to him to dwell in by the other tribes.

8–12. '*Judah, thou, may thy brethren praise thee :*
May thy hand be on the neck of thy foes ;
May thy father's sons bow down to thee.
A lion's whelp is Judah ;
From the prey, my son, art thou gone up :
He couched, he lay down like a lion,
And like a lioness ; who can rouse him ?
The marshall's staff shall not depart from Judah,
Nor the leader's staff from between his feet,
Until he come to Shiloh ;
And may the obedience of the peoples be his.
Binding to the vine his foal,

> *And to the Sorek vine his ass's colt :*
> *He washes in wine his garments ;*
> *And in the blood of grapes his raiment :*
> *Dark are his eyes with wine,*
> *And white his teeth with milk.'*

8. The *name* here suggests the form of the blessing; cf.
29, 35, as though it were, '*Praise . . . thy brethren shall
praise thee.'*

אתה prefixed as a nom. abs., like אנכי in 24, 27; cf. the
note on that passage, also Ewald, § 309 b; Ges., § 145. 2.

ידך בערף וגו″ . Cf. Job 16, 12 ואחז בערפי ויפצפצני.

בני אביך . Not אחיך or בני אמך, but בני אביך; for all
Jacob's sons—not only those Leah bore him—shall praise
Judah.

9. גור אריה יהודה . The comparison with a lion is
not uncommon; see Deut. 33, 20 (where Gad is compared
with a lioness), and 22 (where Dan is spoken of as a lion's
whelp); cf. also Num. 23, 24. 24, 9 (which bears a striking
resemblance to this passage, כרע שכב כארי וכלביא מי יקימנו),
Mic. 5, 7.

מטרף בני עלית . '*From the prey, my son, art thou gone*
up,' i.e. Judah is like a lion reascending to the mountain (cf.
Song of Songs 4, 8) after having devoured his prey. LXX
render עלית with ἀνέβης, and מטרף with ἐκ βλαστοῦ, taking it
as in Ez. 17, 9 כָּל־טַרְפֵּי צִמְחָהּ '*all its fresh springing leaves.'*
עלה Hif'. is found in Ez. 19, 3, meaning '*to bring up* (of a
lion);' but as עלה is generally only used of vegetation in the
sense to '*grow up,'* the rendering, '*From the prey, my son,*
art thou gone up,' is preferable. If Judah were compared
to a lion growing up, the addition of כאריה וכלביא would be
hardly necessary.

כְּלָבִיא. The lioness, defending her young, is fiercer than the lion (Herod. iii. 108).

10. לֹא יָסוּר . . . עַמִּים. The rendering given above is that adopted by Di. and Del.; but as will be shewn below it cannot be regarded as satisfactory. First of all let us examine the rendering of the A.V. and A.V.R., '*until Shiloh come.*' שִׁילֹה[1] is here taken as a personal name, possibly meaning '*peaceful,*' or '*peace-bringer.*' But, as is generally admitted (see Professor Driver, in the *Cambridge Journal of Philology*, xiv. 2, and in *The Expositor*, July, 1885), there are serious philological difficulties in the way of this view. As pointed in our present texts, the ending ה must either stand for the suffix of the third pers. masc. sing., or mark the word as a pr. n.; cf. שְׁלֹמֹה, דוֹדוֹ, עֵדוֹ, יִתְרוֹ, etc. From these examples the word might, as far as its form goes, be a personal pr. n. If it be a pr. n., it must obviously, in a passage like the present, have some special significance. שִׁילֹה apparently must be connected with שָׁלָה, which denotes '*to be at ease,*' or '*quiet.*' The only exact parallel is גִּלֹה, the name of a place. But neither גלה nor שילה can be derived from גלה and שלה respectively, after the analogy of קִיטוֹר, כִּישׁוֹר; for—as Tuch argues, and Del. allows—they would, if derived from ל״ה verbs, following analogy, be גִּלוֹי and שִׁילוֹי. But the Gentile names גִּילֹנִי and שִׁילֹנִי (2 Sam. 15, 12. 1 Kings 11, 29) shew that שִׁילֹה and גִּלֹה are really apocopated from שִׁילוֹן and גִּילוֹן, and have to be regarded as coming from the roots שׁוּל* or שִׁיל, and

---

[1] The word שׁילֹה is pointed שִׁילֹה, שִׁלֹה, and שִׁלוֹ. The first punctuation with the *scriptio plena*, being of a later date than שִׁלֹה, שִׁלוֹ, is only found a few times. It is worthy of notice that the *scriptio plena* is not found on the Moabite stone, nor do the Versions have it in שִׁלֹה.

*נול or ניל. Further, if שׁילה could possibly be derived from שׁלה, ' שׁלה is not a full and significant word like שׁלם (Zech. 9, 10); at the most it denotes *mere* rest (Ps. 122, 6. 7), and is often associated with the idea of careless worldly ease (e. g. Job 12, 6. Ez. 16, 49).' So the rendering, '*peaceful one*,' or '*peace-bringer*,' can hardly be got out of the root שׁלה. Further, there is no allusion in any other part of the O. T. to *Shiloh* as a personal name. Del. and Di. adopt the rendering given in the translation of vers. 8–12, above, arguing that the philological difficulty just mentioned, the absence of any allusion in subsequent parts of the O. T. to Shiloh as a personal name, and the fact that שׁילה everywhere else in the O. T. is the name of a place, favour the rendering, '*until he come to Shiloh ;*' cf. 1 Sam. 4, 12 ויבא שלה '*he came to Shiloh.*' They then, following the course of history, suppose that the prophecy was fulfilled in Josh. 18, 1, where the settlement of the land is described, pointing out that at an early date pre-eminence was assigned to Judah,—e. g. Num. 10, 14, the tribe marched first in the wilderness; Judg. 1, 2, advanced first to battle (cf. Judg. 20, 18); Josh. 15, was the first to receive its share when the land was divided,—and urge that the arrival of the Israelites at Shiloh was really a turning-point in their history,—the period of wandering was ended, the period of rest began,—a turning-point of sufficient importance to be noticed in the blessing; cf. Josh. 21, 42. 22, 4. The position Judah had gained was in subsequent years confirmed; the 'obedience of the peoples' was realised in the victories of David (2 Sam. 8), while it also included the ideal relation of Israel to the heathen, which is more distinctly spoken of by the prophets. The Messianic idea is thus not excluded in this view, though it cannot be attached to the word Shiloh. This view is also adopted by Herder (*Vom*

Geist der Hebr. Poesie, ii. 6); Ewald, *Jahrbücher*, ii. 51; *Hist.*, ii. 283 f. (Eng. trans.), and others. It is objected to by Schultz (*Alttest. Theologie*, 1878, pp. 668–672), Cheyne (*Isaiah*, vol. ii [eds. 1, 2], Essay iv), and by Professor Driver, who points out that Judah is represented as possessing not only supremacy, but royalty; for שבט standing in ver. 10 alone, without any qualification, suggests rather a *sceptre* than a '*commander's staff*' (in Judg. 5, 14 שבט ספר may = 'a commander's staff;' cf. הספר in 2 Kings 25, 19, but here שבט has no such qualification). The מחקק מבין רגליו represents rather a king sitting on his throne than a commander on active service, and the view that Judah will have not only supremacy, but royalty, is confirmed by a comparison of 8 b with 37, 7. Judah, too, enjoyed no royal power till long after Josh. 18, the passages in Num. and Josh. attributing only supremacy, not royalty, to him; and if שבט can bear the meaning assigned to it by Di. and Del., the context contains indications that the picture is one of royalty, and not mere supremacy; see further, Driver, l. c.

As Professor Driver has shewn in his two articles already referred to, the word שלה is first connected with the Messiah in a passage in the Talmud, *Sanh.* 98 b, where the pupils of Rabbi Shila compliment their master by connecting his name with a title of the Messiah, calling him 'Shiloh,' on the ground of the present passage. The versions, as will be seen, have not interpreted it in this way, and it is doubtful whether the rendering, '*until Shiloh come*,' appears at all before the sixteenth century. The LXX render the verse, Οὐκ ἐκλείψει ἄρχων ἐξ Ἰούδα, καὶ ἡγούμενος ἐκ τῶν μηρῶν αὐτοῦ, ἕως ἐὰν ἔλθῃ τὰ ἀποκείμενα αὐτῷ· καὶ αὐτὸς προσδοκία ἐθνῶν. Variants are ᾧ ἀπόκειται; so Ignatius, Irenaeus, Tertullian, Leo, Ambrosius, and Theodoret; see Lagarde, *Gen. Graece*, p. 203: ὁ ἀπόκειται αὐτῷ and ὁ ἀπόκειται, see *Journ. Phil.*, l. c., p. 4. The last two variants are unimportant. τὰ ἀποκείμενα αὐτῷ is a paraphrastic rendering, which takes שלה as=שֶׁלֹּה, i. e. אֲשֶׁר לֹו (see 2 Kings 6, 11. Song of Songs 1, 7; and cf. the note on 6, 3). ἐὰν ἔλθῃ ᾧ ἀπόκειται, this rendering is not a faithful reproduction of the Heb., as it supplies the subject ('until he comes, whose [it is]'), which is wanting in the Hebrew. ἐκ τῶν μηρῶν αὐτοῦ=מבין רגליו; cf. Deut. 28, 57 מבין רגליה: LXX διὰ τῶν μηρῶν αὐτῆς. προσδοκία for יקהת seems to connect it with תִּקְוָה, קִוָּה. Pesh. has לָ ܬܚܠܶ ܫܳܒܛܐ ܡܶܢ ܝܺܗܘܕܐ ܘܡܚܰܘܝܳܢܐ ܡܶܢ ܒܶܝܬ ܪ̈ܓܠܰܘܗܝ ܥܕܡܐ ܕܢܺܐܬܶܐ ܡܳܢ ܕܕܺܝܠܶܗ ܗܘ ܘܠܗ ܢܣܰܟܘܢ ܥܰܡ̈ܡܐ 'The sceptre (שֵׁבֶט) shall not depart from Judah, nor an interpreter from between his feet, until he come whose it is, and him the nations expect.' ܡܚܰܘܝܳܢܐ='an interpreter,' 'announcer.' The Pesh. in Deut. 33, 21. Judg. 5, 14. Is. 33, 22 uses the same word again for מחקק. Possibly this is a free translation on the part of the Syriac Vers.; in the two passages in the Psalms (60, 9. 108, 9) where מחקק occurs, the Pesh. gives ܡܰܠܟܝ 'my king.' The מחקק in both the Psalms is Judah. ܡܳܢ ܕܕܺܝܠܶܗ ܗܘ, the Syriac renders שלה, like the LXX,=שֶׁלֹּה. In the present text the Pesh. has nothing to explain the fem. ܗܘ. Possibly the original form of the text has been preserved by Aphraates (330–350 A. D.), who gives ܡܰܠܟܘܬܐ,= 'kingdom,' after ܗܘ. This version also connects יקהת with תִּקְוָה, קִוָּה in its rendering ܢܣܰܟܘܢ. Onq. has לָא יְעְדֵי עָבֵיד שׁוּלְטַן מִדְּבֵית יְהוּדָה וְסַפְרָא מִבְּנֵי בְנֽוֹהִי עַד עָלְמָא עַד דְּיֵיתֵי מְשִׁיחָא דְּדִילֵיהּ הִיא מַלְכוּתָא וְלֵיהּ יִשְׁתַּמְעוּן עַמְמַיָא 'A ruler (lit. one exercising authority) shall not depart from those of the house of Judah, nor a scribe from among his sons' sons for ever, until Messiah comes, whose is the kingdom, and him the peoples shall obey.' Onq. takes שבט as 'ruler,' and מחקק as 'scribe,' מבין רגליו is interpreted similarly to the LXX, 'from his

descendants,' 'for ever,' and *' Messiah'* are insertions, and שלה
is taken as שֶׁלּה, following the construction of ᾧ ἀπόκειται,
' kingdom' being inserted after it. For traces of a various
reading in Onq., see Berliner, *Targum Onk.,* ii. p. 18. The
Targ. Jerus. is substantially the same as Onqelos; but the
Targ. Ps.-Jon. takes שלה as מַלְכָּא מְשִׁיחָא זְעֵיר בְּנוֹהִי=*'King
Messiah, his youngest son,'* שילה being connected with שִׁלְיָתַהּ,
Deut. 28, 57, where Onq. has זְעֵיר בְּנָהָא *' her youngest son,'*
and Rashi בָּנִים הַקְּטַנִּים. This interpretation afterwards found
considerable favour, and is perhaps embodied in the Massoretic punctuation שִׁילֹה (=*' his son'*). The Old Latin has
' donec veniant quae reposita sunt ei,' with the variants *' donec
veniat cui repositum est'* (or *' cui reposita sunt'*); cf. the LXX
translations. The Vulgate has *' donec veniat qui mittendus
est,'* reading שלה as though it were שָׁלוּחַ. The Sam. Vers.
has ᚲᚻᚷᛐᚷᚼ for רגליו *' his ranks.'* The Heb.-Sam. has מבין
דגליו *' from between his banners,'* דֶּגֶל for רֶגֶל. It retains the
word שילה, and renders מחקק *' leader'* with the LXX (ἡγούμενος) and Vulg. (*' dux '*).

Thus it will be seen that most of the versions took שלה as
שֶׁלֹּה, which would be a poetical equivalent of אֲשֶׁר לוֹ (see
above, on the LXX translation); the sentence being then
rendered, (1) *' until there come that which* (or *he that*) *is his,'*
or (2) *' until there come he to whom* (or *he whose*) *is.'* In the
second case the sentence is without a subject, and requires
some word, e. g. הוא or יהיה, referring back to שבט, or some
expression denoting *' dominion;'* cf. the renderings of Onq.
and (possibly) the Pesh. The suffix ה for ו does not occur
with ל elsewhere; but בֹּה is only found once (Jer. 17, 24),
and we have סוּתֹה and עִירֹה in ver. 11. Possibly Ez. 21, 32
עד בא אשר לו המשפט may be a reference to this passage; if so,
it favours the punctuation adopted by most of the Vss. As

may be seen from the extracts given by Professor Driver, the rendering of the Targ. Ps.-Jon. (*his son*) is adopted by Yepheth Ben Ali (c. 950–990), Abulwalid (11th cent.), David Kimchi (d. 1235), etc. If שִׁיל means '*son*' in this verse, it is the only passage in the O. T. where the word occurs. The verse was interpreted in ancient times, by both Christian and Jewish writers, as Messianic; but this Messianic idea was derived, not from the word שׁלה, but from the context of the verse, especially from the promise of supremacy and success which is held out to Judah.

Other renderings of the passage that have been proposed are : (1) '*So long as one comes* (=*people come*) *to Shiloh*,' i. e. as long as the worship at Shiloh is continued shall Judah retain his supremacy, i. e. for ever; so Tuch and others, comparing the use of עַד שֶׁ in Song of Songs 1, 12 = '*as long as*.' (2) Reading לה (ם)שׁ(יו) or (ת)שׁ(יו) יבא כי עד. This is the reading suggested by Prof. Cheyne (*Isaiah*, ii. Essay iv), who thinks that the LXX rendering presupposes a fuller text than שׁלה. The rendering with this reading would be, '*for whom it* (*the dominion*) *is appointed*.' Cf. Judg. 5, 14 מני בעמלק שרשׁם אפרים '*out of Ephraim* [*came down*] *they whose root is in A*.' (3) '*Till he come to that which is his*,' or '*his own*;' cf. Deut. 33, 7, the rendering adopted by C. von Orelli, *O. T. Prophecy*, § 15; see further, Di., Del., and Tuch in their commentaries, Professor Driver, l. c., and the various authorities cited by them [1].

שׁבט. In the rendering adopted by Del., Di., and others, שׁבט means '*the leader's*' or '*commander's staff*.' In Judg. 5,

---

[1] See also the two articles by the Dean of Peterborough in *The Churchman*, Oct. and Dec., 1886, who, after pointing out the difficulties of the rendering '*till Shiloh come*,' adopts the rendering of Kurtz and Oehler, *Theology of the O. T.*, § 229, '*until he come to rest or tranquillity*.'

14 it certainly has this meaning, but in that passage it is
qualified by ספר. Di. remarks that the term שבט is not
exclusively applied to a king, and points out that it is used
here, as מחקק in Ps. 60, 9. Num. 21, 18, of the leader's or
chief's staff.   מחקק, Di. and Del. '*leader's staff;*' cf. מחקק in
Num. 21,18. Ps. 60, 9 (Del.). If the view, defended by Professor
Driver, be adopted, as שבט must then mean '*sceptre,*' מחקק
must in the parallel clause = '*ruler's staff.*'   The Syriac has
ܡܚܘܩܢܐ, which perhaps favours the rendering '*law-giver,*'
and which could be applied to a '*leader*' or '*ruler;*' LXX
ἡγούμενος; Onq., Targ. Ps.-Jon. (of actual '*scribes*' [teachers of
law]), Jer. Targ. '*scribe;*' Vulg. '*dux;*' Sam. Ver. שבדי =
'*leader;*' all (excepting perhaps the Targums) renderings that
could be used of a commander or a king.   The meaning of
מחקק must be similar to that assigned to שבט, whether שבט
be rendered '*sceptre*' or '*leader's staff,*' as the two portions
of the verse are parallel.

מבין רגליו.   '*From between his feet,*' the picture representing the leader with his staff of office between his feet
(Di., who compares the figures on the old Persian and
Assyrian monuments), or the king on his throne, with the
sceptre between his feet.   The meaning, '*from among his
descendants,*' is favoured by the LXX, Onq., Targg. Ps.-Jon.,
Jer., Vulg. ('*de femore ejus*'), but depends on a comparison
with Deut. 28, 57, and is unsuitable here.   Tuch renders
רַגְלָיו as the plural of רגלי a '*foot soldier;*' cf. the Heb.-Sam.
text, and the Sam. Vers. referred to above, a meaning which
would suit the word if the picture is that of a military commander.   Di. condemns this rendering as devoid of taste
and ungrammatical, as רַגְלָיו cannot stand for רִגְלָיו; cf.
Böttcher, *Heb. Gram.,* § 827.   Di. also rejects the Heb.-Sam.
rendering, '*banners,*' as incompatible with the מחקק.

עד כי חדל ‎41, 49; ‎עד כי נדל ‎13 ‎,26 ‎.Cf ‎. עד כי יבא;
‎2 Sam. 23, 10 ‎עד כי יגעה ידו; and ‎עד אשר ‎in 27, 44.

ולו יקהת עמים. יְקְהַת with the *dag. forte dirimens;* see
Ges., § 20. 2 b; Dav., § 7. 4. note; Stade, § 138 a; so עֹנְבֵי,
Deut. 32, 32; קַשְׁתֹתָיו, Is. 5, 28; חַלְּקֵי־נַחַל, Is. 57, 6.

יקהת. The meaning '*obedience*,' which is also adopted
by Onq. (see above), agrees with Prov. 30, 17 (where it also
has *dag. dirimens*), the only other passage where the word
occurs, and is corroborated by the Arabic وَقِهَ '*to obey.*' The
A.V. renders, '*gathering of the people*' (but A.V.R. '*obedience*'),
following Aq. (σύστημα), Tauchuma (9th cent.), Rashi (אֲסִיפַת
הָעַמִּים). The Sam. Vers., Heb.-Sam., and Saadiah render
יקהת similarly, possibly connecting the word with מִקְוֶה, נִקְוָה.

11. אסרי לגפן עירה. אסרי, the construct state with the
binding vowel ‎ִ־י, so בְּנִי; cf. 31, 39 and the note on that
passage. On the cstr. state before a prep., see Ges., § 116. 1;
M. R., § 73. Rem. a ; so (with the archaic connecting vowel
‎ִ־י) Is. 22, 16 חֹקְקִי בַּסֶּלַע; Obad. 3 שֹׁכְנִי בְחַגְוֵי־סֶלַע; Mic. 7,
14 שֹׁכְנִי לְבָדָד; Ps. 123, 1 הַיֹּשְׁבִי בַּשָּׁמָיִם.

עירה. On the archaic orthography ה (for ו), see the note
on 9, 21. עירה is for עִירֹה (the abs. state is עַיִר); cf. בֵּיתֹו, בַּיִת,
לֵיל, and לַיְל; so שַׁיִת in Is. 10, 17 makes שִׁיתֹו, not שִׁיתֹו; see
Stade, § 100; Ewald, § 255 b, who also cites דִּישֹׁו, Deut. 25, 4,
as though from דַּיִשׁ; but דִּישֹׁו may be inf. cstr. of דִּישׁ. Onq.
and the Sam. Vers. and Heb.-Sam. take עירו as = '*his city!*'

שרקה. '*The sorek vine*,' so called from the red colour
(شَقِرَ) of the grapes. Both the grapes and the wine were of
a specially choice kind. In the territory of Judah the vine
flourished; cf. Joel 1, 7 ff. 4, 18. 2 Chron. 26, 10, and Num.
13, 23 f., where the vineyards near Hebron, and Song of
Songs 1, 14, where those of En-gedi, are mentioned.

כבם. Cf. the use of רחץ in Job 29, 6. Di. considers this a continuation of the part. אסרי; cf. Ges., § 134. 2. Rem. 2; Driver, § 117. In this construction the second verb is usually connected with the part. by waw conv., or simple waw and the perfect, the perfect being separated from the waw by some word or words; cf. ver. 17 הנשׁך ... ויפּל. It seems more natural to disconnect כבם and אסרי, following the accents, and to render as above.

סותה. This word only occurs in this passage; on the suffix ה, see on עירה. The Heb.-Sam. reads כסותו, which is possibly the correct reading. But as there seems to be no authority for the elision of the כ (תֶּן for נְתֶן is not parallel), it will be better to derive the word from a root סוה ' *to envelop*,' '*wrap up*,' סוּת being contracted for סוּוֹת; cf. the noun מסוה, which comes from the same verb סוה. סוה may=the Arab. زَوَى (the ס in Heb. corresponding exceptionally to an Arabic ز) =*abdidit celavit*, conj. VII, *abdidit se*.

12. חכלילי עינים. The י is not the binding vowel, as in בני, אסרי, but חכלילי is an adj. from חכל (see Ewald, § 164 a), with a repetition of the last two letters of the root (see Stade, § 149). (Del. compares שַׂעֲרוּרִי, but this word does not actually occur, though the fem. form שַׂעֲרוּרִיָה, Hos. 6, 10, is found in the Ktb., and might presuppose a masc. שַׂעֲרוּרִי.) The adjectival ending י– is common, e. g. פְּלִילִי, נָכְרִי, פַּרְזִי, רַגְלִי. The root חכל (which, however, is not found) corresponds (apparently) with حَكَلَ ' *to be obscure and doubtful*.' Del. on Ps. 10, 8 compares also the Arab. حَلِكَ ' *to be jet black*.'

חכלילי עינים. Cf. Prov. 23, 29 לְמִי חכלילות עינים. The construction is the same as in יפת תאר, 29, 17; see on 12, 11.

וּלְבֶן־שׁנַּיִם. לְבֶן cstr. state of לָבָן, from an abs. state לָבָן; so חֲלֵב cstr. state of חָלָב, from an abs. state חָלָב, which

with Maqqef would be חֶלָב; so אֶבֶל־, Ps. 35, 14, from אֵבֶל;
see Stade, § 202 a; Ges., § 93. 2. Rem. 1. With this verse,
cf. Joel 4, 18. Amos 9, 13. The pasture lands of Judah
were celebrated; see 1 Sam. 25, 2. Amos 1, 1. 2 Chron.
26, 10.

13. '*Zebulon—on the shore of the sea shall he dwell:*
    And he himself shall be on a shore of ships,
    With his border by Sidon.'

There is possibly an allusion here to the meaning of the
name Zebulon ('*dweller*') given in 30, 20.

לחוף ימים ישכן. In Judg. 5, 17 Asher is spoken of
thus, יֵשַׁב לְחוֹף יַמִּים, and in Deut. 33, 19 Zebulon and
Issachar '*suck the abundance of the seas*' (שפע ימים יינקו).
Zebulon's territory did not in reality lie on the seashore, so
perhaps we ought to render עַל צ״ with Del. '*towards Sidon,*'
i.e. his border lay in the direction of Sidon, but was not
actually on the seashore, only towards the coast district.
The Sam.Ver., Heb.-Sam., LXX, Syr., Vulg., and apparently
Onq. (מְטֵי עַד) read עד='*up to S.,*' which would express the
meaning '*in the direction of*' more clearly than עַל. According to Jos. (*Ant.,* v. 1. 22; *Bel. Jud.,* iii. 3. 1) Zebulon inhabited
the district from the lake of Gennesareth to Mount Carmel
on the Mediterranean, and in support of this Tuch compares
Josh. 19, 11 with Matt. 4, 13.

והוא לחוף אנית. On the rendering '*he himself,*' see
Ewald, § 314 b (והוא added in a new proposition, with special
force, as the subject). Cf. 2 Sam. 17, 10, where further
emphasis is produced by the addition of גם.

14, 15. '*Issachar is a strong ass,*
        Lying down between the sheep-folds:
        And he saw a resting-place, that it was good,

And the land, that it was pleasant;
So he bowed his back to bear,
And became a servant in bondage.'

14. חֲמֹר גָּרֶם, lit. '*an ass of bone,*' i. e. a strongly built, powerful ass; so Aq. ὄνος ὀστώδης, Vulg. '*asinus fortis.*' The Sam.Vers. has ᛘᛋᛘᛈᚾᛉᚿ, reading גֵּרִים ('*sojourners*'), which Geiger defends as the correct reading (*Urschrift*, p. 360), Issachar being '*an ass of strangers,*' i. e. bearing the burdens of strangers, and subject to them. But Del. points out that this rendering destroys the force of the figurative expression חמר, and some other word, such as זרים or נכרים, would be expected rather than גֵּרִים. The Heb.-Sam. has גרים, which Tuch punctuates גְּרִים, =the Arab. جَرِيم '*bony.*' The LXX have τὸ καλὸν ἐπεθύμησεν, which presupposes some such reading as חָמֵד גָּרַם (Geiger); see Ps. 119, 20, LXX.

הַמִּשְׁפְּתַיִם. This word is only found once again, Judg. 5, 16, though we find שְׁפַתָּיִם in Ps. 68, 14 = '*sheep-folds.*' משפתים is probably from שפת='*to fix.*' Ewald, § 180 a, explains the word as = '*double pen,*' with reference to the cattle being usually separated into two portions in the pen; while Stade, § 340 b, classes the word with those that denote ' instruments or other things consisting of two parts belonging to one another, or standing in pairs, one opposite to the other; so חמתים;' see also Ges., *Thes.*, 1471 f. The word in this verse, and Judg. 5, 16, is used as a proverbial expression for the easy life of the agriculturist. Onq. renders בֵּין תְּחוּמַיָּא '*between the boundaries,*' so Vulg. '*inter terminos,*' while the LXX have ἀνὰ μέσον τῶν κλήρων (but in Judg. ἀνὰ μέσον τῆς διγομίας), and the Syr. ܒܝܬ ܫܒ̈ܝܠܐ '*between the paths.*'

15. מנוחה, either '*rest*' or '*a resting-place,*' as the word occurs with both meanings.

טוּב must be taken as a neuter subs.=*'a good thing.'* The Heb.-Sam. has טוֹבָה (fem. adj.), which perhaps suits the parallelism better (נָעֵמָה).

ויהי למס עבד, lit. *'and was (reduced) to the forced service of a labourer.'* The phrase היה למס עבד recurs Josh. 16, 10; cf. 1 Kings 9, 21, and היה למס (without עבד) is found in Judg. 1, 30. 33. Is. 31, 8, both expressions always meaning the compulsory service rendered by slaves, prisoners, or conquered nations. Del. points out that Issachar is not a פֶּרֶא, i.e. *'a wild ass'* wandering about at will, but a חֲמוֹר, i.e. *'a beast of burden,'* and sees in the last clause of the verse an allusion to the meaning of the name יששכר (=ישא שכר or יש שכר; cf. 30, 16. 18). Issachar, though strong and active, prefers a life of ease and indolence, sinking even into the condition of bond-slave. Cf. Judg. 5, 16, where Reuben is reproached in similar language for his inactivity and aversion from active exertion. The LXX render the words ויהי למס עבד καὶ ἐγενήθη ἀνὴρ γεωργός, an attempt to do away with the reproach contained in the verse, and Onq. completely changes the meaning of the last clause of the verse in his paraphrase, *'He will subdue the provinces of the peoples, destroy their inhabitants, and those who are left among them shall be servants unto him, and bringers of tribute;'* cf. Geiger, l. c., p. 360.

16, 17. *'Dan shall judge his people,*
> *As one of the tribes of Israel.*
> *Let Dan be a serpent in the way,*
> *A horned adder in the path:*
> *That biteth the horse's heels,*
> *So that his rider falleth backwards.'*

16. Dan, though a tribe by no means powerful, and possessing only a small territory, will maintain the cause of

Israel, in its conflicts with the heathen nations, as valiantly as the other tribes; cf. Judg. 13–16.

דָּן יָדִין. Notice the play upon the name דן in the choice of the verb ידין.

יָדִין = '*will judge*,' i. e. plead the cause of, render help to; דן always has this meaning, cf. 30, 6. Deut. 32, 36. Jer. 22, 16, and not the meaning '*rule*' or '*govern.*'

עַמּוֹ = the people of Israel, as in Deut. 33, 7. Others (Vatablus, Rosenmüller, etc.) understand עמו as the people belonging to the tribe of Dan, and explain the verse as meaning the small tribe of Dan will have its own administration and its own jurisdiction; or Dan, though a small tribe, will maintain its own independence (Tuch, Wellh.). But both these views take ידין = '*will rule*' or '*govern,*' a meaning which, as above remarked, דן does not have.

17. עֲלֵי דֶרֶךְ, so עֲלֵי אֹרַח, עֲלֵי being the poetical form for עַל; cf. אֱלֵי, poetical for אֶל (but only in the book of Job); עֲדֵי, poetical for עַד.

שְׁפִיפֹן, a ἅπαξ λεγόμ.; perhaps the ending ‑וֹן is diminutive in this word (see Stade, § 296 c), the word being probably from the root שָׁפַף = '*to crawl.*' שְׁפִיפֹן is the horned adder, a small and very dangerous species of snake, of a bluish yellow or sand colour. Hieronymus renders it by '*regulus*' in his *Quaest.*, ed. Lagarde, p. 69; the Syriac ܚܘܝܐ = '*a basilisk,*' the Vulg. '*cerastes,*' Onq. פִּיתְנָא = '*an adder.*' The LXX, not understanding the word שְׁפִיפֹן, render it, in harmony with the context, ἐγκαθήμενος. In Arabic شفة = '*a serpent with black and white spots.*' In Deut. 33, 22 Dan is compared with '*a lion's whelp that springeth out of Bashan.*'

עִקְּבֵי, *dag. dirimens*, see on יְקְהַת, ver. 10.

הַנֹּשֵׁךְ . . . וַיִּפֹּל. Cf. the note on 27, 33.

The meaning of the verse is, Dan, like the serpent lurking in the path, attacks his foes, not in open fight, but with stratagem; cf. Judg. 18, 27, and the history of Samson.

18. *'For thy help I wait, O Yahweh.'*

This verse breaks the connection of the poem, hence it is regarded by some (Maurer, Olshausen, etc.) as an interpolation; but if this is the case it must have been added at a later date by the redactor of the book, as a protest against Dan's idolatrous devices. It is found in all the Vss. Tuch explains it as 'an exclamation from the patriarch Jacob, who is exhausted and nerving himself for another effort before his death.' Kn., whom Di. follows, says, 'The patriarch here speaks in prayer, in the name of his descendants, who must, in the wars with the nations, e.g. the Philistines, put their trust in Yahweh, and look for His assistance.' So the Targg. Ps.-Jon. and Jer., Wright, Del., and Driver.

19.　　*'Gad—a troop shall press upon him,*
　　　　Yet he shall press upon their heel.'

Gad, though exposed to the attacks of his foes (cf. Josh. 13, 25. Judg. 11, 15), and probably often engaged in border warfare with marauding bands (cf. 2 Kings 5, 2. 6, 23), successfully defends himself and puts his enemies to flight (cf. Judg. 10 f. 12. 1 Chron. 5, 18 ff. 12, 8 f.); cf. Deut. 33, 20. 21. The name גד is here connected by the writer with גור *'to assail,'* and גדוד = *'a marauding band'* (see 2 Kings, l. c.), in the sense *'assailer'* or *'attacker.'* In 30, 11 another explanation of the name is suggested.

לעלות לעם יגודנו Cf. Hab. 3, 16 .גד גדוד יגודנו

עקב, the rendering given above, follows the reading עֲקֵבָם, which is adopted by Bleek, Knobel, Ols., Wright, and others, the ם of מאשר being taken away and appended to עקב. The LXX, Syriac, Vulg., and Saad. in a measure support this reading, as they do not translate the commencement of the next verse מאשר, but אשר. עקב by itself, as Di. remarks, is sufficient, but, as Del. points out, with the rendering '*their heel*' (A.V. R. margin), 19^b and 20^a alike gain in clearness. All the other 'blessings,' except Joseph's in ver. 22, begin with the name of the person blessed, without any preceding word.

The rendering '*heel*' is more forcible than '*rearguard*.' Gad is depicted as pressing hotly on his foes, almost on the heels of the retreating enemy. עקב cannot = אחור '*back-wards*' (Vulg. '*retrorsum*'), nor '*at the last*,' A.V. The A.V. R. renders correctly, '*upon their heel*.'

20. '*Asher—fat is his bread,*
       And he shall yield kingly dainties.'

This rendering follows the reading אשר, the pr. name being a *casus pendens*, like גד in ver. 19; cf. Deut. 32, 4. Ps. 11, 4, etc.

If the reading מאשר be adopted (so the Sam. Ver.), the rendering will be either, '*From Asher (comes) fat—his bread*,' so Tuch; cf. שמנים, Is. 25, 6 ; or, '*For Asher—his bread is too fat*,' Ewald. With the first rendering, מאשר = א״מארין, which is perhaps not quite suitable to the context, and שמנה fem. is not found as a noun; with the second, לחמו must be taken as feminine; see Bött., § 657, who distinguishes between לֶחֶם = '*bread*,' masc., and לֶחֶם = '*abundance of bread*' (Brotfülle), fem. The Sam. Vers., according to one reading, has שמן masc.

מעדני מלך. '*Dainties fit for kings*.' Cf. לחם אבירים, Ps. 78, 25. It is not necessary to think of a king of Israel in the term מלך.

The fertility and productiveness of Asher are again alluded

to in Deut. 33, 24 f. Di. suggests that as the Phoenicians procured all sorts of country produce from the Hebrews (Ez. 27, 17. Acts 12, 20; Jos., *Antiq.*, xiv. 10. 6), Asher, from his geographical position, would participate largely in this traffic.

21.   *' Naphtali is a hind at large,*
                 He that utters goodly words.'

אילה שלחה = '*a hind let loose,*' so A.V. and A.V.R.; Aq. ἔλαφος ἀπεσταλμένος, Vulg. '*cervus emissus.*' The Syriac paraphrases, but with the same meaning, ܡܠܐܟܐ ܩܠܝܠ '*a swift messenger;*' cf. Job 39, 5 מי שלח פרא חפשי וגו". Del., Tuch, and others take שלחה in the sense '*stretched out,*' so '*graceful,*' but there seems to be no authority for this rendering in the case of living beings. Knobel, comparing Is. 16, 2 (קֵן מְשֻׁלָּח), renders, '*a scared hind,*' but this thought is very unsuitable, and quite out of harmony with the context. The allusion in this part of the verse is probably to the swiftness of the heroes and men of the tribe of Naphtali (cf. for the expression, Ps. 18, 34. Hab. 3, 19. Is. 35, 6; also 2 Sam. 2, 18. Song of Songs 2, 9). The Syriac seems to interpret the first half of the verse as meaning that Naphtali is specially adapted for the duties of a messenger, while Christian writers see an allusion in שלחה to the apostles (Syriac ܫܠܝܚܐ)!

הנתן אמרי שפר. The allusion here is to the poets of the tribe, Barak, however, being the only one of whom we hear anything (Judg. 5, 1). הנתן naturally refers to נפתלי, and not to אילה, which is fem.

The reading of the LXX, Νεφθαλὶ στέλεχος ἀνειμένον ἐπιδιδοὺς ἐν τῷ γεννήματι κάλλος, seems to rest on some such reading as נַפְתָּלִי אֵילָה שְׁלֻחָה הַנֹּתֵן אֲמִירֵי־שֶׁפֶר, i.e. אילה =

'*terebinth*,' for אַיָּלָה, and אֲמִירֵי (cf. Is. 17, 6. 9) = '*topmost branches*,' for the poetical אֹמֶר. Di., Ewald, Ols., and others follow this reading, comparing for the epithet שְׁלֻחָה, Jer. 17, 8. Ez. 17, 6. Ps. 80, 12, and the noun שֶׁלַח '*shoot*,' '*blossom*,' Song of Songs 4, 13, and for the figure, ver. 22; the אמירי are then the leaders produced by the tribe of Naphtali; cf. Judg. 4, 6. 5, 18. 6, 35. 7, 23. If this reading be adopted, the rendering would be '*Naphtali is a slender terebinth, that puts forth beautiful branches*.' Onq. has נַפְתָּלִי בְּאֲרַע טָבָא יִתְרְמֵי עַדְבֵיה וְאַחְסַנְתֵּיה תְּהֵי מְעַבְּדָא פֵּירִין יְהוֹן מוֹדָן וּמְבָרְכִין עֲלֵיהוֹן '*Naphtali, in a goodly land shall his lot be cast, and his possession shall be yielding fruits, they shall praise and bless over them*,' which apparently supports this reading.

22–26. '*A son of a fruit tree is Joseph,*
    A son of a fruit tree by a fountain;
    His branches run over the wall.
    The archers harassed him,
    And shot at him, and lay in wait for him;
    But his bow remained firm,
    And the hands of his arms were strong:
    From the hands of the mighty One of Jacob,
    From thence, (from) the shepherd, the stone of Israel:
    From the God of thy fathers—so may he keep thee,
    And with the Almighty—so may he bless thee,
    With blessings of heaven above,
    Blessings of the deep, that lieth beneath,
    Blessings of the breasts and womb.
    The blessings of thy father have prevailed over the
        blessings of the ancient mountains,
    The desire of the eternal hills:
    May they be upon the head of Joseph,
    On the crown of the prince among his brethren.'

22. בֵּן פֹּרָת יוֹסֵף. '*Son of a fruit tree is J.*,' i.e. '*a young fruit tree;*' cf. בֵן, Ps. 80, 16. בֵּן—though elsewhere pointed ‑בֶּן or ‑בִּן, with Maqqef—must be taken as construct state, cf. שֵׁם, cstr. state, 12, 8, and שֶׁם‑, 16, 15, or we must read בֵּן with Di. The Massoretes may, as Del. suggests, have taken בֵּן as sing. abs. fem., pl. בנות, with the meaning '*branch,*' and פרת as an adj. qualifying it = '*a fruitful branch.*'

פרת with the archaic ending ‑ת, (see Ges., § 80. Rem. 2 b; Ewald, § 173 d), = the later פֹּרָה, means '*a fruit tree;*' cf. פֹּרִיָּה, Is. 17, 6 (of the olive tree); probably a vine, cf. גפן פריה in Is. 32, 12. Ez. 19, 10. Ps. 128, 3; so Onq., Tuch, Ewald, Di. The בנות are the branches of the vine that grow over the wall. Possibly there is an allusion here to the name אֶפְרַיִם (perhaps '*double fruitfulness*'), 41, 52.

עֲלֵי עָיִן. The moisture would promote the growth of the vine; cf. Ps. 1, 3. Jer. 17, 8.

בָּנוֹת צָעֲדָה. On the construction of the plural, where inanimate objects are spoken of, with the sing. fem. expressing (as in Arabic) the *collective*, see Ges., § 146. 3; Ewald, § 317 a; cf. Joel 1, 20 גם בהמות שדה תערוג; Zech. 6, 14 והעטרת תהיה לחלם, and the construction, common in Greek, of the neuter pl. with a sing. verb, as τὰ θηρία ἀναβλέπει. Ewald reads the text here בְּנוֹת צֶעֱדָה '*daughters of ascent,*' but this alteration is unnecessary. Wright takes the verse quite differently. פֹּרָת = '*a heifer,*' '*a hind,*' as antelopes are called by the Arabs بَقَرُ ٱلْوَحْشِ '*wild oxen;*' the בנות are then the hinds that accompany the stag, and שׁוּר = '*an ambuscade*' (see Ges. in *Thes.* s. v.) made by the huntsmen near the pool where the deer come to drink. But even if פרה can = '*hind,*' and שׁוּר '*ambuscade*' (Ps. 92, 12 is not conclusive, as שׁוּר = rather '*lier in wait*' than '*an ambuscade*,' and שׁוּר in every other passage means '*wall*'), as Naphtali has already been compared to a hind, ver. 21, we should hardly expect the same comparison in this verse in the case of Joseph. The Vss. appear to have entirely misunderstood the verse.

23. וימררהו = '*they embittered* or *irritated him*.'

וָרֹבּוּ with pretonic qameç, as in תהו ובהו, 1, 2; see the note there. רֹבּוּ is from רבב, with the intransitive punctuation (see Stade, § 385 b. 2; Ges., § 67. Rem. 1), meaning '*to shoot*;' so Ps. 18, 15 וברקים רב ויהמם; related to רבה and רמה; cf. רַבָּיו, Job 16, 13. Jer. 50, 29. The LXX, Sam., Onq., and Vulg. seem to have read וירִיבו, but בעלי חצים does not suit this.

בעלי חצים. Cf. בעל החלמות, 37, 19; בעלי ברית, 14, 13, and the note on that passage. Compare with this verse the narrative in Judg. 6 ff. 1 Chron. 5, 18 f., of the hostility shewn to Ephraim and Manasseh by the neighbouring Arab tribes; and Josh. 17, 16 f., where the children of Joseph are commanded to drive out the Canaanites from the territory Joshua assigns them.

24. ותשׁב באיתן קשׁתו. '*Yet his bow remained in firmness*.' On the adversative force of the waw conv., see Driver, § 74 β; Ewald, § 231 b; so in 19, 9. 32, 31.

באיתן. Del. explains איתן as a subst. = בְּמָקוֹם אֵיתָן; Ewald, § 299 b (cf. § 172 b), considers that the adj. here must be taken as neuter, '*in* or *with firmness*,' and the בּ conceived as forming the predicate, comparing Ex. 32, 22 ברע הוא. The form איתן, cf. אכזב, אכזר, in Hebrew corresponds to the Arabic formation for adjectives أَفْعَل, with the signification of our comparative and superlative, and so called '*the noun of pre-eminence*' or '*elative.*' In Hebrew the forms have lost their original significance and are used as simple adjectives; see Wright, *Arab. Gram.*, i. p. 159; Ewald, § 162 b.

The LXX have καὶ συνετρίβη μετὰ κράτους τὰ τόξα αὐτῶν, reading וַתִּשָּׁבֵר, and the Syriac ܘܦܟܠ ܚܝܠܢܐ ܩܫܬܗ '*his bow turned in strength,*' reading וַתָּשָׁב; so apparently Onqelos.

וַיְפֹזּוּ . פּוז means '*to be nimble,*' '*pliant;*' cf. the Arabic فَزَّ '*to be nimble.*' The root only occurs once again in the Pi'el in 2 Sam. 6, 16 מְפַזֵּז וּמְכַרְכֵּר '*skipping and dancing*' (cf. Ges. in *Thes.* s. v.). The LXX have καὶ ἐξελύθη, Syr. ܘܐܫܬܪܝ, Vulg. '*dissoluta sunt* [*vincula*],' reading perhaps וַיִּפָּצוּ, from פּוּץ.

מִידֵי אֲבִיר יַעֲקֹב, i. e. Joseph's strength comes from the hands of the mighty One of Jacob, which support him. אביר יעקב, cf. Is. 1, 24 (אביר ישראל). 49, 26. Ps. 132, 2. 5, where the phrase is borrowed from this passage.

מִשָּׁם רֹעֶה וגו׳. In the rendering given above, which seems relatively the best in this difficult clause, רעה is taken as explaining מִשָּׁם, which probably means '*from heaven,*' cf. Eccl. 3, 17 (?), and אבן יש׳׳ is a second name for God, in apposition to רעה. For the term רעה applied to God, cf. 48, 15. Ps. 23, 1. 80, 2. אֶבֶן must be taken as equivalent to the common title of God צוּר (Ps. 18, 32. 1 Sam. 2, 2. Deut. 32, 4. Is. 30, 29); אבן, however, never has this meaning anywhere else. Another rendering which is possible is that adopted by Tuch (cf. Ewald, § 332 d), '*whence is the Shepherd the Stone of Israel:*' מִשָּׁם = '*inde ubi;*' cf. מֵאָן = '*ex quo tempore,*' Ps. 76, 8; cf. the Vulgate, '*inde pastor egressus est*

lapis' etc. Ewald renders similarly, but reads רֹעֶה אֶבֶן יִשְׂרָאֵל
('*Shepherd of the Stone of Israel*'), the allusion being to 28,
18 f. 22, a reading Di. approves of, as רעה without the art.
or ישראל following is awkward, and God is never elsewhere
called אבן. Rosenmüller renders, '*From that time he* (*Joseph*)
was the shepherd and stone of Israel;' cf. מִשָּׁם in IIos. 2, 17
(Heb.); A.V. R. renders, '*From thence is the Shepherd, the
Stone*' etc., which may be explained as meaning, '*From thence,*'
i. e. from God, Joseph became a guardian and defence of his
people, viz. in Egypt. The Pesh. and Onq. (apparently)
read מִשֵּׁם, instead of מִשָּׁם; cf. Ps. 20, 2, but this, though
removing the awkward expression מִשָּׁם, does not stand very
appropriately in parallelism with מִידֵי. In all probability the
text, as it stands at present, is corrupt.

25. **מֵאֵל אָבִיךָ**. The מן continues the thought contained in ver. 24, connecting ver. 25 with the preceding
verse; but in this verse two blessings are inserted. 'The
same God, who has hitherto helped him, will also give him
the following blessings,' Di. מאל אביך, cf. 31, 5. 42. 48, 15.
Ex. 15, 2. 18, 4.

וַיַעְזְרֶךָּ = וְיַעְזְרֶךָּ, the suffix being strengthened by the
demonstrative nun. Render, '*So may He help thee;*' cf. Ex.
12, 3. 15, 2. Ps. 59, 13. The weak waw with the imperf. (voluntative) takes the place of the perf. with waw conv., after words
standing alone, in language of an excited and impassioned
character; see Ewald, § 347 a; Driver, § 125; so ויברכך in
the next clause.

וְאֵת שַׁדַּי. '*And with the Almighty,*' i. e. with the help
of the Almighty. The Syr., Sam. Ver., and IIeb.-Sam., and
a few MSS. read ואל, a reading which is perhaps supported

by the LXX [1], Vulg., Saadiah. Bleek, Hitzig, Tuch, Ewald, and Di. adopt this reading, as being more suitable, the shorter title שדי being first used without אל at a later period of the language (it is very common in the book of Job). If this reading be preferred, the force of מן in מאל אביך extends to אל שדי; so Judg. 5, 9. Is. 15, 8. Hab. 3, 15; see Ewald, § 351 a.

ברכת שמים וגו׳. ברכת is the acc. after ויברכך = 'may he bless the blessings of,' i. e. with the blessings of.

מעל. Cf. 27, 39 ומטל השמים מעל. The ברכת שמים are the dew, rain, sunshine; cf. 27, 28. 39. The ברכת תהום are the springs, rivers, brooks, which are regarded as springing from the subterranean תהום. The ברכת שדים ורחם are · every kind of animal fruitfulness [contrast Hos. 9, 14 (Tuch)]. Compare Joseph's blessing in Deut. 33, 13 ff. with this verse, where the similarity in thought and language is most striking.

26. The translation given above follows the reading הוֹרֵי עַד, or perhaps better הַרְרֵי עַד, as הור only occurs as a proper name, and gives to תאוה its ordinary meaning 'desire.' This rendering suits the parallelism (גבעת עולם), and is supported by Deut. 33, 15 (הַרְרֵי־קֶדֶם). Hab. 3, 6 (הַרְרֵי־עַד), and the rendering of the LXX, ὀρέων μονίμων, and is adopted by Ges., Ewald, Tuch, Wright, Di., and A.V.R. (margin). The Massoretic text is supported by the Syr., Onq., Vulg., Saadiah, the Jewish commentators, A.V., and A.V.R. (text). The rendering then must be, ' *The blessings of thy father have prevailed over the blessings of my parents, up to the boundary*

---

of the eternal hills.' הוֹרַי must be separated from עַד, following the accents, and taken in the sense *'parents,'* while
תאוה must be translated *'boundary,'* from תָּאָה = *'to mark,'*
'limit;' cf. Num. 34, 7 f.; also תָּוָה in 1 Sam. 21, 14.
Ez. 9, 4; see Ewald, § 186 b. The word הוֹרַי, however, =
'my parents,' seems very doubtful. Neither the plural הוֹרִים,
nor dual הוֹרַיִם occur with this meaning, and though the
fem. הוֹרָה = *'mother'* is found in Song of Songs 3, 4. Hos.
2, 7, the original meaning of the root, i. e. *'to conceive,'*
is still present in this word in both of the passages where
it occurs. The reading of the Sam. Vers. is uncertain,
but the Sam. Codex (Heb.-Sam.) has הָרֵי עַד. The later
Samaritans, however, pronounced the words הָרֵי עַד *'my
mountain, up to'* etc., and understood it of Mount Gerizim,
which was situated in the territory of the tribe of Joseph;
see Tuch, p. 501. The LXX and Sam. Vers. follow a
reading ברכת אביך ואמך, while the Jer. Targ. exhibits
traces of both the renderings discussed above, viz. *' my
parents,'* and *'everlasting mountains;'* see Geiger, *Urschrift*,
p. 250.

לראֹש יוסף ולקדקד נזיר אחיו. Cf. Deut. 33, 16
where these words recur. נזיר אחיו = *'the prince of his
brethren.'* The Vulg. and Saadiah take נזיר in the sense
'Nazirite,' a meaning which is unsuitable here. It is best to
take נזיר = *'the separated one;'* cf. Onq.'s rendering of the
passage, גַּבְרָא פְּרִישָׁא דַּאֲחוֹהִי *'the man (who is) separated
among his brethren,'* in the sense of *'prince'* or *'leader;'* so
Saadiah and most moderns (cf. Lam. 4, 7), though with no
allusion to a kingdom in the tribe of Joseph. The meaning
cannot, however, be regarded as certain.

Del. remarks that לראֹש is chosen intentionally, as בראֹש is
the usual expression for a curse coming upon any one, while

לְרֹאשׁ is used for a blessing; cf. Deut. 33, 16. Prov. 10, 6. 11, 26.

Joseph receives not only the blessings of the eternal hills, i. e. the rich and fruitful hill country of Ephraim and Manasseh (cf. Jer. 50, 19. Deut. 32, 14), but the blessings that surpass these, viz. the promises made by God to his forefathers.

27. '*Benjamin is a ravening wolf:*
    In the morning he devoureth the prey,
    And at even divideth the spoil.'

That Benjamin was a most warlike tribe is shewn by the share it took in the struggle for freedom under Deborah (Judg. 5, 14), and by the war it carried on with the other tribes (Judg. 19 ff.) after the outrage committed at Gibeah. Ehud, Saul, and Jonathan were also Benjamites.

זְאֵב יִטְרָף, lit. '*a wolf that ravens,*' the relative pronoun being omitted. Cf. Is. 51, 12 אֱנוֹשׁ יָמוּת='*mortal man;*' Hos. 4, 14 עַם לֹא יָבִין '*a people without understanding;*' and see Ges., § 123. 3 a; M. R., § 159 a; Ewald, § 332 a; Driver, § 34.

יִטְרָף, pausal for יִטְרֹף; see on ver. 3, עָי. Kn. remarks on the·comparison of Benjamin with a wolf, 'The figure of the wolf occurs elsewhere in the O.T., only in a bad sense (Zeph. 3, 3. Hab. 1, 8. Jer. 5, 6. Ez. 22, 27); hence in this passage it does not signify a full measure of praise, though it recognises Benjamin's warlike capabilities.' Di. supplements this remark by pointing out, 'that the lion has already been used in ver. 9, and that only a comparison with some small beast of prey would be fitting in the case of Benjamin, the smallest of the tribes. The wolf was used in comparisons by non-Semitic peoples of antiquity in a good sense.'

יֹאכַל עַד. Cf. Num. 23, 24 עַד יֹאכַל טֶרֶף.

28. ‫אתם‬ ‫ברך‬ ‫כברכתו‬ ‫אשר‬ ‫איש‬. '*Each one with
that which was according to his blessing he blessed them,*' ‫בֵּרַךְ‬
being construed with a double acc., as in Deut. 12, 7. 15, 14;
cf. ver. 25. The LXX, Syr., and Sam. omit ‫אשר‬. As the
text is very awkward, Del. emends to ‫כב"‬ ‫איש‬ ‫איש‬; cf. 2 Sam.
23, 21, where the Kri directs that ‫איש‬ is to be read instead
of ‫אשר‬, and Num. 21, 30, where the Kri marks the ‫ר‬ of ‫אשר‬
with a point, as suspicious. With this emendation, the verse
may be compared with Ex. 36, 4 ‫ממלאכתו‬ ‫איש‬ ‫איש‬; Lev. 15,
2 ‫יהיה‬ ‫כי‬ ‫איש‬ ‫איש‬; Lev. 24, 15 ‫יקלל‬ ‫כי‬ ‫איש‬ ‫איש‬, and often.
Perhaps, however, it is better simply to omit ‫אשר‬.

30. ‫השדה‬ ‫את‬ . . . ‫קנה‬ ‫אשר‬. Cf. 50, 13, and see the
note on 13, 16.

32. ‫וגו"‬ ‫מקנה‬. It is perhaps best to regard this verse
as in apposition to ver. 29. Tuch prefers to regard it as a
parenthesis, referring to ver. 30; cf. Ps. 72, 14.

50.

2. ‫אביו‬ ‫את‬ ‫לחנט‬. '*To embalm his father.*' Embalm-
ing the dead was an Egyptian custom, which was due to the
popular belief in a permanent union of the body and the
soul. The art was practised by a special class named ταριχευταί; see Herod. ii. 86 ff.; Diod. i. 91; Ebers in Riehm's
H. W. B., 352 f. The ταριχευταί are here called ‫הרפאים‬.
Joseph probably had his own special body of physicians.

3. ‫החנטים‬. The plural is used according to Ges., § 108.
2 a; Ewald, § 179 a ('to embrace the scattered units into a
higher idea, thus to form the meaning of an abstract').

‫יום‬ ‫שבעים‬. For a king the Egyptians used to mourn
seventy-two days (Diod. i. 72). Jacob's death was mourned
for by the Egyptians out of respect to Joseph. On the

mourning customs of the Egyptians, see Herod. ii. 85; Diod. i. 91; Wilkinson, *Manners and Customs* (ed.², 1878, iii. c. 16).

4. בכיתו. Object. gen.; see on 9, 2. בכית is formed like שבית, חנית, by adding the ending ת to the third radical י; see Ewald, § 186 b; Stade, § 192 b.

5. כריתי לי. LXX ὤρυξα, so the Vulg. and most moderns; cf. 26, 25. 2 Chron. 16, 14, a rendering which suits בקברי better than that adopted by Onq. and the Syr., '*I bought*,' with which Deut. 2, 6 וגם מים תכרו מאתם may be compared.

10. עד גרן האטד. '*To the threshing-floor of thorns;*' probably not '*the threshing-floor of Atad.*' The locality is not further known.

בעבר הירדן, i. e. on the eastern side of Jordan, the narrator being in Palestine.

שבעת ימים. Cf. 1 Sam. 31, 13. Judith 16, 29. Ecclus. 22, 12.

11. אָבֵל מצרים. אָבֵל may be taken either as a verb, '*Egypt mourns*,' or as a noun, '*the meadow of Egypt;*' cf. the proper names, אבל מחולה, אבל השטים, אבל מים, אבל בית מעכה, אבל כרמים; but this rendering '*meadow of Egypt*' being hardly suited to the context, the narrator explains from '*mourning.*' The LXX have here Πένθος Αἰγύπτου, and the Vulg. '*Planctus Egypti*,' and it is not improbable that the author pronounced אבל, אֵבֶל; while the punctuators took it as אָבֵל, either '*meadow*,' or as a verb 3rd pers. perf. sing. The position of אבל מצרים is not known. It has been identified by some (Knobel, Ritter, etc.) with בית חגלה, on the southern boundary of Benjamin, the modern *Ain Ḥagla*, a little north of the Dead Sea, following Hieron., who in the Onom. identifies *Area Atad* with בית חגלה. But this identification is precarious, as Hieron.'s account is not trustworthy; and further,

בית חגלה is on the western, and not the eastern side of Jordan; see further, Di., p. 455; Del., p. 524.

13. את השדה. 'With the field;' cf. 49, 30.

15. לו ישטמנו יוסף. 'If Joseph were to hate us!' cf. Ez. 14, 15. Ex. 4, 1 והן לא יאמינו לי 'and if they will not believe me!' LXX here, μήποτε μνησικακήσῃ ἡμῖν Ἰωσήφ. The imperf. in the protasis, where no apodosis follows, denoting either a *wish* or (as here) a *fear;* see Driver, § 142; Ewald, § 358 a, who compares a similar aposiopesis in Ps. 27, 13; see also M.R., § 165.

16. ויצוו. 'And they sent a message.' LXX καὶ παραγενό-μενοι, Pesh. ܣܡܟܘ, possibly a free translation, the translators not understanding ויצוו.

17. אָנָּא is only found once again in the Pent., viz. Ex. 32, 31 אָנָּא. Ewald, § 262 a, remarks that the Massora regards אנא always as consisting of two words (אָהּ־נָא); hence the double accents here and in Ex. l. c. The tone is on the penult.

שָׂא נָא פֶשַׁע ... שָׂא נָא לִפֶשַׁע. נשא='to forgive' (cf. 18, 24) is here construed, for the sake of variety, with the acc. and dat.; see Ewald, § 282 d.

19. כי התחת אלהים אני. 'For am I in God's place?' so in 30, 2; see the note there. Del. proposes a slightly different meaning here as an alternative, 'Am I authorised to interfere in what God does, am I not obliged to submit myself to it?' Aq. ὅτι μὴ Θεὸς ἐγώ; Symm. μὴ γὰρ ἀντὶ Θεοῦ ἐγώ εἰμι; Onq. renders אֲרֵי דַחֲלָא דַיְיָ אֲנָא 'for a fearer of Y. am I,' possibly reading חְתַת אל״ (from חָתָה), or more probably rendering freely; so Saadiah, أَخَافُ ٱللّٰهَ 'I fear God.'

20. עשׂה. See on 48, 11.

21. וידבר על לבם. See on 34, 3.

23. וירא יוסף לאפרים.   The ל as in 44, 20 ויותר הוא לבדו לאמו.

בני שִׁלֵּשִׁים = ' *sons of the third degree*,' i. e. not great-grandchildren, but great-great-grandchildren, שִׁלֵּשִׁים (cf. Ex. 20, 5. 34, 7. Num. 14, 18. Deut. 5, 9) being the children of the third generation,· the first ancestor not being counted. Elsewhere they are called רִבֵּעִים; so Di. and Ewald (*Antiq.*[3], p. 225, Eng. trans., p. 169). LXX, Vulg., Pesh., Targ., Tuch, and Del. understand '*great-grandchildren ;*' but then either בנים must be read (so Sam.), or the cstr. בני be taken according to Ewald, § 287 e (the cstr. state used where there is really only an appositional relation between the two words, and = ' *consisting of*').

על ברכי יוסף.   Cf. 30, 3.

26. וַיִּישֶׂם.   See on 24, 33.   Render, ' *they brought*,' 3rd pers. sing. imper.

בארון = here '*in the coffin.*' The article, by Ewald, § 277 a; Ges., § 109. 3 c. 'The Egyptians used to place the embalmed body in a wooden coffin, and carefully preserve it in the vault (Her. ii. 86),' Kn. in Di., p. 457. With these verses, cf. Ex. 13, 19. Josh. 24, 32.

APPENDIX I.

THE book of Genesis, like the other books of the Hexateuch (for it is now generally admitted that the book of Joshua must be attached to the Pentateuch, and the whole regarded as one work), was not the production of one author. A definite plan may be traced in the book, but the structure of the work forbids us to consider it as the work of one writer. This is clear, not only from the (apparently needless) repetitions that occur (e.g. 21, 1a and 1b; 4, 25 f., and 5, 1–6; 47, 29 ff., and 49, 29 ff.', but also from the different accounts of one and the same event which we meet with, not merely such as may be explained on the supposition that the author is really describing *different* events, or reproducing *different* traditions (e.g. the narratives contained in 12, 10 ff.; 20, 1 ff.; and 26, 7 ff.; in 16, 1 ff., and 21, 12 ff.; the double covenant with Abram, chaps. 15 and 17; the double blessing of Jacob by Isaac, 27, 1 ff., and 28, 1 ff.; the double promise of a son to Sarah, 17, 17; and 18, 10 ff.; the three explanations of the name Isaac, 17, 17; 18, 12; 21, 6; the two explanations of the names, Edom in 25, 25. 30; of Issachar, Zebulon, and Joseph, in 30, 16–18. 20. 23 f.; of Mahanaim, in 32, 3. 8), but such as mutually exclude one another, because the event narrated can only have happened once (e. g. the two accounts of the creation, in chaps. 1 and 2; the number of the animals that went into the ark at the time the flood was on the earth, in chap. 6 f.; the dispersion of the nations, in chaps. 10 and 11, 1 ff., cf. 10, 25; the varying explanations of the names Beersheba, in 21, 31; 26, 33; Israel, in 32, 29; 35, 10; Bethel, 28, 18 f.; 35, 14 f.; the different accounts of the relations between Jacob and the Shechemites, in chaps. 34 and 48, 22; and the variations in the narrative in 37, 19–36,—the sale of Joseph by his brethren). Many other notices in Genesis also militate against the unity of authorship (e. g. that Abraham begat many sons after the death of Sarah, 25, 1 ff. against 18, 11 f. 17, 17; that Esau had already settled in Seir when Jacob returned from Mesopotamia, 32, 4 ff. against 36, 6; that all Jacob's sons were born in Paddan Aram, 35, 26 against ver. 16 ff.; the different names of Esau's wives, 26, 34. 28, 9 against 36, 2 f., etc.; the differences in chronology, e. g. in the age of Sarah, in 17, 17, cf. 12, 4, and in 12, 11. 20, 2 ff.; as to Isaac's approaching death, in 27, 1 f. 7. 10. 41 and in 35, 28 and 26, 34; in the account of Rachel's death in 35, 19, while in 37, 10 she is represented as still living, etc.); even narratives are found in which some parts do not agree with the remainder of the narrative (e. g. 31, 48–50 and the rest of the chapter, and 24, 62–67 and the beginning of the chapter).

These discrepancies and difficulties in the book of Genesis, and similar ones in the other books of the Pentateuch, had been perceived as far back as the eleventh century [1], but it was not until the middle of the eighteenth century that a serious attempt was made to examine systematically the structure of the Pentateuch. This was first undertaken by Astruc [2], a Paris physician, who, following the opinion already expressed by Vitringa, that Moses had made use of older sources in composing the Pentateuch, arrived at the conclusion that the book of Genesis was composed from these older sources, which Moses had embodied in the work without any essential alterations; and that two main documents were clearly discernible, which are distinguished by the peculiar use of the names of God, Elohim occurring exclusively in the one, and Jehovah in the other; and several (nine) minor documents which were less frequently employed, and which are recognisable by certain individual peculiarities. Astruc's work may be regarded as the beginning of the criticism of the Pentateuch. His views were adopted, or arrived at by independent investigation, by several scholars subsequently, and many additional points were discovered. The gradual growth of the criticism of the Pentateuch cannot be fully entered into here, but some of the more important discoveries may be noticed, and the reader referred to the Introductions to the Old Testament etc. [3] for further details. Eichhorn not only arrived independently at the same conclusion as Astruc with regard to the two documents, but made the further observation that the usage of language in these two documents differed greatly., De Wette was the first to draw attention to the fact that the book of Deuteronomy was essentially different from the preceding books, and really formed a separate document, a view that is now generally accepted; while to Bleek belongs the merit of having discovered that the book of Joshua reveals traces of the same hands as the Pentateuch, and must be taken as forming the real conclusion of the work. Further advances were made by Ewald and Hupfeld; Ewald drawing attention to the fact that

---

[1] See Zoeckler, *Handbuch der Theolog. Wissenschaften*, i. p. 133 f.; Bleek's *Einleitung* (ed. Wellhausen), p. 16, Eng. trans. (ed. Venables), p. 193.

[2] In his *Conjectures sur les mémoires originaux dont il paroit que Moyse s'est servi pour composer le livre de la Genese*, Brussels, 1753.

[3] See Bleek, *Einleitung* (ed. Well.), p. 57 f., and Eng. trans., p. 257 f.; also the Introductions in Kuenen's *Hexateuch*, and Wellhausen's *History of Israel*, Eng. trans.

the two main documents do not only extend to Exodus 6, 2 (as had been previously supposed), but are clearly discernible in the remaining books of the Pentateuch, and also in Joshua; while Hupfeld demonstrated that the Elohim document was not the work of one and the same writer, but was really two documents[1]. Hupfeld considered that Genesis was founded on three continuous historical writings, which were quite independent of one another, two Elohistic and one Jehovistic[2], and this view, with certain modifications, may be regarded as the one generally accepted at the present time. As the results of the investigations of these and other scholars, the following points were regarded as fixed, that, firstly, the Hexateuch was mainly composed of four documents, the so-called 'Grundschrift' or 'main stock[3],' called by Dillmann A, but usually cited as P (the Priests' Code); the second Elohist, Dillmann's B, usually quoted as E; the Jehovist, Dillmann's C, usually referred to as J; and the Deuteronomist or D; secondly, that several portions of the Pentateuch are really much older than the documents themselves in which they have been preserved (e. g. the Decalogue, Ex. 20, 22–23, 19, the Song in Ex. 15, and other passages containing laws and poetical fragments); thirdly, that the Elohistic documents were older than the Jehovistic document; and, fourthly, that these three documents were worked up into a whole before the Deuteronomist. Opinions differed as to the plan adopted in working up these documents into one work, but most scholars considered that P, E, and J were united by a redactor, and that D was added subsequently; some scholars even being of the opinion that D himself was the redactor. This view of the origin of the Pentateuch was, however, combated by Graf[4], who, following the opinion that had already been put forth by Reuss, George, and Vatke[5], independently of each other, propounded the view that the so-called 'Grundschrift' was not the oldest of the three documents, but the youngest. This was not, however, the original form of Graf's hypothesis. He first divided the 'Grundschrift' into two parts, and then endeavoured to shew that the priestly or ritual laws usually regarded as belonging to the 'Grundschrift' were post-deuteronomic, while the remainder of the 'Grundschrift' was prae-deuteronomic, and

---

[1] This had already been pointed out by Ilgen (died 1834). Hupfeld's views will be found in full in his *Quellen der Genesis und die Art ihrer Zusammensetzung*, Berlin, 1853.

[2] See below, however, p. 366.

[3] This is the term used by Wellhausen's translator for the German word.

[4] In *Die geschichtlichen Bücher des Alten Test.* (1866).

[5] See Wellhausen, *Hist. of Israel*, Eng. trans., p. 5, and Kuenen, *Hexateuch*, Introduction, p. xxxiv; Zoeckler, l. c., p. 136.

antecedent to the Jehovist. · When, however, Riehm[1] and Nöldeke[2] had shewn that this division of the 'Grundschrift' was, on philological grounds, impossible, Graf modified his view, and assigned the whole of the 'Grundschrift' to the post-exilic period[3]. This view is also held by Kuenen[4], and has been brought into greater prominence by Wellhausen[5], and since adopted by various scholars. The reasons alleged by Graf and his followers in support of this view are that the history contained in the books of Judges, Samuel, and to some extent in the books of Kings, is in contradiction to the laws usually regarded as Mosaic, and that these laws themselves were quite unknown at the period to which they are supposed to belong; further, that the prophets of the eighth and ninth centuries are unacquainted with the Mosaic code. Those who maintain Graf's view regard the Jehovistic laws (Ex. chaps. 20–23. 13, 1–16. 34, 10–27) and the Jehovistic narratives as prae-deuteronomic, and consider that Ezekiel is older than the redaction of the Ritual code and the laws contained in P. Thus the question of the age of P is the chief point that is at present undetermined, though the real date of the other documents cannot be regarded as definitely fixed. Other questions that are still matters of controversy are whether the Jehovist (J) utilised the Elohist (E) in composing his own work, whether the redactor who combined P and J had E before him, and also whether P is a composite production, the result of a long period of priestly activity, or the work of a single author. These points cannot be discussed here, but must be studied in full in the works of Nöldeke, Delitzsch, Schultz, Wellhausen, Kuenen, and others[6]. The existence of various documents may be considered to have been proved, also that the number of these documents in Genesis is three, viz. P, J, and E; that J and E are not only closely akin to one another in matter and in the way things are viewed by their authors, but also have come down to us so closely interwoven one with the other, as to form almost one document; and, lastly, that these three documents were combined into one whole by a redactor or redactors.

These three documents, P, J, and E, are distinguished one from the

---

[1] *Studien und Krit.*, 1868, pp. 350–379.

[2] *Untersuchungen zur Kritik des A. Test.*, Kiel, 1869.

[3] In Merx, *Archiv für Wissensch. Erforschung des A. T.*, i. 466–477.

[4] In his *Onderzoek*, 1st ed., chap. 1, § 18, and *Hexateuch*.

[5] In his *History of Israel*, and *Composition des Hexateuchs*, printed at first in the *Jahrbücher für Deutsche Theologie*, xxi, 1876, pp. 392–450, 531–602; xxii, 1877, pp. 407–479, and since issued separately as part ii of his *Skizzen und Vorarbeiten*, 1885; see also his article '*Pentateuch*' in the *Encycl. Britannica*, 9th ed.

[6] The reader will find the opinions of these and other scholars briefly sketched and discussed in Zoeckler, l. c., p. 139 fol.

other, not only by a difference, more or less distinctly marked, in their contents, but also by a peculiar usage of language. P, which has been largely employed in the composition of Genesis, can be more clearly separated from J and E, than these from one another, the points of demarcation between them being less clearly defined than in the case of P. P chiefly contains legislation, setting before us the various precepts and ordinances that were to be observed by Israel, and explaining their origin. The history contained in it is merely the framework in which to arrange the legislative matter. The thread of the narrative is very thin, and often only serves to carry on the chronology. Important events, however, are treated more in detail (e. g. the story of the creation, the deluge, the covenants with Noah and Abraham, the journey of the patriarchs into Egypt), especially such events as are narrated to explain the origin of various laws (e. g. 17, 23), in which case the narrative is generally full and detailed. Other events of less importance are only briefly described, partly in the form of genealogies (e. g. chap. 5. 11, 10 ff. 35, 22 ff.), and partly in the form of short summaries (e. g. chap. 10. 25, 12 ff. chap. 36). In its method of representation P is detailed and circumstantial, everywhere aiming at strict accuracy, especially in all legal points, and exhibiting a marked fondness for recurrent formulae. Its language is formal and precise, technical words and phrases and certain turns of expression not found elsewhere frequently recur. The manner in which the author handles his materials gives evidence of research and reflexion, and a capacity for justly weighing and estimating the sources of information at his disposal (e. g. chaps. 1. 5. 10 f. 36. 46), while in describing the events of the past, and in the accounts of foreign peoples, remarkable accuracy is displayed (e. g. 25, 16. 36, 15). Some of the peculiarities of the language of P have been pointed out in the notes. The portions of Genesis that are usually assigned to this document are the following: 1, 1–2, 4 a. 5, 1–2S. 30–32. 6, 9–22. 7, 6. 11. 13–16 a. 18–21. 8, 1–2 a. 3–5. 13 a. 14–19. 9, 1–17. 28–29. 10, 1–7. 20. 22–23. 31–32. 11, 10–27. 31–32. 12, 4 b–5. 13, 6. 11 b–12 a. (chap. 14 ?). 16, 1a. 3. 15–16. 17. 19, 29. 21, 1 b–5. 23. 25, 7–11 a. 12–17. 19–20. 26 b. 26, 34–35. 27, 46–28, 9. 29, 24. 29. 31, 18 b. 33, 18. 34, 1–2. 4–10. 13–18. 20–25 (partly). 27–29. 35, 5. 9–15. 23–29. 36 (in the main). 37, 1–2 a. 41, 46. 46, 6–27. 47, 5–6 a. 7–11 (as in LXX [=5 b from ἦλθον δὲ to 11]). 27 c–28. 49, 28 b–33. 50, 12–13.

The remaining documents differ widely from P.

In Genesis the legislative element is almost entirely absent, the object of the narrators being to present in a brief and attractive form the chief historical events of the past, with a view to instruction and

edification. One of these documents, E, is called by Dillmann the
Traditional History of Israel. It probably is based on older written
sources, but in the main draws its information from tradition, and
preserves unchanged in its narratives both the colouring and tone of
tradition as current among the people. To this document we are
indebted for many important details which are not given in P or J (e. g.
Eliezer, Deborah, Rachel's nurse, and Potiphar are known to us only
from E), and for many peculiar notices and brief statements, which,
bearing the impress of the highest antiquity (e. g. 21, 27 ff. 15, 2. 20,
16. 48, 22), are unfortunately only preserved in a fragmentary form.
In E many traditions attaching themselves to certain localities (e. g. 31,
51 ff. 33, 19. 35, 8. 20) are to be found, and the origin of several of the
sacred places in central and eastern Palestine is frequently referred to
(21, 31. 28, 17 f. 32, 3. 31. 33, 20. 35, 4. 7. 46, 1 f.). It contains a full
account of the honour gained by Joseph, and brings into prominence
the consideration in which Reuben was formerly held (37, 21 f. 29 f.
42, 22. 37). E contains no account of the flood, but makes frequent
mention of the many sanctuaries of the Israelites (28, 22. 33, 20),
though it condemns the Teraphim-cultus and other idolatrous practices
(35, 2 ff.). Angels and visions in dreams are frequently spoken of,
Abraham bears the title of Prophet (20, 7), and attention is directed to
the gradual accomplishment of God's promises as revealed to Abraham
and his descendants. It has been already remarked that E has been
incorporated with J into one work, and it frequently happens that the
parts of the two documents can be severed one from the other with not
more than approximate certainty.

The third document, J (for a long time called the supplemental
document, as though it were composed to supplement P; a view that is
now generally abandoned), may be designated, as distinguished from P,
the Prophetic Narrative. In the account of the family of Noah, the
deluge, and in the table of nations, it is in substance closely akin to P,
also in the portion of Genesis containing the history of Abraham it has
several narratives in common with P (e. g. the separation of Lot and
Abraham; the destruction of Sodom and Gomorrha; the story of
Dinah; also cf. 47, 1–11. 29 ff. and 49, 29 ff.), but elsewhere in the
history of the patriarchs, and in that of Joseph and Jacob, it is more
closely connected with E, so much so, that from chap. 27 onwards, most of
the narratives in J have their complete parallels in E, the passages in E
being rich in material details, while J is distinguished by a fondness for
picturesque description, by breadth and variety of ideas, and by the
polish and artistic finish of its narratives. Many passages of J, which
we possess in their full form, are masterpieces of narrative art, with

which only a few out of E can be compared (e. g. chap. 22). Of all three documents J betrays the profoundest appreciation of the existence, origin, and growth of sin in man, and of God's counteracting influence, of the plan of man's salvation (3, 15 f. 5, 29. 8, 21 f. 9, 26 f. 12, 2 f. 18, 19), of the call of the divinely chosen instruments, and their training in faith, obedience, and a virtuous life, and of the divine purpose of making Israel a source of blessing to the nations. In the usage of language, as well as in its style, J is more closely allied to E than to P, and although subtle differences between J and E are discernible, the criteria for definitely distinguishing one from the other are often not clearly marked.

How these documents were worked up into one whole cannot be determined without fixing the date of P. If P is the oldest portion of the work, then the view that this is the framework, into which the other documents were fitted, is tenable. If P, on the other hand, is the latest of the three sources, then it is probably best to suppose that J and E were first united into one whole, and that D was added to this, the last redactor of the Hexateuch combining P with the whole thus formed J, E, D.

The following remarks may perhaps give a general idea of how Genesis arose out of the three documents P, J, E. It has been already remarked that a definite plan can be traced throughout the whole book. To put it as briefly as possible, the object of the book is to give an account of the history of Israel from the earliest times until the death of Joseph, to shew how God created the world and mankind, preserved Noah from the deluge and made a covenant with him, chose Abram the descendant of Noah through Shem, and made a covenant with him, promising to him and his descendants the land of Canaan, and taking him under his especial protection, and imposing upon him the observance of several precepts. The history is carried on in the person of Isaac, to whom the promises made to Abraham are renewed; some account is given of Ishmael, who then disappears from the narrative, which employs itself with the fortunes of Jacob and Esau, the latter being dismissed after a short account of the relations between him and Jacob, and the course of the narrative confined to Jacob. We are next told of the birth of Jacob's sons and the sale of Joseph into Egypt, Joseph now becoming the prominent figure in the narrative. After some account of the journeys of Joseph's brethren into Egypt, and their meeting with Joseph who was regarded as dead, the history tells us of Jacob's descent into Egypt, and finally relates Joseph's death, after he had removed his father's remains to Canaan and buried them in the Cave of Machpelah.

In compiling this history from the materials at his disposal the compiler chose from his sources what was most suited to the plan of his work. Sometimes he merely makes small extracts from one document (e.g. 4, 17-24. 6, 1-4. 30, 32-42, merely small portions of fuller accounts), or notices individual points (e.g. 11, 29, Jiska mentioned; 20, 12, the relationship between Abram and Sarai, cf. 28, 22 (see 35, 7); 48, 22). At other times the portions taken from the documents are quoted in full, and for the most part are verbally transferred from the original (e.g. the narratives in P up to 11, 26), and sometimes again, whole passages from one document are omitted, possibly because they were at variance with the accounts given by the others (see in P the brief accounts in 11, 27-32; the omission of the introduction to the history of Abram, previous to chap. 11; of the divine manifestation to Isaac; of the sojourn of Jacob in Paddan Aram; of all the history of Joseph prior to Jacob's arrival in Egypt). When combining his sources the compiler, as far as possible, or as far as he deemed necessary, appears to have taken the narrative verbally from each and inserted both in his work (cf. chap. 2 f. side by side with chap. 1, chap. 27 side by side with 26, 34 f. and 28, 1-9; 48, 3-7 side by side with 48, 9-22). Elsewhere, as for example, where the event need only be quoted from one document (e.g. the birth or death of any person), he selects his account from one source, even though the same event be recorded in more than one document. In other cases the compiler found two accounts in the documents before him, agreeing in the main but differing in details, he would then weave one account into the other, omitting from each what could not be reconciled, and choosing from both what best suited the plan of his work (cf. chaps. 7 f. 10. 16. 25. 27-37. 39-50).

To the redactor also probably may be attributed the accommodation necessary to preserve consistency in the use of the names Abram and Sarai, in all passages previous to chap. 17, of the double name Yahweh Elohim in chaps. 2-3; also the change of Elohim into Yahweh in 17, 1. 21, 1. It is also probable that slight changes were made by him at the juncture between different narratives (e.g. 11, 1-9. 12, 10-20. 25, 5 f. 11 b. 25, 21 ff. 35, 16-20. 47, 12 ff.). In other passages the sources are loosely combined (e.g. 7, 7-9. 22. 15, 7 f. 31, 45 ff. chap. 36. 46, 8-27), the compiler now and then making additions of his own to bring the documents into harmony (e.g. 21, 32. 34. 27, 46. 35, 5. 46, 12-20). Sometimes possibly use was also made of materials taken from other sources than P, J, and E (e.g. perhaps in chap. 14)[1].

---

[1] For full details of the various works bearing on the criticism of the Pentateuch, see Dillmann's *Genesis*, 5th ed., p. xix ff., or Zoeckler, l. c., p. 145 ff., from whom most of the above particulars are derived.

APPENDIX II.

יהוה‎, אֱלֹהִים‎ and אֵל‎.

THE first two names of God, אֵל‎ and אֱלֹהִים‎, as may be seen from
the Concordance, are of frequent occurrence in the Old Testament. The
plural of אֵל‎ and the sing. of אֱלֹהִים‎, on the contrary, are rare; the
plural forms of אֵל‎ occurring about five times, and the sing. of אֱלֹהִים‎
about 57 times. אֵל‎ (sing.), on the other hand, occurs (including
proper names of people and of places compounded with אֵל‎) over 300
times, and אֱלֹהִים‎ over 2500 times[1]. It will be found, on a closer
examination of the various passages, that אֵל‎, though of common occurrence, is essentially a poetical word, being very common in the poetical
part of Job (about a quarter of the passages where אֵל‎ is found are in
Job). It is also found in the Psalms (but not so frequently as
אֱלֹהִים‎) and in other poetical passages, and is used by the prophets
from Hosea to Deutero-Isaiah and his contemporaries. אֵל‎ is found in
the Pentateuch in certain special phrases, such as אֵל־קַנָּא‎, אֵל־שַׁדַּי‎, but
otherwise the less poetical parts of the Pentateuch and Prophets avoid
it. אֵל‎ apparently formed no part of the ordinary spoken language, as
it is never used in Judges, Samuel, or Kings, and even in Chronicles
only occurs in poetical passages. In proper names of persons and of
places it is found from the earliest times. Thus from the O.T. it may
be inferred that אֵל‎ was a very old name of God, which, however, at a
tolerably early date ceased to be used, and was only preserved in poetry,
elevated prose, and in a few special phrases. אלהים‎ was the common
name of God, the word being used for the sing. and plural. The
singular אֱלֹהַּ‎ is most common in the book of Job, and it is found elsewhere in only a few poetical passages. In pure prose it occurs only in
two very late passages (2 Chron. 32, 15 and Dan. 11, 37–39); and even
in the prose parts of Job is replaced by אֱלֹהִים‎. אֱלֹהַּ‎ may thus be
regarded as an artificial sing. of אֱלֹהִים‎[2]. So in Hebrew the ordinary

---

[1] Cf. Nestle, *Theologische Studien aus Württemberg*, 1882, p. 243 f.

[2] Nöldeke, *Sitzungsberichte der Berliner Akad.*, 1882, p. 1177; cf.
Nestle, l.c., p. 249.

word for God was אֱלֹהִים, without a real singular, אֵל and אֱלֹהַּ being nearly entirely confined to poetry.

In the other Semitic dialects אֵל is common, being found in Assyrian, Phoenician, and Himyaritic, but whether it is found in Northern Arabic and Aramaic is a disputed point[1]. אֱלֹהַּ is found, on the contrary, only in Aramaic and Arabic, the word both in Aramaic and Arabic being probably indigenous and not borrowed from the Hebrew[2]. In Sabean אֵל and אֱלֹהַּ occur, both words being used in much the same way as in Hebrew[3].

Various explanations of these names אֵל and אֱלֹהִים have been offered by different scholars, but no certain derivation for either appears yet to have been obtained.

Fleischer[4], whom Delitzsch and others[5] follow, takes אֱלֹהִים as the plural of אֱלֹהַּ (a noun of the form קְטוּל = قَتُول), deriving אֱלֹהַּ from an unused root אָלַה = the Arabic أَلِيَ (وَلِيَ), which has the notion of '*wandering about*,' '*going hither and thither*' in perplexity or fear, and followed by إلى '*to betake oneself*' to a person, by reason of fright or fear, seeking protection[6]. אֱלֹהַּ would thus, it is argued, = '*fear*,' and then '*the object of fear*' (cf. σέβασμα in Greek, and the Heb. מוֹרָא, פַּחַד, see Gen. 31, 42. 53), and so '*God*.' This derivation would appear, however, to be questionable. For in the verb the idea of 'fear' is altogether subordinate, and though in a particular case it may express the idea of seeking protection *with* a person, in fear (of course) of *other* things, it is difficult to understand how a substantive derived from it could be used to denote God as the *direct* object of fear. It might, conceivably, denote Him as a *refuge*, but hardly as *fear*, or the object of fear. אֵל is regarded by these scholars as belonging to a root אול, with the primary meaning '*strength*[7].'

---

[1] Lagarde, *Orientalia*, ii. p. 3 f. (cf. Nestle, l. c., p. 251), denies the existence of אֵל as a real Aramaic and Arabic word : Nöldeke disputes this, and appears to have shewn that Lagarde is in error. See *Monatsberichte der Berliner Akad.*, 1880, p. 768 f., and *Sitzungsberichte* of the same *Akad.*, 1882, p. 1182.

[2] See Nöldeke, *Sitzungsberichte*, 1882, p. 1189; but cf. Nestle, l.c., p. 252.

[3] See *Über* אל *und* אלה *im Sabäischen*, by Prof. D. H. Müller, Leyden, 1884.

[4] Del., *Comm.*[4], p. 57.

[5] Oehler, Schultz, Mühlau, Volck.

[6] See Lane, *Arabic Lex.*, p. 82.

[7] Cf. Ges., *Thes.*, pp. 42, 48.

Ewald[1] connects אֵל and אֱלֹהַ, regarding אֵל as abbreviated from אֱלֹהַ, and holding אלה '*to be strong*' to be the root of both.

Lagarde[2] has proposed an entirely different derivation for אֵל (the origin of אֱלֹהַ he does not discuss). He regards אלי (אלה) as the root of אֵל, and compares the form אֵל with גֵּו (from גוה), Is. 50, 6, שָׂמִים=שָׂמַיִם (from שׂטה), and כֵּלִים (but cstr. state כְּלֵי). אלי (אלה) he conjectures had the meaning '*to stretch out to*,' and God he considers called אֵל, as '*one whom men strive after*.' The vowel in אֵל Lagarde regards as originally short, evading the analogy of words like נֵר, נֵד, מֵת, by the remark that such a word as אֵל, '*God*,' can hardly be, what its vowel — would indicate that it is, a neuter passive participle (see more fully *Mitteilungen* (1884), p. 103 f.).

Nöldeke[3] holds that אֵל is a noun with a long vowel like בֵּן, פַּך, שֵׂר, etc., almost all of which belong to verbs ע"ו and ע"ע, and refers it to a root אול = *to be in front*, so אֵל = *the leader, Lord*. He expresses no decided opinion as to the connection between אֵל and אֱלֹהִים, but thinks a connection may be possible[4].

Dillmann[5] regards אֵל and אֱלֹהַ as inseparable, considering the latter to imply an extended form of the former, like אֲמָהוֹת from אמה, and مَعْمُوذَا from غَمّ, خُذْبَا('[?] from خُذْ, in Aramaic, and شَقَاء from شَقَف in Arabic: אֵל (with an original short i), however, being from אלה, and having the meaning '*might*.'

Nestle[6], lastly, has proposed another explanation of the relationship between אֵל and אֱלֹהִים. He infers from the usage of language that אֱלֹהִים is the real plural of אֵל, and that אֱלֹהַ is a secondary derivation from אֱלֹהִים. אֱלֹהִים he thinks has arisen out of אֵל, just as אֲמָהוֹת out of אָמָה.

The above is a brief account of the various views that are held as to the origin of אֵל and אֱלֹהִים, but none appears to be entirely free from objection.

That אֱלֹהַ comes from a root אָלָה, as Fleischer and Delitzsch maintain, is, as has been already shewn, doubtful. In favour of Ewald's

---

[1] *Jahrbuch*, x. 11, and *Lehrbuch*, § 178 b.

[2] *Orientalia*, ii. p. 3 ff.

[3] *Monatsberichte der König. Preuss. Akad.*, 1880, pp. 760–776.

[4] Nöldeke's view, as far as the derivation of אֵל from אול is concerned, is the same as Gesenius' referred to in note 7, p. 372, differing only as to the meaning borne by אול.

[5] *Commentar über die Genesis*, I, I.

[6] In his article in the *Theologische Studien aus Württemberg*, 1882, Heft iv.

view may be urged the fact that it connects both אֵל and אֱלֹהִים, by
deriving them from a root אָלָה, and the existence of proper names
compounded with אֵל exhibiting traces of י, e.g. אֱלִיהוּא, אֱלִימֶלֶךְ, and
others[1], though it is only fair to admit that the evidence from proper
names ought not to be pressed, as the י may be the suffix of the first
person and not the third radical. But it does not account for the presence
of the ה in אֱלֹהִים, and if אֵל is abridged from אֱלֹהִים, it is not clear why
אֵל is found chiefly in poetical passages where we should naturally
expect antique forms.

Lagarde, in so far as he derives אֵל from a root אלה, agrees with
Ewald, though he assigns to this root a different meaning, viz. *'to
stretch out to.'* Apart from the fact that the meaning thus assigned to
אלה is conjectural, he can hardly be said to have proved against
Nöldeke that the e of אֵל is short, and that it does not belong to a root
ע״ו. The evidence Nöldeke adduces from the occurrence of Semitic
proper names in Greek inscriptions, in favour of a long e in אֵל[2], does
not seem to have been met by Lagarde, and in failing to observe the
Aramaic use of אֵל[3], he has exposed himself to Nöldeke's objection,
supported by the Syriac, that formations like כֵּן, כַּף, etc. point to ע״ע
or ע״ו stems[4]. Nöldeke's own view of אֵל (which is in the main the
same as Gesenius held[5]) does not appear adequately to account for the
shortening of the e in אֵל in the proper names אֱלִיהוּא, אֶלְקָנָה, etc.[6],
nor for the י in the latter name, which would seem to imply a root ל״ה[7].
It also does not take into account the Assyrian *ilu*, which has always a
short *i*, and which never appears as *êlu* or *êlu*[8].

Nestle's view has been examined by Nöldeke[9], who points out that
the usage of language is against it, that the explanation of אֱלֹהִים as an
extended form of אֵל is precarious, for only one clear case of this occurs
in Hebrew (viz. אֲמָהוֹת from אָמָה), and the cases that are found in the

---

[1] This also applies to Dillmann's view.

[2] See *Monatsberichte der König. Preuss. Akad.*, 1880, p. 760 f.

[3] See *Monatsberichte*, etc., p. 772.

[4] See *Monatsberichte*, etc., p. 773.

[5] Cf. note 4 on p. 373.

[6] Nöldeke accounts for this on the ground that an unusual shortening of
vowels is often found in proper names.

[7] Though, as has been just said, this might be the pronom. affix.

[8] Del., *Par.*, pp. 163-165. Brown in *The Presbyterian Review* (New York),
1882, p. 407.

[9] In the *Sitzungsberichte der Berliner Akad. der Wissenschaften*, 1882,
pp. 1175-1192.

other Semitic dialects always have, in the expanded form, the plural feminine ending, whether the word itself be masc. or fem.[1] Nöldeke also remarks that long o for long a is difficult (the long a in אֲמָהוֹת goes back to short a[2]), and that if the e of אֵל is long, the ◌ֱ in אֱלֹהִים is difficult to explain.

The following points seem to require a satisfactory explanation before the derivation of אֵל and אֱלֹהִים can be definitely fixed. (i) Are the two words really connected one with the other, and derived from the same root? (ii) Does אֵל really come from אוּל, or from a root אלה (i. e. אלי)? (iii) How is the ה of אֱלֹהִים to be accounted for? (iv) Can the evidence which Nöldeke brings forward to prove that the ◌ֵ in אֵל is long be accepted as conclusive in the face of the fact that the vowel in the corresponding word in Assyrian (*ilu*) is short? (v) If the ◌ֵ is really long, is Nöldeke's explanation of the shortening of ◌ֵ in אֱלִיהוּ, אֶלְקָנָה, and other similar proper names adequate[3]?

The above is a brief sketch of the views held by scholars as to the derivation of אֵל and אֱלֹהִים. Both אֵל and אֱלֹהִים (אֱלֹהַּ) are old words in Semitic, and, *prima facie*, would appear to be distinct : their original derivation, however, is at present obscure.

יֶהוָה

It is well known that the vowels with which the Tetragrammaton is punctuated in the ordinary editions of the Massoretic text do not really belong to it, but have been supplied from the word אֲדֹנָי, with the composite shewa changed into a simple shewa, unless this word precedes יהוה, when the points of אֱלֹהִים are used, e. g. Is. 28, 16. 30, 15. 49, 22. Ez. 2, 4. 7, 2. Amos 5, 3, etc. This is clear from the following considerations : (1) With the prefixes ב, ל, מ, ו we find בַּיהוָה (e. g. Ps. 11, 1. 32, 10. 11. 64, 11); לַיהוָה (e. g. Ps. 7, 1. 16, 2. 24, 1); מֵיהוָה (e. g. Ps. 33, 8. 37, 39. Is. 40, 27); וַיהוָה (Gen. 13, 14. 1 Sam. 12, 12. Is. 53, 10), i. e. בַּאדֹנָי, לַאדֹנָי, מֵאֲדֹנָי, and וַאדֹנָי (cf. Ges., § 23. 2ʻ. (2) If the word that follows יהוה begins with one of the letters ב, ג, ד, כ, פ, ת, the dagesh lene is inserted, e. g. Gen. 13, 10. Ex. 15, 6. Num. 11, 25.

---

[1] Cf. *Sitzungsberichte*, p. 1180 f. The masc. forms that occur in Syriac are, as Nöldeke points out, late. Nöldeke's remarks on this point also apply to Dillmann's explanation.

[2] Nöldeke, *Sitzungsberichte*, p. 1181.

[3] See note 6, p. 374.

Judg. 21, 15. 1 Sam. 28, 19. 2 Sam. 23, 2. (3) Ewald in his *Lehrbuch*, § 228 b, draws attention to the fact that in Num. 10, 35, cf. ver. 36, קוּמָה is accented on the last syllable, though the ה is ה cohortative, because the next following word יהוה begins with a guttural, e. g. א, יְהוָֹה=אֲדֹנָי, cf. Ps. 3, 8 קוּמָֽה; 6, 5 שׁוּבָֽה; 7, 7. 10, 12, etc. (4) The abbreviations יְהוּ‎, יָהּ‎, יְהוֹ cannot come from יְהֹוָה. The objection to using the real punctuation of יהוה arises from an old misconception of the two passages, Ex. 20, 7 (לֹא תִשָּׂא אֶת שֵׁם יְהוָה אֱלֹהֶיךָ לַשָּׁוְא). Lev. 24, 16 (וְנֹקֵב שֵׁם יְהוָה מוֹת יוּמָת), which were interpreted as meaning that the divine name was to be treated as a *nomen ineffabile*. This interpretation of these two verses is mentioned by Philo, *De vita Mosis*, iii. pp. 519, 529; Josephus, *Archaeol.*, ii. 12, § 4; Talmud, *Sanhedrin*, chap. 2, fol. 90; Maimonides, *Yadh Chasaka*, chap. 14, § 10; Theodoret, *Quaest.* 13 in Exod.; Eusebius, *Praep. Evang.*, ii. p. 305; the passages (excepting that from Eusebius) being quoted by Gesenius, *Thes.*, p. 575 f. The LXX render the Tetragrammaton always by ὁ Κύριος (their ordinary translation of אדני), and the Samaritans used שׁימא ('*name*') for יהוה, when they had to pronounce the word.

There is every reason to assume that the punctuation adopted by modern scholars for יהוה is correct, viz. יַהְוֶה, the form being an imperfect Qal (according to another view Hif'il) of הוה, which is an archaic and North Palestinian form of the verb היה (cf. the note on 27, 29); compare the other proper names formed after the analogy of the imperf. of the verb, e. g. יִצְחָק, יָאִיר, יַעֲקֹב, etc. That this assumption is correct is proved by the fact that the abbreviations יְהוּ (out of יַהְוּ), יְהוֹ and יוֹ (out of יַהְוֹ=יְהוֹ), and יָהּ (יָה=יַהְו=יַהְוֶה) can easily be derived from יהוה, and by the statement of Theodoret that the pronunciation of the Samaritans was IABE, while Epiphanius, *Adv. Haer.* 20 (40) cites IABE as one of the names of God, explaining it (from Ex. 3, 14) as ὃς ἦν καὶ ἔστι καὶ ἀεὶ ὤν, see Ges., l. c. If this punctuation be conceded it will next be necessary to explain the meaning of the name. The class of words to which יהוה belongs is not very wide in Heb., and is practically limited to a few proper names (see Stade, *Lehrbuch*, § 259). The form יַהְוֶה, as far as the punctuation is concerned, may be the imperf. Qal or Hif'il of הוה; and the meaning we must assign to the word will obviously depend on which of these two conjugations we consider the form to come from. If it be imperf. Qal, it may mean, '*he that is;*' if it be imperf. Hif'il, '*he that causes to be.*' If the former view be adopted, the word being taken as imperf. Qal, we must, in interpreting the meaning of the name, be guided by the passage in Exodus, viz. 3, 14;

for though the name יהוה may have been known to the Hebrews prior to
the time of Moses—cf. the name of Moses' mother, Ex. 6, 20 יוֹכֶבֶד, and
the formula '*God of thy father*,' Ex. 3, 6 [1]—it was through him that it
received its first explanation. The name has been considered by various
modern scholars [2], reviving the view held by Le Clerc, and thrown out as
a suggestion by Gesenius, as a Hif'il derivative, although the interpreta-
tions differ; e. g. Kuenen interprets the name as '*the giver of existence;*'
Schrader and Schultz, as '*the giver of life and deliverance;*' Lagarde and
Nestle, who follow Le Clerc, as '*he who brings to pass,*' i.e. '*the performer
of his promises;*' Land, as '*life-giver,*' so Ges. in *Thes.* The objection to
the derivation of the word from the Hif'il stem is that though היה is used
of the fulfilment of a promise or prediction (e. g. in 1 Kings 13, 32), it
requires the object of the promise to be at least indicated in the context,
and further, that scarcely any Semitic language uses the causative form
of היה [3]. If this derivation be regarded as too uncertain, the alternative one, in which the word יהוה is treated as a neuter (Qal), must be
adopted.

In the passage in Exodus (3, 14) God, in His answer to Moses, says
אֶהְיֶה אֲשֶׁר אֶהְיֶה, then calls Himself אֶהְיֶה, and finally יהוה. It is clear
from this that הָוָה (see above) is presupposed to be equivalent to היה,
and that אֶהְיֶה, the shorter expression, must be explained by אֶהְיֶה אֲשֶׁר
אֶהְיֶה. Then אהיה אשר אהיה must not be taken as a refusal to answer
Moses' question '*I am* just *who I am,*' i. e. it is a matter of indifference
to you who I am, and you should not seek to know (Le Clerc, Lagarde);
as the following אהיה cannot bear this sense, and אהיה אשר אהיה more
naturally gives an explanation of the name. An explanation of the
name is certainly found in the rendering adopted by Wellhausen, following Ibn Ezra, '*I am, since I am,*' אהיה being regarded as the name, and
אשר אהיה as its explanation; but אֲשֶׁר for כִּי in this context is hardly
probable, and Moses did not ask '*What is thy name?*' but '*What shall
I tell them?*' Therefore אהיה אשר א" must be taken as a simple
sentence, which has been variously rendered. The LXX and Knobel
translate, '*I am he who exists,*' i. e. '*he who is;*' but it is doubtful whether
אשר אהיה can = ὁ ὤν. Rashi renders, '*I will be with them what I will
be with them in the subjection of their future captivities;*' while Ewald
explains, '*I will be it,*' viz. the performer of his promises; both sup-

---

[1] See Nestle, *Eigennamen*, p. 80 ff.

[2] Comp. Prof. Driver, in *Studia Biblica*, i. Oxford, 1885.

[3] Comp. Prof. Driver, l. c., p. 14, foot-note.

porting their renderings by ver. 12 אֶהְיֶה עִמָּךְ. Robertson Smith renders similarly, '*I will be what I will be*,' i. e. your God and Helper (cf. Driver, l. c., p. 16). The objection to this view is that what Jehovah will prove Himself to be is not expressed, but must be understood (see Di. on Ex. 3, 14). But it may be (as Del.[1] and Oehler[2] suggest) that היה is to be understood in a pregnant sense, '*give evidence of being*.' The most probable view is that the passage means, '*I am that I am*,' not that which fate or caprice may determine, but what my own character determines. היה has the idea not of fixity, but of change; not a capricious change, but a conscious one. The verb means properly not '*to be*,' but '*to come into being*' (cf. Del., *Comm.*, pp. 26, 60); so יהוה is a living active God, a God of the past, but also of the future, who cannot be named or defined, but whose divine nature is ever expressing itself, and manifesting itself under fresh aspects; a God who enters into personal relations with His worshippers, who is consistent with Himself, true to His promises, and unchangeable in His purposes (comp. Del., l. c.; Oehler, l. c.; Driver, l. c., p. 17; Di. on Ex. 3, 14)[3].

---

[1] *Comm.*, pp. 26, 60.

[2] *Theology of the Old Testament*, § 39.

[3] On the various views held by scholars concerning the origin of the Tetragrammaton, the reader may be referred for further particulars to the paper by Prof. Driver, and to König's *Hauptprobleme der altisrael. Religionsgeschichte*, 1884, pp. 29–33 (translated in *Hebraica*, April, 1885, pp. 255-257).

CORRIGENDA.

	for	read
Page 7, line 7 from bottom,	*for* prefix בְ	*read* prefix יְ
,, 11, ,, 4 ,, ,,	,, defined שְׁנִי. On	,, defined שְׁנִי; on
,, 25, ,, 4 ,, ,,	,, اَلنِّيلُ	,, اَلنَّيِّلُ
,, 27, ,, 11 from top,	,, וְּשֶׁנֶה	,, וְשֶׁנֶה
,, 34, ,, 4 from bottom,	,, חית	,, חית ונו"
,, 36, ,, 16 from top,	,, it rejects it	,, they reject it
,, 41, ,, 4 from bottom,	,, ܢܣܘܚ	,, ܢܣܘܚ
,, 41, last line on page,	,, דְּעָבַדְתְּ	,, דְּעָבַדְתְּ
,, 50, line 16 from bottom,	,, דִּינָא	,, דִּינָא
,, 50, ,, 5 ,, ,,	,, اَلرَّابِض	,, الرابض
,, 55, ,, 11 from top,	,, עֵשֹה	,, עֵשֹה
,, 68, ,, 13 from bottom,	,, דְּאִינּוּן	,, דְּאִינּוּן
,, 70, ,, 7 ,, ,,	,, כְּמֵימְרֵה	,, בְּמֵימְרַה
,, 72, ,, 5 from top,	,, 'arcani'	,, 'arcam'
,, 87, ,, 7 ,, ,,	,, נה ובארצה	,, בארצה
,, 87, ,, 8 ,, ,,	,, בו וּבְאַרְצוֹ	,, בְּאַרְצוֹ
,, 87, ,, 8 ,, ,,	,, ובביתה	,, ¹ובנהה
,, 94, ,, 10 ,, ,,	,, Targ.	,, Targg.
,, 94, ,, 11 from bottom,	,, דְדָנִים	,, בְּנֵי דְדָן
,, 125, ,, 5 from top,	,, Sir.	,, Ecclus.
,, 125, last line on page,	,, דְּשִׁעֲבִּידוּ	,, דְּשִׁעֲבִּידוּ
,, 142, line 7 from top,	,, 'experienced.' LXX	,, 'experienced,' LXX
,, 143, ,, 3 ,, ,,	,, Jerome	,, Hieron.
,, 155, ,, 13 from bottom,	,, sees	,, saw
,, 166, ,, 15 from top,	,, הָיָה	,, הָיֹה
,, 175, ,, 2 ,, ,,	,, Araba	,, Arabah
,, 178, ,, 3 from bottom,	,, نَعِيلُ	,, فَعِيلُ

---

¹ These passages are corrected from Smend and Socin's edition of the
Moabite Stone (Freiburg I. B., 1886), p. 12.

Page 181, line 9 from top,   *for* וְנִבְחַת   *read* וְנִבַחְתְּ
   ,, 194, ,, 12 from bottom, ,, הברון   ,,   חברון
   ,, 204, ,, 1 from top,   ,, וַיָּבֹא   ,,   וַיָּבֹא
   ,, 205, ,, 2   ,,   ,,   ,, *or the left*   ,,   *or to the left*
   ,, 218, ,, 6   ,,   ,,   ,, וַנַּעֲשֶׂה   ,,   וַנַּעֲשֶׂה
   ,, 272, ,, 5 from top, after *with* insert etc.
   ,, 288, ,, 2 from bottom, *for* וַעֲשִׂית   *read* וְעָשִׂית
   ,, 305, ,, 14 from top,   ,, שָׁאָה   ,,   שָׁאָה
   ,, 329, ,, 4 from bottom, ,, שֹׁמְעוֹן   ,,   שִׁמְעוֹן
   ,, 339, ,, 6 from top,   ,, זֵעֵיר   ,,   זְעֵיר
   ,, 341, ,, 3 from bottom, ,, רַגְלָיִו   ,,   בַּגְלָיִו
   ,, 342, ,, 11 from top,   ,, Tauchuma   ,,   Tanchuma
   ,, 346, ,, 15 ,,   ,,   ,, of bond-slave   ,,   of a bond-slave

אל

THE END.